Additional praise for *The Decline of Representative Democracy*
by Alan Rosenthal

*This book does an admirable job of providing a comprehensive yet interesting
view of the current state of state legislatures, as well as a compelling argument
for why they find themselves in their current state. Rosenthal is to be commended for making abstract notions about representation relevant [to readers]
by tying them to the actions of state legislators, and by bringing into the
discussion the move toward expanding mechanisms of direct democracy.*

Peverill Squire
The University of Iowa

*This is a thought-provoking book that should be required reading for those
who want to understand the nature of state legislatures in the 1990s.*

Keith E. Hamm
Rice University

*Given that the last comprehensive discussion of the state legislature was
written almost twenty years ago, and also penned by Rosenthal,* The Decline of Representative Democracy *is long overdue.*

Thomas H. Little
The University of Texas at Arlington

THE DECLINE OF REPRESENTATIVE DEMOCRACY

Process, Participation, and Power in State Legislatures

Alan Rosenthal
RUTGERS UNIVERSITY

A Division of Congressional Quarterly Inc.
Washington, D.C.

To Vivian—
who expanded my horizons

Printed in the United States of America

Cover design: Debra Naylor

Library of Congress Cataloging-in-Publication Data

Rosenthal, Alan
    The decline of representative democracy : process, participation,
and power in state legislatures / Alan Rosenthal.
        p.   cm.
    Includes bibliographical references and index.
    ISBN 0-87187-975-1 (cloth : alk. paper). — ISBN 0-87187-974-3
(pbk. : alk. paper)
    1. Legislative bodies—United States—States. 2. State
governments—United States. I. Title.
JK2488.R658   1997
328.73—dc21   97-38196
                                                                    CIP

Contents

Tables and Figures

Preface

I have spent most of my professional career observing legislatures, trying to figure out how they work, why they function as they do, and what they mean in a political system built around representative democracy. No matter how long and how hard I have looked, I still have not succeeded in nailing things down. But I keep trying.

This book reports on my latest attempt to figure legislatures out and discern where they are headed. It is a product of a confluence of factors.

One factor that led to the present enterprise was my book, *Legislative Life,* which was published in 1981, years after I arrived at the Eagleton Institute of Politics to begin my association with state legislatures. *Legislative Life* described the processes and politics of state legislatures, focusing on individual behavior and institutional performance. Its purpose was to inform legislators and legislative staff, as well as interns and undergraduate and graduate students in political science. From all accounts, it fulfilled its purpose. After it went out of print and was no longer available, a number of my colleagues in political science who had used the book in their courses inquired as to whether I would be preparing a new edition. For years, I fended them off.

The present volume is by no means a revision of *Legislative Life.* It is a completely new book; yet it covers some of the same ground and has comparable objectives. My hope is that, like its predecessor, it will be used as a text that offers a comprehensive overview for practitioners and students alike.

Another factor that is responsible for this book relates to my efforts in the area of legislative modernization and reform, and principally those that have been supported by the Carnegie Corporation. Thanks to Carnegie, Eagleton conducted an annual retreat for specially selected legislators from 1966 to 1975. The subject of five days of seminars in Florida each summer was legislative reform and modernization. Over the course of the ten years, a total of 432 outstanding legislators from the fifty states participated. In 1990 Carnegie funded a follow-up program, one in which a number of alumni of the conferences came together in Williamsburg, Virginia. Background papers were prepared by several legislative scholars, including Malcolm Jewell of the University of Kentucky; Karl Kurtz of the National Conference of State Legislatures; and Burdett Loomis of the University of Kansas. Discussion by participants focused on changes in the composition of the legislature, the development of legislative capacity, the professionalization of legislative bodies, and the impact of campaigns and elections. Our intention was to publish a book assessing state legislatures and drawing on the Williamsburg materials. This assessment of the state of state legislatures is designed in part to accomplish that project's goal.

The final factor to which this volume can be credited is the recent democratic trend in and around state legislatures. Despite the popular perceptions that legislatures are autocratic, arbitrary, isolated, unresponsive, and up for sale, legislatures are in fact extraordinarily democratic institutions. They have been becoming more democratic of late, so that a systemic shift from representative democracy to participatory democracy now seems to be under way. This change and its implications are the thematic focus of this book.

The Decline of Representative Democracy was an easier book to write than *Legislative Life,* mainly because of the remarkable progress made in the field of state legislative research. The literature today is far richer than it was fifteen years ago. Much of the advance can be attributed to the intellectual leadership of Malcolm Jewell and to those political scientists who have been following in his scholarly footsteps. The University of Nebraska series, *Politics and Governments of the American States,* edited by John Kincaid, also deserves credit. Thanks to the volumes in this series, we currently have basic and essential information on legislatures in one-third of the states. Anyone writing in the field thus has a solid base on which to build. I have built on it.

Much of what is reported here derives from interviews I conducted especially for this study. These interviews were with legislators and legislative staff in five states: California, Florida, Maryland, New Mexico, and Ohio. I quote, paraphrase, and refer to these interviews and cite them in notes, but I do not name those who were interviewed. As far as my argument is concerned, it is not necessary for individuals to be identified; as far as the respondents are concerned, it cannot hurt for them to remain anonymous.

In addition, I have made general use of my observations of legislatures and casual conversations with legislators, staffers, and lobbyists with whom I have visited over the years. On every trip to a state capital to consult or participate in an orientation session or seminar, I manage to acquire some grist for my mill. If one listens and watches, there is always something that can be learned and usually something that can be applied.

Some of what I have written recently is reflected in these pages. Chapter 1 draws on "The Nature of Representation: An Overview," which was part of a project conducted by the Collins Center for Public Policy in Florida. Chapter 2 makes use of "State Legislative Development: Observations from Three Perspectives," which appeared in the May 1996 issue of *Legislative Studies Quarterly*. Chapter 6 draws on *The Third House: Lobbyists and Lobbying in the States* and chapter 9 on *Governors and Legislatures: Contending Powers,* both of which were published by CQ Press.

Like much of my other writing, this book is aimed at several audiences.

First, it is aimed at the practitioner community, and specifically the state capitol crowd of legislators, legislative staff, and lobbyists. They are much nearer to the process than I am, but their experience is necessarily narrow, limited for the most part (except in the case of some lobbyists) to a single state. One of my intentions is to expand the horizons of these practitioners, affording them a context in which to reflect on their own experience. Another of my intentions, frankly, is to alert them to what might be considered threats to the legislature as an institution and to the system of representative democracy.

Second, this book is aimed at the community of participating citizens, those people who are willing to take upon themselves civic responsibilities. My hope is that they can learn more about the political system under which they live, and that such learning will help them become more sensitive participants in legislative politics.

Third, this book is aimed at scholars and students who constitute the political science community. I hope that this work is useful to those who, like myself, are fascinated by state legislatures. If it encourages my colleagues, engages them, or provides them with an insight or a lead, it will have served one of its purposes. I hope also that this work is read by students of state politics and of legislatures, and especially those who might be interning at the capitol. What I would hope is that students reading this will find legislative life and politics to be interesting and well worth their commitment. I would be elated if it contributed to their greater appreciation of representative democracy.

In trying to appeal to different communities, each with a diverse membership, I may be reaching too far. But I believe it is important for political scientists—at least those who feel so inclined—to make efforts to bridge the gap between the political and academic realms. That is something to which I have devoted a career, deriving substantial gratification for what might appear to be very limited results.

I am indebted to many people for their help throughout the course of my career. Were it not for them, the present book could not have been written. Legislators and members of legislative staffs from New Jersey to California and from Vermont to Florida have had a profound influence on my work. They are too many to mention by name, but that does not limit my indebtedness or my gratitude. The national legislative organizations—the National Conference of State Legislatures, Council of State Governments, and State Legislative Leaders Foundation—have been of continuing assistance to me, and I hope what I write here will do the same for them.

Although I may venture beyond the boundaries of political science research, I am thankful for the valuable work my colleagues have done. I have tried to bring their writing to the attention of practitioners, and I have leaned heavily on it in my own writing. It more than stands up under my weight. I am grateful, in particular, to the scholars—Keith Hamm, Thomas Little, and Peverill Squire—who read this book in manuscript form and whose suggestions led to important revisions. It is a better book than it would otherwise have been, thanks to them.

The Eagleton Institute of Politics at Rutgers University has nurtured my passion for legislative bodies. It has permitted me to work with them in a public service capacity, teach students about them, and write books and articles on practically nothing else but legislatures. Eagleton has afforded me the most pleasurable way I can imagine to forge a career and make a living. I am somewhat embarrassed to have had it so good.

The Carnegie Corporation of New York, which funded several legislative projects in earlier years, also provided partial funding for this project. I am grateful for the foundation's support.

As usual my work at Eagleton depends on the assistance I receive from a pleasant, accommodating, and resourceful group of people. They manage, administer, reimburse, organize, untangle, remind, type, and generally prop me up. Chris Lenart and Sandy Wetzel, I am happy to say, do much of my job for me. Joanne Pfeiffer of Eagleton did most of the typing on the manuscript and responded to the pressure of deadlines better than I did. She was joined by Patty Moran, secretary of the Department of Public Policy, who pounded out one of the drafts.

This is the third book of mine that CQ Press has published. CQ's staff of editors and marketeers can be proud of the job they do. I want to extend special thanks to Brenda Carter, who has guided me through the publishing process and has seemed to appreciate, or at least put up with, my peculiar sense of humor.

My family, of course, deserves much more than thanks, but that is all I can give them here. They may not be legislative enthusiasts, but they are supportive of what I do. So I want to acknowledge John, Lisa, Patrick, and Kelly; Kai; Tony and Kathleen; Lisa, Garrison, and Chas; and Vinnie. And then there is Hex, who put a roof over my head while I was writing the spiciest parts of this book. Among the near and dear, I want to single out Vivian, who even more than state legislatures has transformed my life—for the better, I think.

Introduction

My book, *Legislative Life,* was published in 1981, when state legislatures were riding high. They had gone through almost fifteen years of reform and modernization and were on their way to achieving independence as a coequal branch of government. State legislatures had taken on additional responsibilities and embarked on new initiatives. Legislators felt good about themselves in the 1980s and were enthusiastic about meeting the challenges that came their way. *Legislative Life* gives an account of the people involved, the processes used, and the performance of legislatures during this period of resurgence. It is essentially an optimistic book, reflecting a confident institution and a vigorous membership. But amidst the many signs of progress, one could discern warning signals.

Legislatures were not being given their due by either the press or the public. The former was hostile and the latter cynical. Since the 1960s, and particularly after the Vietnam War and Watergate, Americans have lost faith in their leaders and institutions—governmental and nongovernmental—and the press has been increasingly intent on searching out blemishes on legislative bodies.

Legislators themselves were not giving legislatures their due. Members treated their institutions with less than tender, loving care. Some, in order to appeal to their electorates, even ran against the legislatures in which they served. With a new breed of individualistic, entrepreneurial legislators emergent, community was on the decline and the powers of leadership were beginning to be whittled away.

Such was legislative life then; it has become more so now. Gone, however, is the sense of confidence and institutional bravura of the 1970s. To the casual observer, legislatures look much the same today as they did then. The process is not markedly different. Bills are introduced, taken up by committees, and allowed to languish or be reported to the floor. Most issues do not arouse partisan passions, but they do engage interest groups on one or both sides.

But anyone who has served in or observed legislatures over a length of time can notice substantial differences between what they used to be like and what they have become. Today, with the New Federalism, devolution, and the federal government in retreat domestically, state legislatures have more on their plates than ever. Competition between the parties is greater, interest group conflict is more intense, and members run higher risks.

As significant as developments within legislatures is the climate outside legislatures. Although the media never gave political institutions a free ride, the press today is more critical, more searching, and more intrusive. The public, too, although never trusting or supportive of legislatures, is nowadays downright hostile. By way of illustration, take a poll of Indiana citizens reported in the *Indianapolis Star* and *Indianapolis News* (February 18, 1996). It found that 36 percent disagreed with the statement that "legislators generally have the public's interest in mind when they are conducting business." As many as 85 percent agreed with the statement that "the voices of ordinary citizens are drowned out by the influence and money of lobbyists and special interests." A 1997 poll in Texas found legislators happy because their unpopularity had declined, with only 48 percent of people saying the legislature was doing a "poor" or "only fair" job. In 1992 as many as 69 percent gave the legislature similar ratings. Even in a state like Vermont, with its citizen legislature, the climate has become negative, with legislators sensing that the voters suspect their honesty. "You'll just get to be like the others," they are told when entering public office.[1]

This book is based on the general belief that legislatures are extraordinarily important institutions—ones that have proved their value to American democracy. Having been in business for roughly 230 years, legislatures have shown remarkable staying power, suggesting they must be functioning reasonably well. T. V. Smith, who served in both the Illinois legislature and the U.S. Congress, extolled representative democracy: America's "general way of life makes legislatures possible," he wrote, "and legislatures in turn keep alive and prosperous its way of life."[2]

From a contemporary perspective, David Broder, a reporter for the *Washington Post* and syndicated columnist, admonished his colleagues for describing the essential characteristics of the legislative process as failures of the system instead of remarking that they were requisites for democracy. In his view, legislatures are "collecting points for conflicting views." The debate and the conflict that occur as interests and agendas clash, he says, is healthy, not patho-logical. "We ought not to make it appear as if debate and fights and even impasses are train wrecks," he cautioned his colleagues. Just as conflict is in-evitable in legislative bodies, so is compromise. Most often, if diverse interests are to be reconciled, if conflicting demands are to be worked out, and if consensus is to be maintained in the society, there will have to be compro-mise. "We don't have to trash deal making; we don't have to trash people who change their positions," says Broder. "We have to be willing to say that this is part of the work of representative government."[3]

Those who have served in state legislatures are almost unanimous in their praise of the legislative institution and process. However frustrating and con-tentious their experiences, former legislators remember their service fondly, their colleagues affectionately, and the system positively. Tom Loftus, a one-time speaker of the Wisconsin assembly, concludes his book on the legislative process with the sentence: "I loved my fourteen years in the legislature, and I am still very much in awe of the institution as the embodiment of represen-tative democracy."[4] Another former speaker, Ralph Wright of Vermont, also gives the legislature high ratings. "There's no place like a legislature," he writes in his memoirs. "If continuity is the very essence of life, then a legislature is eternal." For Wright, the bottom line is that *"the system works."*[5]

In writing this book, I have two principal objectives in mind. The first is to revisit the description and analysis of state legislatures and the legislative pro-cess, which was the main task of *Legislative Life*. Much has happened in the last seventeen years, and it is worthwhile to bring things up to date.

Chapter 1, "Shifting Bases of Representation," looks at the subject from two perspectives. The first is that of the individual legislator in terms of the delegate-versus-trustee dichotomy. The second is that of the legislature and its institutional responsiveness and systemic performance.

In chapter 2, "The Development of State Legislatures," I explore the build-ing of legislative capacity, the emergence of professional legislatures and leg-islators, and the institutionalization and deinstitutionalization of legislatures. Considered here are the people who make laws, the resources they have at their disposal, and the vitality of legislative bodies.

"The Transformation of Legislative Cultures," chapter 3, describes the capital communities in which legislatures function, the impact of ethics on these communities, and the role of an aggressive press. It concludes with an assess-ment of legislative norms, or rules of the game, which, although never bind-ing, are even less constraining today.

"The Process of Lawmaking," chapter 4, attends to the fundamentals of legislative procedure—that is, the steps by which a bill becomes a law. Sponsorship, committee deliberation, and floor action are the key subjects.

Electoral politics, which have become a central part of legislative life, is assessed in chapter 5, "Competition for Legislative Control." Competition, at both the individual and party levels, drives the system. The campaign is hardly over when it begins again, permeating the legislative process.

"The Dispersion of Interest Group Influence," chapter 6, focuses on the interest group struggle on legislative terrain, the business of lobbying, relationships between lobbyists and legislators, and the role of money. It concludes by pointing to new directions in lobbying—grassroots, public relations, and media campaigns.

Chapter 7, "The Job of Leadership," tackles the change in the role and powers of the presiding officers. Selection and tenure are examined. The leader as manager, partisan politician, and consensus builder receive primary attention.

"Balancing Executive Power," chapter 8, assesses the relationship between the legislature and the governor given their particular powers and predispositions. It examines, in particular, their respective roles on the budget.

The second objective of this book is to assess the legislature according to democratic standards. The legislature is portrayed in the press and perceived by the public to be essentially undemocratic—unrepresentative, unresponsive, unethical, serving special interests, and controlled by a few. That is not the legislature I have been observing for all these years, and it is surely not the legislature now in place. The legislature is a much more democratic institution, operating in a much more democratic environment, than is popularly conceived.

I seek to support this argument, chapter by chapter, regarding internal and external democracy. The argument for legislative democracy is brought together in this book's conclusion, chapter 9, "The Democratic Challenge." The key democratic characteristics guiding this assessment relate to the nature of representation, especially the responsiveness of legislators; the extent and intensity of participation by extra-legislative groups and individuals; and the distribution of power within the legislature. With regard to each of these characteristics, we find that legislatures are not only democratic institutions, but also that they have become more so in recent years.

Indeed, what I refer to as "participatory democracy" (which is not quite "direct democracy") has been growing in strength at the expense of representative processes. Government is no longer conducted with the consent of the governed, according to the original Federalist plan. It is conducted with significant participation by the governed, and by those who claim to speak for the public's interest, according to a more populist plan. The voices of elected representatives are being drowned out by pronouncements made on behalf of the public. The legislature and the legislative process are in the throes of greater democratization. Representative democracy, as the states had experienced it for several centuries, is now in decline. We may or may not be comfortable with the situation, but that is the conclusion that follows from this account of contemporary state legislatures.

NOTES

1. The Texas poll was conducted by the Office of Survey Research, University of Texas, and reported in *Austin American-Statesmen,* May 10, 1997. The characterization of the Vermont climate was made by a new member at an orientation session for Vermont legislators, Grafton, Vermont, November 19, 1994.

2. T.V. Smith, *The Legislative Way of Life.* Reprinted by Office of Urban Policy and Programs, Graduate School and University Center, the City University of New York, December 1973.

3. David Broder, address at Collins Center Florida Legislative Project, St. Petersburg, January 11, 1996.

4. Tom Loftus, *The Art of Legislative Politics* (Washington, D.C.: CQ Press, 1994), 171.

5. Ralph Wright, *All Politics Is Personal* (Manchester Center, Vt.: Marshall Jones, 1996), 11–12.

CHAPTER 1

Shifting Bases of Representation

Americans feel they have lost control of their government. Indeed, they no longer regard it as *their* government, serving their interests, but rather as a government of *others* serving special interests. For many members of the public in states across the nation, even the legislative branch of government, designed to be closest to the people, is no longer considered democratic.

The irony of this perception is that government, the first branch in particular, has in recent years become more, not less, democratic. "While Americans feel increasingly powerless, cynical, and frustrated about government," writes Lawrence Grossman, "the distance between the governed and those who govern is actually shrinking dramatically."[1] If by democracy we mean, among other things, rule by the people and political equality, then legislatures have been moving in a decidedly democratic direction. In fact, the very nature of representation is undergoing democratization, and more democracy rather than less can be anticipated in the near future.

MODELS OF DEMOCRACY

According to Robert Dahl, democracy is characterized by a distinctive set of institutions and practices, a body of rights, and a process of making collective and binding decisions. Generally, democracy (or "polyarchy," as Dahl refers to democracy in actual practice) requires officials who are elected; free and fair elections; inclusive suffrage; the right to run for office; freedom of expression; authoritative sources of information; and autonomy of associations. Presidential, congressional, or parliamentary government may fulfill these requirements. Form is not fundamental as long as other conditions are met. Anthony King portrays two models that apply nicely to the legislative branch. The first he calls the "division of labor" model, in which there are governors on the one hand and governed on the other. The function of the former is to make decisions in what they believe to be the state's best interests. The function of the latter is not to determine policy, but to choose who will do so. In this model, governors need not be responsive to public opinion. The second model is that of "agency," according to which those who govern function as agents of the people who are governed. In this model, governors must not only heed public opinion but also reflect citizen views in a narrower sense.[2] Another model, which can be labeled "direct democracy," is one in which no middlemen are necessary to act on behalf of the *demos*. The people govern directly. They themselves vote on the issues rather than elect representatives to vote in their stead.

The latter model is just that—an ideal. Direct democracy, or "pure democracy," as Madison referred to it, has little basis in practice. Besides the city-states of classical Greece and the town meetings of New England, we have little experience to go by. Furthermore, Athenian democracy excluded large elements of the population, and in this respect would not meet the requirements set for democracy today. Even if it did work in the fifth century B.C., it could not work under contemporary conditions, mainly because the modern state is not homogeneous in its interests as was the Greek city-state.

The democratic ideal of rule by the people was joined with the less-democratic practice of representation to give democracy the form it took in the new American republic. A republican form of government, in which interest is balanced against interest and branch against branch, was one principal outcome of the struggle over the U.S. Constitution. A system of representation, in which the Congress had the major representational role, was the other. Within the broad range available, the "division of labor" and "agency" models competed for predominance. The former was espoused by the Federalists, led by James Madison and Alexander Hamilton; the latter by the Anti-Federalists.

The Anti-Federalists subscribed to the idea of classical Greek democracy, in which public officials were tightly controlled. They saw representation as a necessary evil, which impeded the people from governing more directly. They opposed House constituencies of thirty thousand as too large, two-year terms as too long, the Senate as too aristocratic, and the powers of the central government as too extensive. The Federalists, in contrast, wanted larger constituencies. They subscribed to Madison's reasoning in Federalist No. 10 that a greater number of citizens means "a greater variety of parties and interests," making it "less probable that a majority of the whole will have a common motive to invade the rights of other citizens." The Federalists also feared too much citizen involvement, which could not only be inefficient but dangerous as well. They put their faith in representatives who would, as articulated by Madison in No. 10, "refine and enlarge the public views by passing them through a chosen body of citizens."

The Federalists emerged victorious. They had the major say in determining the initial structure of representative democracy in the American nation. Although the direct-majoritarian vision of the Anti-Federalists lost out, the battle over the Constitution did not end the struggle over representation. The Jacksonian era bought a resurgence of direct-democratic tendencies, as did Populist movements in the late nineteenth and early twentieth centuries. Direct primaries, initiatives and referendums, and public opinion polls, among other developments, have reshaped systems of representation in the United States.

THE LEGISLATOR'S REPRESENTATIONAL PERSPECTIVE

In his speech to the electors of Bristol in 1774, Edmund Burke advanced the case for the representative in the role of trustee: "Their [constituents'] wishes ought to have great weight with him; their opinion high respect; their business unremitted attention. It is his duty to sacrifice his repose, his pleasures, his satisfactions, to theirs—and above all, ever, and in all cases, to prefer their interest to his own. But his unbiased opinion, his mature judgment, his enlightened conscience, he ought not to sacrifice to you. . . . Your representative owes you, not his industry only, but his judgment; and he betrays, instead of serving you, if he sacrifices it to your opinion." Burke's representative is a free agent, left unfettered to do his work in the legislature. Burke, in fact, did not think that the act of representing even required that the represented be consulted. If the interests of a constituency are objective and unattached to individual constituents, as Burke believed, it is possible for the representative to promote the interests of constituents without consulting their wishes.

Many political theorists support the Burkean position, agreeing that representatives must do what is best for those in their charge, using judgment and wisdom in making their decisions.[3] Yet other political theorists maintain that the representative's duty is to reflect accurately the wishes and opinions of those who are being represented. According to this position, the representative is an agent or even a servant of the constituency. As a delegate, the representative acts in response to the wishes of constituents even if they conflict with the representative's own judgment.

Where do legislators position themselves with regard to this trustee-delegate distinction? Political scientists have given considerable attention to this question. In 1962 John Wahlke and his associates published a study of legislative behavior that soon assumed the status of a classic. In it the authors analyzed the representational role orientations of members of the California, New Jersey, Ohio, and Tennessee legislatures, characterizing legislators as "trustees," "delegates," or "politicos" (the latter being those representatives who do not fit neatly into either of the two other categories). The role that predominated in each of the four states was that of trustee, with 55 percent in California, 61 percent in New Jersey, 56 percent in Ohio, and 81 percent in Tennessee identifying with that style of representation. In contrast, only 20 percent, 17 percent, 15 percent, and 6 percent respectively were identified as delegates. The rest fell in the middle category.[4] Other studies have produced similar results. For example, a survey of Minnesota legislators found that 85 percent viewed their role mainly as that of trustee, while only one out of ten saw their role mainly as that of delegate, with the rest responding that they had mixed roles.[5]

In her theoretical work on representation, Hannah Pitkin allows for a continuum, ranging from a "mandate" theory of representation, where legislators assume delegate roles, to an "independence" theory, where they assume trustee roles. At the mandate/delegate end, representation occurs only when the representative acts on explicit instructions from constituents. The representative is an agent of the constituency, a tool or instrument by which the constituency acts. Further along the continuum, the representative exercises some discretion but is required to consult on controversial issues and then do as the constituency wishes, or else resign. Toward the middle of the continuum, a representative acts as he or she thinks constituents would want, unless they give instructions to the contrary, which the representative must obey. Proceeding further toward the independence/trustee position, the representative acts as he or she thinks is in the interests of constituents, unless they give instructions to the contrary, which have to be obeyed. Near the independence/trustee position, the representative must do as he or she thinks best, except insofar as the representative is bound by campaign promises. At the very end of the continuum the representative, once elected, is entirely free to use his or her own judgment.[6]

In a seminar discussion of representative democracy seventeen members and former members of the Florida house were probed about their views on the role of the representative and the functioning of representative democracy.[7] They were asked, among other things, to place themselves on the continuum from delegate to trustee. The distribution of self-identification is shown in figure 1.1.

The distribution of responses conforms to evidence provided by other studies. Not one legislator (or former legislator) self-identified as a delegate per se. Five placed themselves at midpoints on the continuum. These members, as one explained, "want to be representative of the mindset of the people," and they believe they are. Another felt he took on both roles: "I have sort of guiding principles, and that is the part where I am a delegate. But I am exposed to parts of that equation that the other folks at home are not. To that extent, I am a trustee." Twelve of the seventeen located themselves near the trustee end of the continuum. These members justified their positions on the basis of:

- *The importance of their own beliefs.* One explained, for example, that no matter what views her constituents expressed, she would vote for more revenues for education. She could not be budged on such a basic issue.
- *Their greater knowledge derived from their role in the legislative process.* One legislator commented that while "the public sees a snapshot, legislators see full-motion video." Legislators are exposed to information that other people simply do not get a chance to see. While apologizing for sounding elitist, a

FIGURE 1.1

Theory and Practice of Representation

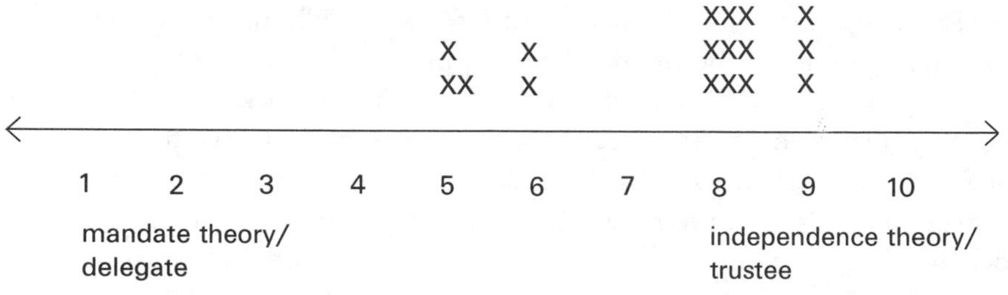

Source: Alan Rosenthal, "The Nature of Representation: An Overview," in Collins Center for Public Policy, *Making Florida Democracy Work* (Tallahassee: Collins Center, Florida State University, n.d.), 9.

former legislator insisted, "You *do* know more." Moreover, as part of their knowledge advantages, those who are there also understand what it takes to make policies and programs work.

• *The nature of their constituency and its beliefs, which on many issues preclude a delegate role, no matter what the legislator's orientation.*

HOW REPRESENTATIVES REPRESENT

Representation, as we have been discussing it, pertains to the relationship between district views or interests on the one hand and a legislator's actions on the other. The relationship is usually framed by public policy issues—with constituencies' views on taxes, welfare, education, and so forth compared with their representative's legislative action on these matters. Political scientists ordinarily seek to determine analytically the fit between constituents' views and representatives' behavior in order to assess the strength of the relationship. However, in his study of the behavior of members of the U.S. House in their districts, Richard Fenno criticizes this traditional approach. He sees representation as more than the "structural relationship in which the congruence between the policy preferences of the represented and the policy decisions of the representative" can be portrayed "by matching and calibrating substantive policy agreements."[8]

Although the representative-constituency linkage is partly a function of policy congruence, according to Fenno and other students of the process, linkage manifests itself in a variety of ways—through the conduct of casework, the acquisition of resources, and the projection of concern. All establish a connection that benefits both the representative, who builds support, and the constituents, whose individual and collective needs are addressed. Just as there is more than one way to skin a cat, so faithful representation can be demonstrated in ways besides the substance of policy.[9]

Being One of "Them"

One method of representation is to keep in close touch with constituency groups and individuals. Perhaps more symbolic than material, this method is important nonetheless. Citizens want to feel their representatives care, that they have not become one of "those people" at the state capitol. As Fenno has discussed in the case of congressmen, legislators therefore present themselves to their constituents both as they are and as constituents might like them to be. Many lawmakers in the states have been born and raised in their districts, and even those who move in as adults quickly grow roots in their new environs. Most of them have organizational and political affiliations in the district, continue to live and work part-time among their constituents, and get home on weekends or, in some states, every night, even during sessions. They make themselves constantly available to one and all.

Legislative districts vary enormously from state to state (as is shown in table 1.1), and the nature of representation depends in part on the size of a district. At one extreme are the more populous states, whose districts contain comparatively large populations. On the senate side, California's 40 members each represent about 744,000 people, Texas's 31 members each represent approximately 547,950, Ohio's 33 members 328,700, and Florida's 40 members 323,450. On the house side, California's 80 members each represent approximately 372,000 people, New Jersey's 80 members each represent about 193,250, Arizona's 60 members 122,170, and New York's 150 members 119,940.[10] At the other extreme, the least populous states have comparatively small populations in each of the legislative districts. On the senate side, North Dakota's 53 members each have approximately 12,620 constituents, Montana's 49 members 15,980, Wyoming's 30 members 15,121, and Vermont's 30 members 18,760. On the house side, New Hampshire's 400 members each have approximately 2,770 constituents, Vermont's 150 members 3,750 constituents, Wyoming's 64 members 7,090 constituents, and Montana's 100 members 7,990 constituents.

In states like North Dakota, Vermont, Wyoming, and Montana, representatives lead significantly different lives than do their counterparts in California, Texas, Ohio, and New Jersey. Their constituencies are more likely to be relatively homogeneous. They can get to know a larger proportion of their constituents, interacting with them on a person-to-person basis. Their election campaigns are door-to-door, allowing for further personal contact. Even in a state like Minnesota, the scale is manageable. There are sixty-seven senate districts, each containing two house districts. Each senate district has 60,000 people, each house district 30,000. Legislative candidates can still run door-to-door political campaigns. In contrast, those from the larger states can never be in personal touch with a very large a segment of their community. They rely instead on mail and media to get their messages across. Presumably (although we have no data on the point), constituents in districts of a few thousand people will feel closer to their representatives than constituents in districts of several hundred thousand.[11]

The nature of representation is also affected by geographical size and shape. In this respect, there is variation within states, generally with urban districts

TABLE 1.1
Population of State Legislative Districts

| | Senate | | House | |
	Seats	District Population[a]	Seats	District Population[a]
Alabama	35	115,450	105	38,480
Alaska	20	27,500	40	13,750
Arizona	30	122,170	60	122,170[b]
Arkansas	35	67,160	100	23,510
California	40	744,000	80	372,000
Colorado	35	94,130	65	50,680
Connecticut	36	91,310	151	21,770
Delaware	21	31,720	41	16,250
Florida	40	323,450	120	107,820
Georgia	56	115,680	180	35,990
Hawaii	25	44,330	51	21,730
Idaho	42	23,970	84	23,970[b]
Illinois	59	193,740	118	96,870
Indiana	50	111,080	100	55,540
Iowa	50	55,540	100	27,770
Kansas	40	61,940	125	19,820
Kentucky	38	96,980	100	36,850
Louisiana	39	108,200	105	40,190
Maine	35	35,080	151	8,130
Maryland	47	101,730	141	33,910
Massachusetts	40	150,410	160	37,600
Michigan	38	244,610	110	84,500
Minnesota	67	65,300	134	32,650
Mississippi	52	49,490	122	21,090
Missouri	34	150,500	163	31,390
Montana	50	15,980	100	7,990
Nebraska	49	32,210	—	—
Nevada	21	57,230	42	28,620
New Hampshire	24	46,210	400	2,770
New Jersey	40	193,260	80	193,250[b]
New Mexico	42	36,070	70	21,640
New York	61	294,930	150	119,940
North Carolina	50	132,570	120	55,240
North Dakota	53	12,620	106	12,620[b]

(Table continues on the following page.)

TABLE 1.1
(continued)

	Senate		House	
	Seats	District Population[a]	Seats	District Population[a]
Ohio	33	328,700	99	109,570
Oklahoma	48	65,530	101	31,140
Oregon	30	94,740	60	47,370
Pennsylvania	50	237,630	203	58,530
Rhode Island	50	20,070	100	10,040
South Carolina	46	75,800	124	28,120
South Dakota	35	19,890	70	19,890[b]
Tennessee	33	147,790	99	49,260
Texas	31	547,950	150	113,240
Utah	29	59,410	75	22,970
Vermont	30	18,760	150	3,750
Virginia	40	154,680	100	61,870
Washington	49	99,320	98	49,660
West Virginia	34	52,750	100	17,940
Wisconsin	33	148,240	99	49,410
Wyoming	30	15,120	64	7,090

Source: Anthony Gierzynski, "Elections to the State Legislatures," in *Encyclopedia of the American Legislative System,* ed. Joel H. Silbey (New York: Scribner's, 1994): 436–437.

[a] Population is given for single-member districts in states with mixed district types. District populations were calculated by dividing the 1990 population of the state by the number of seats.

[b] Population for districts with 2 seats.

being more concentrated and rural districts more dispersed. In California districts range from 18 square miles to 28,991 square miles. New York's range from 1 square mile to 4,731 square miles. Colorado's districts range from those in the city, which are roughly 6 square miles, to a district of 12,916 square miles, covering the entire northwest corner of the state.[12] The larger the territory of the district, of course, the more difficult it is for representatives—either routinely or during the reelection campaign—to meet face-to-face with their constituents.

In smaller states, legislators soon develop a feel for the rhythm, tempo, and timing of different groups. The Chambers of Commerce may gather for breakfast, the Rotary Clubs for lunch, and the Board of Realtors for dinner. The

League of Women Voters may meet on Sunday afternoons, while the sportsmen's club gets together on Saturday night. Add to all of that the town hall meetings and the special sessions that legislators themselves set up. In larger states, legislators are given district offices or allowances to pay for them and staff aides to support their efforts at home. They also have budgets for newsletters to inform constituents of what they are doing on their behalf, and for questionnaires to find out what is on people's minds. Some legislatures facilitate communications by providing studio facilities for producing audio- and videotapes that can be broadcast on radio and television back home.

Nowadays, few legislators choose to take lightly their relationships with the people back home. Most respond to constituents' requests, make time for their calls, and juggle busy schedules in order to be available for their visits. One veteran Maryland lawmaker addressed the following advice to those who were newly elected: "Above all else, answer your constituent mail and phone calls first. This is more important than being schmoozed by the governor or anyone else."[13]

Although there is no hard evidence, practitioners agree that lawmakers, when they are not actually legislating, have been spending more and more of their time "coming around" to visit with constituents and listen to their concerns. In a few of the states that still have citizen legislatures, the people's representatives are granted a sabbatical from their governmental duties when the legislature is not in session and allowed to resume their regular employment in order to earn a living. They are not expected to represent the folks back home when they are back home themselves and not engaged at the capital. But in most states today, representatives have no time off. People expect them to be available when the legislature is in and out of session and on weekends as well as weekdays, during the night as well as the day. Few legislators are willing to disappoint their constituents or risk being perceived as unavailable.

Providing Service to Them

Legislators also fulfill their representational function in rendering constituency service by means of redressing grievances—that is, by doing casework—for individuals having problems with government at one level or another. Constituents request assistance from their representatives on issues involving welfare, health and hospitals, unemployment compensation, roads and highways, traffic, nursing-home care, drivers' licenses, occupational licenses, insurance, taxes, and public jobs.

Some legislators can go further, making awards on their own. In Louisiana, Maryland, and Illinois, they can give out a few college scholarships. Legislative scholarships have been a perquisite of members of the Illinois General Assembly for almost a century. Currently each member can hand out two four-year scholarships annually, as long as the recipients live in their districts. Most make their awards on the basis of merit, but some use them as a perk in the political game.[14]

Years ago legislators were much less involved in the service function than they are today. Of the 474 members in four states interviewed almost four decades ago by Wahlke and his associates, only about one-quarter spontaneously mentioned service as an important aspect of the job.[15] Depending on the state, anywhere from one-third to two-thirds would now cite constituency service as an important, or even *the* most important, part of the job of being a legislator. Research conducted several years ago by Malcolm Jewell shows that constituency service looms extremely large in California, Massachusetts, Ohio, and Texas; is less so in Indiana, Kentucky, and Tennessee; and is relatively unimportant in Colorado and North Carolina. The differences are attributable, at least in part, to the availability of staff to take on constituency service tasks in some places but not in others.[16]

Where legislators have district offices and staff, such as in California, Florida, New York, and New Jersey, casework becomes a normal part of the legislative routine. Staff takes on much of the burden, although legislators always bear some of it. A California assemblyman, for example, has his administrative assistant in the district office meet periodically with directors of the state's local offices (such as motor vehicles and employment development), and his aide in Sacramento works regularly with the legislative liaison personnel of a number of state agencies. Casework becomes routine. Those legislators who see the psychic benefits of cutting through bureaucratic red tape and those who see the electoral benefits of handling constituent problems go further. They are likely to advertise their services, by word of mouth or even in the press, to generate more business.

Even in places where staff for constituency purposes is scarce or nonexistent, legislators have entered into a casework mode. Take Vermont, for instance. The legislature here has a small staff that provides bill drafting and fiscal analysis assistance, but not constituent service. Legislators, nevertheless, have much more casework than they had in the past, and they have started to complain about the load and the costs that they personally have to pay. The Arkansas legislature faced a similar situation, but responded by hiring additional staff for a newly created bureau of constituency services.[17]

Some legislators go even further than those who incur out-of-pocket expenses, usually for long-distance telephone, in helping constituents. An Oklahoma representative is an example. A constituent called him at home to complain about the overgrowth of weeds on the median strip of the local highway. The representative knew there was no way he could get the highway department bureaucracy to do anything, so he took his own lawnmower, drove to the highway, and cut down the weeds himself.[18] A Colorado representative acted in similar fashion. In going door-to-door in his district, he asked constituents if he could help them in any way. One woman told him, "Yeah, you can water my petunias." The representative thereupon went outside, turned on the hose, and watered the petunias.[19] In another instance of service beyond the call of duty, a Massachusetts senator would regularly pick up clothes that constituents wanted exchanged at Filene's Basement department store in Boston.[20] Assuming he did not select the wrong size or color (there were risks even here), he could count on building and solidifying support in his district.

"In the case of casework, I am certainly a delegate," a Florida legislator declared for himself and, no doubt, for just about all of his colleagues. In the discussion of representation, members and former members all agreed on service as an important part of their job. Helping constituents, in their minds, is what they are supposed to do.

Casework in Florida as elsewhere may create difficulties for the contemporary legislator. Constituents come to a legislator with problems like the following: "We are having trouble getting a permit," or "I want my daughter to go to Florida State." Legislators write letters and make phone calls to help constituents out. Then they get accused of abusing their power. In a few cases they do abuse their power, and in more than a few cases they appear to be doing so. Florida's legislators are conscious of the problem. Several are wary lest their intervention affect a state administrator's decision. It is all right for them to cut through red tape, but they distinguish between helping to handle the constituent's case and advocating a particular decision. Yet they want to act on their constituents' behalf. "The extremes," said one house member, "are ambivalence on the one side and being a bully on the other side, and the tightrope that we must walk is in between." In performing this representational role, legislators have to watch their step.

Acquiring Resources for Them

If constituent service, which has generally been viewed as an inoffensive activity, raises ethical issues, efforts by legislators to bring resources to their districts (and prevent resources from being taken away) raises even more. Little is more salient to legislators than state aid channeled to local units of government—counties, municipalities, and school districts. Legislators try to ensure that the funding formula enacted into law benefits their constituencies as much as possible. How does the allocation of funds compare with that made to a neighboring district? With most allocations? When it comes to devising or revising an aid formula for education, public welfare, highways, or general support, legislators have their constituencies foremost in mind. In these situations, such a thing as a state interest is almost completely lost from view. The local interest is virtually all that matters.

As representatives, legislators also seek projects for their districts that range from the expensive (including convention centers, community colleges, and county courthouses) to the paltry (such as funds for boxing clubs, boys' choirs, and the trips taken by high-school bands). Projects like these that find their way into state budgets are known generally as "pork," but in New York they are known as "member items," in Pennsylvania as "walking-around money," and as "turkeys" in Florida. Often, a legislature will set aside a sum of money to be divided between the senate and house and then among the members. New York reportedly dedicated $48 million to such items in a recent state budget.[21] Sometimes the representative has to choose which among a number of worthy district causes to endorse. For example, one New Mexico legislator in a normal year might have about $300,000 on which to draw. He would review all the requests from his constituency and then choose three or four as priorities, making sure they were spread around (with one from Los Alamos, where the most votes are) and could be justified on the basis of need and merit.[22]

Although bringing home the bacon is standard practice nowadays, legislators draw distinctions based on the nature of their districts. In some places, spending on construction and facilities may be less welcome. Constituents would rather not have roads laid, prisons constructed, or landfills sited. In other places, where the economy has declined and unemployment has risen, virtually any project is looked on favorably.

Expressing Their Policy Views and Interests

When it comes to gestures that express concern, constituency service that helps individuals with their government-related problems, state aid, or pork, the role of the representative is relatively straightforward. Problems may arise along the way, such as the ethical questions confronting a legislator who champions the case of a constituent who also happens to contribute to the legislator's campaigns. Still, it is not difficult for the representative qua delegate to know which way to go in pursuit of the district's interests. On symbolic matters on the one hand and material concerns on the other, the mandate is clear: heed and express constituency concerns, bring home the bacon, and help the folks back home who have run afoul of government.[23]

It is much more difficult, however, for representatives to act as agents of their constituency on policy matters. Let us assume for the moment that representatives want to play the delegate role on issues. To do so, they must determine who their constituents are, what views—if any—their constituents hold, how strongly they feel, how they divide, and whether a constituency mandate can be said to exist.

Legally, a representative's constituency consists of all those people living within a specified district. Demographically, a constituency may be mainly urban, suburban, or rural. It may be largely white or predominantly black or Hispanic. It may be affluent or poor. The more heterogeneous the district, the more difficult it is to represent because its interests are more diverse. Politically, a constituency is less than the entire population; rather, it consists of those people who vote or who are eligible to vote. Even the electorate as constituency can be subdivided—into "primary" and "reelection" constituencies, the former being a representative's strongest supporters and main source of campaign funds and endorsements, and the latter being those who voted for the representative at the last election.[24]

These several demographic and political constituencies must be factored into a representative's thinking. A member of the Florida house, who is from a Republican district, explained he got 40 percent of the vote in the primary and 54 percent in the general election, in which 14,000 people elected him and sent him to Tallahassee. That, he figured, is about 20 percent of the electorate. The other 80 percent either did not vote for him or simply did not vote. But as a representative, according to his understanding, he had to accommodate the 80 percent as well as the 20.

If the very definition of constituency is unclear, then the distribution of constituency views on issues before the legislature is even blurrier. Suppose the representative wants to take on the role of delegate. Can it be done? The representative, according to mandate theory, must do what his or her principal would do if the principal were acting. But in the case of political representation, there is not one principal, but an entire constituency of anywhere from a few thousand to hundreds of thousands of principals.[25]

In much of their work, political scientists have reduced constituencies to major dimensions—liberal or conservative, white-collar or blue-collar, white or black, rich or poor. Knowing a district's sociodemographic composition is to know much, but by no means enough. Political scientists, furthermore, would distinguish among constituencies on the basis of their homogeneity.[26] Homogeneous constituency characteristics no doubt help representatives interpret district views on some issues; yet on other issues they are of no help whatsoever.

As Pitkin points out, a constituency is not a single unit with an opinion on every topic. A representative, thus, cannot reflect what is not there to be reflected.[27] The overwhelming majority of issues addressed at a legislative session engage only a small proportion of citizens in any one district. This does not mean these issues are not important to at least some constituents. Many of them are what might be called "special interest" issues—of concern to optometrists and ophthalmologists, dentists and dental hygienists, mayors and municipal officials, a corporation or business, and so forth. They affect the well-being and the livelihoods of relatively small professional and occupational groups, industries, or businesses. But they are not matters that command public interest or concern, and therefore constituency views on these issues, if they exist, are few and far between. One Florida legislator, for instance, pointed out that there was virtually no opinion in her district on 95 percent of the issues on which she had to vote. She recalled that one of her early votes (she sat on the regulated industries committee) affected the disposition of the Florida stamp on a beer can. "It is rare," she commented, "that I have a sense of really what my district feels on any issue, except the most major questions." Not surprisingly, her constituents had no feelings about beer-can labeling.

Constituents can express themselves rather directly on issues before the legislature, communicating by telephone, mail, or fax. Some letters are thoughtful, but much of the correspondence legislators receive is uninformed, unclear, and unconvincing. Moreover, much of it is inspired by organized interest groups and does not accurately represent the true feelings of constituents. Aware of the ability of special interests to affect the thinking of their constituents on a given issue, some legislators discount the messages they receive. Others, not at all sure of what the communication means, would rather not run the risk of neglecting any possible reflection of constituency views.

On some occasions, voters have the opportunity to express themselves very clearly. In Florida, for instance, citizens voted county by county on whether to raise the local sales tax to finance school construction. Most such proposals were defeated overwhelmingly, presumably sending a message as to how people felt about taxes, even for education. But one Florida house member, whose constituency defeated such a proposal, declared she would not feel at all bound by the results of the referendum. The defeat of the proposal, she said, was not an expression of antitax fervor or lack of support for education, but rather a demonstration of anger toward the government and the school board. This legislator could justify behaving as a trustee in this instance, but realized she might have to pay an electoral price.

Should all expressions of opinion count equally to the representative, or should more intensely held views matter more than those that seem to be only loosely anchored? If legislators assign greater importance to more intensely held views, then participation by those concerned should be especially valued. Although voter turnout has generally declined, evidence suggests that the number of politically active constituents has increased. These constituents are joining interest groups, writing letters, and contributing to campaigns.[28] Such activists make up a larger portion of the electorate than before, and are likely to hold more intense views, be more vocal, and be susceptible to mobilization. They are very different from the disengaged, inattentive majority.

A Missouri legislator describes changes in participation that have brought constituents closer to their legislators than they were twenty or forty years ago. "When I came into the system as a senator, I got six letters, threw five in the wastebasket and said to the secretary, 'Tell the other S.O.B. he doesn't know what he's talking about'. That was about the relationship and attitude we all had." Not anymore. Transportation improvements have made it easier for citizens to visit the capital, and district offices have made the legislator more accessible.[29] Still, the question remains, just who participates? How typical are these politically active voters? An Ohio senator doubts the representativeness of the activist minority. "If you go to 100 meetings in my district," he commented, "you'll meet the same people 85 times."[30]

Should the representative be attentive only to the *desires* of the constituency (assuming such desires can be determined), or should the representative care as much or more about the *interests* of the constituency (and how would such interests be determined)? Burke recognized the distinction between the desires of a voter on the one hand, and a voter's interests on the other. Similarly, the desires of a constituency and its interests may also differ. Does a large, heterogeneous constituency or a small, homogeneous constituency have an interest for the representative to pursue? On some issues, perhaps; but on many, the constituency may have no, or conflicting, interests. Is it possible for representatives to know their constituents' interests any better than they can know their constituents' opinions?[31] Not likely, but representatives are guided by their interpretation of what those interests are. They are also guided by what appears to be in, or on, their constituents' minds. Often they cannot be sure of either, for there is no guarantee that either interests or opinions really exist.

THE REPRESENTATIONAL PROCESS

A 1991 newspaper survey of 110 members of the South Carolina legislature found that 24 percent named constituent service and district funding as their most important role as legislators. Another 38 percent ranked constituency service and setting state policy as equally important. The remaining 37 percent ranked setting policy above constituency service in importance.[32] For three out of four members, therefore, policy-making for the state of South Carolina constitutes a most significant part of their job. These legislators, among the many in other states, recognize their responsibilities to their state as well as to their districts.

Burke expressed in vivid fashion the idea that the representative must pursue the interest of the state and that the legislative body "is a *deliberative* assembly of *one* nation, with *one* interest, that of the whole; where, not local purposes, not local prejudices ought to guide, but the general good, resulting from the general reason of the whole." Madison similarly urged against legislators sacrificing the interest of the state for the particular and separated views of their counties and districts.[33]

Although locally elected, legislators have little recourse but to work to advance the interest of the state. The interest of the state, however, will not necessarily emerge as the sum of local constituency desires.[34] For the state interest to be well represented, legislators must think in terms of the whole as opposed to only the part that elects them. The legislative process itself facilitates their doing so. The legislature and the process by which policies are enacted introduces additional obligations for the legislator to assume. These added duties can hardly be ignored. The representative does not act alone, on behalf of his constituency or otherwise. The representative works with colleagues in an institutionalized context trying to hammer out policies for the state. Pitkin summarizes the context of the representational process in the legislature. "The modern representative," she writes, "acts within an elaborate network of pressures, demands, and obligations."[35]

To represent their districts, let alone the state, representatives must deliberate, negotiate, and collaborate with one another. They are responsible to the

committees on which they serve, the legislative parties with whom they affiliate, and the chamber or party leaders who wield influence over their agendas. In their actions as legislators they are answerable to many individuals, as
well as to the voters who elect them. And they listen to them all. For example,
when Ohio legislators were interviewed in 1993, they were asked whom they
consulted in making their decisions. About 60 percent said they consulted
their constituents, another 30 to 40 percent reported consulting interest groups,
party leaders, ranking committee members, legislative experts, and the like.[36]

It is likely that newer legislators put more stock in what they think their
constituents might desire, while more senior legislators balance their obligations a bit differently. Particularly nowadays, incoming members feel they
have been elected to transmit the voices of their constituents to those who
govern. But, as a member of the Florida house described the metamorphosis:
"The longer you are in the process, the more you tend to become a trustee. . . .
When I think back on my career, I certainly see how I have moved from
being a delegate advocating for my constituents to being a trustee in trying to
advocate . . . what I think is in the best interest of all of the people in Florida."
Changes in position result from changes in perspective that derive, in turn,
from greater information, longer experience, additional responsibilities, increasing obligations, more of a historical sense, and a developing institutional
commitment. All of these build over time.

Tenure affects representative roles; so does the issue. On most issues, relatively few constituents have opinions, and legislators need not be constrained
by constituency mandates, for nothing near to a mandate exists. Not many
issues meet the criterion of "mandate," but some do. In every state and every
district, there are scattered matters about which people care a great deal, and
a number of issues around which they can be mobilized. Legislators must be
concerned about constituency views on these matters before they themselves
take a position. A veteran senator in Minnesota advised: "You can stay out of
trouble if you keep away from hunting, fishing, and daylight-saving time"—
salient issues in his district and elsewhere in the state.

How does a legislator determine the existence of a mandate and, if it exists,
what it is? Although constituents may express concern on some issues, what
they want done is far from clear. "But there are some issues where it is so
overwhelming," said a Florida house member, "you hear it from so many
people in so many different walks of life that it is clear. That is a mandate."
This particular representative, like so many others, was able to derive what he
called "guiding principles" from the voices in his district. One of these principles was, "Be tough on crime."[37] The representative explained that "my

constituency has said over and over again, you have to lock them up, you have to be tough." For one Florida member, supporting bingo was a "guiding principle," and she was not hesitant about assuming the delegate role on that. Another Florida member personally favored legalized gambling, but his district voted overwhelming against it in a state referendum. "From that point on," he acknowledged, "I became antigambling." His colleagues agreed with him. On an issue like gambling, they felt, the personal preferences of the people should be weighed heavily, although on the large majority of issues, the people's representatives have a superior vantage point.

Despite there being few issues on which constituency mandates can be said to exist, legislators are becoming more attentive than ever before to the views of individuals and groups in the district. William Bryant, a former legislator from Michigan, describes the situation as he saw it:

> I watched one decent, hardworking legislator sit frozen with fear on a
> controversial issue because he did not know the immediate, momentary
> majority view of his constituents. . . . A far less worthy legislator, in contrast,
> brought only his eyes to the legislative session, for he wanted to know only
> how the others from his geographic region of the state were voting in order to
> determine his own vote. That was his measure of public opinion . . . and . . .
> public opinion was all that mattered to him. Once in a while he would run a
> quick phone poll or do a mailed questionnaire and then act as if the results
> were divine truth.[38]

Judgment and trusteeship are still requisite, but representatives increasingly feel obliged to take soundings of their constituents so as not to run aground.

Legislators themselves appear to be more parochial than was formerly the case. Single-member districts tend to engender stronger local orientations among their legislators than do multimember districts. Constituency groups are more insistent and grassroots-issue campaigns more common. When legislators are in their districts, which is most of the time (even in states like California, Michigan, and New York), they are constantly subject to the problems, requests, and demands of their constituents. A former member of the California assembly described the representational experience: "In Sacramento you could be a ruler without fear of overthrow. Back in the district, you're brought down to earth."[39] And more and more frequently, legislators back home are being pounded into the earth.

Even legislators who seem to have a lock on their seat may feel electorally insecure. They never know when a well-funded opponent will challenge them in a primary or general election. They have witnessed electoral lightning striking colleagues considered "safe" but who somehow lost touch with their districts. They do not want the same to happen to them. Of course, those with a history of freedom from partisan, well-financed, and bitter campaigns have some leeway to behave as trustees. But they, too, can be called to account.

One Florida legislator from a safe district told how she was targeted in a primary because of the positions she took. As a consequence, she had to raise more money and run harder than she ever had in order to win. Another Florida legislator recalls two votes he cast in Tallahassee that did not reflect his constituency's feelings. One involved a proposal to establish a new law school at Florida Agricultural and Mechanical University (FAMU), which the Board of the Regents opposed because it had recommended a scholarship program for minority students instead. The representative offered a bill encompassing the regents' idea, which aroused the FAMU community throughout the state and in his district. "I took the position knowing the people were opposed to it," he explained, "but I felt it was the best thing for my constituents." He maintained his position, was soundly criticized, but still emerged in one political piece. On another occasion, where he went against his constituency, this representative not only explained why he took the position he did but also promised he would never do it again. No strong opponent arose in the next election, so presumably his constituents had been sufficiently reassured.

Elections are the mechanism by which representatives are held accountable. If legislators stray too far afield, they risk challenge and defeat at the polls. "Because of their vulnerability," Anthony King writes, "officeholders are extraordinarily sensitive to opinions and demands of voters in their districts." They are subjected, continuously, to a level of electoral pressure that is extremely high by the standards of other democratic nations.[40] They feel under constant scrutiny—as, indeed, they are—particularly, but not only, at election time.

One Florida representative expressed his feelings: "I think they [the voters] know a lot more about us than we think. I mean, I pick up the paper every once in a while and I learn things about myself that I hadn't even thought about yet." Another Florida representative pointed out that when an elected public official—involved for some time in the community—engages in a campaign for reelection, citizens will "know exactly who you are, where you are coming from, what kind of background you have." It is during the campaign, moreover, that legislators must explain their votes, particularly the unpopular ones, to constituents and organized groups within their districts.

Legislators have far less to fear from rejecting constituency mandates, which they rarely do, than from simply angering one side or the other by taking a position on an issue about which constituents care but on which opinion is divided. One Florida legislator calls these "coin flip" issues: concerns that find as many people feeling one way as the other. Frequently, these are issues legislators prefer to avoid, sensing they will lose either way—voting "yes" or "no." Many coin-flip issues engage relatively few voters. Not infrequently these few feel strongly about the issue, are readily organized, and have the potential for influencing others.

The political task of legislators, be they trustees or delegates, is damage control as much as anything else. In order to remain in office, they have to be careful not to annoy too many people. They deal in electoral margins or increments and are never certain how many disgruntled people are too many. The more secure they are (or the more secure they feel) and the more they conceive of the representative's role as that of trustee, the greater the risks they are willing to run. But even the most courageous and independent will try not to expose themselves on all the issues that confront them as members of the legislature. So, if there is a way to straddle a fence, vote on both sides, or not have to choose sides at all, legislators will jump at the opportunity. This should not be surprising.

Legislators believe they should act in the interests of their constituency and with the views of their constituents in mind. Even if they were in their last term of office, they would feel this way because this belief is rooted in our representational culture. Were there any doubts as to their representatives' devotion, voters can take comfort in the ever-approaching election. Elections are more than a mechanism for choosing representatives; they also help to prevent representatives from veering away from constituency interests and desires.[41]

Somewhere between the poles of delegate and trustee, in Pitkin's words, the representative acts "in the interest of the represented, in a manner responsive to them." The representative's action inevitably involves discretion and judgment, and the potential for conflict between the representative and the represented about what is to be done is seldom absent. But such conflict must be the exception and not the rule, for a representative cannot be persistently at odds with the wishes of the represented.[42] In view of the desires of representatives to be in step with their constituents, the frequency of elections, and the potential (if not the guarantee) of opposition, it is extremely unlikely that representatives will get very far out of line with their constituencies—writ large—but in the normal course of affairs they will be unable not to offend one constituency group or another.

THE LEGISLATURE AS REPRESENTATIVE ASSEMBLY

Although it is essential to examine the legislator as a constituency representative, it is also necessary to examine the *legislature* as a representative institution. The two are related, but the relationship is by no means simple and direct. Even if all legislators represent perfectly the districts that elect them, the collectivity of perfect representatives might not add up to a perfectly representative body. Yet just as individual legislators have become more responsive to their constituencies, so legislatures have become more democratic bodies and more subject to democratic currents beyond their institutional boundaries. As the function of representation has changed in recent years, legislative democracy has changed in four ways: politically, descriptively, participatorily, and deliberatively.

Political Representation

Representation is certainly more democratic since the U.S. Supreme Court rulings in *Baker v. Carr* (1962) and *Reynolds v. Sims* (1964) changed apportionment and districting laws. Prior to these Court reapportionment decisions, the populations of districts deviated considerably within a state—more markedly in some legislative bodies, but to some degree in all. Generally, a rural member of a state senate or house had substantially fewer constituents to represent than did an urban or suburban member. The fewer the citizens who shared a representative, the greater their representation in the legislature as individuals. Thus, not all people were equal in political terms.

After the Supreme Court's intervention into the political thicket of reapportionment, the doctrine of "one person, one vote" became the standard and the population variations among senate districts and among house districts within each state became negligible. In effect, every person has political, or legal, representation equal to that of everyone else.

With the reapportionment revolution, the major issue of political representation had been resolved. But other issues, such as gerrymandering, persisted. Gerrymandering is a practice that allows the dominant political party to seek advantage through the drawing of district lines. The objective of the party in control of the process is to maximize the distribution of its own partisan voters and minimize the distribution of its opponent's partisan voters. Thus, state electoral systems tend to overrepresent majorities of one party or the other. This results partly from district lines being drawn to waste an opponent's votes, while fully utilizing one's own. For example, the dominant party will try to put as many opposition voters in one district as possible, ceding the seat; meanwhile, its own districts will have comfortable, but not wasteful, majorities of its own voters. Even in fairly apportioned districts, a minority's votes can be wasted. So it is not unusual to see a party with 55 percent of the statewide vote winning 60 percent of the legislative seats.[43] The case of *Davis v. Bandemer* (1986) opened the federal door to challenges aimed at partisan gerrymandering. But as of yet, the U.S. Supreme Court has not ruled definitively on just what is permissible and what is not.

Another democratizing trend in political representation has been the decline since the 1960s in multimember districts and the concomitant increase in single-member districts. Currently, only seven senates and fifteen houses of all ninety-nine chambers have some members from multimember districts. In Alaska, Idaho, Vermont, West Virginia, and Wyoming both chambers are multimember in composition. In Arizona, Arkansas, Georgia, Indiana, Maryland, New Hampshire, New Jersey, South Dakota, and Washington, only the house, and in Nevada only the senate, is multimember.[44]

Ordinarily, multimember districts impede the minority party. Because candidates are not likely to be very visible, most people will vote for one party's slate or the other's. This means that even if 40 or 45 percent vote for the minority party, it might fail to win any seats at all. If the district were to be divided up, however, it is more likely that minority voters concentrated in one area or another would elect one of their candidates.

Multimember districts are also supposed to hinder minority groups for the same reasons they thwart minority parties. The use of multimember districts has been challenged on civil rights grounds in the federal courts. As a result of the U.S. Supreme Court's decision in *Connor v. Johnson* 402 U.S. 690 (1971), Mississippi was forced to divide Hinds County into single-member districts, and as a result of the Court's decision in *White v. Regester* 412 U.S. 755 (1973), Texas had to create single-member districts out of two multimember districts.

Within a mixed system, any organized indigenous interest, or for that matter any resourceful constituent, would appear to benefit from multimember representation in comparison with constituents represented by single members. In the multimember districts, groups or individuals may enlist multiple legislator allies and not merely one. A multimember arrangement therefore enables certain constituents and constituency interests to have more voice in the state legislature than others, even though each district has the same ratio of members to population. The fewer such disparities, the more democratic the representational system.

Single-member districts, moreover, tend to bring members and constituents closer together. Legislators' districts are smaller. Legislators are more identifiable. They cannot hide in a crowd or seek protection by voting in a bloc. They are on their own—fully exposed. They do not have the luxury of running for reelection as a team; they have to wage individual campaigns. These legislators become more parochial—as we see in the case of Florida, which went to single-member districts in 1982. Their concern for local interests increases, and their concern for statewide interests diminishes.

"Descriptive" Representation

In theory, descriptive representation is a system in which one person stands for others "by being sufficiently like them." If descriptive representation is a goal, the legislature should "mirror" or "picture" the people of the state. As John Adams said during the debate over the U.S. Constitution, a representative legislature "should be an exact portrait, in miniature, of the people at large." According to this notion, representation is not to do something on behalf of, but rather to reflect typical characteristics of, one's constituency.[45]

Although it would be nearly impossible for representatives to supply a perfectly accurate reflection of the citizenry, other suitably representative arrangements are conceivable. Stratified random sampling would best produce a microcosm of the people. Selection by lot would be more *descriptively* representative than the recruitment process we have now. But must a legislature mirror the citizenry in order to be representative? And which characteristics—sociological, ideological, educational, occupational, gender, or racial— must it seek to mirror?

Legislatures today, as in the past, do not reflect state populations. They are elitist bodies, at least in the sense that members tend to be from the more privileged and achieving sectors of society. Legislators are better educated and have higher incomes than average citizens. Almost half have postgraduate education, and a total of 82 percent of state legislators have at least college. Almost one-third earned more than $85,000 in their outside jobs.[46] But in several respects legislative bodies have been becoming more descriptively representative and, by that measure, more democratic in composition.

One of the most important changes has been in the number of women serving in state legislatures. One estimate is that in 1940 only 2 percent of the nation's legislators were women. By 1969–1970 the percentage had doubled, but still to only 4 percent. As of 1997, 21.5 percent of the total number of state legislators were women—18.2 percent in senates and 22.6 percent in houses.[47] Earlier, women had uphill campaigns with serious obstacles in the way of their election and little chance of winning. Since the mid-1980s, however, the electoral fortunes of women running for the legislature have been equal to those of men, with incumbent women having an equal success rate to that of their male counterparts.[48] In some states—Washington, Arizona, Colorado, Vermont, New Hampshire, Nevada, and Minnesota—women constitute 30 percent or more of the legislators today.

The progress made by women is representationally significant. Research shows that female legislators do differ from their male counterparts in their policy priorities, their more liberal and feminist voting records, and their view of themselves as representatives of women's concerns.[49] They have introduced new issues onto legislative agendas, stressing women's, children's, and family concerns. Particularly pertinent here, 57 percent of women legislators consider representing women "very important," while only 33 percent of men legislators feel this way.[50]

The gains made by African Americans in the legislative ranks are not nearly as great as those made by women. Still, the number of black state legislators has also been on the rise since 1973–1974, when they constituted just 3 percent of the total. They have made considerable gains in the South, so that currently the African American proportion of the national total is a little more than 6 percent.[51]

In the past decade African American representation has been abetted by the federal courts and their interpretation of the 1982 amendments to the Voting Rights Act. In *Thornburgh v. Gingles* (1986), the Court ruled that the states must draw legislator district boundaries so as to create minority districts whenever possible. The states followed the ruling in both the congressional and state legislative redistricting of 1991–1992, stretching lines in order to produce a number of new majority minority districts. But in recent opinions, the courts have reversed field, saying in *Miller v. Johnson* (1995) that race cannot be the "predominant factor" in drawing boundaries. This decision has left in some doubt just how much of a factor race can be. In 1996 a federal court panel declared nine South Carolina districts unconstitutional, saying they were drawn solely on the basis of race.

The representational effects of "racial gerrymandering," as it is called by opponents, have occurred primarily in southern states at both the congressional and legislative levels. More African Americans were elected to office by districts with black majorities. With African American voters jammed into designated districts, however, the adjoining districts have become more white, more conservative, and more Republican. Racial districting has thus benefited black populations in one respect but cost them in another. They have gained black representatives but have lost moderate or moderately conservative white Democrats (most of whom have been replaced by very conservative white Republicans). In South Carolina, for instance, the number of African American members of the 124-member house increased from 3 in 1971, to 14 in 1981, to 17 in 1990, to 18 in 1993. Concurrently, the number of Republican members rose from 11 to 17 to 42 to 50.[52]

The occupations of state legislators, too, have changed. Although the original assemblies were dominated by colonial elites, in the nineteenth century the proportion of the extremely rich in the state legislatures fell from one-half to one-quarter. Meanwhile, the proportion of merchants and lawyers also declined in the northern states.[53] The legislature of the 1960s and 1970s continued to be dominated by business and law, with about two-fifths of the members engaged in the former and almost one-fourth engaged in the latter. By 1993 the proportions in business and law had declined significantly. Only one out of six legislators was a lawyer and one out of five was in business. A growing number of members nowadays are not only full-time legislators, but have had no other profession but politics in their lives. In some places—such as Maine, New Hampshire, North Carolina, South Dakota, and Vermont—retirees comprise a substantial cadre among legislators.[54]

Probably the chief occupational change has been the decline in the number of attorneys. Plenty of them still serve in Virginia, Texas, Louisiana, New Jersey, Kentucky, Florida, and South Carolina.[55] But the time demands and the financial disclosure laws deter many practicing attorneys from seeking legislative office. In some states—New Hampshire and Delaware are examples—only a few lawyers still serve, and in some places there are not enough even to fill the ranks of judiciary committees. Legislative bodies are no longer dominated by the legal profession. The contemporary legislature is thus at least somewhat more descriptively representative than it used to be.

Participatory Representation

A system of participatory representation is characterized by high input from voters in decisions made on issues before the legislature. Such participation ranges from citizen initiatives that bypass legislatures entirely to issue campaigns that involve substantial grassroots lobbying efforts.

In the early 1980s futurist John Naisbitt called attention to a "massive shift" from representative to participatory democracy or, more accurately, representation with greater and greater participation by citizens. We have moved the locus of political power, he observed, and given it to citizens through direct ballot vote and grassroots participation. He not only identified this change as a "megatrend" but also applauded it. "The fact is," he wrote, "we have outlived the historical usefulness of representative democracy, and we all sense intuitively that it is obsolete."[56]

THE INITIATIVE AND REFERENDUM. The initiative, which is permitted in twenty-four states, is the principal way for citizens to vote directly (or indirectly in the case of indirect initiatives and referenda) on issues, enacting them into the state constitution or statute, or rejecting them entirely. The initiative provides for maximum citizen participation. Populists and Progressives were deeply mistrustful of the legislatures, accusing them of being captives of the special interests. Between 1898 and 1918, nineteen states provided for the initiative, and the other five adopted the initiative since 1959, with Mississippi being the last.

The referendum is a common procedure. Voters in all states but Delaware must formally approve changes in the state constitution by referendum. Legislatures, on their own, often place issues on the ballot (including bond measures for capital expenditures) as a way to secure a public decision. The popular referendum, however, is different; it bypasses the legislature's wishes and permits citizens to place a measure enacted by the legislature on the ballot for a ratifying or rejecting vote.

The initiative process allows citizens to draft laws or constitutional amendments, place them on the ballot, and have the voters decide their fate. If a proposed law goes directly to the ballot, it is a direct initiative. If the legislature is authorized to consider the proposal and possibly adopt on its own a law or constitutional amendment, the process is called an indirect initiative. The initiative is seen by proponents as a way to correct legislative "sins of omission," while the referendum is a way to correct legislative "sins of commission."[57]

The states have varying requirements for initiatives and referendum, such as the number of signatures that have to be collected and the percentage of the vote needed for adoption. They also vary in their use of this end run around the legislature. In the period since 1950 the citizens of California, Oregon, North Dakota, Washington, Colorado, Arizona, Montana, and Michigan have voted on the most initiatives. In recent years initiatives have been used on a wide range of issues—fiscal limitations, the death penalty, abortion, insurance, and English as a state's official language, among other things. The November 1996 ballot in twenty states had a total of ninety-four initiatives, including proposals on term limits, taxes, gambling, education, and the environment and wildlife. Electorates in Idaho, Michigan, and Washington could decide whether to forbid the use of bait or dogs in hunting bears, and electorates in Colorado and Massachusetts could decide whether to ban the use of leghold traps.

California is clearly the nation's leader when it comes to the initiative. From 1981 to 1990 California on average considered twelve initiatives per general-election cycle, approving five. It had as many as twenty-six on the primary-election ballot in March 1996 and twelve on the general-election ballot in November of that year. Proposition 209, the California Civil Rights Initiative, which would have done away with affirmative action in the state, was the most well known. But two more initiatives were extremely important for attorneys. One was designed to bar the state from regulating their fees, and the other would have made it easier to sue corporations for financial performance. Two other measures had as their objective the regulation of the managed health care industry, barring practices that had been used by health maintenance organizations (HMOs) to control costs. The California Nurses Association and consumer groups placed these initiatives on the ballot.

Proponents of an initiative usually argue the following points.[58] First, the initiative is important as a last resort, when a legislature has refused to act; further, because the initiative presents a threat, it is able to spur legislative action. Second, it allows all issues, not just special-interest concerns, to be included on the public agenda. Third, it expresses the popular will directly, without the filtering or distortion introduced by the representational process. Fourth, it reduces alienation toward government because voters who express themselves directly on issues can see government as their own and not someone else's. Fifth, the initiative maximizes the full human potential of citizens as they engage in democracy. Sixth, it results in more informed constituents. Seventh, it reduces the incidence of abuse and corruption endemic to the legislative process. Eighth and finally, it lessens the protection of turf by various interests and encourages change.

Despite proponents' claims, the initiative process has a mixed record. To begin with, a number of proposals are simply unconstitutional—having been declared so either before making it to a vote or after having been adopted by the electorate. Some major initiatives have received majorities and gone into effect, with questionable consequences. Among the most notably dubious initiatives are California's Proposition 13, which passed in 1978, and Proposition 2½, which Massachusetts voters passed in 1980—both served to limit local property taxes. One thing is certain, however. These initiatives have re-

duced the power of elected officials to make policy and allocate fiscal resources. They have no doubt reflected the popular will, at least at the time of
the referendums. But over the years they have also harmed both the structure
of government and the performance and policies of the state.

Studies of the initiative process have revealed a number of problems. To
begin with, signature drives have sometimes been misleading or deceptive.
Voters frequently sign initiative petitions without knowing anything about
the contents. In any case, signature collectors on the big issues in the large
states are no longer primarily volunteers. They are paid workers, put on the
streets by a booming signature-collection industry. Even the League of Women
Voters and Common Cause relied on paid help to collect signatures to put a
campaign-finance initiative on the ballot in California.[59]

The drafting of the initiative has also created confusion, with sponsors
casting their language in the terms most advantageous to their cause. A number of initiatives have placed minority rights in jeopardy. Colorado's antigay
measure in 1992, recently overturned by the Supreme Court as unconstitutional, is one example. More often than not, discriminatory propositions do
not survive the process, although there is always a risk that they will.

There is also the danger of voter incomprehension or sheer exasperation.
Even with the explanation of propositions in the California voter's guide,
Californians had an extraordinarily difficult time sorting out the issues on at
least half the measures on the November 1996 ballot. In his wry "Observer"
column in the *New York Times* (November 2, 1996), Russell Baker describes
his dilemma in trying to vote on all the issues that occupy space on the ballot:
"Making sensible judgments on these things would have required bringing a
lawyer and an accountant into the booth with me. Since there wasn't room
enough for three I decided to simplify the problem. So with my first vote, I
pulled down 'yes' on all the bond issues and 'no' on all the constitutional
amendments. Next election I reversed field: 'yes' on all constitutional amendments; 'no' on all bond issues."

By their nature, many initiative campaigns appeal to passions and prejudices and wind up fostering greater disagreement and conflict than there was
to begin with. These conflicts are often fueled by media campaigns for and/or
against an initiative that frequently misrepresent the issue in an effort to win.

One student of the process examined fifty issues in four states during the
1970s and found that in most instances the higher spenders won at the polls.
According to her study, grassroots campaigns (which could on occasion overcome high-spending groups) appeared to communicate information rather
reliably. But where substantial money was involved, campaigns tended to be

manipulative rather than informative. With so little enlightenment being offered the voters, this researcher wondered how they were able to reach an informed decision.[60]

In the twenty years since then, initiative campaigns have become costlier, particularly when a powerful group is involved. California has been a particularly bloody battleground for the special-interest initiative wars. In 1988 the brawl over automobile insurance, which pitted the insurance industry against trial lawyers and consumer groups, cost $100 million. Although the measure passed, it was tied up in legal and regulatory disputes for years. In March 1996 tort reform propositions 200, 201, and 202 again found trial lawyers battling business, this time at a cost of $25 million and with all three going down to defeat. Here again was the ultimate clash of special interests. A recent study of the initiative process in California concluded that it failed to make government more responsive to the demands of its citizens.[61]

The very existence of the initiative enables advocacy groups to demand action from the legislature under threat of a ballot initiative bearing a more extreme measure. This forces legislators to give in to demands, lest they have to live with something even worse, from their point of view. If the legislature complies, these groups achieve their purposes without having to resort to the ballot. It is not possible, therefore, to calculate precisely the effects of the initiative in states like California, Colorado, Oregon, Washington, and Massachusetts. Either directly or indirectly the initiative has become a significant part of representative democracy in a number of states.

PUBLIC OPINION POLLING. The public has also made its voice heard in less authoritative ways. The rise of grassroots-issue campaigns and their impact on the legislative process is one of them. (We will consider grassroots participation later, in chapter 6.) Another way in which citizen views affect the representational process is through public opinion polls. In *The American Commonwealth,* Lord Bryce predicted a time in America when public opinion would "be ascertainable at all times, when it would not only reign but govern," and when the will of the people would become manifest "without the need of its passing through a body of representatives." We have reached the point where the opinions of the people, but not their will, are made manifest regularly through the mechanism of the public-opinion poll. Has this given legislators a better handle on what citizens want?[62]

We do not intend to document here the rise over the past thirty years of public opinion polling in American politics. Suffice it to say that over the past several decades polls have proliferated. Major newspapers, magazines, and the networks, along with Gallup, Harris, Roper, and Yankelovich, all conduct national polls periodically. We can find distributions of public opinion on virtually any major issue, and on many minor ones as well. State polls have come into fashion as well. In 1971 when the Eagleton Institute of Politics at Rutgers University established a New Jersey poll, only a handful of state polls existed—California's Field Poll, the Iowa Poll, and the Texas Poll.[63] Today thirty-nine states have a statewide poll, although only fifteen or so are firmly established and produce results on a regular basis. Some are university-based, others are conducted by newspapers or television stations, and still others are business operations. In addition, Mason-Dixon, a private polling firm, is commissioned by media outlets and groups in states throughout the nation.

Although legislators and legislative leaders rarely commission polls other than for purposes of their campaigns, they are on the receiving end of polling information on many major issues. Their campaign polls, and perhaps those done for the governor (if they share partisan affiliation), provide issue information which legislators value, especially if the poll pertains to their district rather than to the state at large. They tend to carry that information into the next session with them.

Increasingly, interest groups commission polls, or buy questions on omnibus surveys, in order to be able to argue that the public is behind their legislative cause. On health care, for example, state polls have been conducted recently for the Arizona Hospital Association, the Kaiser Family Foundation of California, the Illinois consumer rights coalition, the Iowa Hospital Association, the Health Maintenance Organization of Massachusetts, the Ohio Hospital Association, and groups in New Jersey, Washington, and West Virginia. Although health care has been the dominant area of polling activity, issues ranging from school reform to endangered species have also been explored as part of interest-group campaigns to buttress their case.

How are the results of polls used, and how do they affect decisions legislators make? Polls rarely have a decisive effect. Occasionally they help to shape legislative strategies. For instance, in response to a poll that indicated that 40 percent of New Jerseyans were concerned about the future of their jobs and 20 percent had actually lost their jobs, state legislators and labor leaders convened a meeting to figure out how to reduce regulations in order to create a favorable environment for business, and hence more secure jobs for employees.

More often polls buttress the position of one side in the debate. Interest groups, their lobbyists, and their legislator allies latch onto those findings that show a majority of respondents in agreement with their proposal. The other side may ignore these findings, explain them away, or criticize their methodological foundations. Editorial writers are probably the principal consumers of public-opinion polls. But like interest groups and legislators, they use findings that support the positions they hold independently of what the public thinks.

A gay-rights coalition, for example, commissioned a poll that found 83 percent of New Jerseyan respondents believed homosexuals were discriminated against, and 72 percent felt it was wrong to do so. The coalition pushed for an antidiscrimination law, which passed the New Jersey legislature. Another poll showed that 60 percent of New Jerseyan respondents favored a ban on handguns. The sponsors of a bill to ban handguns pointed to the opinions revealed in the poll in support of their proposal.

Poll products are among the grist for the legislative mill. Legislative outcomes are frequently generally consonant with poll results. Sometimes they are not. A New Jersey poll indicated that 59 percent of the respondents did not favor a sales-tax cut if it would mean a reduction in state services. The Republican majority in the legislature had pledged a cut in their campaigns and were not about to renege because of a public opinion poll. Indeed, the chairman of the assembly appropriations committee pointed out that the poll results were inconsistent with the election results of November 1991, in which the Republicans enjoyed a huge victory. In any case, the Republicans believed and claimed that essential services would not be jeopardized. Another poll found that 70 percent of New Jerseyans favored an increase in tobacco and alcohol taxes to pay for charity care by the state's hospitals. Legislators, however, were reluctant to raise taxes of any kind, no matter what a statewide poll indicated.

A recent study on the national level concludes that, on highly salient issues, polls allow politicians to act in a manner consistent with the public's will. This enables them to behave as delegates, while on less salient issues politicians follow a trustee strategy. Probably the chief impact of such polls, however, is to caution legislators, rather than to embolden them. They greet the finding that a majority, or even a sizable majority, of people favor a proposition with some skepticism (unless they themselves are champions of what the majority favors). Most would not rush ahead on the basis of such information alone. They need to know where the significant players stand. But legislators take rather seriously the finding that a considerable proportion of people oppose something. It makes them think twice or more about the risks they may be running. Take another example from New Jersey, a state with 587 municipalities, 36 percent of which have populations of less than five thousand, and almost all of which have their own school districts. For years reformers and rationalists have pressed for regionalization. When the concept, with which most respondents were unfamiliar, was explained, 44 percent supported regionalization if it could reduce costs (this constituted a majority of those expressing an opinion). Majorities also favored regionalization of a number of services, such as library and street maintenance. But only 35 percent favored consolidating school districts (which was still more than those who opposed consolidation). Legislators already knew their constituency did not want to lose its high school or the separate identity of its high school. The poll, which showed only one-third of the respondents in favor, reinforced the conventional wisdom. Pushing regionalization, especially where education was involved, would entail too great a risk. The poll results served as further warning, if legislators needed it.

ELECTRONIC DEMOCRACY. Legislators are nothing if not extraordinarily sensitive to the currents of opinion swirling about them. Their antennae are constantly probing the environment to detect threatening signs. Veteran legislators, who were used to several degrees of greater freedom, cannot understand the behavior of their newer and less secure colleagues. William Bulger, who retired from the presidency of the Massachusetts senate in 1995, regretted the new emphasis on responsiveness. He said: "Instead of acting out of firm conviction, we far too frequently play the role of weathermen. We get consultants to tell us what everyone out there is thinking. Then, once we know it, we fashion our positions or responses."[64]

Participatory representation makes its presence felt through issue initiatives, grassroots campaigns, and public-opinion polls. In the future, its presence promises to be even greater, thanks to the communications revolution we are undergoing. Political scientist Robert Dahl in 1981 predicted that the new telecommunications technology would change the democratic process by allowing citizens to place questions of their own on the public agenda.[65] More recently, Lawrence Grossman, in a provocative Twentieth-Century Fund study, offered the prospect of Americans sitting at home or at work, able to use telecomputer terminals, microprocessors, and computer-driven keypads, pushing the buttons to tell their elected officials what they want done about important (and, perhaps, less important) matters.[66] John Geer offers the prospect of constant referendums taking place via telephone, computer, or TV, allowing a member of the legislature to sample thousands of households on a particular bill before voting on it.[67]

What would this technology mean for representative democracy? Could public policy be made through electronic polling? Why not? asks James Fishkin.

Just hook up the electorate to a two-way cable system such as Warner-Amex Qube. "Teledemocracy" would not replace the legislature entirely. The legislature could be kept as an agenda setter, with committees devising proposals that would be put to an electronic vote if supported by petition signatures.[68]

With instantaneous reporting of electronic referendums of voters in their districts, and with the good possibility that the results would be reported in the press, many representatives would be hard-pressed to ignore whatever predominant opinion happens to be that day. An election opponent could make a lot out of such defiance. Some representatives would be happy to be taken off the hook. "You can ask them," one of the Florida house members said facetiously, "I have to vote on Thursday, what would you like me to do?" Under such a scenario, legislators would become principally agents of their constituency, while the legislature would become principally the reactor to successive public-opinion majorities.

According to some commentators, electronic democracy might lead to more public support for the political system, as greater participation induced the public to buy into governmental decisions. But if the legislature does not go along with an electronic poll, which after all is only advisory, then public cynicism would increase even further. Or, suppose the legislature followed public advice, yet the enacted policy did not work in practice. Then the public would be hard-pressed to use the legislature as a scapegoat; it would have to accept responsibility itself.

According to Grossman, the big losers in electronic democracy will be the traditional institutions that have been the main intermediaries between the government and its citizens. These include political parties, unions, and civic associations,[69] which have already been losing influence. A further loss of influence could be crippling. But interest groups with important issues at stake would not throw in the towel. They have not done so yet, and they can be expected to exploit the same communications technologies to get their images across in order to try to manipulate the electorate and win a majority of their votes.

Deliberative Representation

In a discussion of the constitutional initiative in Florida, legislators were asked whether they could recall any issues where the legislature refused to act despite public sentiment favoring action. Two were mentioned. One was the fishing-net ban and the other was the lottery. The first was opposed by the fishing industry, the second by the parimutuel industry. Both were passed, with the backing of organized interests, as constitutional amendments through the initiative process. The legislature was criticized for not allowing these measures to be reported out of committee for a floor vote. But the legislature normally disposes of many matters in committee; one of the purposes of a committee system, after all, is to separate the wheat from the chaff. Florida legislators discussing the issue appeared to agree that, whatever the popular vote, the legislature was making a reasonable judgment in each case and may well have been right.

Even though groups that lose in the legislative arena can resort to the ballot, legislators argue that the introduction of initiatives can mean that the legislature *is* doing its job rather than *not* doing it. Three-strikes-you're-out, tort reform, casino gambling, and campaign-finance proposals were all bottled up in the legislature. In the view of Senate President Pro Tem Bill Lockyer: "Usually [a surge of initiatives] means we're doing our jobs and turning down ill-advised proposals that are little more than special interest efforts."[70] Most ballot propositions, of course, are the product of organized interests—not of an unorganized public. Their aim is to achieve their goals by end-running the legislature.

The legislative process, which provides deliberative representation, is very different from direct democracy or even participatory democracy. In republican theory, deliberation is crucial to the governmental process. The framers of the Constitution intended to establish a legislative body that would restrain public demands and through deliberative processes arrive at reasoned settlements. For Alexander Hamilton, John Jay, and James Madison, as they expressed the wisdom of founding fathers in the *Federalist Papers,* representative government was preferable to direct democracy. In Federalist No. 10 Madison warned against the "majority faction," which is "united and activated by some common impulse or passion, or of interest, adverse to the rights of other citizens, or to the permanent and aggregate interests of the community." One protection against such factions is a large and diverse republic in which interests balance out and are less able to coalesce. Another protection is the representative assembly deliberating on the common good, with representation functioning as a filter that will "refine and enlarge the public views, by passing them through the medium of a chosen body of citizens."[71]

No legislative body can be expected to live up to the Madisonian ideal. The legislative process is imperfect. It is not sufficiently deliberative. But the judgments rendered by a representative body, like those of the individual representative, derive in part from the give-and-take of discussion. More of a premium is on information, reason, commonality of interests, and even farsightedness than is the case in public judgments recorded by a poll or a referendum. Citizens are extraordinarily weak when it comes to deliberation. They are constrained by time, competing interests for whatever leisure hours they have, and the complexity that is usually involved.[72] As Fishkin points out, on many issues on which they are polled, four out of five citizens do not have stable opinions. They have nonattitudes or pseudo-opinions, with answers to questions invented on the spot. Referendums, too, lack a deliberative element. Initiatives can be passed because people are angry at government or because of the ability of a campaign to manipulate images effectively.[73] And there is little recourse once a snap judgment is reached.

Information is a necessary part of a deliberative process. Naisbitt argues that with contemporary technology, "we [the people] know as much about what's going on as our representatives, and we know it just as quickly."[74] That is simply not the case. Legislators have far more information available to them than do rank-and-file citizens. And they have far greater incentive to make use of it. Moreover, they have probably worked with the issues in question longer, perhaps specializing by virtue of a standing committee assignment. They, or trusted colleagues to whom they can turn, will know the ins and outs of many of the issues that come before the legislature for resolution. Citizens, in contrast, are more apt to be satisfied with their feelings and with the images and slogans that get their attention.

Skill fits into the deliberative process. It is not just a matter of deciding yes or no on issues, but of settling on the specific provisions and language of law. In legislation, especially, the devil is in the details. While many initiatives show little knowledge of existing law or drafting, legislative bills are more likely to be modified and clarified along the way to enactment. Some enacted legislation still is technically deficient. Some enactments are not implementable. But, for the most part, legislatures get done what they aim to do. Furthermore, while anyone can learn the legislative ropes, there is no substitute for the learning that comes on the job and with time. Those engaged in the legislative process, particularly those who have been at it for a while, are more skilled at lawmaking than citizens. It is a specialized business. Thus, respected political philosophers and political scientists—Walter Lippmann, E. E. Schattschneider, Joseph Schumpeter, and V. O. Key—were strong believers in a division of labor, with those elected to govern governing.

Linkage is an essential component of the deliberative process. Legislators decide on proposals in context, while voters face measures that are separated from one another.[75] Pitkin makes the point: "Issues do not come before representatives in isolation. They are interrelated."[76] The speaker of the Florida house makes the same point, almost in the same words:"Issues are not isolated and voted on one by one without being in relationship to others."They are linked to past issues, ones that may have taken on somewhat different form. Some legislative remedy might have been tried but did not work in the past, and that has to be factored in the discussion today. The electorate lacks the continuity that the legislature has (even under current limitations on legislator tenure and legislative memory).

Just as the public does not see linkage vertically, it also fails to see it horizontally. There are connections among bills. People never have to confront trade-offs and the implications of proposals. They need not take into account the balance sheet when it comes to needed programs on one side of the ledger and necessary revenues on the other side. They do not have to consider priorities. A Florida legislator put the dilemma simply: "Do you want to spend $1 billion on prisons? The answer is yes. But if you knew you had to take $1 billion away from education, would you say yes?"

Often people think they can have their cake and eat it too, as long as "waste" is eliminated from government. Legislators would like to think that way, but they are not permitted the luxury of doing so. Constitutionally or statutorily, state budgets must be balanced everywhere except in Vermont (which normally balances its budget anyway). These constraints are built into the legislative process, imposing reality and forcing legislators to make hard choices.

Bargaining and compromise are totally absent from citizen decision making but are critical ingredients of the legislative process. To get what they want, proponents have to negotiate with the opposition, giving on one point in order to gain on another. The two sides may "logroll," trading one issue in return for another or agreeing to an increase for a budgetary item here if there is also an increase there. Sometimes, the two sides on an issue conflict head on, with a floor vote settling the issue. More often, a compromise, which pleases neither side but "satisfices" for both, resolves the issue. In either case, in order to reach a majority, legislators must negotiate, bargain, and compromise along the way. One student of public opinion makes the case that elected officials do represent the full diversity of interests and thus are more likely to weigh the intensity of different opinions on an issue. They are more likely, therefore, to arrive at a policy that is an acceptable compromise for all affected groups.[77]

When citizens are involved, compromise becomes questionable. Citizens are used to making decisions individually in terms of either yes or no, this candidate or that candidate, up or down. They do not vote on alternate bills and they cannot amend a proposal to make it more acceptable. All they can do is vote affirmatively, negatively, or abstain. Deliberative representation, however, requires thoughtful consideration, give and take, and continuing efforts to forge majorities. Anticipating the impact of electronic democracy, Grossman writes: "Whenever the public becomes directly engaged in a major controversial issue, the process of negotiation, compromise, and deliberation—the essence of effective policy making—becomes difficult, if not impossible."[78]

Responsibility for one's decisions is another aspect of the legislative process missing from a process dominated by citizens. In a legislature, every member, or practically every member, takes a stand (except on the very few matters that are intentionally swept under the rug rather than voted down in public). Whatever passes into law does so by the vote of a majority or near majority. In contrast, most ballot measures that pass do so with substantially less than a majority of eligible voters in support. Voters, of course, do not have to explain their votes, or defend them. Indeed, no one knows how or whether a particular citizen voted. Legislators are on record, not for everything they do, but for quite a lot. They have to defend their records, justify their decisions in terms of constituency interests, and fend off attack if their election is contested.[79]

Deliberative representation tends, more than popular democracy, to take into consideration long-term interests. Legislatures can be faulted for not looking ahead, at least not ahead beyond the next election. As present-oriented as they may be, they are less likely than citizens to sacrifice the intermediate term for more immediate gratification.

Deliberative representation, furthermore, takes some of the direct confrontation and conflict out of the policy-making process. Through negotiation, bargaining, and compromise, it helps build consensus for policy outcomes. In doing so, it may tend to dilute policy, so that neither side gets quite what it wants. Sometimes, the result is a Rube Goldberg–type contraption that can command a majority in the process but cannot work in practice. Sometimes, if both sides buy in, a compromise will prove workable. The alternative would be for cohesive party majorities simply to enact their own policies, outvoting rather than compromising with their opponents. Such, of course, is a predominant feature of parliamentary systems. Even if legislative parties were that cohesive, in two-party states such an arrangement would lead to policy by fits and starts. The party in power would enact its programs, but the opposition would repeal them when it won power. Could such programs be administered? Could bureaucrats cope? What could citizens expect? Under conditions of popular democracy, this could be the situation, as the voters changed their minds and altered direction from referendum to referendum.

REPRESENTATIVE DEMOCRACY

Legislatures in the states combine elements of political, descriptive, participatory, and deliberative representation. Whatever their deficiencies, the resulting systems allow the will of the state's citizens to shape the broad contours of public policies—not directly but through the deliberations and actions of the assembled representatives whom voters have chosen.

What representation by state legislatures entails is not any single action, "but the overall structure and functioning of the system, the patterns emerging from the multiple activities of many people." The legislature has the responsibility for making policy, but its responsibility is exercised by representatives who are tied to their districts and who respond to their constituents' views and interests. These representatives are continuously sensitive to the opinions, demands, and interests of their constituents. "There need not be a constant activity of responding," according to Pitkin, "but there must be a constant condition of responsiveness, of potential readiness to respond."[80] On issues of import, constituents and the public at-large are always part of the policy equation, more so today than ever before. Public opinion forms the backdrop, the context in which policy is deliberated. It also acts as a veto on some policies and is a force propelling others.

Direct democracy is not a serious option in the United States. It should be noted, however, that in 1994 Canada approved the accreditation of the Democratech Party of British Columbia. This party advocates turning all governmental decisions over to the public, to be resolved through electronic referenda. With modern communications, the party maintains, representative government is unnecessary. The people can make their own decisions, "relegating politicians to the scrapheap of history."[81] Even if it is difficult to conceive of a nation of states without elected legislators, representative democracy must confront the challenges of new modes of participation that promise to link representatives and the electorate closer than ever before.

NOTES

1. Lawrence K. Grossman, *The Electronic Republic* (New York: Viking, 1995), 3–4.

2. Robert A. Dahl, *Democracy and Its Critics* (New Haven, Conn.: Yale University Press, 1989), 5, 220; Anthony King, *Running Scared* (New York: Free Press, 1997), 53–56.

3. Hannah F. Pitkin, *The Concept of Representation* (Berkeley and Los Angeles: University of California Press, 1967), 4, 209–210.

4. John C.Wahlke et al., *The Legislative System* (NewYork:Wiley, 1962), 267–286.

5. Royce Hanson, *Tribune of the People* (Minneapolis: University of Minnesota Press, 1989), 232.

6. Pitkin, *Concept of Representation*, 125, 145–146.

7. The seminar, held in Tallahassee on November 6, 1995, was part of a project conducted by the Collins Center for Public Policy. The quotations of participants are from a two-volume transcript of the discussion. Subsequent quotations of Florida legislators are from that transcript. The following discussion in this chapter appears, in shorter form, in Alan Rosenthal, "The Nature of Representation: An Overview," in *Making Florida Democracy Work* (Tallahassee: Collins Center, Florida State University, 1996), 8–23.

8. Richard F. Fenno Jr., *Home Style* (Boston: Little, Brown, 1978), 240.

9. See Linda L. Fowler, "Constituencies," *Encyclopedia of the American Legislative System*, ed. Joel H. Silbey (New York: Scribner's, 1994), 399–418.

10. New Jersey and Arizona have two members in each house district.

11. It should be pointed out that district size was considered to be a problem by the California Constitutional Revision Commission of 1995–1996. The commission initially recommended that the constitution be amended to provide for a unicameral, instead of a bicameral, legislature so that the size of the population in each district could be smaller. The commission abandoned its recommendation when it became obvious that it would not receive legislative approval.

12. Anthony Gierzynski, "Elections to the State Legislatures," in *Encyclopedia of the American Legislative System*, ed. Joel H. Silbey (New York: Scribner's, 1994), 435–449.

13. Howard A. Denis, "To a Young Legislator," *Baltimore Sun*, January 10, 1995.

14. Michael Hawthorne, "A Nice Political Plum," *Illinois Issues*, May 1996, 22–26.

15. Wahlke et al., *Legislative System*, 304.

16. Malcolm E. Jewell, *Representation in State Legislatures* (Lexington: University Press of Kentucky, 1982). See also Patricia K. Freeman and Lilliard E. Richardson Jr., "Explaining Variation in Casework Among State Legislators," *Legislative Studies Quarterly* 21 (February 1996): 41–56.

17. Robert S. McCord, "Revival in the Arkansas House," *State Legislatures*, July–August 1995, 40–41.

18. Alan Rosenthal, *Legislative Life* (New York: Harper and Row, 1981), 104.

19. Thomas E. Cronin and Robert D. Loevy, *Colorado Politics and Government* (Lincoln: University of Nebraska Press, 1993), 156.

20. Interview with the author, November 28, 1995.

21. *New York Times*, June 9, 1994.

22. Interview with the author, May 17, 1995.

23. It should be noted that pork-barrel practices also lubricate the legislative pro-

cess, providing leaders with resources that they can hand out in building majorities for major legislation.

24. Fowler, "Constituencies," 406.

25. Pitkin, *Concept of Representation*, 144–145.

26. Fowler, "Constituencies," 406.

27. Pitkin, *Concept of Representation*, 147.

28. Fowler, "Constituencies," 407. Also Sidney Verba et al., *Voice and Equality* (Cambridge: Harvard University Press, 1995), 49–96.

29. Quoted in Kurtz, "Old Statehouse," 7–8.

30. Interview with the author, February 22, 1995.

31. Pitkin, *Concept of Representation*, 197, 215.

32. Cole Blease Graham Jr. and William V. Moore, *South Carolina Politics and Government* (Lincoln: University of Nebraska Press, 1994), 136.

33. Joseph M. Bessette, *The Mild Voice of Reason* (Chicago: University of Chicago Press, 1994), 26.

34. Pitkin, *Concept of Representation*, 147.

35. Ibid., 219.

36. Samuel C. Patterson, "Legislative Politics in the States," in *Politics in the American States*, sixth edition, ed. Virginia Gray and Herbert Jacob (Washington, D.C.: CQ Press, 1996), 196–197.

37. This has been interpreted as a mandate practically everywhere, as is evidenced by the enactment in the 1990s of laws requiring "truth in sentencing," "three strikes, you're out," longer sentences for those convicted of serious crimes, and the registration of sex offenders.

38. William R. Bryant Jr., *Quantum Politics* (Kalamazoo: New Issues Press, Western Michigan University, 1993), 115.

39. Interview with the author, March 16, 1995.

40. Anthony King, "The Vulnerable American Politician" (paper prepared for delivery at the annual meeting of the American Political Science Association, Chicago, August 31–September 3, 1995).

41. Bessette, *Mild Voice of Reason*, 46.

42. Pitkin, *Concept of Representation*, 166, 209.

43. Patterson, "Legislative Politics in the States," 164–165.

44. Gierzynski, "Elections to the State Legislatures," 440.

45. Pitkin, *Concept of Representation*, 60–61, 75–76, 80.

46. Lillian C. Woo, "Today's Legislators: Who They Are and Why They Run," *State Legislatures,* April 1994, 28–29.

47. Data provided by the Center for the American Woman and Politics, Eagleton Institute of Politics, Rutgers University.

48. Patterson, "Legislative Politics in the States," 176–177.

49. Cindy Simon Rosenthal, "Women's Ways of Political Leadership: Gender Differences in a Cross-Jurisdictional Study of State Legislative Committee Chairs" (paper prepared for delivery at the annual meeting of the American Political Science Association, Chicago, August 30–September 3, 1995), 2. Yet a recent study could find no differences between men and women in orientations toward power and "hardball" politics. Both were based on concepts of power that stressed compromise, consensus-building, and honesty. See Beth Reingold, "Conflict and Cooperation: Legislative Strategies and Concepts of Power Among Female and Male State Legislators," *Journal of Politics* 58 (May 1996): 464–485.

50. Sue Thomas, *How Women Legislate* (New York: Oxford University Press, 1994), 68–69, 74–75, 141–143.

51. Patterson, "Legislative Politics in the States," 177–178.

52. Graham and Moore, *South Carolina Politics and Government*, 122. For a persuasive analysis of the effects at the congressional level, see Kevin A. Hill, "Does the Creation of Majority Black Districts Aid Republicans?" *Journal of Politics* 57 (May 1995): 384–401.

53. William G. Shade, "State Legislatures in the Nineteenth Century," in *Encyclopedia of the American Legislative System*, ed. Joel H. Silbey (New York: Scribner's, 1994), 195.

54. Dianna Gordon, "Citizen Legislators—Alive and Well," *State Legislatures,* January 1994, 24–27. See also Eric Hirsch, *State Legislators' Occupations, 1993 and 1995* (Denver: National Conference of State Legislatures, March 1996), 11.

55. Ibid., 25.

56. John Naisbitt, *Megatrends* (New York: Warner Books, 1982), 160, 177, 179.

57. David B. Magelby, *Direct Legislation: Voting on Ballot Propositions in the United States* (Baltimore: Johns Hopkins University Press, 1984), 219–222.

58. Some of the arguments presented here are from Thomas E. Cronin, *Direct Democracy: The Politics of Initiative, Referendum, and Recall* (Cambridge: Harvard University Press, 1989), 207–219.

59. *New York Times,* July 9, 1996.

60. Betty H. Zisk, *Money, Media, and the Grass Roots: State Ballot Issues and the Electoral Press* (Newbury Park, Calif.: Sage, 1986), 103, 109, 137, 152–158. A recent study suggests that voters can make rational decisions on the basis of "signals" rather than information. See Arthur Lupia, "Shortcuts versus Encyclopedias: Information and Voting Behavior in California Insurance Reform Elections," *American Political Science Review* 88 (March 1994): 63–76.

61. Steve Scott, "Ballot Bulge," *California Journal,* July 1996, 12, 14; Edward L. Lascher Jr. et al., "Gun Behind the Door? Ballot Initiatives, State Policies, and Public Opinion," *Journal of Politics* 58 (August 1996): 760–775.

62. John G. Geer, *From Tea Leaves to Opinion Polls* (New York: Columbia University Press, 1996), 68.

63. This section on polls relies on assistance provided by Tom Silver, editor of *The Polling Report*, and Janice Ballou, director of the *Star-Ledger*/Eagleton Poll.

64. Quoted in Garry Boulard, "The Compleat Politician," *State Legislatures,* June 1996, 15.

65. Dahl, *Democracy and Its Critics*, 339.

66. Grossman, *Electronic Republic*, 12.

67. Geer, *Tea Leaves*, 192.

68. Fishkin, *Democracy and Deliberation*, 21–25.

69. Grossman, *Electronic Republic*, 16.

70. Scott, "Ballot Bulge," 17.

71. Pitkin, *Concept of Representation*, 193–194

72. Bessette, *Mild Voice of Reason*, 21, 214–215.

73. Fishkin, *Democracy and Deliberation*, 59, 83.

74. Naisbitt, *Megatrends*, 176–177.

75. Hans A. Linde, "On Reconstituting 'Republican Government'," *Oklahoma City University Law Review* 19 (Summer 1994): 207–208.

76. Pitkin, *Concept of Representation*, 220.

77. Jack Citrin, "Who's the Boss? Direct Democracy and Popular Control of Government," in *Broken Contract: Changing Relationships Between Americans and Their Governments*, ed. Stephen C. Craig (Boulder: Westview, 1996), 279.

78. Grossman, *Electronic Republic*, 172.

79. Linde, "On Reconstituting 'Republican Government'," 207–208.

80. Pitkin, *Concept of Representation*, 221–222, 233.

81. Graeme Browning, "Ballot Lines," *National Journal,* April 20, 1996, 882.

CHAPTER 2

The Development of State Legislatures

Criticism of American state legislatures was probably as severe in the 1960s as it is today. The difference is that thirty years ago, few were listening. The action was in Washington, D.C., and the states took their cues from the federal government. Governors, their executive appointees, and the permanent bureaucracies ran state government, while legislatures busied themselves with matters of lesser salience.

Political scientist Alexander Heard described legislatures of that earlier era as poorly organized; technically ill equipped; functioning with inadequate time, staff, and space; and operating with outmoded procedures and committee systems. "State legislatures," he summed up in a plea for reform, "may be our most extreme examples of institutional lag."[1] Others also saw the need for legislative reform. In 1967 North Carolina's former governor Terry Sanford observed, "We have so much riding on state legislatures that they are going to have to rise to their challenges." He predicted that they would, "notwithstanding the enthusiastic invective ... heaped upon them."[2] Sanford was right. State legislatures during the period from about 1965 to 1980 responded as few political institutions have ever done.[3]

During this time, state legislatures undertook the task of developing themselves as political institutions. They did so partly because of the changes in their composition as a result of reapportionment and partly because of the actions of reformist legislative leaders and national organizations. As we shall show here, legislators made substantial progress. First, they built capacity. Second, with improved capacity came the professionalization of the legislature and greater careerism among legislators. Third, legislative institutionalization, a consequence of these and other changes, was followed by a period of deinstitutionalization, which pertains to legislatures today.

Ironically, perhaps, legislative modernization and the unanticipated changes accompanying the movement may have something to do with the serious problems and low standing of state legislatures today. The current dissatisfactions may have their roots in the reforms adopted years ago. Many believe, for instance, that the institutional development of legislatures and legislators' professionalism went too far. As William Schneider told a meeting of state legislators, "Professionalism and politics do not mix. The notion of a professional politician is antithetical."[4] Legislative modernization, at least in the most advanced states, has come to a standstill in the face of a public that has found little in state legislatures to applaud but much to condemn. The governmental reforms of yesterday have become what so many citizens believe to be the governmental tyrannies of today.

BUILDING LEGISLATIVE CAPACITY

The legislative reform movement of the 1960s and 1970s was a loosely articulated campaign involving legislators, academicians, and citizens and designed to reshape state legislatures.[5] Although legislators and their allies had no explicit plan, the models they had in mind were the U.S. Congress and the California legislature. These institutions had developed in a way that not only appeared to improve their job performance but also seemed to confer benefits on members.

Recommendations for reform ran the gamut from those with profound implications, such as reducing the size of a legislative house, to those that were mainly administrative, such as eliminating the time lag between introducing or amending bills and having them available in printed form. The reform agenda focused principally on ways to enhance the legislature's capacity so that legislatures would have the wherewithal and the ability to do their jobs. Reformers specified capacity in terms of what one of them, Donald G. Herzberg, called the five S's—space, sessions, structure, staff, and salaries.

Space had to be expanded so that more room and additional facilities would be available for committees and individual members. In many states committees had to meet wherever they could find a room available, and members had to use their desks on the floor of the chamber as their office. The expansion of facilities was a major accomplishment, with the renovation of capitol buildings and the construction of legislative office buildings going on practically everywhere. Typical improvements made by many legislatures included electronic data processing and roll-call voting equipment, individual offices (and in some places district offices) for members, and hearing rooms for standing committees. Because of these physical changes, the legislature of the 1980s and 1990s looked very different from that of the 1960s. Technically and technologically speaking, it worked better.

Sessions had to provide more time, and more flexible time, so that legislatures could accomplish their objectives. This imperative led to the removal of constitutional limitations that had restricted the length of regular sessions or the time that legislatures could spend in the interim. It also led to the amendment of constitutions so that legislatures could call themselves into special session if they thought it necessary. Reformers had in mind more frequent and longer sessions. In 1969 annual sessions were the practice in twenty-six states, and by 1985 legislatures were meeting annually in forty-three states. Progress was made in other respects as well. All told, legislatures spent more time on task, both during regular and special sessions and in the periods between sessions. During the 1964–1965 biennium, twenty-four of them spent one hundred or more legislative days in regular and special sessions. By 1979–1980 as many as forty were in session for at least a hundred days, with twenty of them close to or exceeding two hundred actual legislative days.

Structure also needed streamlining, according to legislative reformers. In a number of states legislative bodies appeared to be too large. As far as the legislative reform movement was concerned, small was beautiful. The size of the Connecticut house was twice reduced, first from 294 to 177 and later to 151. In Ohio and Vermont houses were decreased by 38 and 96 seats, respectively, and in Massachusetts the house was cut from 240 to 160. Several states made smaller reductions, and recently Rhode Island decreased the size of its house from 100 to 75 and its senate from 50 to 38 (effective after the 2000 census and redistricting). The objective of reductions in size was to increase efficiency and reduce expenses. Whatever gains were achieved in efficiency, however, they came at a price. With fewer legislators, the size of legislative districts grew, so more people had to share a representative. Furthermore, with fewer legislators, the talent pool within the chamber diminished. A larger number of members allows for a more effective division of labor and specialization, with more legislators to draw on for leadership and committee assignments; a smaller number has to be spread more thinly.

Unicameralism was another structural recommendation that appealed to reformers. Although the idea of one chamber instead of two has made little progress, it deserves some attention here. Our nation's Constitutional Convention adopted bicameralism as a way of satisfying both the large and small states. At the time, ten of the thirteen colonial legislatures were bicameral. By the Civil War all the states had bicameral legislatures, but in 1934 Nebraska left the nation's ranks and, by initiative, went unicameral. Here, there is a single chamber, with members bearing the title "senator" and the presiding officer bearing the title "speaker." In the years following Nebraska's action, unicameral proposals were introduced in almost half the states; none were adopted.

A number of knowledgeable people have recommended unicameralism as an important reform. The most prominent, and one of the relatively few legislators, to advocate it was Jesse Unruh, speaker of the California assembly from 1961 to 1968 and later elected four times to the office of state treasurer in California. In Unruh's judgment, the most effective way to improve state government was to consolidate the legislature into one house; the two-house system, he argued, was "a costly and inefficient anachronism that thwarts the popular will, caters to private interests, and hobbles responsible and responsive decision making."[6] Others have argued in favor of unicameralism on the grounds that it (1) ends the bickering and possible deadlock between two houses; (2) lowers costs; (3) makes the individual legislator more accountable; (4) reduces the influence of lobbyists, and (5) strengthens the legislature vis-à-vis the governor.[7] Moreover, it used to be that the two houses of the legislature were differently based—one on population and the other on geographical areas and governmental units as well as population. With the reapportionment decisions of the U.S. Supreme Court, that rationale for bicameralism no longer exists.

Although both houses are currently apportioned on the basis of population, significant differences between the two bodies still exist. In most states senators are elected for four-year terms and representatives for terms of two years. The latter are more likely to reflect momentary mandates, while the former are less affected by tides. In every state, houses are substantially larger than senates, usually twice or three times the size, and in New Hampshire almost seventeen times the size. Partly because of their larger size, houses tend to have more centralized power. Speakers in most places have greater authority than their counterparts in the senate.

Senators tend to be more experienced than representatives, since many of them served previously in the house (only rarely has a house member had prior service in the senate). In the 1995 California legislature, for example, thirty-one of forty senators had served previously in the assembly, and of the eight senators newly elected in 1994, seven had been in the assembly. Legislative experience makes for greater autonomy or independence on the parts of senators. Senate leadership thus faces a harder job than its counterpart in the house in controlling its troops and building consensus. One California senator, for instance, compared senators to walruses:"They sit on top of their own rock, protecting their turf. They don't move much, but they roar when anybody gets close."[8] Senates are less-partisan bodies. Collegial relationships are more apt to cross the aisle, party lines are less rigid, and bipartisan agreement is easier to achieve. Members of the minority play a larger role in the senate, operating more as individuals rather than as members of the opposition party.

Although unicameralism has gotten no further than the discussion stage, the reshaping of standing committees has made considerable progress. In many places committees played only a nominal role, serving as much to afford members letterhead affiliation as to provide for a division of labor and policy expertise in the process. The late 1960s and the 1970s brought many changes in standing committee systems. In about three-quarters of the states the numbers of committees and the number of committee assignments for members were reduced. Each committee was given more serious jurisdictional responsibility and each member had the opportunity to better focus his or her attention. By 1985, furthermore, three out of five states were making use of standing committees to explore issues and formulate proposals during the interim period.

Staffing provided the single greatest boost to legislative capacity. Recommendations for increased professional staffing were at the very top of practically every reformer's list of priorities. In its manifesto, which evaluated legislatures in all fifty states, the Citizens Conference on State Legislatures (CCSL) in 1971 advocated the strengthening of staff support in thirty-eight states, committee staffing in thirty states, staff for legislative leaders in thirty states, and staff for rank-and-file in thirty-three. Staff was the major panacea for what ailed legislatures. Since then, progress made in staffing legislatures has been substantial. By 1980, forty-three states had permanent legislative research councils, as compared with only thirteen two decades earlier, and forty states furnished staff for all committees, as compared with only eleven two decades before. By 1980, thirty senates and twenty houses provided members with personal staff, a marked gain over the earlier period.

Until the 1960s professional staffs were small and removed from the hurly-burly of the legislative process. But in the period from 1968 to 1974, legislative staffs grew by more than 100 percent and then by another 25 percent between 1979 and 1988. As the 1980s ended, the number of full-time professionals exceeded two hundred in all but ten legislatures. The largest staff complements were found in New York, California, Pennsylvania, Texas, Florida,

Michigan, and Illinois. The ratio of staff per member was 23.9 in California, 17.0 in New York, 9.9 in Florida, 8.7 in Michigan, 8.1 in Texas, and 7.8 in Pennsylvania. At the other end of the spectrum, Idaho, New Hampshire, New Mexico, North Dakota, Vermont, and Wyoming employed one staffer for every three to five members.

The growth in staffing slowed in the 1980s and has come to a virtual halt in the 1990s, with tight budgets and public criticism of bureaucracy acting as constraints on further staffing. In California, Proposition 140, adopted in a 1990 referendum, resulted in a substantial cut in staff for the legislature. Other states began to undertake internal examinations of their staff structures in order to figure out how to do as much or more with less.

Salaries in the 1960s were considered to be inadequate everywhere. It was believed that talented individuals would not be able to serve in the legislature, even on a part-time basis, if they had to make too much of a financial sacrifice. Among the major reform recommendations were increases in salaries and expenses and the provisions of pensions and related benefits for members of state legislatures. CCSL proposed higher salaries for forty-two states. But in almost half the states in 1970 compensation could be changed only by amending the constitution. By 1985 only nine states (and by 1995 only five) set legislator compensation in their constitutions and increases in compensation had occurred in most places. The 1965 average annual salary of $3,900 had almost quadrupled by 1979, and it kept rising during the next decade.

LEGISLATIVE PROFESSIONALIZATION

With modernization substantially achieved in many states, the issues confronting state legislatures began to change. Professionalization of the legislature and its members was one of the most significant of these emerging issues.[9] The creation of a professional legislature, like those serving in Washington, D.C., and Sacramento, was a principal reform objective.

Professional Legislatures

Political scientists generally agree on what factors constitute professionalization at the state legislative level. Included are "the five S's" discussed above as features of legislative capacity. These elements can serve as measurable indicators. Among them are session length, staff, and compensation, as employed by Peverill Squire in his work.[10] Some confusion surrounds the concept, since "professionalization" can refer either to the attributes of the legislative institution or to the characteristics and behavior of the people who hold legislative office; frequently it refers to both.

One political scientist notes that "state legislative professionalism generally refers to the enhancement of the capacity of the legislature to perform its role in the policy making process."[11] Another recognizes that "institutional professionalism" is distinct from what he calls "careerism."[12] The use of the concept *professionalization* suggests the need for institutionally connected factors to be used as indicators. Session length and staff suffice, while legislative compensation is conceptually unlike the other two. Session days and staff have a very direct impact on the way the legislature works, but only an indirect impact on legislators as individuals. Compensation, in contrast, is of direct relevance to individual members, but has no direct effect on the legislature itself and is thus an individually (not institutionally) connected factor.

Legislative professionalization can best be operationalized in terms of schedule and staff, with the former specified as legislative work days and the latter as total staff support. One can then distinguish between the professional legislature with a heavier schedule and larger staff, as in California and New York, and the amateur legislature with a lighter schedule and smaller staff, as in Idaho and Wyoming. A number of legislatures have relatively heavy schedules, but smaller staffs. Colorado, Delaware, Maine, New Hampshire, and Rhode Island are examples. These are not fully professionalized legislatures, but are work-intensive, resembling the amateur legislature more than the professional one. And a few, such as those in Florida and New Jersey, have comparatively light schedules but large staffs, and can be thought of as support-intensive legislatures. The latter resemble the professional legislature more than the amateur one. (See fig. 2.1 for a depiction of the general scheme.)

Professional Legislators

Along with reform and modernization has come the professionalization not only of state legislatures but also of legislators themselves. Indeed, the building of institutional capacity encouraged career politicians, even though that might not have been the intent. For example, the 1965 Illinois Commission on the Organization of the General Assembly (COOGA) did not intend to create professional legislators, just a professional legislature. But by providing for annual sessions, offices, secretaries, and professional staff and by increasing salaries and benefits, modernization established conditions in which career legislators might thrive.[13]

FIGURE 2.1

The Professionalization of Legislatures

	Larger Staff	Smaller Staff
Heavier schedule	Professional legislature	Work-intensive legislature
Lighter schedule	Support-intensive legislature	Amateur legislature

Source: Alan Rosenthal, "State Legislative Development: Observations from Three Perspectives," *Legislative Studies Quarterly* 21 (May 1996): 175.

Several elements give appropriate meaning to professionalism at the individual level: whether legislators are full-time or part-time; how they identify themselves; whether or not they have substantial outside employment; and their political ambitions.

OCCUPATION, IDENTIFICATION, AND TIME. Since the 1960s the time demands on legislators have increased just about everywhere. Within any legislature, some members put in more hours per day, days per week, and weeks per year than do others. Legislative leaders and those who chair major committees have to do so. Others may want to do so. Retirees, who have no other employment, women who are second wage-earners in the family, and those who simply love the work and are willing to sacrifice outside income set the pace for their fellows.

Still, as expected, full-time legislators are more likely to be found in the more professionalized legislatures. In Pennsylvania 77 percent of the members report that they are full-time, in New York 69 percent, Wisconsin 63 percent, Massachusetts 56 percent, Michigan 51 percent, Illinois 42 percent, Ohio 39 percent, and California 37 percent.[14] The remainder of members, although part-time, may still devote many hours to legislative affairs. In Minnesota, for example, only 28 percent of the members claim they are full-time. Yet on average, Minnesota members spend sixty-five hours a week on the legislature near the close of a session and fifty-three hours a week during the middle. In the interim, legislative activities require about eleven hours a week.[15] Wisconsin has an eight-month session in odd years and a four-month session in even years, plus interim committees and legislative council commissions. Many legislators come to their offices in Madison every day, whether they are in session or not. Even in Kentucky, which surely has a part-time, biennial, citizen legislature, members devote almost half their time to legislative work, when district and political tasks are included as part of the job. New Mexico's legislature takes pride in its "citizen" status, but nonetheless legislative leaders and retirees spend almost half-time, and fewer than one-quarter of the membership can keep their legislative commitments much lower.

Another way to determine the degree of legislator professionalization by state is by legislators' identification of their occupations. Thirty years ago, almost all lawmakers in their biographical sketches for the blue book or state directory identified themselves by their occupations outside the legislature. With the exception of California, hardly any categorized themselves as "legislator." That changed in the 1970s and 1980s, as increasing numbers came to see themselves first as legislators and second as something else. The percentage of New York legislators noting their occupations as legislator went from zero in 1964 to 65 percent in 1988.[16] In 1963 only 7 of 236 Illinois legislators described their commitments as full-time; in 1993, 84 of 177 so described it.[17] By 1990, of the 202 house members and 50 senate members in Pennsylvania, 149 and 31 respectively listed their occupation as legislator.[18] Yet, in California, which is indisputably a full-time legislature, only 43 percent of the 80 members of the assembly identified as legislators in 1991; of newly elected legislators in 1992–1993, only 31 percent so identified. In Wisconsin not one lawmaker recently admitted to being a legislator occupationally, although well over half the members consider themselves essentially full-time.[19] Of 135 house members in the 1991 Minnesota house, 19 percent identified as legislators, although more would claim that they work full-time at the job.[20]

Self-identification allows for plenty of wiggle room and, thus, varies with the esteem in which legislators are held by the public. With government and politicians so unpopular today, what legislators publicly call themselves is not a completely accurate estimation of the number of officeholders who are principally legislators rather than principally attorneys, business people, educators, farmers, and so forth. Currently, at least, self-identification underestimates the full-timers and careerists who would prefer not to be labeled "professional politician." This is not to say that legislators do not have outside employment. Most do earn income in addition to their legislative salaries. But with the exception of someone like Willie Brown, who managed to earn more than $100,000 from the practice of law while serving as speaker of the California assembly, outside earned income is supplemental.

In assessing commitment to public life, we ought not be misled by the occupational designations of legislators, as reported in state directories or surveys. Those who claim outside occupations are not necessarily "citizen legislators," although they might like such cover. Many who say they are attorneys practice little law; many who say they are business owners let others in their family attend to the business; and many who teach at the elementary, secondary, and higher educational levels have left the classroom entirely to go to the capital for the spring semester of the year.

MOTIVATION AND AMBITION. To understand the professionalization of legislators, it is useful to factor in the motivations of individuals, specifically with regard to their ambitions to hold public office. If time on the job and desire to stay in it or move up the ladder are important, then we might conclude that most legislators no longer fit into the citizen mold. The purest citizen legislators are people who intend to serve for a while, but not for long. They keep one foot rooted in their private-sector careers and have no difficulty returning after their stint in the legislature. These people still constitute a sizable proportion of legislators in Montana, New Hampshire, North Dakota, Vermont, Wyoming, and maybe another half-dozen states. But even in these places the ranks of citizen legislators are thinning. Elsewhere this breed is barely hanging on. Take Maine, where the number of citizen legislators is diminishing as the number of professional legislators is growing. For several years now Augusta has been filled with young men and women whose entire means of earning a living is government-related.[21] The trend in Maine and elsewhere, however, may change with term limits.

One of the most striking statistics of legislative life recently is the low rate of voluntary departure from it. Some who are elected follow their original game plan and leave within a short span of time. A few become frustrated because they cannot get enough done. A few simply do not like it; they decide not to run again. Some are discouraged by the hostile climate surrounding public officials and refuse to tolerate the media's abuse and the invasion of their privacy. Others cannot bear the financial burden and have to attend to the demands on their income and savings imposed by their children who are approaching college age. A number, who have achieved veteran status, feel burnt out. "I got tired and lost my energy," said a former member of the South Carolina house, "It was time. I lost my support group, which peeled off. And I didn't want to go through the same issues again."[22]

A member who served fourteen years in the New Mexico house described his reasons for dropping out. He could have gotten reelected easily, but he had the feeling that it was time to retire. He no longer looked forward to the session and was becoming more passive, not initiating things the way he did when he first went to the legislature. He also felt that as he got older, he was finding the stresses and strains of legislative life harder to take. He did not want to put in twelve- to fifteen-hour days and undergo the tension that was part of the routine. Nor did he feel he could keep on sacrificing income and the goodwill of his wife.[23]

Less voluntary departures are the lot of those who do not want to risk defeat. There are those who are frightened off by an unfavorable redistricting after a decennial reapportionment or by a district whose demographic and political composition undergoes natural change, but for the worse as far as the incumbent's reelection prospects are concerned. In either case, reelection is questionable. The risk is not worth it anymore. Some exit for health reasons. Others depart as soon as they have a shot—even a long shot—at higher office. Members of the house tend to run for the senate when a seat becomes open; and members of both bodies jump at a chance to run for a congressional seat or for statewide office when and if the opportunity arises. Occasionally, legislators decline a run for Congress, preferring to remain nearer to home. A number of presiding officers, who feel other members are ready to take their turn at leadership (such as Tom Loftus, former speaker of the Wisconsin assembly) or whose terms are limited by tradition (such as Alan Karcher, William Hamilton, and Chuck Hardwick, all former speakers of the New Jersey assembly) choose to run for governor as a respectable way of exiting from the legislature, and possibly being elected governor as well.

In a study done in eleven states during the 1970s, it was found that about two-thirds of nonreturning senators (who did not seek higher office) left the legislature because of business demands and two-fifths because of financial burdens. And 30 percent of them mentioned that they had never intended to serve any longer.[24] A later study, of forty-three legislators from Indiana and Missouri who exited for reasons other than election defeat, found that twenty-one left because they were seeking another office, four because they anticipated defeat, seventeen mentioned professions and families to which they wanted to return, and seven departed because they were dissatisfied with the legislative experience.[25]

The fact is that relatively few people have been leaving legislatures of their own volition, except in furtherance of their ambition for higher office. California and Illinois have been losing only about 5 percent of their members voluntarily at any single election. In Florida, Michigan, Wisconsin, and Ohio the rate has only been a bit higher. Indiana's voluntary turnover was down to about 7 percent and Connecticut's and Maryland's was about 10 percent. Kentucky and Tennessee have moved along a similar path. Some of the smaller states with citizen legislatures are exceptions to this trend. New Hampshire, where a third of the members voluntarily leave the legislature at term's end, is one of them. Montana is another; here on average one out of five members in the house and one out of four in the senate leaves voluntarily at each election.[26] Lately, however, voluntary retirements—which briefly soared in Congress—are increasing at the state legislative level.

Legislators in the states that have professionalized and in those states that have moved even modestly in that direction have tended to have political careers in mind—in the back of their minds, if not the very front. They are politically ambitious, although their goals may not be set in stone when they enter the legislature. They shift and veer with the opportunity structure and the progress of their careers. Relatively few start out with the firm intention of serving a short while and then leaving—having, in Joseph Schlesinger's term, *discrete* ambitions.[27] That may be changing, however. Among the classes of Republicans brought into state legislatures on the Gingrich tide of 1994 are more legislators with a sense of immediate mission. Their avowed purpose is to enact a conservative agenda rather than a personal one and then to return home rather than make public office their career. On entering the legislature, at least, these lawmakers say their ambitions are discrete; but they too may change with time.

Ambitions, according to Schlesinger, may also be *static,* with individuals wanting to make long-run careers out of a particular office. They, too, are ambitious politically, even though they do not want to achieve "higher" office. Some legislators, and especially ones in citizen legislatures, start off this way; others decide after a while that legislative office is all they want; and a number feel compelled to settle for it, because it is the highest office they believe they can achieve. Ambitions may also be *progressive,* writes Schlesinger. Individuals aspire to attain an office "higher" or more important than the one they are holding. My guess is that progressive ambitions are widespread, although they can be abandoned when legislators realize they no longer have a realistic chance of climbing or there are simply too few offices to go around.

In his book on the Colorado legislature, which is still regarded as a citizen legislature, John Straayer writes that members "are rarely apolitical citizens who just come to Denver to do a good-hearted and brief public service stint for the benefit of their fellow citizens."[28] They are in it for the longer run. A survey of Ohio legislators produced similar results: one-third of the representatives and two-fifths of the senators were definitely interested in running for other offices, and another one-quarter of lawmakers in each house expressed a tentative interest. How many others harbored such an interest, but chose not to express it on a survey? Royce Hanson's study of the Minnesota legislature runs along the same lines. Half the members want to continue serving as long as possible; one-fourth would like to run statewide or for Congress; and only one-fourth want to return to private life.[29]

Until they have to make a choice, incumbent legislators have several options. Why preclude any of them? Why shut doors? They can wait for the opportunity—however they define that possibility—to run for a congressional seat or statewide office. Legislators can work toward leadership within their own chamber. If in the house, they can look for an opening in the senate. They can settle in, gaining influence with time and experience. Or they can return to private life.

Even among those who run for the legislature without a thought of a long-term career, a large number get hooked after a while. A senate leader characterizes Florida's legislature as composed of "citizens" like himself, even though he and other "citizen" colleagues have spent almost two decades in office. Although he never anticipated a lengthy career, "I got good at it, I liked it, I got satisfaction." Whenever he thought about quitting, he was "promoted."[30] A former California assemblyman's experience was similar. He did not start out to become a career politician, but legislative life for him was seductive and reasonably secure. Service evolved into career. "You become a career politician when you're in the legislature, if not before," was the way he saw his experience in California.[31]

A careerist orientation grows out of a legislator's personal ambitions. One way to determine these ambitions might be to look at the political experience of newly elected legislators. Do they appear to be on a political track? Those who have already held office probably are. In New Jersey roughly three out of five legislators have been mayors, council members, or elected county officials before taking up business in Trenton. In Ohio a 1988 survey suggested that 73 percent of representatives and 83 percent of senators had held party or elective office before election to the legislature.[32] In Alaska's 1993–1994 legislature, of the sixty members, seventeen had served as legislative aides and fifteen had been elected mayor or to the borough assembly or school board. More than half had prior governmental experience upon entering the legislature.[33] According to a recent review of the literature, new legislators with experience in elected positions made up 30 percent of the legislatures in Oregon, Utah, Minnesota, and Washington, and 50 percent in Massachusetts, North Carolina, and Connecticut.[34] These individuals are not political neophytes when they arrive at the legislature.[35] However short a state's legislative session and low a state's legislative compensation, those who have already been in politics and those who are looking forward to higher office are indisputably on a careerist path. Even after term limits were being felt in the California assembly, almost half the eighty members had worked as congressional or legislative aides or been in local governmental office.

The distinction commonly made between the "professional" and the "citizen" legislator requires clarification. The two can best be distinguished along two dimensions, time and term. Full-time and part-time legislators differ. So do those with careerist records and/or ambitions and those who are novices without political ambitions. Those who are full-time at the work and long-term in their experience and/or aspirations are without question professional legislators. They want to continue in public office. In contrast, those who are part-time and with little political mileage behind or ahead of them are clearly citizen legislators. They may seek higher office but are not in it for the long run. The mixed types include those who are part-time, but have a political past and, they hope, a political future. They can be labeled dual-careerists because they pursue two careers simultaneously. Still, they are closer to the professional than to the citizen type, and would probably welcome higher office. The mixed types also include those who are full-time but think of themselves as merely on temporary leave from regular life. They are nearer to the citizen end of the spectrum and can be labeled citizens-on-leave. Wherever they land, their stay will be relatively short. Although it is doubtful that many of this last type exist, there are some, such as retired people or those who can afford to take a sabbatical from their jobs and want to fulfill what they believe to be their civic obligations. These types are portrayed in figure 2.2.

Contributors to Professionalization

The professionalization of the legislature itself, in terms of enhanced legislative capacity, has contributed to the professionalization of legislators themselves. The improvement of facilities, the provision of services, the employment of staff, and the growing power of the legislative branch all appealed to men and women who might have been interested in political careers anyway. In-

FIGURE 2.2

The Professionalization of Legislators

	Full-time Service	Part-time Service
Long-term Service	Professional legislator	Dual-career legislator
Short-term Service	Citizen-on-leave legislator	Citizen legislator

Source: Alan Rosenthal, "State Legislative Development: Observations from Three Perspectives," Legislative Studies Quarterly 21 (May 1996): 181.

creases in compensation—salary, stipends, expenses, and benefits—made continued legislative service more feasible for people than it would have been otherwise.

THE INFLUENCE OF COMPENSATION. For many members, legislative pay affects not only the amount of time they can devote to their duties but also how long they can afford to remain in office. Sufficient compensation is requisite for a legislature filled with professionals. Higher salaries were instrumental in the conversion of the Wisconsin legislature to a body of professionals from one populated mainly by citizen types. The salary of legislators doubled in the 1970s, reaching $17,800—enough to match teachers' salaries. More educators then began declaring their candidacies. By the 1990s Wisconsin was paying almost $35,000 (and a $64 per diem), which was estimated to provide three-quarters of the average member's total income.

In the professionalized legislatures, salaries are more attractive. Currently, California's legislators are paid $72,000, and $101 per diem. All told, members in California realize about $93,000 in compensation a year. The speaker of the assembly and the president pro tempore receive an additional $14,100, and the floor leaders of the two houses receive an extra $7,200. Most members do not need much additional income and can afford to devote practically all their energies to the legislature. The yearly salary of New York legislators is $57,500. This sum is supplemented by per diems of $89 and leadership stipends, known as "lulus," of between $6,500 and $30,000, which are so liberally dispensed that every member of the senate and 114 of 115 assembly members receive them.

In states where citizen legislators predominate, salaries lag far behind or are abysmally low. Unless they are wealthy or supported by a spouse's income, people find it difficult to abandon outside occupations when legislative compensation is $15,000 or less a year, as it is in about half the states. There is little danger of being overrun by professional lawmakers in Utah, where the salary is about $3,000, or in New Hampshire, where it is only $100 a year, with no per diem to ease the pain.

PARTISAN AFFILIATION. A professional legislature encourages the recruitment of professional legislators. Moreover, professional legislators increase the time spent on legislative work and generate more tasks for more staff, thus further professionalizing the legislature and further encouraging the recruitment of professional legislators. All this may have been facilitated by the predominance—until 1994—of Democrats in state legislative office.

Alan Ehrenhalt makes the point that political office is simply more appealing to Democrats.[36] In his view, people nominate themselves for office in this age of entrepreneurial candidates. Those who do tend not only to enjoy politics but also to believe in government as an institution. Democrats fit this mold, and Republicans do not. Ehrenhalt writes: "It is not easy to find conservatives willing year after year to put up with long hours and low pay for the privilege of being part of a government they essentially distrust." Democrats, in short, are more likely to be professional legislators simply because they like the profession enough to make the sacrifices required.

Morris Fiorina agrees that Democrats are more professionally inclined to enter politics. But he argues that this inclination results from a difference in opportunity costs rather than a difference in belief. According to him, amateur legislatures appeal to Republicans while professional legislatures appeal to Democrats, because in the former, legislators have more flexibility to combine legislative service with an outside career, and the outside careers of Republicans are attractive and difficult to abandon. In professional legislatures, on the other hand, outside careers have to be sacrificed; since Democrats have less going on the outside than Republicans, sacrifice comes to them more easily.[37]

Ehrenhalt's conclusions are based partly on his thoughtful contrast of Democrats and Republicans in the Wisconsin legislature. He quotes the Republican senate leader's explanation of the partisan difference:

> Democrats can go out and find a whole slew of people making less than $30,000 a year . . . who want to go out and change the world. You come in here at eight o'clock on a Monday and all the Democratic parking places are filled. This is their career. This is what they do with their lives. It's it. Republicans will show up at nine o'clock on Tuesday when the session starts at ten. They leave at four on Thursday. They come and vote on the bills and then they leave. The Democrats come back on Friday to work out what they are going to do the next Tuesday and Thursday.[38]

The difference in behavior may, however, have something to do with the fact that the Democrats were the majority party and had control over the agenda for many years. Recently the differences have been narrowed.

In 1992 Wisconsin Republicans won control of the senate and in 1994 they added control of the assembly. Republicans tried to recruit and fund better candidates, and Republican incumbents began to work as hard as Democrats at their legislative jobs. The new Republican breed in Wisconsin and elsewhere may not like government as Democrats do, but they still want to affect it and its policies. Ideology does not discourage Republican candidates, perhaps because conservatives can gain as much pleasure from limiting government as liberals can from expanding it.[39]

Fiorina's findings, which are based on indirect evidence, are also qualified by Republican gains in 1992 and 1994 in California, Illinois, Michigan, New Jersey, Ohio, and Pennsylvania, states where legislative salaries and legislative professionalization are both high. Yet legislative party leaders have intensified their recruitment efforts and allocated funds and other campaign resources, efforts that have diminished the differences in orientations toward government or in opportunity costs. Furthermore, the boost given Republicans everywhere by their congressional, gubernatorial, and legislative electoral gains, along with the advancement of more conservative policies, may erode such effects further.

Legislative Institutionalization

Modernization and professionalization have had important effects on the legislature as an institution. One of the most profound is the institutionalization

FIGURE 2.3
Membership Turnover in State Legislatures

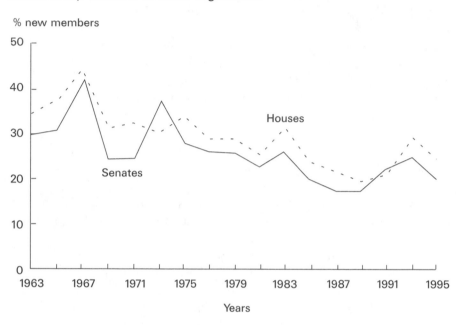

Source: Samuel C. Patterson, "Legislative Politics in the States," in Politics in the American States, 6th ed., ed. Virginia Gray and Herbert Jacob (Washington, D.C.: CQ Press, 1996), 180.

of the legislature, so that it is well bounded or differentiated from its environment.[40] The concept of institutionalization was first applied to the U.S. House of Representatives by Nelson W. Polsby. He showed how over time the House had become a more institutionalized body, particularly with regard to the continuity of its personnel. More recently, Squire examined the institutionalization of the California assembly and showed that this body also had developed well-defined boundaries.[41] Indeed, in the 1970s and 1980s many legislatures were going through a process of institutionalization; Florida, Iowa, Minnesota, New Jersey, New York, Ohio, and Wisconsin to name several.

Legislatures are differentiated from their outside environments by, among other things, their personnel. On the basis of tenure and turnover data, it is possible to observe just how legislatures became more institutionalized. Turnover declined generally, as shown in figure 2.3. In some states, such as Michigan, New York, and Ohio, it dropped to 10 percent. Overall, turnover in lower houses fell from 45 percent in the 1950s to 32 percent in the 1970s to 28 percent in 1981–85, and then to 20 percent in 1984–90. In thirteen out of the eighteen houses examined over four decades, turnover decreased and retention increased. For example, retention rose from 65 to 80 percent in Ohio, 57 to 73 percent in Iowa, 39 to 77 percent in Kentucky, 45 to 60 percent in Utah, and 50 to 69 percent in Oregon. Legislatures were also retaining many legislators, from biennium to biennium, in Rhode Island, New York, Pennsylvania, Michigan, and California.

Low turnover rates can be explained by the high proportion of incumbents—seven or eight out of ten—who had committed to political careers (or dual careers) and sought reelection. They can also be explained by the many legislators—roughly nine out of ten—with the skill and other resources necessary to win reelection. There can be little doubt, therefore, that professionalization had stabilized the membership of the state legislature.

One expects an institutionalized organization to possess managerial autonomy—that is, to manage its own interval life without substantial control or outside intervention. Public agencies cannot be entirely insulated from outside control. Yet if control is mainly in the hands of outsiders, then the legislature's autonomy to manage itself and the legislature's separation from the environment are in question. The institutionalized legislature should, with minimal intervention, determine its own organizational structure and procedures, working conditions, and personnel. Legislatures have been able in the past to a greater extent than presently, in effect, to govern themselves.

THE WANING OF THE INSTITUTION

The development of state legislatures through capacity building, professionalization, and institutionalization has had consequences other than those legislative reformers had in mind. Modernization and strengthening made the legislature not only more attractive to politically interested men and women, but more effective as well. Yet by the 1990s the mood of the nation had become hostile to government and to legislative bodies. Although legislatures had improved themselves in many respects, democratizing their memberships and procedures, they were under siege. The institutional fabric was unraveling, and legislatures appeared to be in decline.

The Public Mood

The evidence of public dissatisfaction today is overwhelming. It can be found in public-opinion polls on the job performance of legislatures. Data from state polls since the late 1980s show that opinions of the legislature are generally low, and no better than the 33 percent approval ratings for Congress in the 1990s.[42] Public evaluations seem to be going even lower. Take New Mexico, for example, where the legislature's approval rating at the end of 1994 was only 25 percent. Approval meant that people rated its job performance as either "excellent" or "good," as compared to "fair" or "poor." That rating was the highest it had been since the beginning of 1991. On a few soundings it had sunk to 15 percent or lower and on several to 20 percent. This was below the ratings given to public servants generally, well below those given the governor, and far below those given police in the respondent's area.[43] Florida provides another example. In one recent poll, only 28 percent of Floridians believed that the legislature was doing a "good" or "excellent" job. An Alabama poll's findings were similar: 23.9 percent positive, 70.6 percent negative. So was a New Jersey poll: 28.9 percent positive, 56.6 percent negative.[44]

Thad Beyle of the University of North Carolina has compiled data on legislative performance in a number of states. In Alabama, from 1980 to 1994, two-thirds to three-fourths of the respondents rated the legislature as "fair" or "poor" (rather than "excellent" or "good"). The Kentucky legislature fared much better in the 1980s, with the ratio of "fair" and "poor" to "excellent" and "good" ratings about five to four. In Missouri, from 1981 to 1992, three-fifths to three-fourths of the respondents were negative, with the pattern roughly the same from 1984 to 1994 in New Jersey. The ratings of the Illinois legislature between 1984 and 1994 have also been low, with grades of C, D, and F given by two-thirds to four-fifths of those surveyed.

The public has lost its confidence in government, at both the federal and state levels. For the past thirty years, the National Election Study (NES) has been surveying national samples, and these show a marked decline of citizen efficacy and trust in government. In 1964, 31.8 percent of those surveyed thought government paid "a good deal of attention" to what people think when it decides what to do; in 1992 only 12.2 percent felt the same way. The percentage who thought public officials did not care "what people like me think" rose from 35.9 percent to 51.7 percent. On the NES's "trust in government" index, three-quarters of the respondents in 1990, as compared with just over one-quarter in 1964, thought government "is pretty much run by a few big interests looking out for themselves." Almost half in the later sample also believed quite a few people running government are "a little crooked."[45]

The decline in trust in government is part and parcel of a decline in trust generally—in business, labor, and institutions—and even a decline in trust in human nature. According to a national survey by the *Washington Post* (reported January 28, 1996), only 35 percent of those polled believe "most people can be trusted," a decline from 54 percent that felt that way in 1964. Citizen distrust in government specifically rests in part on the widespread belief that ordinary people are shut out. Politics is no longer theirs, but has been taken away by a system made up of lobbyists, political action committees, special interests, and the media. This is a central conclusion of the Harwood Group, which conducted a series of focus groups for the Kettering Foundation a few years ago.[46] As far as the public is concerned, the legislature as a system and legislators as individuals are, at best, ethically suspect and, at worst, completely corrupt. People's cynicism is not confined to politicians, but politicians are held in lower esteem than other elite groups. According to a Times Mirror survey, Americans are most cynical with respect to public officials in Washington, whom 77 percent give a low rating for honesty and ethics. A low rating is given state and local officials by 52 percent. Community leaders, business leaders, and even professionals from national and local media also rated public officials in the survey, but they were not as critical as rank-and-file citizens.[47]

Focus groups conducted by the Center for Public Interest Polling at Rutgers University in California, Minnesota, and New Jersey reinforce these disturbing findings. In Minnesota, for example, throughout the discussion state legislators were described as "power hungry," "out of touch," "interested in personal gain," and "not representing the people." As one focus-group participant commented, "I don't trust them—any politician, not a single one." Nowhere does cynicism appear as high as in California, where a scandal that had dragged on for years had a profound impact. People felt so burned by the legislature that they were sure that no member could stand thorough scrutiny. One participant said: "If I look through their financials and through all their dealings and saw who was giving them gifts, I guarantee I could find something. Pick one [legislator], it doesn't even matter whose." The population in New Jersey is no less suspicious. The Center for Public Interest Polling asked New Jerseyans to guess what percentage of legislators in Trenton took bribes. Five percent answered that they thought none took bribes, and 4 percent thought all of them did. Between these extremes, assessments were scattered. Of the total number who ventured an estimate, an astounding 36.6 percent thought that *half or more* of the legislators took bribes.[48]

Many explanations have been advanced to account for the public's hostility toward legislatures and other governmental institutions. I will mention a number now, and elaborate on others later on. First, legislatures simply do not *look* good, no matter how well or democratically they function. In the words of the former speaker of the Rhode Island house, "Whatever we've done in the assembly, we've never looked good doing it." Or as the aphorism cautions:

"There are two things you do not want to see being made—legislation and sausage."

Second, legislatures are often made to look bad by the media reporting on them. For the press, good news (for example, a competent legislature hard at work) is no news at all. The best story—that is, the one that attracts an audience and promotes the journalist's career—accentuates the negative, uncovers scandal, and gets (as in "gotcha journalism") legislators and the system.

Third, the increasing competitiveness of politics and the rise of negative campaigning lead the public to conclude that since candidate A says Candidate B is untrustworthy and Candidate B says Candidate A is untrustworthy, both are right. They're all untrustworthy.

Fourth, scandals are an unfortunate feature of the legislative environment. "Shrimpgate" in California, Arizona's "AzScam," and "Operation Boptrot" in Kentucky all started with law-enforcement stings that led to the indictment and conviction of legislators and lobbyists. Other scandals have also left their mark in Florida, Louisiana, Maine, Maryland, Massachusetts, Michigan, Minnesota, New Jersey, New Mexico, Ohio, Rhode Island, Tennessee, Texas, Washington, and Wisconsin. Thus, some empirical evidence buttresses public beliefs.

Fifth, social changes and political events have combined to produce a heightened sense of entitlement among the American people. Government feeds citizen expectations, in part by dealing with more issues and mandating more programs. Politicians campaigning for office contribute to citizen cynicism, holding out solutions and making promises that cannot be kept. Popular discontent grows as the gap (actual and perceived) between the norm and the reality of popular government widens. The result is public anger, with governmental institutions getting much more blame than they deserve.[49]

Sixth, one way or another many problems have gotten onto the agendas of Congress and state legislatures; yet solutions are not in sight. Crime remains a problem, race relations have not improved markedly, employment is always uncertain, and improvement in public education is glacial. Had all these issues diminished or stood still, the strengthened legislatures might have dealt with them. Nevertheless, the issues have not gone away, and legislatures have been unable to find solutions.

Seventh, professionalization has contributed to public discontent. It may indeed have weakened the legislature as an institution, by diminishing the values of teamwork. Equality and individualism have encouraged legislators to go their own ways. But legislatures require leadership, discipline, and the willingness of individuals to submerge their personal preferences for the common good.[50] Professionalization may also have placed greater emphasis on the retention of office and, thus, on the continuing political campaign, which has intruded mightily in so many places.

In the case of amateurs, the risks of losing are modest; defeated amateurs may return to their private occupations and do better financially than they did in the legislature. Both psychologically and economically they can afford to lose. On the other hand, professionals have pretty well severed their connections with occupations outside of politics, or never have had connections at all. For them the costs of losing a legislative seat, in terms of status, prestige, and income are substantial. As incumbents, they will do a great deal in order to protect their positions. A member of the California senate described what happened when the legislature became the sole source of revenue for many of his colleagues:

> After a while, legislators became *more* dependent upon the job than before. . . . The longer he is a full-time legislator, the more dependent he becomes upon his salary. His former occupation and his business contacts are in the past and difficult to reestablish; going back to his old occupation seems like a step backward. It becomes all the more important to keep his legislative job. . . . Keeping the job becomes a matter of personal survival.[51]

Professional legislators can easily become risk-averse. They are closely tied to their district's apron strings. Upon retiring from the Minnesota legislature, John Brandl warned: "The more one needs the job, the less one is bold and creative, the less concerned with the state in the twenty-first century, the more with one's own district between now and the next election."[52] According-ing to others, they have too much time on their hands, are undisciplined, and fail to perform as well as citizen bodies. The natural inclination of a part-time lawmaking is to be rather more selective in the issues it addresses, to prioritize its time, and to resist the impulse to micromanage the executive.

All this has a cumulative impact on citizens, who perceive professional legislators as distancing themselves from the voters who elected them. To citizens, these officeholders become remote figures—insiders who speak a different language and live a better lifestyle. They travel at taxpayers' expense, dine at lobbyists' expense, and manage to feather their nests at everyone's expense. This is how the public views legislators today, as professionals rather than amateurs. Confidence in citizen legislatures probably exceeds that in professional legislatures. For example, North Dakotans are thought to have maintained confidence in their legislature over the years mainly because it is a citizen body that allows for participation. Even in an era of heightened cynicism, the public perception of the North Dakota legislature is of an uncorrupt institution composed of honest, hardworking members.[53]

Deinstitutionalization

Legislators are painfully aware of the public mood today. A survey of legislative leaders, for example, found that 107 perceived the public as increasingly dissatisfied while only 13 perceived the public differently. One commented that "public criticism of government is Oklahoma's number-two sport, behind football."[54] Three-quarters of the leaders attributed dissatisfaction, not to governmental failings, but to public misperception. As much as anything else, the hammering by citizens has demoralized the legislature. In a study of Minnesota legislators, two-thirds of those interviewed believed their dissatisfaction on the job stemmed mostly from the public's perceived lack of respect.[55] Recently, veteran legislators throughout the nation are talking more about getting out, and those who actually leave are growing in number.

After a period of becoming institutionalized, state legislatures have entered a period of deinstitutionalization.[56] In the 1990s, the direction has changed largely because of public insistence. Legislatures now are less separated from their environments, more permeable, and less able to keep outside influences from penetrating internal structures and processes.

Currently turnover is on the rise. The California assembly, which Squire characterized only a few years ago as an institutionalizing operation, is now deinstitutionalizing. From 1972 to 1990 assembly turnover averaged 20 percent; from 1990 to 1994 it averaged 36 percent. As of 1995 more than half the members had been in the California assembly less than three years; of the 80 members, 27 were newly elected in 1992 and 27 were newly elected in 1994. As of 1995, more than half the members of the Florida house had been there less than three years; of the 120 members, 47 came into office in 1992 and 29 in 1994. When Republicans became the house majority, only 8 of 41 members had served longer than two years. Maine is similar. In 1992, 47 percent of the 35 senators and 33 percent of the 151 representatives turned over and in 1994 the percentages were 46 and 47 respectively. Maryland's turnover in 1994 was 43 percent. Overall, one out of three senates and almost one out of two houses experienced a turnover of at least 33.3 percent in either 1992 or 1994, or in both years.

If one looks at the change of personnel during the past decade, it is possible to see that relatively few legislators are around very long. Of those members of state senates in 1997, only 28 percent were also serving in 1987. Of those members of statehouses in 1977, only 16 percent were also serving in 1987. The turnover figures for the decade are shown in table 2.1.

Probably the major deinstitutionalizing force of late is the term-limits

TABLE 2.1
State Legislative Turnover, 1987–1997

	Senate			House		
State	Total	New Members	Turnover (%)	Total	New Members	Turnover (%)
Alabama	35	24	69	105	74	70
Alaska	20	17	85	40	36	90
Arizona	30	28	93	60	55	92
Arkansas	35	20	57	100	75	75
California	40	31	78	80	80	100
Colorado	35	27	77	65	54	83
Connecticut	36	30	83	151	119	79
Delaware	21	13	62	41	19	46
Florida	40	31	78	120	95	79
Georgia	56	45	80	180	132	73
Hawaii	25	21	84	51	42	82
Idaho	35	26	74	70	51	73
Illinois	59	34	58	118	90	76
Indiana	50	29	58	100	64	64
Iowa	50	39	78	100	84	84
Kansas	40	33	83	125	110	88
Kentucky	38	31	82	100	72	72
Louisiana	39	33	85	105	80	76
Maine	35	35	100	151	149	99
Maryland	47	28	60	141	94	67
Massachusetts	40	34	85	160	119	74
Michigan	38	26	68	110	84	76
Minnesota	67	41	61	134	99	74
Mississippi	52	41	79	122	86	70
Missouri	34	22	65	163	130	80
Montana	50	39	78	100	84	84
Nebraska	49	35	71	Unicameral		
Nevada	21	11	52	42	32	76
New Hampshire	24	20	83	400	340	85
New Jersey	40	24	60	80	63	79
New Mexico	42	31	74	'70	47	67
New York	61	29	48	150	95	63
North Carolina	50	40	80	120	92	77
North Dakota	49	33	67	98	82	84

(Table continues on the following page.)

TABLE 2.1
(continued)

State	Senate			House		
	Total	New Members	Turnover (%)	Total	New Members	Turnover (%)
Ohio	33	20	61	99	61	62
Oklahoma	48	30	63	101	89	88
Oregon	30	22	73	60	52	87
Pennsylvania	50	26	52	203	150	74
Rhode Island	50	38	76	100	75	75
South Carolina	46	28	61	124	100	81
South Dakota	35	31	89	70	61	87
Tennessee	33	19	58	99	76	77
Texas	31	25	81	150	116	77
Utah	29	24	83	75	65	87
Vermont	30	26	87	150	127	85
Virginia	40	26	65	100	64	64
Washington	49	39	80	98	88	90
West Virginia	34	28	82	100	90	90
Wisconsin	33	24	73	99	72	73
Wyoming	30	26	87	60	50	83
Total	1,984	1,433	72	5,440	4,258	84

Source: National Conference of State Legislatures, May 1, 1997.

movement. Between 1990 and 1996 the electorates of nineteen states expressed their unhappiness with state legislative systems by voting for initiative (or referendum) propositions that, either constitutionally or statutorily, limited the terms of legislators. Where citizens had the opportunity to put the legislature in its place, they did so—and usually by large majorities—in every case but two. In Mississippi (which in 1992 had passed a law allowing for an indirect initiative) term limits was voted down by 54 to 46 percent, primarily because it applied too broadly and to local appointed as well as elected officials, possibly including fire chiefs, school superintendents, and members of county hospital boards. Term limits were also rejected by the North Dakota electorate (which also extended house terms from two to four years). In two other states the legislature itself adopted term limits—under threat of an initiative in Utah and of electoral retaliation in Louisiana. The Nebraska court, however, invalidated two different term-limits measures. A federal judge in California ruled that Proposition 140's term limits, by providing a lifetime ban after service in a particular office, was unconstitutional. At this writing, the case is on appeal to a higher federal court. The latest reversal occurred in Massachusetts in mid-1997, where the state's Supreme Judicial Court struck down term limits on the grounds that the law adopted by initiative could not modify the qualifications for seeking office as set by the state constitution.

As of mid-1997, therefore, twenty-one states had enacted term limits, as shown in table 2.2. In eighteen states, term limitations are intact, with about one-third of the nation's legislators affected.

TABLE 2.2
Term Limits in State Legislatures, 1990–1997

State (year of enactment)	Number of years in term	
	Senate	House
Arizona (1994)	8	8
Arkansas (1992)	8	6
California (1990)*	8	6
Colorado (1990)	8	8
Florida (1992)	8	8
Idaho (1994)	8	8
Louisiana (1995)	12	12
Maine (1993)	8	8
Massachusetts (1994)*	8	8
Michigan (1992)	8	6
Missouri (1992)	8	8
Montana (1992)	8	6
Nebraska (1994)*	8	—
Nevada (1994)	12	12
Ohio (1992)	8	8
Oklahoma (1990)	12	12
Oregon (1992)	8	6
South Dakota (1992)	8	8
Utah (1994)	12	12
Washington (1992)	8	6
Wyoming (1992)	12	6

* Term limits have been struck down by the courts in California, Massachusetts, and Nebraska, and an appeal is under way in California. In other states challenges have been brought before the courts.

Source: Compiled by the author.

The chances are still slim that legislators in noninitiative states will choose to put a provision on the ballot to limit their own terms. Legislators generally oppose such a requirement, although a number of them favor the limitation. A survey of seven states (four of which adopted term limits by initiative) shows that most legislators oppose the idea, although Republicans are more supportive of it than Democrats.[57] Yet if pressure from the public becomes great enough, legislators might be forced to put term limits on the ballot for people to vote in a referendum. The Louisiana legislature, by votes of 88-10 in the house and 31-7 in the senate, was the first to surrender to the popular will (without the threat of an initiative) and on its own propose a term-limits amendment to the constitution for popular referendum. With an election looming and several newer members pressing hard, majorities in the Louisiana house and senate felt they had to accept term limits as the public will. What they did do, however, was to draft an amendment providing for a longer term—twelve years—instead of a shorter one.

The effects of term limits are already being felt. Members are not necessarily waiting for their terms to expire. They are leaving whenever the opportunity to win another office arises. A number of legislators in California, for instance, exited years before their terms were due to expire so they could compete for other elective positions, causing a marked increase in the number of special elections and a disruption of the legislative process. The full impact of term limits occurred in California in 1996. Every member serving in 1990, when term limits was adopted, had to step down. That meant that after the 1996 elections thirty-two of the eighty members were newly elected to the assembly, although four of them had served in earlier years. Only twenty lawmakers had more than two years of experience. If upheld in the courts, term limits would not fully affect the California senate until two years later. In any event, ten new members were elected in 1996, although nine of them had served previously in the assembly.

Of the 1990 assembly contingent, twenty-one were elected to the senate, eleven won seats in Congress or statewide or local office, three became judges, ten lost races for higher office, seventeen retired or were defeated along the way, two were recalled, one was convicted of corruption, and one died. The remaining fourteen went home when their terms ran out.[58]

Term limits affected the California assembly and Maine house and senate first, but by 1998 an additional eight chambers would feel the effects. In the Michigan house 67 of 110 members would be ineligible to run for reelection, in the Arkansas house 50 of 100 members, in the Washington house 32 of 98 members, and in the Oregon house 22 of 60.

Once legislators are elected under a term-limited system, they start thinking about where to go next—higher office or another job. This is especially problematic in full-time legislatures like California and Michigan, where house members may have little to which to return after six years in office. It may well be, as Rauch points out, that "instead of getting careerists out of politics, term-limits might just shorten their attention span."[59]

One expects an institutionalized organization to manage its own internal affairs without substantial control or intervention from outside. Although political scientists have neglected "managerial autonomy" in their analyses of institutionalization, it is a crucial dimension. Moreover, it is one that shows change lately. Although the authority of legislatures to govern themselves has always been somewhat restricted, that authority is more severely restricted now. The outside environment intrudes into, and sometimes determines, what once was regarded as an internal process.

The greatest loss of managerial control has occurred in the same states that have ratified term limits. These are the ones that provide for the direct or indirect initiative to amend the constitution or enact a statute. Several propositions approved by the voters in these states restrict the legislature's power over public policy, particularly concerning taxation and expenditures. Such measures are certainly significant, yet they do not directly restrict the legislature's managerial prerogatives. The measures that infringe on management are those that reduce the size of the legislature, shorten the legislative session, or reduce the legislative budget.

Although a dozen or so states witnessed outside drives designed to reshape life inside, the most notable and successful assaults occurred in Colorado and California. Colorado voters in 1988 passed the GAVEL (Give a Vote to Every Legislator) amendment. It required that every bill referred to a legislative committee be voted on in committee, thus preventing a committee chair from allowing bills to die by default; bills reported out of committee go to the floor, thus negating the power of the rules committee; and legislators not be permitted to commit themselves through a vote in party caucus, thus ending the binding nature of the caucus, especially on the budget bill.

California voters went even further. They adopted Proposition 24 in 1984, which would have stripped the speaker of the authority to appoint committees and required the proportional division of legislative resources between the parties. This initiative never went into effect, having been invalidated by the state courts on the grounds that the California constitution gave the legislature sole authority over its organization. Proposition 140 in 1990, however, did survive judicial review at the state level (if not the federal level). It not only brought term limits to California but also required a 38 percent cut in the legislative budget, necessitating a reduction of about six hundred staff positions. In addition, it abolished the legislature's retirement system, established more than twenty years earlier when the California legislature was professionalizing.

Outside control is also evidenced by the electorate's refusal in several states to allow the legislature to set the length of sessions. The public has voted to restrict the length, even though legislators believe they need more time to do their work. Even more salient is the control the public now has over legislators' compensation. Either by denying proposals to change salary levels frozen into the constitution or by sheer intimidation, state electorates have kept compensation in many places at an exceedingly low level.

New Mexico has a constitutional restriction that prohibits any compensation, except for a per diem of $75, and $0.25 per mile for one roundtrip to the capital each session. Since 1951 the legislature has put compensation provisions on the ballot on eleven occasions, but has been overruled by the electorate eight times. Only in 1996 did New Mexico's citizens approve a proposition that raised compensation moderately, but only because the proposition was worded in a way that led voters to believe they were limiting per diem. The Massachusetts legislature, which in 1994 had not had a pay raise for a number of years, enlisted the support of Gov. William Weld and increased their pay substantially, to $46,410. The public was furious and retaliated with an initiative it hoped to put on the 1996 ballot. It cut the amount in half, to $23,205; provided for payment in six monthly installments, through June; and for good measure eliminated legislative pensions and free parking places at the statehouse. Fortunately for legislators, the court declared this initiative unconstitutional on a technicality.

Even where legislatures have had the statutory power to raise salaries, for political reasons they have been very hesitant to do so. A number have figured out a way to avoid direct responsibility, establishing independent compensation commissions to take the heat for salary hikes and deflecting public criticism. Some have tied legislator pay to that of state employees.

In about half the states now, legislatures do not control the salaries of members. Control is directly in the hands of the people, who have to assent to a change in the constitution, or it is wielded by an independent commission, or it is specified by formula; it is not with the legislature itself. Although legislative autonomy over salaries has always been restricted, it is even more restricted today.

In most states, legislative districting has been the responsibility of legislators themselves. Their leaders and designated committees put together plans, while rank-and-file legislators have input along the way and then a final vote. In a number of states and on a number of occasions, however, the courts have overruled legislative redistricting plans and done the redistricting job themselves. In nine states, moreover, legislatures have surrendered the responsibility for redistricting, giving it instead to independent commissions, which now have the job of formulating and promulgating plans. In Iowa the Legislative Service Bureau draws district lines, and members have little say in the matter. Almost half of them, in fact, wind up in districts with other incumbents.[60]

Legislatures are also losing control over the lifestyles and conduct of their own members, an area that used to be almost entirely within the legislature's dominion. They were once able to handle challenges to the ethics of members within the legislature itself. Today legislatures have far less autonomy in this area. The press and the public often set the agenda, insisting on stricter laws to govern the conduct of their representatives. When a scandal or the appearance of scandal occurs, the legislature finds itself in a reactive mode and tailors its action to stemming the public assault and protecting the political fortunes of members.[61]

At a formal level, in almost one-third of the states, independent commissions currently have jurisdiction over the ethics of legislators. Some have been imposed by initiative and some by political necessity. Commissions, such as those in California, Connecticut, and Rhode Island, see themselves as representing the public in their watchdog function vis-à-vis the legislature. They need to demonstrate their credibility to the citizens of the state, but, as a consequence, their relationship with the legislature is uneasy at best and adversarial at worst. Legislatures learn to live with these commissions that regulate them. But in 1996 the Kentucky legislature struck back, diminishing the authority of its ethics commission and increasing legislative control over the appointment of its members.

At an informal level, legislators are responding to the public mood and altering their conduct in a number of respects. Many of them are reluctant to travel at taxpayers' expense to out-of-state legislative meetings of a professional nature. They are fearful of how the media will report the trip, how the opposition will treat it in the next campaign, and what their constituents who do not get to travel on business will think of their representative's style of life. In response to the press and the public, legislators are less likely to accept entertainment or gifts from lobbyists, even if it is permitted and no matter how much they insist that such largess has no bearing on their legislative behavior.

The institutionalization of state legislatures in the 1970s and 1980s came about mainly because of the desires and behavior of legislators themselves. They were the ones who created professional bodies in which both citizens and careerists could gain gratification for their service. The deinstitutionalization of state legislatures in the 1990s has come about, not because of the wants of members, but because of the demands of those on the outside—principally the media and the public. State legislative bodies can no longer be characterized as organizations that displace goals and focus resources on internal processes at the expense of external demands. Legislatures today are beset by external demands, and most of their attention is therefore focused on these demands. As for their internal processes, legislatures are also more willing to do the public's bidding. They have run the cycle of development, from institutional revitalization in the 1970s and 1980s to institutional decline in the 1990s.

NOTES

1. Alexander Heard, ed., *State Legislatures in American Politics* (Englewood Cliffs, N.J.: Prentice-Hall, 1966), 3.

2. Terry Sanford, *Storm Over the States* (New York: McGraw-Hill, 1967), 182.

3. This is not to suggest that reform suddenly commenced at a precise point in time or ended at another. Modernization was under way in California before the 1960s, and it continued beyond the 1980s in a number of states and in various respects. But the period in which a national movement was under way is the span from roughly 1965 to 1980.

4. National Conference of State Legislatures, *Leader's Letter*, November 1991, 3.

5. This section is based in part on Alan Rosenthal, "Reform in State Legislatures," in *Encyclopedia of the American Legislative System*, ed. Joel H. Silbey (New York: Scribner's, 1994), 842–845. One other objective of the reform movement was legislative independence, a subject that will be addressed in chapter 8.

6. Unruh, who was regarded as a powerful leader, used to joke that he initially favored unicameralism because he thought it meant "one man."

7. Craig Grau and Dale Olsen, "The Unicameral Option" (University of Minnesota at Duluth, March 1986).

8. Richard C. Paddock, "The Mixed Legacy of a Practical Politician," *California Journal,* March 1992, 147.

9. This section is based largely on Alan Rosenthal, "State Legislative Development: Observations from Three Perspectives," *Legislative Studies Quarterly* 21 (May 1996): 169–197.

10. See Peverill Squire, "Legislative Professionalization and Membership Diversity in State Legislatures," *Legislative Studies Quarterly* 17 (February 1992): 70–72. Karl Kurtz, in his index of professionalization, adds to those items employed by Squire the "continuity of service" by legislators, in "The Changing State Legislatures (Lobbyists Beware)," in *Leveraging State Government Relations*, ed. Wesley Pedersen (Washington, D.C.: Public Affairs Council, 1990), 23–32. For a general review of measurements, see Christopher Z. Mooney, "Measuring U.S. State Legislative Professionalism: An Evaluation of Five Indices," *State and Local Government Review* 26 (spring 1994): 70–78.

11. Mooney, "Measuring U.S. State Legislative Professionalism," 70–71.

12. Richard A. Clucas, *The Speaker's Electoral Connection: Willie Brown and the California Assembly* (Berkeley: Institute of Governmental Studies Press, University of California, 1995).

13. David Everson, "COOGA Redux?" *Comparative State Politics* 17 (April 1996): 10–11.

14. Dianna Gordon, "Citizen Legislators—Alive and Well," *State Legislatures,* January 1994, 24–27.

15. Royce Hanson, *Tribune of the People* (Minneapolis: University of Minnesota Press, 1989), 225.

16. Daniel M. Shea, *Transforming Democracy* (Albany: State University of New York Press, 1995), 85.

17. Samuel K. Gove and James D. Nowlan, *Illinois Politics and Government: The Expanding Metropolitan Frontier* (Lincoln: University of Nebraska Press, 1996), 81.

18. Patricia McGee Crotty, "Pennsylvania Individualism Writ Large," in *Interest Group Politics in the Northeastern States*, ed. Ronald J. Hrebenar and Clive S. Thomas (University Park, Penn.: Pennsylvania State University Press, 1993), 288–289.

19. Peverill Squire, "The Theory of Legislative Institutionalization and the California Assembly," *Journal of Politics* 54 (November 1992): 1034–1035, and Gordon, "Citizen Legislators," 27.

20. Theodore Rueter, *The Minnesota House of Representatives and the Professionalization of Politics* (Lanham, Md.: University Press of America, 1994), 52.

21. Kenneth T. Palmer, G. Thomas Taylor, and Marcus A. Librizzi, *Maine Politics and Government* (Lincoln: University of Nebraska Press, 1992), 195.

22. Interview with the author, February 7, 1995.

23. Ibid., May 15, 1995.

24. E. Lee Bernick, as cited in Alan Rosenthal, *Legislative Life: People, Process, and Performance in the States* (New York: Harper and Row, 1981), 44, 49. A response, of course, can cloak other reasons. I can think of an outstanding New Jersey legislator who, some years after retirement, recalled that he never intended to make a career in politics and had it in mind to stay no longer than ten years (his actual length of service). What he failed to mention was that he had run in a primary for a congres-

sional seat, but lost. He had also lost a bid for the speakership. His defeats may have led him to shorten his career. While in office, another New Jersey legislator told an interviewer that he was going to serve until he became speaker or until he knew he would not become speaker. He was defeated in an election before his ambition could be fully tested.

25. Wayne L. Francis and John R. Baker, "Why Do U.S. State Legislators Vacate Their Seats?" *Legislative Studies Quarterly* 11 (February 1986): 119–126.

26. Jerry W. Calvert, "Reform, Representation, and Accountability—Another Look at the Montana Legislative Assembly," in *Legislative Reform and Representative Government in Montana*, ed. Jerry W. Calvert (Bozeman: Burton K. Wheeler Center, Montana State University, 1993), 6–7.

27. Joseph A. Schlesinger, *Ambition and Politics: Political Careers in the United States* (Chicago: Rand McNally, 1966), 10.

28. John A. Straayer, *The Colorado General Assembly* (Niwot: University Press of Colorado, 1990), 65.

29. Samuel C. Patterson, "Legislative Politics in Ohio," in *Ohio Politics*, ed. Alexander P. Lamis (Kent, Ohio: Kent State University Press, 1994), 240; Hanson, *Tribune of the People*, 233.

30. Interview with the author, March 30, 1995.

31. Ibid., March 16, 1995.

32. Patterson, "Legislative Politics in Ohio," 240.

33. Gerald A. McBeath and Thomas A. Morehouse, *Alaska Politics and Government* (Lincoln: University of Nebraska Press, 1994), 146.

34. John R. Hibbing, "Modern Legislative Careers," in *Encyclopedia of the American Legislative System*, ed. Joel H. Silbey (New York: Scribner's, 1994), 497.

35. Newer generations of Republican legislators may contain more citizens among them. This appeared to be the case with the classes elected in 1994.

36. Alan Ehrenhalt, *The United States of Ambition* (New York: Times Books, 1991), 17–18, 20, 203.

37. Morris Fiorina, "Divided Government in the American States: A By-product of Legislative Professionalism?" *American Political Science Review* 88 (June 1994): 304–316. See also the criticism of Fiorina's analysis in Jeffrey M. Stonecash and Anna M. Agathangelou, "Trends in the Partisan Composition of State Legislatures: A Response to Fiorina," *American Political Science Review* 91 (March 1997): 148–155.

38. Ehrenhalt, *United States of Ambition*, 126.

39. Fiorina, "Divided Government," 304–316.

40. This section is based in part on Alan Rosenthal, "The Legislature: Unraveling of Institutional Fabric," in *The State of the States*, 3d ed., ed. Carl E. Van Horn (Washington, D.C.: CQ Press, 1996), 108–142.

41.Nelson W. Polsby, "The Institutionalization of the U.S. House of Representatives," *American Political Science Review* 62 (March 1968): 144–168; Peverill Squire, "The Theory of Legislative Institutionalization and the California Assembly," *Journal of Politics* 54 (November 1992): 1026–1054. See also Rueter, *Minnesota House*, 1–12.

42. Karl T. Kurtz, "The Public Standing of the Legislature" (paper prepared for delivery at the Eagleton Institute of Politics Symposium on the Legislature in the Twenty-first Century, Williamsburg, Virginia, April 27–29, 1990; revised August 1991). See Joseph N. Capella and Kathleen Hall Jamieson, "Public Cynicism and News Coverage in Campaigns and Policy Debates: Three Field Experiments" (paper prepared for delivery at the annual meeting of the American Political Science Association, New York, September 4, 1994).

43. Citizen evaluations of a state legislature often depend in part on their appraisal of the governor's performance. Legislatures generally lag behind governors in their ratings.

44. University of New Mexico Institute for Public Policy Survey Research Center, *Quarterly Profile of New Mexico Citizens* 7 (winter 1994–1995): 5; Survey Research Laboratory, Policy Science Center, Florida State University, *Florida Annual Policy Survey 1995*; Institute for Social Science Research, University of Alabama, March 1994; and *Star-Ledger*/Eagleton Poll, August 1994. In at least one state, Washington, the numbers are running in the other direction. Polls done for the Republican Party by Public Opinion Strategies show that as of early 1997, 56 percent approve and 23 percent disapprove of the legislature's performance, with the positives up 10 points and the negatives down 10 since early 1995.

45. Stephen C. Craig, *The Malevolent Leaders: Popular Discontent in America* (Boulder: Westview, 1993), 10–11, 13.

46. Kettering Foundation, *Citizens and Politics: A View From Main Street America* (Dayton, Ohio: Kettering, 1991).

47. Times Mirror Center for the People and the Press, *The People, the Press, and Their Leaders 1995*.

48. Alan Rosenthal, *Drawing the Line: Legislative Ethics in the States* (Lincoln: University of Nebraska Press, 1996), 41–47.

49. Craig, *Malevolent Leaders*, 63, 78; Robert J. Samuelson, *The Good Life and Its Discontents* (New York: Times Books, 1995).

50. Ehrenhalt, *United States of Ambition*, 274–275.

51. H. L. Richardson, *What Makes You Think We Read the Bills?* (Ottawa, Ill.: Green Hill, 1978), 92.

52. John Brandl, "Reflections on Leaving the Minnesota Legislature," *Humphrey Institute News*, June 1990, 14.

53. North Dakota Consensus Council, "North Dakota Legislative Branch Consul-

tation," September 7, 1994. See Peverill Squire, "Professionalization and Public Opinion of State Legislatures," *Journal of Politics* 55 (May 1993): 479–491.

54. State Legislative Leaders Foundation survey, April 6, 1993.

55. Hanson, *Tribune of the People*, 233.

56. See Rosenthal, "State Legislative Development."

57. Glenn Sussman, Nicholas P. Lovrich, Bryan W. Daynes, and Jonathan P. West, "Term Limits and State Legislatures," in *Extension of Remarks* (APSA Legislative Studies Section Newsletter), ed. Lawrence C. Dodd (July 1994), 3.

58. O. Mark Katches and Daniel M. Weintraub, "The Tremors of Term Limits," *State Legislatures*, March 1997, 21–25.

59. Jonathan Rauch, *Demosclerosis: The Silent Killer of American Government* (New York: Times Books, 1994), 164.

60. The Iowa redistricting system actually calls for three plans. The first cannot be amended. If it is voted down, a second plan is developed by the nonpartisan staff. That plan also has to be voted up or down. If it is rejected, a third plan is offered, which cannot be amended until an up or down vote is taken; but then it can be changed. After the 1990 census both parties gambled and accepted the first plan.

61. For a case study of a legislature retreating under intense fire, see Rosenthal, *Drawing the Line*, 184–210.

CHAPTER 3

The Transformation of Legislative Cultures

Legislatures throughout the states have much in common, but in no two states is the process quite the same. Legislatures differ in large part because the states differ. The New Hampshire legislature would be unthinkable in New Jersey; the Texas legislature could not make it in Utah; the Oregon legislature is ill-suited for Illinois. Legislatures are interwoven in the fabric of their states; and the legislative process cannot be considered in isolation from the prevailing ethos and the capital community of the state in which it operates.

CAPITAL COMMUNITIES

In their efforts to explore the present, political scientists tend to skim over the past. Yet there is little doubt that political history and tradition affect state institutions. To some extent, legislatures are prisoners of their state's past, escaping it—if at all—only slowly. The Minnesota legislature is still influenced by the Democratic Farmer Labor Party, whose leaders emerged in the 1940s and 1950s. The Wisconsin legislature has the progressivism of Bob LaFollette at its roots, which helps to explain the state's moralistic tone and activist government. The legislature in Louisiana, despite changes in recent years, still reflects the politics of the Huey Long era.

California's political past has had notable impact on its political present. In the early decades of the twentieth century, the Progressives, spearheaded by Gov. Hiram Johnson, launched a successful battle against corruption. State politics were dominated by the Southern Pacific railroad and heavily influenced by other interest groups. Bribery was a principal political tactic of the day. In reaction, the Progressives took on the entire political system—the railroad and interest groups, the political parties, the politicians, and the political institutions. The result was the weakening of parties, the glorification of nonpartisanship, the establishment of the initiative and the referendum, and the undermining of politics. Political institutions suffered from the Progressive onslaught, although the large interests survived intact and went on to dominate California politics again in the 1940s and 1950s. California's contemporary political system, with weak parties and popular involvement in policy-making, is rooted in the movement that swept the state more than a half-century ago.

Political Culture

The past has stamped each state with its own distinctive political culture. *Political culture* is a term that political scientists find useful, if not exact, for summing up the political habits built up by a group of people and transmitted from one generation to another. In popular language, it is the "personality structure" of the state. Although few agree on how to measure or classify a state's political culture, it is easy to appreciate the overall utility of the concept. It sensitizes us to distinctive and persistent qualities of each state—its political style, the orientations of its citizens, and its heterogeneity.

Anyone who spends time in a number of states is aware of the differences among them. In New York hard-ball politics, wheeling and dealing, and unabated activity are characteristic. In Virginia, until most recently, one could sense tradition, conservation, and gentility. The Illinois culture has been individualistic, with politics and elective office seen as one way to make a decent living. Politics in Louisiana is still wild and flamboyant, while in Iowa political practices are still moderate and cautious. A strong disposition to compromise, which once characterized Oregon, has been replaced lately by a more dogmatic politics with the liberal and conservative extremes squeezing out the pragmatic middle. In Kansas hard work, respect for authority, fiscal prudence, and a general conservatism and resistance to rapid social change continue to be features of the state environment.

In Hawaii the political dominance of Japanese, and the secondary status of Chinese, native Hawaiians, and *haoles* (whites), make for tough ethnic politics. Ethnicity also characterizes New Mexico, whose minorities account for about half the population and Mexican and Indian cultures blend with the Anglo overlay. Rhode Island is a small state whose parochial inclinations and close-knit ethnic communities have given politics a tribal quality. Yankee Republicans used to run Massachusetts, but then the Irish took over and Italian ethnics made their bid. The Irish qualities of personalism and loyalty are still very much in evidence. The conservative politics of Utah derives from the influence of the Mormon church, with its emphasis on moral conduct, private initiative, self-sufficiency, and work.

Capital and Capitol

Just as the state settings vary, so do the capital settings in which state legislatures are more immediately located. The cities that house the legislatures range from the smaller ones, with populations of less than 100,000—such as Juneau, Montpelier, Bismarck, Pierre, Concord, Carson City, and Jefferson City—to Boston (3.2 million), Atlanta (3 million), St. Paul (2.7 million), Phoenix (2.5 million), and Denver (700,000). Capital cities naturally vary in ways other than size. Some are cosmopolitan, with good hotels and restaurants. These, of course, tend to be the larger places. Some, like Atlanta, Denver, and St. Paul, have international airports that make them very accessible. Others are much harder to get to. Juneau can be reached only by air or boat. In 1974 Alaska's voters approved moving the capital, but eight years later they voted down a bond issue to finance construction at a new location. The capital remains Juneau. In some places state government is practically the only game in town; others places can boast universities, commerce, and the arts. A few— Madison, Austin, Raleigh, and Phoenix—rank among the fifty most livable cities in the nation. A number—Harrisburg, Hartford, Trenton, Albany, and Springfield—are at the other end of the livability scale, ranking in the lowest fifty of three hundred cities rated by *Money* magazine in 1996.[1]

Within each of the fifty capital cities, there is the state capitol, the building in which the legislature (and usually the governor's office, the supreme court, and perhaps the secretary of state) is lodged. In twenty-seven states the official name for the building is the "State Capitol," in five states it is the "State Capitol Building," and the "State House" in eleven more. The other seven states have conceived of their own names: "Legislative Building," "Legislative Hall," "State Legislative Building," "Main Capitol Building," and "New Capitol."

Despite similarities, each capitol is unique, and very much a reflection of a state's tradition. The capitol in Richmond, Virginia, is a splendid example. Designed in part by Thomas Jefferson, the building's rotunda contains a famous marble statue of George Washington and the busts of seven other presidents, all of whom are identified with Virginia. In the capitol is the old hall of the House of Delegates, where Aaron Burr was tried for treason and Robert

E. Lee accepted command of the Confederate Army. Most other states have historical capitols of similar design, with a portico, two wings, and a dome atop a tall rotunda. A few, such as Honolulu's impressive, modernistic capitol building erected about twenty years ago and the high-rise tower from the period of Huey Long's governorship in Baton Rouge, deviate from the conventional model. Florida prides itself on its 1978 capitol, a 22-story structure with two thousand doors, sixty-six public restrooms, eleven private bathrooms and showers, thirty miles of telephone cable, a public observation deck on the top, and legislative chambers on the fourth level. In three states—Arizona, Nevada, and North Carolina—the legislative chambers are located in legislative buildings separate from the capitols.

The architecture of the capitol buildings is not without its effects on the legislative process, attesting to Winston Churchill's aphorism, "We build our buildings and then our buildings build us." The high-rises in Baton Rouge and Lincoln, for example, tend to impede informal communication among members, particularly among staff. That is because people are less likely to meet and chat on elevators and staircases than in corridors and hallways or space in the rotunda between senate and house chambers. In Columbus, while senators' offices are in the Senate Building, representatives' offices are in a skyscraper more than a block away. House members, and staff of the Legislative Services Commission who are also located there, are cut off. Formerly, everyone would bump into one another and often share tables for lunch in the statehouse. Although the food was nothing to write home about, collegiality and conversation more than made up for it. With the construction of the new state office building and restoration of the capitol, members of the senate and house seldom get a chance to mingle anymore.

Collegiality can suffer not only from structural features but also from the provision of offices to legislators. Before the legislative reform movement and its boost of legislative capacity, members in only a few states had offices to themselves. In many states rank-and-file had to use the desks in the chamber as work space. When their house was not in session, they would remain in the chamber making phone calls, catching up on correspondence, reading bills, and conversing with colleagues who were doing the same. In some places, members had the comparative luxury of shared space in what was sometimes called the "bull pen," an area where they could hardly help getting together with one another. In Ohio this space was called "the pit," and was shared by a representative with about fifteen others. Under such circumstances, privacy was limited and everyone knew what everyone else was doing. When legislators acquired their own offices and their own secretaries, a marked change took place. The old social structure crumbled; it was replaced by a new one in which legislators were more independent. Recently legislators in Connecticut and Kentucky acquired their own offices; they could close their doors, engage their computers, and have their privacy. But the result is less communication with one another and less opportunity to develop a set of shared norms in the capital community.

The Capitol Crowd

The capitol crowd consists of legislators and others, usually lobbyists, who play a part in the governmental business that takes place under the capitol dome. For many of these participants, legislative business and legislative community are practically all-consuming. A former Michigan legislator describes the appeal that few legislators have been able to resist: "The capitol is a world unto itself. It is a zoo and a womb. It is busy, gossip-ridden, boisterous, complex, and family-like. To some it becomes family. For those who have no other family or none for whom they deeply care—especially for those who stay in the capital city all week or all session, by inclination, or distance to home, or workload—the legislature may become or overshadow all other family."[2]

Many legislators are, at best, on the fringe of this action. If their districts are in or near the capital city, then they can commute to work daily when the legislature is in session. In a number of places, where the capital and its suburbs have a substantial share of the state's population, as in Arizona, Hawaii, and Indiana, a large proportion of legislators do commute. Since Lincoln and Omaha are near one another in Nebraska, legislators representing both these cities can return home in the evening after the legislature recesses, and consequently they interact less with their colleagues. About half the members of the Minnesota legislature live in the Minneapolis–St. Paul metropolitan area; they normally return home after the day's session. Salem is fifty miles south of Portland; therefore, about half the members of the Oregon legislature are within commuting distance of the city. About the same proportion of New Mexico's legislative membership are from Santa Fe or Albuquerque, and they too can get home when the legislature recesses for the day. Only during the session's final weeks do members from Albuquerque stay over in Santa Fe from one day to the next.

Legislators who do not live in or near the capital cities in most of the states spend much of their time there when the legislature is in session. Most members of the California, Florida, Michigan, Ohio, Pennsylvania, and Texas legislatures maintain a residential presence during sessions. They normally travel to the capital city from home each week, driving or flying in on a Monday morning for a noon session or on Monday evening for a session starting early Tuesday morning. They will then remain at the capital until their house recesses on a Thursday afternoon or Friday morning, at which time they will return home and put in as much time as practicable practicing law, selling real estate, or whatever. Early in the year, a few days a week may be spent at the capital, but as the session approaches the date of adjournment, members may not even get back to their districts for the weekend.

The capital communities, as they existed in the 1970s and into the 1980s, have undergone marked change in recent years. The physical environment is different, collegiality has diminished, ethics issues have taken a toll, the media have become more intrusive, legislative norms—never very strong to begin with—have weakened, and the strains of legislative life have increased. These changes and their impact on the capitol crowd and the legislature are discussed below.

THE EROSION OF COMMUNITY

When the legislature was in session the community of legislators used to be collegial, even fraternal. Members would work and play together, staying at the same hotels or motels and frequenting the same restaurants and the haunts later in the evening. In the old days legislators would congregate at one or two hotels in the capital. In Albany Democrats stayed at the DeWitt Clinton and Republicans at the Ten Eyck. In Springfield, Democrats went to the St. Nicholas, Republicans to the Leland. Legislator locales in Des Moines were the Ft. De Moines and the Savery, in Jackson, the Heidelburg and King Edwards, and in Harrisburg, the Penn-Harris and the Harrisburger. Legislators were all together and could be reached after a tough session by legislative leaders and lobbyists alike. It was easier in those days to communicate face-to-face and for majorities to mobilize overnight.

Many of the old hotels, which served as Democratic or Republican headquarters, no longer exist. They have been torn down or converted for other uses. Nowadays legislators are dispersed in their capital living—spread out among apartments and condominiums and Ramada Inns, Holiday Inns, and Howard Johnson motels. The change, even in a citizen legislature like North Dakota's, is detailed by David Nething, a former president pro tem of the senate:

Our capital city underwent quite a change in downtown—the old hotels that used to house the legislators when I started aren't there anymore. Instead, we have better and newer hotels in the outlying areas. So that had a way of breaking apart that evening structure. Then, in addition to that, a few years ago we provided a housing allowance for our legislators of $600 a month—which meant the room rates immediately went to that level. Now, all of the snow-birds in Bismarck that like to go to Arizona or Texas are willing to rent their house to us for $600 a month. Many of us like that because we can bring our wives with us, some even bring their children over and enroll them in school. That's another factor that diminishes that evening relationship that all of us had experienced. But, we still have one advantage in our state: we see each other a lot because we don't have office space for legislators. Our desk where we cast our vote is our office. Now at least we have a telephone with a WATS line on our desk, which is a help with that constituent service that we generate. Our relationship is pretty good because of that.[3]

Montpelier used to have a large hotel, which shut down after a flood and never reopened, leaving Vermont legislators without a place to congregate. Concord does not have any facility that can accommodate all 424 members of the New Hampshire legislature, so there is not even a place to hold an event for the whole legislature. Wyoming may be one of the last states re-maining where a large proportion of members stays in the same hotel—the Hitching Post. But even in Cheyenne, legislators are finding other motels and beginning to rent homes.[4]

Talbot "Sandy" D'Alemberte, now president of Florida State University, served in the Florida legislature during what is referred to as its first "golden age" of the late 1960s and 1970s. It was an extraordinarily collegial place, where Democrats and Republicans and urban and rural members shared a sense of mission. D'Alemberte reminisces: "It seemed to me that by and large we were united in a way that was almost spiritual. . . . You would be surprised how many of them shared the same idea of what it was like to be in public service."[5] Such collegiality is much diminished today. Public service may not be in complete disrepute, but it is tarnished—no longer the laudable goal it was during the Kennedy administration.

Moreover, the overall contemporary culture is highly individualistic, and today's legislators are a product of that culture. They are better educated, better informed, more professional, more ambitious. They are independent—sometimes compulsively so. Preoccupied with their constituencies, their causes, their campaigns, and their careers, today's legislators have little spare time to get very involved with their colleagues. One recent study examined relationships among the forty-seven members of the Maryland senate and found that members developed significant personal or political friendships with no more than five or six of their colleagues.[6] The current scene is wonderfully described by a former member of the Michigan house: "With more ambitious, hardworking, highly educated, and political career-minded legislators, there is less camaraderie, less seeking after common wisdom. There are more attempts at personal attainment."[7] Even the culture on Beacon Hill, home of the Massachusetts legislature, is undergoing substantial change. It is no longer defined by longevity, party discipline, and cozy relationships with lobbyists. As one observer notes: "There used to be people around here called "Knocko" [Edward McCormack Sr.] and "Onions" [William Burke]. They are gone."[8]

Just as individualism has eroded collegiality, so have the members' party affiliations. Party is more of a factor today than ever before. Other affiliations are also more fragmenting today than they used to be—gender and race among them. Women, for example, have progressed organizationally from informal social networking to ad hoc coalitions to formal caucuses. Women's caucuses, which by 1970 existed in ten states, have had a marked impact on process and policy, but they have also helped to divide the legislature along gender lines.[9] African Americans also have coalesced on certain issues and organized as a caucus in several states.

Camaraderie and mutual respect are diminished—in Arkansas, Texas, Minnesota, and other states. In earlier times, according to a veteran staffer in Florida, legislators "liked each other" and "laughed their butts off." Not anymore. When the 330 legislators in the survey of veterans were asked whether "there is less socializing and personal interaction, and fewer friendships among members today," 58.0 percent of them agreed and only 29.5 percent disagreed.[10]

THE CULTURAL IMPACT OF ETHICS

"Ethics" have taken a toll on legislative life in recent years and have further undermined the sense of legislative community. Ethics problems in state legislatures are real; they are not just attributable to media sensationalism or to unreasonable public standards. Corruption has been ferreted out in several states, and minor scandals have surfaced in many others. California, Arizona, South Carolina, and Kentucky were all subject to undercover operations, or "stings," by the FBI or local law enforcement agencies. In each state legislators were indicted and convicted. In California everyone who was tried— fourteen individuals, including three senators and two assemblymen—were convicted. In South Carolina, of twenty-eight individuals indicted, all but one pleaded guilty or was found guilty; and of the seventeen legislators involved, sixteen were sent to jail.

Bribery and extortion by legislators and lobbyists are not typical legislative practices. In fact, the conduct of legislators is better today than it used to be, when public expectations and standards were far less demanding. Nevertheless, ethics issues are constantly cropping up; they have shaken legislative bodies in several states and affected legislators practically everywhere. A member of the house was convicted in New Mexico. The top aide to the speaker in Maine was found guilty of electoral fraud. In Ohio, a few legislators pleaded guilty to having failed to disclose the source of honoraria paid them, and another was accused of shaking down interest groups for invitations to speak in return for honoraria. Florida legislators failed to disclose the costs of trips for which lobbyists paid, arguing that they did not realize that travel would be interpreted as a gift and that its disclosure was required by law. The speaker of the Massachusetts house pleaded guilty to federal tax evasion for filing false expenses and lying under oath about them. In New Jersey and Washington, the legislative parties were shown to have made use of state staffs and facilities for their political campaigns, which they were not supposed to do. Personal ethical problems beset Minnesota's Democrat Farm Labor Party, with one member standing trial for fraud, another convicted of shoplifting, another charged with slapping his estranged wife in public, and still another accused of threatening to cut funding for the Public Safety Department because he was refused a state patrol plane ride to a former governor's funeral.

Ethics have become politicized. Candidates use ethics in their campaigns to get elected, accusing their opponents of either exhibiting moral flaws themselves or ignoring the moral flaws in their legislative or governmental colleagues. Legislators who aspire to higher office see a hard stand on ethics as politically advantageous. Partisanship propels the new "politics of ethics." One party accuses the other of being soft, forcing it to adopt severe restrictions on legislators. And legislatures appear today to be trying to "out-ethics" one other, enacting what members can claim are the toughest ethics laws in the nation. All of this is not helping to maintain trust or civility in legislative bodies. A diminution of trust and civility makes governance more difficult. When distracted by ethics controversies and provoked by assaults on their character, members have a harder time developing the consensus required to resolve public policy disputes. When people cannot deal with each other, deadlock and gridlock are more likely to be the outcomes. Politicization, it should be noted, also does the subject of ethics an injustice. As Dennis Thompson writes, "When ethics charges become yet another political weapon, they lose their moral authority." The danger occurs when ethical conduct is less important than the votes that can be won wielding ethics as a weapon—when ethics becomes the means, while winning elections becomes the end.[11]

The Effects of Scandal

Scandals have weighty effects on legislatures, as demonstrated by subsequent events in states that endured sting operations. Scandals undoubtedly alert some legislators who otherwise might have wandered off the ethical map. And they certainly improve the immediate culture in which the legislature does its business. Yet the fallout from scandals can also hurt legislatures, at least in the short run. Legislators grow fearful lest they inadvertently become implicated in something that might initially have seemed innocent, but might appear otherwise on video or audiotape produced by a sting operation. They walk on eggshells, afraid to run risks and act in a way that might cast suspicion on them. Appearance becomes the standard by which legislative behavior gets judged; so legislators worry more over how they look than what they do.

The effects of AzScam illustrate some consequences. As the Arizona sting broke, members started asking themselves the question, "Did I ever say anything that could be misinterpreted?" Subjects of the ongoing investigation were shunned by their colleagues; no one wanted to get too close to or be photographed with them. The tapes released by authorities included, among other things, legislators putting down their colleagues. Feelings were hurt, reputations were damaged, and the institution suffered. Moreover, the news story kept running, and the pall did not lift. Members became weary, relations between legislators and lobbyists became chillier, and the entire fabric of legislative relationships was badly torn.

No legislature, however, was as wounded as badly by the aftermath of a sting as California's. Aware that members were cooperating with authorities and hearing rumors of colleagues wearing wires to secretly tape conversations, legislators in Sacramento became distrustful of practically everyone. The new style of communications in the capital was to keep discussions brief and speak in official language, leaving nothing to the interpretation or imagination of a grand jury that might listen to audiotapes.[12] Several years after Shrimpgate, the ripples were still observable in California.

Legislating Ethics

In part because of scandals, but also because of the overall climate, legislatures have been enacting laws to regulate the conduct of members with regard, first, to conflicts of interest and, second, to gifts from lobbyists.[13] Each type of regulation leaves a residue of problems.

Most states restrict or ban members from using their official positions for personal gain, taking part in outside business activities that may conflict with public service responsibilities, or favoring relatives or friends. The fundamental prohibition applies to the legislator who would personally benefit from some piece of legislation in a way or to a degree that other people would not. In citizen legislatures where members have outside-employment conflicts of interest are more likely to occur than in professional legislatures where outside employment is more limited.

One way to reduce conflicts of interest would be to do away with the citizen legislature, making legislative service a full-time occupation as it is in Congress. This is certainly not what voters in most places would seem to want. The public has been trying to *de*-professionalize legislatures (as discussed in chapter 2), not the other way around. Nor have state electorates seen fit to raise legislator salaries so that members might be less dependent on extra-legislative income. Therefore, people have little choice but to live with the ambiguity entailed when legislators are teachers, insurance salespersons, attorneys, and businesspersons in their private careers. Nonetheless, legislatures endeavor to reduce conflicts insofar as possible.

First, codes of ethics serve as a general standard and a means of raising the consciousness of members. In New Mexico, for example, members at the opening of the session recite on the floor: "I shall not use my office for personal gain and shall scrupulously avoid any act of impropriety or any act which gives the appearance of impropriety."

Second, legislators are required to disclose their financial interests. The purpose of financial disclosure laws is to make available sufficient information to allow citizens to judge whether officials are favoring their own interests or not. Although requirements vary by state, information subject to disclosure normally includes assets, income, transactions, liabilities, and gifts.

Third, legislators are prohibited from engaging in various activities. Several states prohibit lobbyists from serving in the legislature. A number also require that legislators wait, usually a year but occasionally two, until they can work as lobbyists after leaving the legislature. Attorneys in thirty-two states are restricted from representing clients before state agencies.

Fourth, legislators are required to declare their interest or abstain from voting on legislation that might appear to affect them. Legislative codes provide for several options. A legislator may disclose a personal interest and declare that he or she can cast a fair and objective vote, and then vote; or a legislator can abstain and inform the presiding officer, and then not have to disclose. Ultimately, it is up to the individual to decide whether to participate or sit it out, either because one's personal interest is too heavily involved or because it appears to be.

In a climate of distrust, or even in one of skepticism, just about anything can look bad or be made to look bad, and much of the behavior of public officials is viewed as suspect, if not unethical or corrupt. The remedy—to insulate legislators from all financial interests apart from their legislative compensation—is not viable and perhaps not even desirable. So legislators have to walk a tightrope, running the risk that their participation will be challenged as a conflict of interest by the press, the public, or the party in opposition.

Distrust is even more in evidence when it comes to the dealings between legislators and lobbyists. The two groups are highly interdependent. Legislators have to rely on lobbyists for information. What does an interest group want? What are the policy ramifications? And what are the likely consequences in both substantive and political terms? Legislators also rely on lobbyists (and their principals or clients) for campaign contributions. Lobbyists, on their part, rely on legislators for support for bills they are advocating and opposition to bills they are fighting.

Over the years lobbyists and legislators have developed relationships based on socializing, campaign support, and a sense of mutual appreciation. Insofar as their relationships are based on entertainment and other gifts from lobbyist to legislator, they have become highly regulated of late. One outcome of any scandal, as a matter of fact, is tighter regulation of what legislators can take from lobbyists. Thus, the process of socializing, through which lobbyists hope to build trusting relationships, is much diminished in state capitals today.

Socializing has suffered—at least the socializing occasioned by hunting and fishing trips, meals after the legislators' session day, or drinks at the local watering hole—even without the new salience of ethics. New generations of members drink less, eat more sparingly, work longer days, and try in their off hours to spend time with their families. They no longer stay over at the same motels or hotels or frequent the same watering holes. They are highly dispersed. As a lobbyist, and former Maryland senator, summed up:"People disappear after work."[14] Younger legislators are less available than their senior colleagues for the blandishments of lobbyists. Some of the old watering holes have closed down, while others are no longer attracting legislators as they used to, the way light bulbs attract moths. Clyde's in Tallahassee is more likely to be visited in the evening by lobbyists than legislators, and the Galleria in Columbus, where the house speaker habitually held forth, has been replaced by Christopher's, whose drawing power is not as great. Nor does Fran O'Brien's in Annapolis have the appeal it once did. Fewer people do business, or even socialize, at bars nowadays. Salem, Oregon, typifies the new order. There are still watering holes here and occasional late-night poker games. Yet compared with a generation ago, the legislators are a much less colorful bunch. They go their own way and do not hang out together. One member described Vera Katz, the speaker of the house, as "almost religious in her devotion to catching the 5 p.m. commuter bus so she could get home to walk her golden retriever."[15] Other members also had compelling reasons to commute back to Portland as soon as they could.

With the regulation of gift-giving and gift-taking, relationship-building is harder. Gifts run the gamut—from recreational trips for hunting or fishing to tickets to sporting events to dinners and drinks to minor mementos. In the face of demands for stiffer ethics laws, legislators maintain that no one's vote can be bought for a dinner (or even for a benefit that is more substantial). Yet there is a lot besides the vote; marginal behaviors and tendencies affect the legislative process. In any case, a pattern of taking from the same lobbyists or interests may create an obligation on the part of the legislator.

In addition to the powerful political motivations for legislators to enact ethics regulation, there are important public-policy purposes as well. It is desirable to reduce legislators' obligations deriving from the benefits conveyed. A sense of obligation is normal in political life and among people in elective office. Legislators feel obligated because of electoral support, alliances, favors, friendships—for many reasons. But they ought not to develop obligations based on gifts bestowed by those who are trying to cultivate political friendships. It is also desirable to discourage, insofar as practicable, the appearance to the public that the largess of lobbyists is influencing legislators. Yet while reducing legislators' obligations and removing some of the basis for an appearance of corruption, regulation should not interfere with communications between legislators and the people who serve as agents of organizations and groups of citizens.

The trend nationwide has been toward limiting, or in some places prohibiting, gifts by lobbyists and the disclosure of anything above a certain value given to legislators. The "no cup of coffee" rule, which bars legislators from taking anything of value from lobbyists, is in effect in a few states. Wisconsin, with its Progressive tradition, has had a prohibition since the 1950s. More recently, states hard hit by scandals enacted such laws. South Carolina went cold turkey after "Operation Lost Trust," and Minnesota did the same after "Phonegate." Massachusetts also abandoned the gift-giving culture, under pressure from press and public and feeling it had no alternative.[16]

More common than prohibition are stringent limits and disclosure requirements. California prohibits legislators from accepting gifts with an aggregate value of more than $250 from a single source per calendar year. Lobbyists are not permitted to make gifts to an individual member of more than $10 a month. New Hampshire limits gifts from a single source to $250 per year and Kentucky's annual limit is $100. Iowa imposes a $3 limit on any meal or gift. Florida's ethics law prohibits legislators from accepting gifts worth more than $100 from lobbyists, their principals, or PACs and requires the disclosure of gifts worth more than $25. Lawmakers in Florida, however, can accept gratis all the food and drink they can consume in a single sitting. Ohio legislators cannot accept gifts valued at more than $75 a year from any lobbyist.

These laws are not universally observed; loopholes always exist, and some lobbyists and some members manage to evade the limitations. But for the most part these laws have had the intended impact on capital cultures and the interactions of legislators and lobbyists. Few lawmakers travel on pleasure trips at a lobbyist's expense. Such travel is either prohibited by law or severely restricted. Few lawmakers are willing to take anything other than perhaps a token of appreciation—such as a fruit basket, can of nuts, flowers, or plaque. In some states—California is an example—they do not even want to disclose that, and many members refuse anything of value. The year following the enactment of Georgia's ethics law, an administrator at Georgia Tech, in charge of choice seating for the university's football games, sent the usual number of box seats for the 1993 season to members of the legislature. Before accepting the tickets, however, legislators called up the lobbyist compliance officer to ask, "What's reported on me?" As a result, 80 percent of the gifts that had normally been accepted were returned by legislators not willing to risk adverse public reaction.[17]

Wining and dining still goes on, but with disclosure most legislators lose their appetites. Some will pay their own way, while others simply pass up the occasion to dine with lobbyists and instead eat alone or with colleagues. Members are afraid of what the press or an opponent might do with reports of lobbyists having spent money on them, so discretion becomes the better part of valor. For many legislators, disclosure is tantamount to prohibition. New Jersey's legislators, for instance, take a lot less than before disclosure. When the requirement went into effect, "benefit passing" (as gift-giving is called in the Garden State) declined from a predisclosure $163,375 (1992) to $112,177 (1993) to $100,167 (1994) to $76,083 (1995).[18] Disclosure can prove embarrassing for members who rank high on a list of gifts received. For example, Rep. Stephen D. Dargan of Connecticut ranked number 1 in his state, receiving $1,450.98 in food and drink and $144.85 in gifts from a number of groups (each of which was limited to $150 for the year). His standing was widely publicized. Although Dargan defended his behavior, he agreed to support a total ban on gifts, explaining, "I don't want to see any more of these stories about the top-ten list."[19]

Nowadays, the primary occasions for legislators and lobbyists getting together socially are receptions. During the legislative session receptions held by state interest groups have been, and continue to be, a way of life. Receptions are held three or four nights a week, when legislators can be counted on to be in town. Every day legislators may receive two or three invitations to these events. In Maryland's ninety-day session, by way of illustration, for the first three weeks or so receptions are held just about every evening. After a while they taper off, as members get down to work, and by the final weeks of the session, receptions have vanished from the Annapolis scene.

Those legislators who commute will stop in at a reception or two on their way home. Those in residence will try to show up at as many as possible. For some members, and particularly those in states where pay and per diem are low, free food is still an attraction. For most members receptions are an extension of their work—places where they visit with interest group representatives, lobbyists, constituents, and (not incidentally) one another. For some members receptions are a burden that they would just as soon avoid. Florida legislators, for instance, have been known to send their aides in their place with instructions to pick up their name tags so it would appear that they had attended.

The lavish receptions of past years have pretty much been discontinued. Associated Industries of Florida used to throw extravagant parties, but no longer does so. The climate is not at all receptive to such affairs, and the press is not inclined to let them go unnoticed. Yet even in those states that ban gifts, receptions are generally permitted as an exception. Along with fund-raisers, they are becoming the principal, and almost only, venue for legislators and lobbyists to get together in a quasi-social way. They are usually large affairs, however, and the conversation under such circumstances is much different from conversations on a pleasure trip or at a small dinner outing. There is little doubt, according to legislators and lobbyists, that interaction between them is less expansive, less relaxed, and less satisfying. In their judgments, communication has been curtailed. Certainly, relationship-building has been impeded.

Legislators still see one another after hours; yet the general feeling is that collegiality has declined largely because the new ethics laws have virtually outlawed lobbyist largess, dissolving the glue that once held the capital community together. With lobbyists no longer entertaining legislators, there are fewer opportunities for legislators—particularly those from different chambers or opposing parties—to get to know each other socially, to build trust, and foster the spirit of compromise. Whatever the benefit, legislators can no longer stand apart from the citizens they represent, enjoying the deference and perquisites of legislative life. In capital after capital, one can hear veteran legislators—and even some of their juniors—lamenting, "It's no fun anymore." The public clearly does not want it to be fun. People's jobs are seldom enjoyable, so why should their representatives' jobs be different?

ASSAULT BY THE MEDIA

Appearance is the ethical, and prudential, standard that guides legislators nowadays. According to the appearance standard, legislators must avoid not only impropriety but also anything that *looks* like impropriety. The ethicist, Michael Josephson, has written that in matters of public trust and confidence appearances are crucial. In a survey of legislators, legislative staff, and journalists, Josephson's ethics institute asked respondents whether they agreed with the following statement: "Because public trust can be undermined by perceptions of wrongdoing as much as by actual wrongdoing, public officials ought to avoid conduct which creates an appearance of impropriety, even though it requires them to refrain from conduct that is not actually improper." Given the sponsor of the survey, it is not surprising that 91 percent of the legislators and staff and 99 percent of journalists agreed or strongly agreed.[20]

The Rule of Appearance

The appearance standard undoubtedly makes political sense for people in public life, an arena in which perception has come to have as much of a bearing on things as reality. Legislators acknowledge the salience of this standard by counseling each other, "Don't do anything that you would not want to read about in tomorrow's newspaper." But appearance has also been given moral weight by ethicists, who assert that "appearing to do wrong while doing right is really doing wrong." According to Dennis Thompson, public officials who appear to do wrong actually do several kinds of moral wrong: they erode confidence in the political system; they give citizens reason to act as if government cannot be trusted; and they undermine democratic accountability.[21]

The appearance standard is written into many state statutes and codes of conduct. At an extreme, it has served recently as the basis of a U.S. District judge's ruling that Massachusetts prosecutors were not required to prove that a quid pro quo existed between gifts lobbyists bestowed and favorable action legislators rendered. A social relationship could be enough to suggest wrongdoing and intent.[22] In the case of *U.S. v. Jackson* (1995), a U.S. Circuit Court of Appeals found that conviction under the California bribery law does not necessarily require the finding of an explicit quid pro quo.

"'Appearance of impropriety'—what the hell is that?" asks Massachusetts senator, Robert Havern.[23] Although the literature on ethics usually defines "appearance" as what a "fair-minded" or "reasonable" person could "reasonably" believe, it leaves a lot to the imagination. The public is the final judge, and although this standard should obligate the public to be informed in order to render sound judgment, that is not the case.[24] Insofar as the public is informed at all, it is informed by the media. So, practically speaking, "appearance" is that which is communicated to the public by the media. And that which is communicated by the media is often intended to give the appearance of impropriety; otherwise, who could possibly be interested in reading or hearing about it? Although the public has the final word, the media in effect serve as the prosecutor and the judge in a forum where the defense counsel is absent.

The Negative Spin

Citizens get a highly stylized picture of their state legislature. It is a snapshot the media chooses to take and then convey to their audience. Rarely is the snapshot a pretty one, and it appears to be getting uglier. In the survey conducted by the Josephson Institute, there was considerable agreement among legislators and legislative staff as to how the media had been changing: 88 percent saw the media as more aggressive; 84 percent as more negative; 87 percent as more cynical; 64 percent as more prosecutorial; 68 percent as more biased; and 61 percent as more unfair.[25] In another survey, of veteran legislators, 86.4 percent agreed that news coverage of the legislature had become more confrontational.[26]

The media can be expected to be critical, and even adversarial. It goes with the territory, with the definition of just what news is and what it is not. The operating rule that "bad news makes for good news" has long been a standard of American journalism. But, maintains Thomas Patterson, the media have raised it to new heights in recent decades. According to Patterson's studies, negativity in the news has been on the rise since the 1960s.[27] The almost natural biases of journalists favor what is new, what is dramatic, what is bad, and what can be readily grasped. Journalists thrive in an atmosphere of change, conflict, and crisis.[28] As one newspaper columnist commented, "If it bleeds, it leads."[29]

Gunnar Myrdal pointed out years ago, with respect to race in American society, that it is more difficult to discern signs of health than of disease. It is even more difficult with respect to legislative bodies, largely because of the coverage by the press corps. The press accentuates the negative, bypassing whatever is positive. The quest is for misdeeds and malefaction. Muckraking is by no means a new phenomenon. Theodore Roosevelt coined the term "muckrakers," while cautioning journalists not to go too far. "The men with the muckrakers," he said, "are often indispensable to the well being of society, but only if they know when to stop raking the muck."[30] Since Woodward and Bernstein achieved celebrity status with their reporting on Watergate, investigative, or watchdog, journalism has been the model for just about everyone covering politics, not excluding statehouse correspondents.

Investigative reporting, unlike traditional story gathering, is designed to prove a preconceived notion. Sources are selected to support the reporter's basic proposition, while contradictory sources are used mainly to add credibility to a story that is largely predetermined.[31] The techniques of this type of journalism are no longer exceptional; they are now part of mainstream reporting.[32] One variant of this phenomenon, described as "gotcha journalism," tries to catch public officials in seemingly compromising positions. The focus is on the faux pas or the mishap, not on what a person might be achieving on the job.

What the media wants are stories built around personalities, not around institutions or processes. Also wanted are stories with conflict and confrontation, winners and losers, good guys and bad guys, and scandals, scandals, scandals. A good story for a reporter is likely to be a bad story for the legislature.[33] Villains and victims sell well. In the political sphere, politicians, lobbyists, and "the system" are the conventional villains nowadays, while citizens are the victims. Reporters want their readers to respond to their stories of how public officials are subverting the public interest with "Holy shit!" and "This is an outrage!"[34] Focusing on Washington, D.C., Patterson notes that, although there is no persuasive evidence that official corruption has risen, scandals increasingly fill the headlines. In the past decade, ethical lapses have accounted for a fourth of the coverage of Congress, compared with less than a tenth in the previous decade.[35] "The press turns every scandal into another Watergate," writes William Schneider, "The challenge is to bring down the president."[36] It is not surprising that we find like dispositions on the part of the press in the states.

The negative bias of the media does not go unnoticed by the public. A Times Mirror survey found people were critical of the media for their lack of objectivity, emphasis on bad news, and sensationalism. Almost one-third believed press coverage was not very responsible or not at all responsible in the way it covered the personal and ethical behavior of politicians.[37] Another Times Mirror survey found agreement by both the public (66 percent) and opinion leaders (71 percent) that the media are too focused on the misdeeds of political figures. Representatives of the media saw it differently; only 18 percent of the local press and 29 percent of the national press agreed with such a contention.[38] According to the survey of veteran legislators, the media have changed their focus. They now concentrate more than formerly on items that show the legislature in a bad light—perceptions of conflicts of interest, perceived misconduct, perks of office, and legislators' relationships with lobbyists.

The print press stands apart from the other media, in that it is where people go for their state news. A recent survey of statewide officials and legislative leaders in all fifty states found that newspapers were considered the most important media in this respect, with television far behind.[39] Whereas the numbers of statehouse print journalists increased in the 1980s, television generally ignored state politics. An analysis of evening news coverage in five California cities found only one minute out of each news hour devoted to legislative activities. The last out-of-town television station closed its capital bureau in Sacramento in 1988.[40] There simply were no ratings in state news. "State government is terrible television," according to the Columbus bureau chief for WH10-TV, "There's not a story that lends itself to pictures." The print press, by contrast, is serious about its coverage. Take Columbus, Ohio. Sixteen news organizations have full-time staffs there, with the *Cleveland Plain Dealer* having the largest statehouse bureau.[41]

Journalistic Incentives

Given the situation today, where newspapers are struggling to survive the competition with television and radio, the pursuit of dirt may be economically obligatory. A New Mexico legislator recalls that at an ethics task force meeting, which he was chairing, he asked a representative of the press how to get the media to be more appreciative of the legislative process. The reply was,

"Remember, we're a competitive business. We're here to sell papers and news time. Unless we give the public what they demand, we're out of business."[42] This justification is not unlike that for negative campaign ads, which consultants defend on the basis that they work because voters remember their messages, and as long as they work, they will be used.

There can be little doubt that the marketplace is at least partly responsible for the way the media covers legislatures. Politics has become like show business, and much of journalism has become part of the entertainment industry. Currently we are drowning in information, or rather noise of one type or another. Everyone wants to break through and attract an audience. The newspaper press, which provides the lion's share of coverage to legislatures, faces the toughest competition from talk radio, talk television, and infotainment like "Hard Copy" and "Inside Edition." Take local talk radio in New Mexico, for example. People simply go on the air excoriating the "worthless legislature." As the house speaker describes the process: "John comes on the line and says, 'Raymond Sanchez is a lying no-good son-of-a gun'. I hear that a lot." The station, which the house speaker has in mind, reaches more than one hundred thousand people, mainly those driving to or from work.[43] To compete successfully for an audience, the print press has to elevate stories to comparable levels of sensationalism in what one journalist calls a "total-trash environment," where each medium is driven to become progressively more outrageous.[44] Anthony Lewis of the *New York Times* calls this the press's version of Gresham's Law (i.e., bad money drives out good)—the tendency, in the competition for readers or viewers, to let the scandalous drive out serious news.[45]

Contemporary standards and practices are shaped not only by the economics of the industry but also by the incentives that motivates reporters. The major objective of any journalist is to produce an exciting story that will appeal to a large audience. The story that nails legislators and/or the legislature to the wall will be rewarded by one's editors with preferred placement and gain plaudits from the profession.[46] One can think of journalists winning Pulitzer prizes for uncovering corruption, one cannot imagine that many awards are bestowed for portraying the good work of public officials. Headhunting statehouse reporters who master contemporary journalism will be able to advance their careers, which usually means leaving the state capital and going to Washington, D.C., where celebrity status and television punditry are much nearer at hand. With this new mode of aggressive journalism the rage, statehouse reporters have become intrusive, relentless, judgmental, and destructive of individuals and institutions both.

Many public officials believe reporters lack a real understanding of the political process. They also believe reporters let personal bias slip into their reporting.[47] This is indeed the case. Reporters, like the rest of us, are products of a contemporary culture. They are critical of legislatures, less because of attitudes specifically toward those legislatures but mainly because of the decline of legitimacy of all social institutions—legislatures, bureaucracies, police, courts, and even families. Legislators, however, may be feeling the brunt more than others.

For some journalists the role of the press is that of exposing the shortcomings of American democracy, which they think to be substantial. The ideologies of members of the press corps are seldom neutral. Most have a reformist bent. They are reacting, moreover, against the "lap dog" journalism of yesteryear in adopting an "attack dog" mode of today. Vietnam and Watergate added to the moral fires of journalists, and turned a natural skepticism into cynicism. In the journalist's view, our public officials and political institutions cannot be trusted. Power, after all, corrupts and legislators get close enough to power to be corrupted.

As watchdogs of the system, journalists see their obligation as blowing the whistle on malfeasance and those who commit it. It is not just a story they are seeking, but a change in societal agendas and public policy. Their muckraking is intended to provoke outrage on the part of the public, and it does, albeit not for long. But public officials fear the press might provoke the public for longer, so they often respond with action in order to head off continued assault by the media. This is the pattern of legislative response when corruption is uncovered or sometimes even alleged. It is predictable, then, that when 330 veteran legislators were surveyed, 64.5 percent said that media influence had been increasing, while only 9.8 percent said it had been decreasing.[48]

Money as the Source of Evil

More than anyone else, journalists believe money is the source of much—if not all—evil in politics and that their investigations into cause and effect simply have to follow the money trail. The contemporary statehouse press shares the ideology of progressivism, going back to the beginning of the century when the muckraker press mobilized against monied power. Thus, although money is hardly the sole ingredient of politics, the press reacts "viscerally and emotionally" as if it were. According to David Broder, a respected member of the journalistic profession: "We think people who contribute ideas to politics are good citizens. We think that people who have the leisure time to go down and volunteer in campaigns are good citizens. But we think that people who put money into politics are probably doing it for some evil, nefarious purpose."[49]

The theme that legislators are selling out for campaign contributions or other benefits is repeated constantly. The periodic disclosure in so many states of lobbying expenses for entertainment provides regular opportunity for the press to imply that legislators do what they do in return for the food and drink. It is not unusual to see articles, such as those in the *Tampa Tribune* (March 12 and 13, 1995), reporting that there are fourteen lobbyists for every legislator, more than three times the national average. The inference one draws is that lobbyists dominate the legislature. But the "evidence" is misleading. The reason that so many lobbyists are registered in Florida has more to do with the state's strict registration requirements than with the way the legislative process operates.

Tallahassee's press corps is relentless. During the course of deliberations on major telecommunications legislation in Florida, industry groups invited members of the committee with jurisdiction over the subject to dinner. Lobster was the fare.[50] By this time, an agreement had been reached and passage of a compromise package was imminent. The dinner was by way of celebrating a job accomplished, and not for the purpose of gaining support for one position or another. Nevertheless, the press reported on the "lobster dinner" as if legislators were bartering their votes for shellfish. Reporters, who livened up their stories with such innuendo, realize that all the industry bought was the dinner, and not the legislators. Nevertheless, that was not the major point. Statehouse reporters do not approve of legislators and lobbyists getting too close, and they see their mission as that of ending such practices. For them, the lobster dinner is symbolic—it goes right to the heart of whether the legislature is trustworthy. As one statehouse reporter from Tallahassee explained: "If enough people go to these dinners and get slapped . . . by the *St. Pete Times* and other papers, these meetings are going to happen a little less frequently." "Slapping" is thus the press's way of curtailing a practice it deplores.

The press is unwilling to hear any arguments to the contrary on the subject of legislator-lobbyist relationships. At a panel discussion in Minnesota, two legislators—Sen. Ember Reichgott Junge and Rep. Charlie Weaver—responded to questions about whether the recently enacted gift ban had changed the life of legislators. They observed that not all the changes were beneficial. For one thing, they observed, constituent groups no longer came to the capital to mingle with their legislators. A few days later a *Minneapolis Star Tribune* editorial chastised the two legislators for advocating a return to the lavish days of old. Yet neither legislator had endorsed such a thing; neither legislator advocated removal of the gift ban.[51]

Campaign contributions are probably the favorite target of the media. Without fail, stories link contributions to a legislator's vote, although no causal relationship can be demonstrated. A perfect example of inference at work is found in the series by the *Indianapolis Star/Indianapolis News* (February 11–15, 1996), which was titled: "STATEHOUSE $ELLOUT: HOW SPECIAL INTERESTS HIJACKED THE LEGISLATURE." A Florida legislator describes how legislators are treated. For example, if he sponsored a liquor bill, the press would write that "Rep. ———— has always been heavily supported by the liquor industry." The implication is that his sponsorship was prompted by the liquor industry's campaign support. "If I happen to believe that the liquor industry is a viable industry and I do something to try and protect it, why wouldn't they support me?" he asks. "I mean, they're not going to give money to their enemies."[52] No allowance is made for the possibility that the money may follow the vote rather than the vote following the money. Nor is there room to explain the benefits to constituency and to state, nor to detail any of the many factors at work in the legislative process. The story instead is simply that legislators do what they do because they are being bribed—albeit legally—to do it. The press seldom offers an interpretation other than that of hanky-panky.

Cumulative Effects

No single exposé or story makes a deep impression on the public consciousness or on the legislative process. But the accumulation of negatives over time has a number of profound effects on legislators as individuals and the legislature as an institution.

First, legislators become demoralized and resentful. They assume a defensive crouch whenever they are dealing with the media. Few lawmakers expect to accomplish much through the media—they may get by as individuals, but they expect their institution to take hits. As the president of the New Mexico senate put it, "the media tells the public we're a bunch of bums." Television, radio, and print all express the same themes.[53] If they escape political embarrassment or damage, legislators consider themselves fortunate. Some, like William Bulger, president of the Massachusetts senate for seventeen years, simply refuse to speak to reporters. Bulger explained that he saw no reason to abet the media in their commercial efforts to sell newspaper advertising or television time. He stonewalled the press and, until the very end of his career in the legislature, was constantly raked over the coals by the *Boston Globe*. The newspaper relented only when Bulger retired from the legislature to become president of the University of Massachusetts. His successor as senate president, Tom Birmingham, had a view of the media that was different only in degree. He said, "I don't mind an adversarial relationship with the media. But it goes beyond. It's an inquisition. At times it verges on the sadistic."[54] Ed Davis, a member of the California senate and former police commissioner of Los Angeles, also could not stand the capital press in Sacramento, calling them "miserable bastards," and ranking criminals slightly higher as just plain "bastards."[55]

Second, legislators are intimidated by the media. For good reason, they are afraid to do what they believe they should do because of how the media may treat their actions. The critical coverage has curtailed the travel of members to national legislative meetings, like those sponsored by the National Conference of State Legislatures (NCSL) and the Council of State Governments (CSG). The print press will routinely report which legislators attended, how much it cost in state funds, how luxurious the conference hotels were, what social activities transpired, and whether legislators spent any time sightseeing or recreating. All this can, and does, become grist for an opponent's campaign mill.

Legislators fear they will be photographed by a television reporter or followed around by a newspaper reporter, waiting to catch them in an indiscretion. A former television journalist understands the reasons for legislative fears. "You can get a picture of an overweight legislator lying by the pool and drinking. It's a fat picture for television crews."[56] Nowadays, fewer legislators run the risk of traveling out of state and fewer use state funds to finance their expeditions. Many of those who continue to participate in activities of their national organizations draw on their own campaign accounts; some play it safer by paying their own way; and some play it safest by remaining at home.[57]

Third, legislators are discouraged by the reward system imposed by the media's standards. But should legislators even care? A poll done by Gov. William Donald Schaefer in 1994 found that only 10 percent of the Maryland population read the *Baltimore Sun*, a mere 1 percent read the front page, and a mere 0.5 percent read the editorial page. This means that about eighteen thousand to twenty thousand out of 4 million Marylanders read the editorial page. How many even recall what they read? Yet that page has a big impact on legislators who want acknowledgment, approval, and endorsements.[58]

To receive media approval, legislators have to play the media's game rather than the legislature's. Legislators who may not be very effective in the process and have relatively little influence with their colleagues inside may do best in being reported outside. Broder notes, regretfully, that the press glamorizes the mavericks, nay-sayers, and crusaders in the legislature. They are easiest to write about. But these are not usually the people who move the legislative process along. The people who are doing their jobs well, the ones who deserve attention and recognition, do not receive it in the media.[59] Honesty, decency, normality, and effectiveness do not make news and, therefore, in the media's scheme merit no praise.

Legislative leaders and members complain that significant policy advances go unrecognized if they are not on the media's agenda.[60] The incentives for the politically ambitious, or merely the politically insecure, are to play to the press. An Ohio legislator, for instance, explains that when the *Cleveland Plain Dealer* runs a story exposing a problem, a legislator who introduces a bill to solve the problem can almost count on an editorial praising him. The urge to play to the press is practically irresistible.[61]

Fourth, partly because of the media, legislative politics has become more confrontational and less adept at building consensus through compromise. When the media are not busy exposing legislative peccadillos, they are depicting the legislative process, not as "crabwise movement from one compromise to another," but as a sports event or horse race in which one side wins and the other loses. The reporting of the legislature emphasizes emergencies, crisis, and disorder, and not the coherence and continuity that still characterize legislative politics when surveyed over time.[62] In a curious way, the practices of the legislature may be adapting to the media's characterization of them. In this way, the media's portrayal is self-fulfilling.

Fifth, the effects of the media on the public have been as consequential as those on legislators and the legislature. The constant coverage of the negative, or the apparently negative, in legislative life has helped increase public cynicism and reduce confidence and trust in the legislative branch of government. The point regarding confidence, trust, and cynicism was made earlier, in a different context, but here responsibility is assigned to the media. Patterson states the general case: "Democracy requires a degree of skepticism if it is to operate properly . . . but the press has gone way beyond the point of responsible criticism, and the effect is to rob political leaders of the public confidence that is required to govern effectively."[63] Probably even more important, political institutions—and especially Congress and state legislatures—have been undermined. For state legislatures today the only good news is no news. Escaping the attention of the media may be the only way in which legislatures can avoid adding further fuel to the fires of public cynicism.[64]

The irony in all of this, according to Broder, is that a free press depends on the maintenance of a democratic society, and the best safeguard for such a society is representative government. In the press's own interests, the denigration of the legislature makes little sense. But the press's short-term interests are more compelling than its long-term ones. The legislature currently enjoys so little confidence that it cannot tolerate many more blows.[65] Another member of the profession of journalism views the situation similarly: "This constant bashing, this constant negative rundown is because our editors want it, because we are competing for audiences, because we want conflict and we want corruption and we want all of those things we assume go on."[66]

Periodic efforts are made to assemble journalists and legislators in a discussion of how the two parties can achieve détente, thus preserving both legislatures and the press as vital institutions of American democracy. Even the possibility of legislators and statehouse reporters getting together is dangerous, according to one Florida journalist. Given the level of public cynicism, he points out, "as soon as the public sees any sort of collaboration between the media and the people the media are covering, . . . you will really see the cynicism go through the roof."[67]

Sixth, the media have chosen sides as representatives of the public, trying not only to win an audience but to air and reflect the views of that audience. Talk radio and talk television are the most prominent manifestations of the democratizing effects of the contemporary media. The talk commentators today, like the newspaper commentators of earlier times, wield considerable power. But the Walter Lippmanns or the James Restons sought mainly to influence the governing elite—the new talkmeisters play to the masses.[68]

In the view of legislators, the public is not interested in the good things they are doing and is convinced they are "doing something under the table."[69] The cynicism of the public appears to inspire the cynicism of the media, just as the treatment of legislative institutions by the media nourishes the cynical appetites of the public. Moreover, representatives of the media see themselves as guardians of the public interest, while they see the politicians who win election thanks to PAC contributions beholden to the special interests. Journalists favor a leveling of the playing field, so that organized interest groups and their lobbyists have no greater access than unorganized citizens. One way to accomplish this is to curtail the independence of the legislature.

A contemporary book that analyzes investigative reporting concludes on the note that the combination of public alienation toward authority and competition in the media for stories about moral disorder will lead to an upsurge of popular democracy, which in turn can result in either enlightenment or mass mobilization.[70] Although the course is not yet played out, one possible casualty is a strong and independent legislature.

THE EROSION OF NORMS

State legislatures, like Congress, have norms that are distinctive from those of other social groups. These norms—"rules of the game" or "folkways" as they are also called—constitute an understanding about what is proper and improper conduct in the legislature. If legislators share beliefs as to how they ought to behave and how the process should work, then the organization of which they are members will be stronger vis-à-vis its environment. We have touched briefly on norms in the context of legislative institutionalization. We shall touch on them in a different context here.

In considering norms, it is useful to take into account three studies. About forty years ago an exploration of legislative orientations in California, New Jersey, Ohio, and Tennessee identified forty-two types of norms.[71] Roughly twenty years ago another study surveyed senators in eleven states, asking them whether they agreed or disagreed with nineteen normative items.[72] Finally, a relatively recent national survey of 330 legislators, who had served fifteen years or longer, asked a number of questions relating to norms. One was whether these veterans thought that "legislators today are less likely to spend time learning the 'norms' or 'folkways' of the chamber and 'paying their dues'." Of those responding, 68.5 percent agreed, while only 20.3 percent disagreed.[73]

As mentioned earlier, socializing among legislators and legislator friendships are much diminished. The principal effect of friendship is a high level of trust; with fewer friendships, we can expect less trust. One item in the eleven-state survey posed questions regarding notions of trustworthiness, integrity, and one's word. It asked for agreement or disagreement with the practice of "concealing the real purpose of a bill or purposely overlooking some portion of it in order to assure passage." Most respondents opposed such a practice. Years later, however, when veteran legislators were asked whether that norm had lost some of its force, they were divided. In response to the statement, "Legislators are more likely today to hide their legislative motives and try to conceal the real purpose of legislative actions," 31.7 percent agreed, while 36.6 percent disagreed, and 31.7 percent took neither position.

Veteran legislators, however, do notice the diminution of trust. They see one another, and trust one another, less. They are more suspicious of their colleagues' agendas. Their word means less than it used to mean. Alaska's speaker of the house, Ramona Barnes, referred to the time sixteen years earlier when she first came to the legislature. "The old-timers—their word was their bond," she recalled. "You did business with a handshake. That's all passing by the wayside." That feeling is echoed in Ohio. Vern Riffe, who retired in 1994, mentioned that the biggest difference between then and now was that,

"You don't see the trust of the members for each other that you used to see."
The former Ohio house majority leader, William Mallory, agreed: "When
you gave your word, you lived up to your word. I don't think somebody
giving their word necessarily is a commitment today. It depends on what
happens in the next moment."[74] In Florida, too, commitments have been
losing their meaning. Time after time, the vote counts taken by party leaders
and by lobbyists are inaccurate. What members tell them is not necessarily
what they do. The biggest change is that twenty years ago, 90 percent of the
legislators could be relied on for their word, according to one veteran. Now
only a handful can be counted on, as far as a commitment is concerned. The
trustworthiness of individuals, and thus, the trustworthiness of the process is
in decline.

In those states that have had FBI stings and where legislators have worn
wires or otherwise informed on colleagues, trust is almost completely cor-
roded. Legislators feel they cannot afford to trust one another. In those states
where partisanship has grown intense, mistrust runs mainly along party lines.
California is illustrative of both types of states, and the assembly there has
assumed some of the qualities of a snake pit. During Willie Brown's struggle
to retain the speakership for the Democrats, one assembly Republican (Larry
Bowler) exhibited his distrust of Democrats in a graphic way. When he no-
ticed microphones in a capitol meeting room where Republicans were discussing political strategy, he borrowed a pocket knife and cut the wires.[75]

"A reasonable level of civility and mutual respect is necessary . . . if a legislature is to function at all," writes former Michigan house member William
Bryant.[76] The norm of civility is certainly in some peril. Twenty years ago, the
eleven-state survey found substantial agreement, except in Texas, on proscrib-
ing the practice of "dealing in personalities in debate or other remarks made
on the floor of the chamber." This norm survives in some states (Tennessee
being a good example) but is waning in others. In the old days, however harsh
debate became on the floor, legislators maintained their friendships. T. V.
Smith noted about a half-century ago that legislators might attack colleagues,
calling one another names and deprecating their motives. But they would
then walk arm in arm the next day acting as the best of friends.[77] A contemporary legislative leader from Indiana makes a similar observation: "It used to
be that we'd curse each other on the floor, then go and have a beer together;
now we're civil on the floor and curse each other in caucus—and I don't
know which is worse!"[78]

Heightened partisanship has taken its toll on civility. Even in a state like
Virginia, which has been acknowledged for its long and decorous legislative

tradition, civility has been severely damaged. And in a state like California, the damage in the assembly would appear to be almost beyond repair. Session after session finds Republicans and Democrats literally shouting across the aisle at one another, with personal invective substituting for debate. "If the Assembly were a hockey game," one observer writes, "the penalty box would be S.R.O."[79]

Other norms may also be eroding because of recent developments, particularly the imposition of term limits. Some believe that members are no longer willing to serve an apprenticeship. The survey of veteran legislators asked for an "agree" or "disagree" response to the following statement: "Legislators today are less likely to be seen and not heard; they are less likely to show respect for, and seek the counsel of, older, more experienced members." The ratio of agreement to disagreement on this item was 65.9 to 20.2 percent. Even though legislative veterans believe it takes about six years to learn the ropes and become effective, they also recognize that few new lawmakers are willing to take the time to do so. The modern professional politician wants to hit the ground running and displays little deference to anyone who has been around for a while.[80] And in states with term limits, members have no investment in the long range and little incentive to learn. They have their objectives to accomplish and very little time in which to accomplish them. The eleven-state survey asked respondents whether they were expected to serve an apprenticeship period when they first entered the legislature. According to the criteria of the investigators, apprenticeship did not exist as a norm in any of the senates under examination. That was twenty years ago. Currently, such an expectation that legislators will serve as apprentices is completely out of the question.

For years legislatures appeared to be rooted in a system of political relationships based on reciprocity and given to compromise. In order to achieve their own goals, legislators had to go along with the achievement of their colleagues' goals. In order to get anything, they usually had to settle for less than a whole loaf. And settle they did. The modern legislature as an institution is built on accommodation and compromise. The remarkable thing is that political compromise and personal integrity can coexist within one framework. T. V. Smith, an ardent exponent of the virtues of representative democracy, justified compromise along the following lines: No man, he wrote, should compromise the core of himself—that is, the final principles by which he lives. "But a man is not a good citizen," he continued, "who does not meet other good citizens halfway."[81]

No longer is compromise the virtue it used to be. Individual legislators today have positioned themselves on ground that makes compromise harder. As candidates, they campaign on the promise, "Send me there; I'll kick the bastards out and make everything happen." Once elected, however, legislators learn that confrontation is not the path to success. So rather than being confrontational, they become more conciliatory. They become what they ran against, and prove a disappointment to their constituents who want results but abhor "deals." In the words of one legislator from Florida, "The people at home are happiest when you are confrontational." They would be perfectly satisfied "if you went through the chamber yelling and screaming and slaying dragons, even if those dragons didn't exist." If the legislator builds bridges instead, he or she is no different from the rest of them, as far as the public is concerned.[82] People do not trust the process; they do not like it; they do not understand it. Legislators cannot help but be influenced by what so many of their constituents think. Whereas they used to agree with their legislative colleagues, nowadays they are becoming more inclined to side with their constituents, whose feelings are strong and sanctions great.

Unlike in the U.S. Senate of the 1950s, the norm of institutional loyalty was never very strong in state legislatures. Years ago, as today, few members were concerned about the well-being of their institution. The survey of veterans found opinion divided on institutional loyalty; about 40 percent agreed and 40 percent disagreed that "legislators today have less commitment to the legislature itself."

THE STRAINS OF LEGISLATIVE LIFE

Reminiscing about the legislature in which he served during the 1960s, Sandy D'Alemberte, now president of Florida State University, painted a glowing picture: "I think about how valuable it was to have a great collegiality, how much fun it was to serve. . . . We were friends, we were doing things we thought were important, and by and large we agreed on a direction."[83] Perhaps, the Florida legislature of D'Alemberte's recollections has been enhanced by the passage of time. But not entirely. For most members today, legislative life is less satisfying than it was years ago. The strains are just as severe, but the satisfactions fewer.

Many members have sacrificed progressing in their private careers. Even those who retain citizen-legislator status lack time to advance much in the outside world. It is extraordinarily difficult to juggle both. Frank Smallwood, a Dartmouth political science professor who served briefly in the Vermont legislature, described his attempt to reconcile two careers: "Every day became a blur of conflicting demands: meeting classes, grading student papers, preparing lectures, serving on college committees, following up constituency chores, studying bills, answering letters, giving speeches, appearing on radio shows, meanwhile with the telephone ringing, ringing, ringing all day long."[84]

Those who are in the practice of law have to leave larger firms, which will not carry them, for smaller ones, in the hope that their new partners will. Those with legal ambitions see their contemporaries with more time at their disposal pulling ahead. Although some lawyer-legislators prosper in their outside professional lives, proportionately few do.

Most legislators have forsaken salaries in order to serve. Except for some larger states, the salaries provided legislators do not compensate for their loss of income. On those isolated occasions nowadays when their salaries are raised, they are likely to have to pay for their compensation in other ways. In Rhode Island, for example, the salary of legislators used to be $5 a day (or no more than $300 a year). When the constitution was revised to provide a $10,000 salary, the pensions that legislators had been receiving were abolished. Even in the high-paying states like Michigan and Ohio, most members come out behind financially by serving in the legislature, despite their being able under some circumstances to hold down part-time jobs.

Legislators suffer huge frustration in their jobs, especially if they bring ambitious agendas. The road to enacting a major bill is cluttered with obstacles. A legislator has to mobilize a coalition of interest groups to lend support, enlist the assistance of legislative leaders, steer the bill through the standing committees to which it is referred, arrange for it to be calendared for consideration on the floor, ensure the necessary votes are there for passage, and persuade the governor to sign the enactment. JoAnn Davidson, speaker of the Ohio house, shared with newly elected members her original feeling that everyone seems to have a roadblock put in their way. There were constitutional and statutory barriers, and the sheer slowness of the process.[85] The chances for success in enacting legislation are not high. Nor can a legislator, even if successful, depend on leaving his or her mark on public policy for very long. William Muir, in writing about the rigors of life in the California legislature, observes how members exhausted themselves and "then watched projects they had given years to destroyed or frustrated by the complexity of events."[86]

Lawmakers must surrender their privacy. They are fair fodder for the press and for anyone who wants knowledge of the minutae of their private lives— ranging from their business affiliations to their spouse's employment. They disclose periodically, risking the embarrassment of appearing to be too rich or the equal embarrassment of appearing to be too poor. A member of the Florida legislature decided to retire rather than disclose his wealth. It was not embarrassment he was concerned about, but rather that his six children might become targets for a kidnapper.[87]

Family life takes a beating from legislative service. Members take time away from a spouse and children. Mothers arrange for daycare; fathers miss Little League games. Even when they are at home, legislators receive telephone calls from their constituents late into the evening. An Ohio legislator commented, "I cannot face telephone calls at 10:30 p.m."[88] Tom Loftus, a former speaker of the house, described the Wisconsin legislature as a "divorce factory."[89] Other legislatures have their share of broken marriages. It is easy for legislators to overlook their families as they respond to the pressures of politics, the public, and policy. Upon voluntarily retiring from the Minnesota senate, John Brandl observed that one was tempted to take family members for granted, "to treat them as appendages," decorations on campaign literature, free help when envelopes have to be licked, lawn signs erected, doors knocked on.[90] Before he chose to leave the California senate, Ed Davis was struck by the realization of how busy life in the legislature was. He had to tell his children to go through his appointments secretary when they wanted to have dinner with him.[91]

The physical stress of legislative life is hard to ignore. There is never a manageable day. The work is never done. The pace is wearing. Take Michigan, for instance, where members are virtually full-time, putting in fifty or more hours a week, three days a week for nine months and then four or five days a week for the equivalent of three months in Lansing, not to mention the time they put into the job back in their districts. Every year is a tough one in Michigan, but some years are tougher than others. A particularly grueling year was 1993, with a brutal session and nonstop pressure, on one occasion lasting forty-eight hours straight without members getting any sleep. It was so physically debilitating that ten members left the legislature immediately thereafter.

Ed Davis, who characterized his California senate job as "the worst job I ever had," developed phlebitis after sitting through lengthy committee hearings and floor sessions without being able to stretch his legs. For him, the legislature was a stressful, unhealthy place to work, where during the final days of a session he often put in eighteen- and nineteen-hour days. Added to all that was the strain of flying back and forth between Sacramento and his district on weekends.[92]

Today's legislators feel especially abused and therefore resentful. Only lobbyists and staff—the capitol crowd—show them any respect. Once legislators leave the capitol, however, the ground shifts. No longer do they go back home and hear people say, "Thanks for doing a good job." Instead, they are figuratively torn from limb to limb. The disdain for politics, politicians, and political institutions is almost universal; it borders on contempt. Upon leaving the Massachusetts legislature after his defeat in 1992, Republican Minority Leader David Locke mentioned that: "Most of us take it, but when it affects your family, your kids, it hurts." In his view, the long-range effect promises to be that well-qualified people "will not subject themselves or their families to the kind of cynicism and public scrutiny that results today."[93]

Perhaps Locke is correct, but although members like Senator Davis opt out, many more choose to stay. That is why many come to the legislature—to stay or to move up, but not to move out. They share this one trait: they are not seeking legislative office with the idea of remaining for only a single term. Once they get there, few want to leave—at least not for a while.[94] The job is anything if not interesting and challenging. It provides an opportunity to serve the public, to accomplish something in the public interest, to do good. A member of the New Mexico legislature, for example, has her priorities clear: to do a good job for the county, working first for the kids, then for senior citizens, and then for the taxpayers.[95] There are those, primarily baby-boomers, who want to change the world and are willing to use the legislature to do so.[96] And there are the so-called single-issue members, who are dedicated to a cause and will serve in order to defend and promote that particular interest.

Some choose to stay because they have little choice. If they are already retired from their outside occupation, they would have nothing else to do without the legislature. If they have spent their full time on the legislature, they have nowhere to return. If they lose an election or if they feel compelled to earn higher incomes, they may try to metamorphose into lobbyists, settling in Tallahassee, Sacramento, and other capitals where they can keep their fingers in it. Few can walk away from the legislature without a sense of loss. "All in all, it's the best job I've ever had" was the way an Oregon legislator put it. In the words of a former senator from Colorado: "When I was in the senate I was bright, good-looking, and in top shape. The minute I left office I became ordinary, ugly, and fat."[97]

But today the stakes are higher, the strains of legislative life greater, and the side-benefits fewer. The capital culture and community are much diminished. They are no longer as independent of the outside environment as they once were. The pressures on legislators from their constituencies are increasing, while the ties of community are on the wane. And the media have helped turn the public's orientation toward their legislature from one of disengagement and skepticism to one of criticism and distrust.

NOTES

1. As reported in *State Net Capitols Report*, June 28, 1996.

2. William R. Bryant Jr., *Quantum Politics: Greening State Legislatures for the New Millennium* (Kalamazoo: New Issues Press, Western Michigan University, 1993), 112.

3. Karl T. Kurtz, ed. "The Old Statehouse, She Ain't What She Used to Be." National Conference of State Legislatures, July 26, 1993, 16. Photocopy.

4. Ibid.

5. Collins Center for Public Policy, "The Nature of Representation: An Overview" (discussion by members of the Florida house, Tallahassee, November 6, 1995), vol. 1, 14, 18. Transcript.

6. Thomas H. Little, "The Contours of Personal and Political Friendships in a State Legislature: We Can Go to Dinner, But." September 12, 1995.

7. Bryant, *Quantum Politics*, 128.

8. John Powers, "Altered State: It's a New Era on Beacon Hill, With New Players, New Rules, and New Attitudes," *Boston Globe Magazine*, June 16, 1996, 19.

9. Many women legislators successfully infiltrated "old boy" networks, adapting to dominant mores, as they organized "old girl" networks and championed legislation designed to help women and families.

10. Kurtz, "Old Statehouse."

11. Alan Rosenthal, *Drawing the Line: Legislative Ethics in the States* (Lincoln: University of Nebraska Press, 1996), 12–13; Dennis F. Thompson, *Ethics in Congress: From Individual to Institutional Corruption* (Washington, D.C.: Brookings, 1995), 48.

12. Rosenthal, *Drawing the Line*, 13–14

13. The conflicts and lobbyists sections are drawn from ibid., 73–102, 103-137.

14. Interview with the author, June 26, 1995.

15. Phil Keisling, "Thrills, Spills, and Bills," *Washington Monthly*, October 1990, 11–12.

16. In 1995 the U.S. House prohibited all gifts and meals, and the U.S. Senate limited the value of any single gift to $50, with an annual limit of $100 from any one source.

17. Eric E. Grier, "Legislator-Lobbyist Negotiations in Georgia Politics" (paper prepared for delivery at the annual meeting of the Georgia Political Science Association, Savannah, Georgia, February 24–25, 1995).

18. New Jersey Election Law Enforcement Commission, *News Release*, April 3, 1996.

19. *New York Times,* May 5, 1996.

20. Josephson Institute of Ethics, *Actual and Apparent Impropriety: A Report on Ethical Norms and Attitudes in State Legislatures* (Marina del Ray, Calif.: Josephson Institute, 1992).

21. Dennis F. Thompson, "Paradoxes of Government Ethics," *Public Administration Review* 52 (May–June 1992): 257.

22. Garry Boulard, "Lobbyists or Outlaws," *State Legislatures,* January 1996, 22.

23. Powers, "Altered States," 35.

24. Carol W. Lewis, *The Ethics Challenge of Public Service* (San Francisco: Jossey-Bass, 1991), 52.

25. Josephson Institute, *Actual and Apparent Impropriety,* 8–9.

26. Gary F. Moncrief, Joel A. Thompson, and Karl T. Kurtz, "The Old Statehouse, It Ain't What It Used to Be," *Legislative Studies Quarterly* 21 (February 1996): 64.

27. Thomas E. Patterson, "Bad News, Period," *PS: Political Science and Politics,* March 1996, 17.

28. Lawrence K. Grossman, *The Electronic Republic* (New York: Viking, 1995), 80.

29. Remarks of David Nyhan, *Boston Globe,* at statehouse session, November 29, 1995.

30. Quoted in David L. Protess et al., *The Journalism of Outrage: Investigative Reporting and Agenda Building in America* (New York: Guilford, 1991), 6.

31. Doris A. Graber, *Mass Media and American Politics,* 4th ed. (Washington, D.C.: CQ Press, 1993), 173.

32. Protess, *Journalism of Outrage,* 252.

33. Martin Linsky, "Legislatures and the Press: The Problems of Image and Attitude," *State Government* 59 (spring 1986): 42.

34. Protess, *Journalism of Outrage,* 9–10.

35. Patterson, "Bad News," 18.

36. *National Journal,* November 27, 1993, 2864.

37. Times Mirror survey, released March 16, 1994, 1:61.

38. Times Mirror Center for the People and the Press, *The People, the Press, and Their Leaders 1995.*

39. Thad L. Beyle and G. Patrick Lynch, "Measuring State Officials' Views of the Media," *Comparative State Politics* 14 (June 1993): 32–42.

40. Karen Fisher, "Legislatures in the Living Room," *State Legislatures,* August 1991, 15.

41. Sharon Crook West, "The News Media and Ohio Politics," in *Ohio Politics,* ed. Alexander P. Lamis (Kent, Ohio: Kent State University Press, 1994), 182, 193.

42. Rep. H. John Underwood, New Mexico, at conference sponsored by the Eagleton Institute of Politics, Rutgers University, Phoenix, Arizona, October 23–24, 1993.

43. Interview with the author, May 16, 1995.

44. The characterization is that of David Nyhan, columnist for the *Boston Globe,* at statehouse session, November 25, 1995.

45. *New York Times,* December 24, 1993.

46. Graber, *Mass Media and American Politics*, 172.

47. Beyle and Lynch, "Measuring State Officials' Views of the Media," 40.

48. Moncrief et al., "Old Statehouse," 61.

49. David Broder, address at session of Collins Center Legislative Project, St. Petersburg, January 11, 1996.

50. Collins Center for Public Policy, "The Legislature and the Press" (St. Petersburg, December 11, 1995), 62, 65, 70–71. Transcript.

51. *Politics in Minnesota* 15 (September 13, 1996): 2.

52. Collins Center, "Nature of Representation," 1:82.

53. Interview with the author, May 16, 1995.

54. Quoted in Mark Lecesse, "A Beacon in Boston," *State Legislatures,* July–August 1995, 23.

55. *Los Angeles Times*, December 6, 1992.

56. Ginger Rutland, *Sacramento Bee*, quoted in Peter A. Brown, "Gotcha Journalism," *State Legislatures,* May 1994, 25.

57. See Rosenthal, *Drawing the Line*, 200–209.

58. Interview with the author, June 7, 1995.

59. Broder, address at Collins Center, 169–170. Transcript.

60. Interview with the author, May 16, 1995.

61. Ibid., February 22, 1995.

62. Grossman, *Electronic Republic*, 89–110.

63. Patterson, "Bad News," 19.

64. There is some evidence from field experiments that cynicism is either stimulated or is not depressed by strategic campaign coverage, issue coverage, coverage of complex issue policy debates, or coverage of issue styles. Only narrative news seems to buffer or reduce cynicism. If the public is left frustrated or confused by the debate or by the rejection of certain solutions, cynicism may also grow. See Joseph M. Capella and Kathleen Hall Jamieson, "Public Cynicism and News Coverage in Campaigns and Policy Debates: Three Field Experiments" (paper prepared for delivery at the annual meeting of the American Political Science Association, New York, September 4, 1994).

65. Broder, address at Collins Center, 158–159. Transcript.

66. Ginger Rutland, quoted in Brown, "Gotcha Journalism," 25.

67. Collins Center, "Legislature and the Press," 233.

68. Howard Kurtz, *Hot Air: All Talk, All the Time* (New York: Times Books, 1996), 10.

69. Collins Center, "Legislature and the Press," 27.

70. Protess, *Journalism of Outrage*, 253–254.

71. John Wahlke et al., *The Legislative System: Explorations in Legislative Behavior* (New York: Wiley, 1962), 141–169.

72. E. Lee Bernick and Charles W. Wiggins, "Legislative Norms in Eleven States," *Legislative Studies Quarterly* 8 (May 1983): 191–200. This article will be referred to as the "eleven-state survey." Bernick and Wiggins concluded that a norm existed if at least 70 percent responded to a statement in the expected direction and if the item received either a high or a low score in the expected direction.

73. Unfortunately, this item combined two separate ideas—one, that of attending to norms generally and, second, that of apprenticeship. Kurtz, "Old Statehouse."

74. Lee Leonard, in *Columbus Dispatch,* December 12, 1994.

75. *Los Angeles Times,* January 31, 1995.

76. Bryant, *Quantum Politics,* 138.

77. T. V. Smith, *The Legislative Way of Life.* Reprinted by Office of Urban Policy and Programs, Graduate School and University Center, the City University of New York (December 1973), 4.

78. Sen. Robert Hellman, Indiana. Information provided to the author by the State Legislative Leaders Foundation.

79. Steve Scott, "Imbalance of Power," *California Journal,* August 1995, 12.

80. Alan Ehrenhalt, *The United States of Ambition* (New York: Times Books), 34–35.

81. Smith, *Legislative Way of Life,* 77–78, 84.

82. Collins Center, "Nature of Representation," 2:221–222.

83. Ibid., 1:19.

84. Frank Smallwood, *Free and Independent* (Brattleboro, Vt.: Stephen Greene, 1976).

85. JoAnn Davidson, remarks at orientation session for new Ohio legislators, November 21, 1996.

86. William K. Muir Jr., *Legislature: California's School for Politics* (Chicago: University of Chicago Press, 1982), 181.

87. Collins Center, "Legislature and the Press," 208.

88. Remarks at orientation session for new Ohio legislators, November 21, 1996.

89. Tom Loftus, *The Art of Legislative Politics* (Washington, D.C.: CQ Press, 1994), 21.

90. John Brandl, "Reflections on Leaving the Minnesota Legislature," *Humphrey Institute News,* June 1990, 14–15.

91. *Los Angeles Times,* December 6, 1992.

92. Ibid.

93. Quoted in *Boston Globe,* December 15, 1992.

94. Bryant, *Quantum Politics,* 104.

95. Interview with the author, May 17, 1995.

96. Loftus, *Art of Legislative Politics,* 55.

97. John A. Straayer, *The Colorado General Assembly* (Niwot: University Press of Colorado, 1990), 76–77.

CHAPTER 4

The Process of Lawmaking

A legislature performs a number of functions in the governmental system. It provides constituents with representation and service. It appropriates monies for the operations of government. It oversees the executive branch and the performance of state programs. Mainly it makes law. When the legislature is in session, its principal business—besides the budget (which we shall consider separately in chapter 8, below)—is processing bills and enacting laws. In the words of a former California assemblyman, "The nature of legislators is to legislate, and that is what they do."[1]

FROM BILL TO LAW

Despite what the public believes, access to the legislative calendar is not difficult to achieve. Practically any organized group in the state, as well as many influential or persistent individuals, can get a bill introduced. A bill is a formal, written legal instrument for the enactment of a new statute or for the amendment or repeal of an existing statute.

As the data in table 4.1 indicate, the fifty state legislatures introduced an average of about 3,800 bills during the regular and special sessions of 1984–1985, and about 4,150 were introduced during the sessions of 1994–1995. At one end of the spectrum are states where 5,000 or more introductions seem to be the practice. They are led by New York, with 33,635 bills introduced in 1984–1985 and 32,263 introduced in 1994–1995, and Massachusetts, with 18,125 in 1984–1985 and 15,020 in 1994–1995. Among the consistently high bill introducers are legislatures in California, Florida, Hawaii, Illinois,

TABLE 4.1

Bill Introductions and Enactments, 1984–1985 and 1994–1995

	1984–1985				1994–1995		
	Bills				Bills		
State	Intro- duced	Enacted	Percent- age Enacted	State	Intro- duced	Enacted	Percent- age Enacted
Alabama	4,376	893	20.4	Alabama[‡‖]	3,672	899	24.5
Alaska	1,279	280	21.9	Alaska	950	246	25.9
Arizona	1,965	773	39.3	Arizona	2,196	704	32.5
Arkansas	1,830	1,140	62.3	Arkansas	2,163	1,358	62.8
California[*]	6,395	1,025	16.0	California[‡‖]	6,111	2,710	44.3
Colorado	1,303	685	52.6	Colorado	1,191	635	53.3
Connecticut	5,488	1,347	24.5	Connecticut	4,542	666	14.7
Delaware	1,265	482	38.1	Delaware	661	296	44.8
Florida	4,933	1,226	24.9	Florida	5,132	853	16.6
Georgia	2,577	1,553	60.3	Georgia	2,854	1,200	42.0
Hawaii	4,896	624	12.7	Hawaii	7,265	561	7.7
Idaho	1,152	577	50.1	Idaho	1,539	846	55.0
Illinois	5,508	1,647	29.9	Illinois	4,353	308	7.1
Indiana	1,564	376	24.0	Indiana	2,392	213	8.9
Iowa	2,272	604	26.6	Iowa	1,836	421	22.9
Kansas	1,997	729	36.5	Kansas	1,947	631	32.4
Kentucky	1,459	395	27.1	Kentucky	1,346	473	35.1
Louisiana	6,150	2,016	32.8	Louisiana[‡‖]	6,801	2,176	32.0
Maine	2,391	1,020	42.7	Maine	2,214	955	43.1
Maryland	5,490	1,784	32.5	Maryland	4,812	1,398	29.1
Mass.	18,125	1,305	7.2	Mass.[‡‖]	15,020	912	6.1
Michigan	2,846	666	23.4	Michigan	3,402	742	21.8
Minnesota	5,111	626	12.2	Minnesota[‡‖]	6,023	597	9.9
Miss.	4,688	1,185	25.3	Miss.[‡‖]	7,043	1,086	15.4
Missouri	2,369	399	16.8	Missouri	2,498	352	14.1
Montana	1,432	763	53.3	Montana	1,032	594	57.6
Nebraska	1,270	548	43.1	Nebraska	1,408	512	36.4
Nevada	1,254	685	54.6	Nevada	1,325	730	55.1
N. H.[†]	1,063	417	39.2	N. H.	1,539	716	46.5
N. J.[*]	7,529	577	7.7	N. J.[‡‖]	5,253	583	11.1
N. M.	2,008	431	21.5	N. M.	4,486	578	12.9

(Table continues on the following page.)

TABLE 4.1
(continued)

	1984–1985				1994–1995		
	Bills				Bills		
State	Intro-duced	Enacted	Percent-age Enacted	State	Intro-duced	Enacted	Percent-age Enacted
N.Y.*	33,635	2,044	6.1	N.Y.‡ⅠⅠ	32,263	1,566	4.9
N. Carolina	2,738	1,033	37.7	N. Carolina‡ⅠⅠ	3,639	789	21.7
N. Dakota	1,175	701	59.7	N. Dakota	1,042	629	60.4
Ohio	1,458	193	13.2	Ohio	1,228	222	18.1
Oklahoma	1,648	656	39.8	Oklahoma	3,352	751	22.4
Oregon	2,072	827	39.9	Oregon	2,731	810	29.7
Penn.*	4,184	494	11.8	Penn.	5,348	398	7.4
Rhode Island	5,237	2,080	39.4	Rhode Island	7,273	1,404	19.3
S. Carolina	2,589	670	25.9	S. Carolina	2,408	539	22.4
S. Dakota	1,267	732	57.8	S. Dakota	1,303	718	55.1
Tennessee†	4,304	1,237	28.7	Tennessee	6,372	1,122	17.6
Texas	4,231	1,061	25.1	Texas	4,814	1,088	22.6
Utah	759	304	40.1	Utah	1,583	691	43.7
Vermont	941	287	30.5	Vermont	1,224	250	20.4
Virginia	2,828	1,396	49.4	Virginia	3,781	1,860	49.2
Washington	3,543	673	19.0	Washington	4,602	766	16.6
Wisconsin*	1,930	4	0.2	Wisconsin	3,315	586	17.7
Wyoming	928	308	33.2	Wyoming	828	314	37.9
TOTALS	191,167	41,866	21.9	TOTALS	202,838	40,107	19.8

* Regular Session in 1983–84

† Special Session in 1983–84

‡ Regular Session in 1992–93

ⅠⅠ Special Session in 1993–94

Louisiana, Maryland, Minnesota, Mississippi, New Jersey, Pennsylvania, and Rhode Island. At the other end of the spectrum are Wyoming, with only 928 and 826 introductions, and, among the larger states, Ohio, with 1,458 and 1,228 introductions during the two biennia. Although the bill-introducing propensities of most states are fairly consistent, some states vary from one biennium to the other. Oklahoma and Tennessee, on the one hand, show substantial increases in introductions between 1984–1985 and 1994–1995. Connecticut, on the other, shows a marked decrease.

All these numbers, it should be pointed out, are not strictly comparable from state to state. In some places, such as New York, multiple introductions of the same bill are permitted and in some, such as Arkansas, the budget is broken down into several hundred separate measures, each of which adds to the overall volume. In Massachusetts the numbers are inflated by the constitutional provision, the right of free petition, which allows any citizen to submit a bill to a legislator for introduction.

The Sources of Legislation

There is much grist for the legislative mill—perhaps too much. But the philosophical assumption and the political imperatives underlying the process are that virtually every idea deserves a hearing. Introduction of a bill is the first step. Not everyone, of course, has a bill to introduce, but many people do. Normally, bills derive from several principal sources.

First is the state administration and its agenda. The governor has his or her legislative program to advance, which is articulated in the state of the state address and in special messages. Welfare reform, education, health care, crime, economic development, and tax relief are the standard initiatives of the 1990s. Cabinet members and department heads have their own items to add to the administration's agenda. Governors can usually find sponsors among legislators for their initiatives; they can pick from the field. Department and agency bills are usually taken on by committee chairs, if they belong to the same party as the governor, or by ranking minority members.

Second are legislative leadership measures. Relatively few legislative leaders, as discussed in chapter 7 below, act as initiators rather than as brokers and mediators. Yet some do. Florida's speaker of the house has traditionally advocated a program, which his leadership team has been expected to support. The speaker's agenda in Florida has been as important as the governor's. After the 1994 elections, which witnessed GOP gains nearly everywhere, Republican legislative parties in a number of states introduced legislation designed to deliver on the "contracts" they made with citizens of their states.

Third, and accounting for well over half the legislative load, are measures backed by organized interests. These are intended to strengthen or weaken regulation, reduce their taxes, increase their share of budgets, or give one interest an advantage over its competitors. An industry, a teachers' association, an environmental coalition, or some other group is constantly seeking out legislators to sponsor bills that will promote its cause. Virtually every group has a few champions in the legislature and can usually depend on them to carry the group's bill.

Fourth, another source of agenda items are entreaties from those who have little connection with government—citizens who may not be organized but still have needs and desires that suggest a new law. Constituents seldom find their own representatives unresponsive, and, as a consequence, all sorts of bills bear the imprint of rank-and-file citizens. On occasion, as part of their training in civics, schoolchildren take on a project to get legislation enacted. For example, a fifth-grade class in Lexington, Massachusetts, had its representative introduce a bill specifying that balloons sold in the state had to biodegrade within sixty days of disposal.

Fifth, many bills arise as a response to events. The discovery that a male nurse in a Florida hospital had been raping patients in the recovery room led to bills requiring that two people be in attendance at all times in the intensive-care facility. Although cumbersome and expensive, action seemed necessary to some as a way to reassure the public. Drunk driving had been an issue in New Mexico for ten years, but a vehicular accident leading to a fatality prompted the introduction of a number of bills and gave the issue priority status in the 1993 session.

Sixth, legislators themselves come up with their own ideas for bills. Many of them do not just wait for petitioners to come their way. They search for proposals to promote in the public or constituency interest and, perhaps, in their own political interest as well. Some proposals come from long-held ideas that members bring with them to the legislature, and others are of later vintage. As Frank Smallwood recounted in his description of the process in Vermont, "Many of the bills were originated by individual legislators who had identified needs or problems they wanted to do something about."[3] Some proposals are borrowed from elsewhere. Legislators reason that bills introduced in a neighboring state, or by one of the nation's leading states in a particular area, can also be introduced in their own state. Some are picked up at meetings and conferences sponsored by one of the national legislative organizations, like the National Conference of State Legislatures (NCSL) or the Council of State Governments (CSG). Newly elected individuals ordinarily come to the legislature with campaign promises to convert into legislation.

Each member has a different mix of legislation that he or she authors or sponsors. Tom Campbell, a California senator, for example, characterizes his agenda as stemming from this own mind, from lobbyists, from constituents, from the governor, and from the attorney general. The governor asked him to carry a bill that would combine the board of equalization with the franchise tax board, because he was the ranking member of the revenue and taxation committee, the first committee to which the bill would be referred. Campbell, moreover, had a reputation of being a good bill manager. Another bill came from an interest group, the Center for Economic and Environmental Balance. A technical measure, it dealt with the disposal of toxins on site through "elemental neutralization" and needed an exemption from local storage rules. Industry and environmental groups had worked out an agreement beforehand. Campbell also had some of his own ideas, which he introduced as legislation. One of them was a pilot program that would allow police to search a person while engaged in a sobriety check, although otherwise they could not search without probable cause. From his constituents Campbell received ideas for, among other things, ways to improve energy conservation.[4]

Another California Republican senator, Bill Leonard, distinguishes among bills he introduces for philosophical or publicity purposes and nitty-gritty bills that have a good chance of passage. With the former, he hopes to make an issue that will sharpen differences with the Democratic Party. Here, he is trying to put the case before the public. Among these types are bills to abolish welfare, establish a school voucher system, or institute a flat tax. He does not expect these bills to pass, or even receive much of a hearing, in the Democratic-controlled senate. When introducing the latter type of bill, he is trying to get something done for some individual or group in the district. It usually requires tinkering, rather than major overhauls of the law, and has a chance to be enacted (unless Leonard's seat is targeted by the Democrats, in which case few or none of his bills will survive). One bill in this category would allow the sheriff of San Bernardino County to market software in the private sector.[5]

Dealing With the Workload

Year by year the natural tendency is for the legislative agenda to increase. That is, in part, because a large proportion of bills are reintroduced session after session, either for symbolic reasons or in an effort, after the lapse of time and given the right circumstances, to get them passed. Even enactment does not settle an issue conclusively. The winning side may try to make further gains a year or two later, while the losing side may try to undo the gains made by the winners. For example, the battle over tort reform and workers' compensation, with trial lawyers on one side and business on the other, is a continuing struggle. In the process there are no permanent winners or losers, but rather constant appeals to the legislature to redress grievances that are never fully resolved. Add to these recurring issues the new ones that emerge because of the increasing number of organized interests and lobbyists and the expansion of the subjects for which the legislature takes responsibility. It is easy, therefore, to appreciate why the legislature, under the pressures of democracy, finds it almost impossible to control its expanding workload.

Most legislatures have limited time in which to accomplish all they have to do. Their state constitutions restrict them to sessions of thirty, sixty, ninety days, or some fixed period. Florida, for instance, has a sixty-day session, of which about forty-five are working days. Because of major state issues, the Florida legislature has scheduled two or three special sessions a year in the past decade or so. New Mexico's sessions are sixty calendar days in odd-numbered years, but only thirty in even-numbered years when the focus is mainly on fiscal matters. As New Mexico's long session starts, legislators come to Sante Fe on a Tuesday and leave by Thursday afternoon. At the outset the main activity is the introduction of bills. By the second week, committees are meeting, and legislators are facing the thirty-day bill-introduction deadline.[6] By the second half of the legislative session, committees are meeting before 10:00 a.m. and after 2:00 p.m., with the time in between spent on the floor of the chamber. By the sixth week, the committees are backed up with work and legislators are spending every weekday at the capital. As the session reaches its end, committees will be meeting on Saturdays. The last two weeks, with conference committees trying to resolve differences between the senate and house, are especially hectic. As one staff member put it, "There's not a lot of down time during the session."[7]

Legislatures whose sessions are of limited duration are active during interim periods as well. Either their standing committees and/or special interim committees or commissions are assigned problem areas to explore and may recommend legislation to the next session of the legislature.

Maryland relies on its standing committees for work between sessions. During the 1995 interim, for example, the general assembly authorized the senate's five standing committees and the six standing committees of the house, as well as eleven statutory committees and two special committees, to function on its behalf. These groups engaged in more than one hundred studies, including studies on health, education, the environment, insurance, and children and youth.

In New Mexico, in contrast, standing committees end when the legislature adjourns, and therefore cannot meet during the interim. The New Mexico legislature is one of a number that rely on special committees and/or commissions or task forces for its interim work. Here, interim committees have only legislators as members while task forces include public members. Among other things, these groups are used to study complex issues that cannot be given a thorough hearing during a sixty- or thirty-day session. More time for exploration and deliberation and the inclusion of representatives of affected interests helps in the development of consensus and agreement on legislation. The number of committees and task forces in New Mexico has grown from ten in 1985 to sixteen in 1989 to nineteen in 1994. In recent years lawmakers on average had three assignments and the study groups met two or three days a month. Service even for a minimal amount of time between sessions is an additional strain on those legislators who depend on outside employment for their income.

The sessions of other legislatures are limited by neither constitution nor statute. California, Illinois, Michigan, New York, Ohio, Pennsylvania, and Wisconsin meet for periods of six months to an entire year, with recess over the summer months. The California assembly's March schedule provides an example of how a full-time legislature spends a week. On Monday morning the assembly meets in floor session, and in the afternoon standing committees hold hearings. Tuesdays and Wednesdays, both mornings and afternoons, are given over to committees. Thursday morning is reserved for a floor session, and the afternoon for select and special committees for those who serve on them. Members travel back to their districts Thursday and spend Friday and Saturday meeting with constituents. This schedule runs until the summer, when legislators have about four weeks off. They are back on schedule in August and the legislature runs at least until mid-September.[8]

Legislatures have attempted to keep their workload manageable by discouraging the introduction of too many bills by individual members. Sixteen legislative bodies, including both chambers in Colorado, Indiana, Michigan, Montana, Nevada, and North Dakota, now limit the number of bills that members may introduce. Other bodies, such as the Florida house, apply informal limits. Should a member want to exceed the limit, he or she can prevail on a colleague to carry a bill, persuade the committee to adopt the bill as a committee bill, introduce the bill in committee or on the floor as an amendment to another bill, or get a waiver. A California senator, for example, whose limit was sixty-five bills in a two-year session, could appeal to the rules committee for exceptions, justifying his requests on account of district need or other reasons.[9] Usually the limits are sufficiently high so that very few legislators feel a pinch. What does happen, however, is that legislators who want one are afforded an excuse for refusing to sponsor bills pressed upon them by constituents or organized interests.

Even with limits, therefore, legislators do not labor under severe restrictions. Opportunities are abundant for injecting proposals for new law into the process. Not everyone has the same opportunity, but few are completely shut out. In some respects, the process is analogous to a slot machine. Anyone who commits minimal resources can play and has a chance to win. Nevertheless, in the legislative process the player has much better odds than the person dropping quarters into the one-armed bandit.

The Job of Sponsorship

The author or sponsor has responsibility for a bill from introduction to enactment. Introduction is easy. The member first has a bill drafted by a legislative service agency and then submits it to the secretary of the senate or clerk of the house. The bill is assigned a number and achieves official status. In about half the states, companion bills work their way through the process simultaneously.

The sponsors are responsible for their bills' progress, but their intention is not always enactment. Members have a tendency to introduce some bills as a political courtesy and are not necessarily disappointed when they drop by the wayside during the legislative process. But in most instances authors are serious about passage. Indeed, many legislators commit as much energy steering their own bills through as they do to reading, studying, and acting on other people's. Whether companion bills are in order or not, the author has to recruit allies in the other chamber. As a California legislator put it, "Make sure you have a good 'floor jockey' on the other side."[10] In Minnesota, for example, typically a representative collaborates with a senator, and each guides the bill through his or her house.[11] Where a bill starts and just how fast it travels are matters of tactics, with sponsor and proponents endeavoring to create the most favorable circumstances possible.

In some legislative bodies, the sponsor can exercise greater control than others. In Connecticut, control is comparatively slight, with committees taking over legislation almost entirely. By contrast, in California the culture has been that the process for each bill is under the management of the individual member. Only in exceptional cases, which usually concern major issues, is management taken away from the individual member by the leadership. In the assembly, this is referred to as a bill becoming "speakerized."[12]

Bills generally must receive several readings on the floor of the senate and house. The first reading occurs with the introduction of a bill and its assignment to a standing committee. The second reading occurs when the bill is reported, by means of a calendar, to the floor for consideration and amendments. Third reading is at final passage, when a roll-call vote is taken (and in half the chambers amendments are in order).[13] Readings in Ohio provide an illustration. The state constitution requires that each bill receive consideration at least three times by each house before enactment. First is reading by title only on the day of introduction, with a bill numbered H.B. 1 or S.B. 1 and so on. The second consideration comes when rules, reference, and oversight committees report to its house with recommendations. The third reading is when the bill is calendared for floor action and can be amended, laid on the table, referred back to a committee, postponed, approved, defeated, or reconsidered.

For the sponsor, the first task is to try to ensure that the bill not be referred to an unfriendly committee. Most bills are assigned to the standing committees that have jurisdiction in the area. Occasionally, the measure is such that the author can choose the committee of referral by having the bill drafted so that its primary substance falls within one committee's bailiwick rather than another's. Nevertheless, in more than nine out of ten cases, referral is routinely to the committee that would normally have jurisdiction.

In some legislative bodies, a "killer committee" exists, and sponsors have to be wary lest their bills wind up there. The way to kill a bill in the Colorado senate, for instance, is to send it to the state affairs committee.[14] Some bills, customarily those with fiscal impact, have to survive scrutiny by the appropriations committee as well as by a substantive committee. These bills may be referred to two committees concurrently or, more often, to two committees sequentially.

Not infrequently, a bill pertains to a subject in which the author specializes. In such cases, the bill will ordinarily be assigned to the committee on which the author serves or which he or she chairs. Authors have a better chance of having these bills enacted, according to a study of bill passage in the Indiana and Missouri legislatures.[15] The sponsor will testify, arrange for friendly witnesses, and negotiate with members of the committee for favorable recommendation. The second committee, especially if it is appropriations, is much more of a hurdle and is the place where bills are more likely to languish and die. According to one California legislator, Campbell, "If there is a Dr. Death, it's the appropriations committee."[16]

Most bills are noncontroversial, and, shepherded by their sponsor, they travel a straight line through one house and then the other. Many bills are unopposed and others, although opposed, have no organized opposition. These bills go through fairly unscathed.[17] An assessment of New Mexico's workload is illustrative. Perhaps 5–10 percent of the bills are controversial but do not usually split legislators along party lines. The other 90 percent or so are uncontested.[18]

Controversial bills travel an indirect and unpredictable route. Bills that help one special interest at the expense of another have to be negotiated through the process. Bills that carry ideological freight are sure to be challenged by the other ideological side. Partisan bills will raise the hackles of the opposing party. Some bills appear noncontroversial, but run into unanticipated trouble. A seemingly unobtrusive Montana measure to exempt golf caddies from the minimum wage demonstrates that in the legislative process nothing can be taken for granted. Supporters of the bill noted that a typical five-hour, eighteen-hole round of golf would require paying the caddy $25 in addition to green fees. But a Catholic priest objected, saying that the bill "would allow three-year-olds to be carrying golf bags until midnight." He concluded: "I urge you to kill this bill. Kill it in the name of justice. It is the most unjust piece of legislation I have seen come before the legislature." The sponsor, a Republican representative, was a former caddy who wanted to let golf courses set up training programs so youngsters could earn money, play golf, and possibly win a scholarship. After the house committee, in response to the priest's opposition, put off a vote, the sponsor summed up: "You never know what you're going to walk into."[19]

Controversial legislation is a prime object for derailment or alteration along the track to enactment. Bills may start out in one direction and then, over the course of amendments, head in quite another direction. Managers of challenged bills are constantly on the lookout for amendments. They may be designed to gut a bill, modify its thrust, add unwelcome provisions, append something completely extraneous, or turn it around completely. In states, such as Florida, the amendment has practically supplanted the bill as the principal lawmaking vehicle. Tacking an amendment onto a bill is easier than managing a bill through Florida's process. An amendment can be attached during committee consideration or on the floor of either house. An amendment has the advantage of receiving less scrutiny than a bill itself. One tactic that is coming into more common use in Florida is the "stealth bill," which is one filed on a general subject, but without specifics. Its nature is irrelevant, but noncontroversial. It serves, however, as a target for controversial amendments that will be added to it along the way. The only requirements are that the amendments be germane (or at least be ruled germane) and that they have enough votes to be adopted. [20]

COMMITTEE DECISION

The standing committee of reference is a primary locus of decision making on legislation and the first important stage of action on a bill. Committee systems vary substantially. In states like Oregon, they are strong and play a critical role in screening and shaping legislation. In states like Illinois and New York, by comparison, they are weak, and decisions on bills are essentially made elsewhere.

Functions and Structures

Every legislative body divides itself into standing committees on which members, with the exception of top leaders, serve. Committees are delegated many functions in the legislature. First and foremost, committees process bills referred to them. This ranges from screening bills and deciding which to report out favorably to rewriting the legislation on their agenda. Second, they provide for a division of labor, whereby the workload of legislation is parceled out among members. Committees are the only means by which the legislature can hope to process the large number of bills introduced in a session. [21] Some committees are referred more bills, some fewer; but each member has at least one assignment and can count on taking part in the screening of legislation. Third, committees also promote the principle of representation, whereby members of committees are appointed to balance out party, region or county, gender, and race. Fourth, the committee system enables members to learn about a variety of subjects (such as revenues, health, education, transportation, and state government in general), specialize in one or several policy domains, take into account details and particulars, become relatively expert, and provide advice and cues to their colleagues. Fifth, committees form the basic blocs of voting coalitions on issues that come to the floor. Sixth, they allocate benefits, of both a budgetary and substantive type to legislators, groups, and publics. As two political scientists characterize the system in Michigan, the committees signify the "generalized acceptance of nearly every Michiganian's right to some piece of what the legislature produces."[22]

Committees of state legislatures do not have the subject-matter expertise they possessed a decade or so ago. Even then, the continuity of committee chairs and membership had been rather low, with Virginia, California, and New York being exceptional cases. Nowadays, chairs change every two or four years, and half or more of the members of a committee are new. This turnover reflects the overall turnover in legislative bodies, and the members' desire to move up the leadership ladder by chairing the more prestigious committees when opportunities arise. In the states now under term limits, committee expertise will be even more affected. Members will have less time to learn and less incentive to remain in one place.

The legislative chamber decides the number of committees and their jurisdictions through its rules committee. In practice, the number of committees is up to the speaker of the house and the presiding officer and/or the rules committee of the senate. On the house side, the number of committees ranges from Missouri's forty-two and New York's and Texas's thirty-six, to the seven apiece of Maryland and Massachusetts, to Maine and Rhode Island, which have six. On the senate side, the range is from New York's thirty-two, Mississippi's thirty, and Georgia's twenty-six, to four in Maine, and six in Maryland and Rhode Island. Maine and Massachusetts have joint committees.[23]

The more committees, the more opportunities for chairmanships. It is not unusual, therefore, for committees to proliferate during a tight race for leadership, when rivals make promises in return for support, or in an effort by an incumbent leader to consolidate his or her position. With term limits, another justification for additional committees exists. The Florida house increased its committees to twenty-eight so that every Democratic legislator could chair a committee or subcommittee and new members could get early training for leadership.[24]

The existence of too many committees, however, creates problems. Some years ago the Maryland General Assembly reduced its committees drastically because most legislators had assignments on relatively unimportant committees. After reform, each member of the legislature had an important assignment, although not all the committees carried equal weight. Recently, the Ohio house reduced the number of its committees, which had been expanded earlier to provide chairmanships for all returning members. The problem with too many committees was that their jurisdictions overlapped; members had too many assignments; attendance was poor; and the quality of work suffered. Even a 25 percent reduction in the number of committees allowed for sufficient chairmanships and vice-chairmanships for members.[25]

If there is any overriding principle in determining how many committees a senate or house will maintain, it is that of satisfying members, or at least members of the majority party. The demands by rank-and-file for committee leadership opportunities and significant work outweigh any abstract notions of efficiency, effectiveness, or centralized control.

The line-up of committees remains roughly the same from session to session, although some changes are made from time to time. In the 1970s and 1980s energy and environmental committees were added to the slate, in keeping with new challenges to public policy. Some states—Iowa, Maine, and Pennsylvania—show only minor changes, while others, like Wisconsin, see changes in form and substance over the years.[26] Committees are divided to decrease the workload or provide chairmanships, and committees are occasionally created to focus attention on emerging issues.

The size of committees also varies. Committees can be as small as those in New Jersey, where other than appropriations and judiciary they have only five members. Or they can be as large as those in Maryland's house, where the ways and means and commerce committees each have twenty-three members. Frequently, appropriations committees are larger than other committees, giving as many members as possible a share in the budgetary action. No one is quite sure what the optimal size of a committee might be.[27] Larger committees are more representative of the chamber's entire membership; smaller committees are easier to manage. If there is a challenge on the floor, the former have an advantage; the latter enable individual members to take a more active part in deliberation.

The total number of legislators in a chamber, the number of committees, the size of committees, and the number of assignments per legislator are interrelated. The fewer committees generally, the fewer assignments; the more committees—and the larger they are—the higher the number of assignments per member. The larger the legislative body, the more members there are to be distributed among standing committees. Because senates tend to be smaller than houses (half or one-third the size), yet have as many, or almost as many committees, senators tend to have more committee assignments than house members. In 1989 senators across the nation had an average of four assignments; representatives had three. In ten houses and three senates, legislators had only two appointments and occasionally only one.[28]

In North Carolina the many committee and subcommittees required that a representative or senator serve on ten or so committees. When the number of committees was reduced in 1989, so were the assignments—down to an average of seven for senators and five for house members.[29] In contrast, nine committees operate in the senate, while sixteen operate in the house in New Mexico. Senators have two assignments each, while representatives have two, three, or four assignments.

Legislators typically complain about their workloads, particularly when they have four or more committees or subcommittees to cover. In the past many of the meetings of committees on which legislators served came into conflict, so it was impossible for members to attend them all. Today many legislatures have organized their committees so that different groupings have different meeting times. That way a legislator can serve on several committees, but only one from each grouping. This eliminates the possibility of meetings coming into conflict. However burdensome, most legislators in most states want multiple assignments. The reason is that they want a variety of benefits: one committee may have special influence over policy, another may have relevance to one's constituency, still another (sometimes called a "juice committee") may have special appeal to large campaign contributors, and still another may cover an area in which the individual has experience and interest. Some members advise their colleagues to serve on as many committees as possible so that they attain broader knowledge, which helps them with constituents.

In recent decades subcommittees have come into more widespread use. They are now found in more than half the nation's legislative chambers, and are often used by large committees or by committees with jurisdiction over the state budget. They also offer leadership the opportunity to reward additional members. Willie Brown of California, for example, created additional subcommittees for members who were loyal to him. A subcommittee chair in turn brought more staff under a member's control.[30] The budget and taxation committee of the Maryland senate, for example, has four subcommittees that report their recommendations to the full committee. The full committee usually goes along, but makes a few changes along the way. The full committee also handles the budgets of special concern to all members.[31]

Each standing committee has an area of jurisdiction it calls its own, although overlapping jurisdictions are not uncommon. Explicit jurisdictions are spelled out in one-third of the chambers and are generally understood in the rest.[32] The most influential committees are the money committees—appropriations, budget, finance, and taxation. In many states, such as Colorado, after consideration by a subcommittee, bills with fiscal impacts are referred to an appropriations committee as well.

Also influential are judiciary committees, which tend to have a heavy workload. Illustrative is the California assembly judiciary committee, whose jurisdiction includes legislation relating to the following items, among others: adoption, antitrust, civil procedure, contracts, courts, domestic violence, family law, judges, landlords and tenants, medical malpractice, real property, surrogate parenting, and torts. In recent years the most active committee in the Ohio house has also been judiciary, largely because of the legislature's concern about crime. But issues shift, and as an Ohio legislator characterizes the situation: "Sometimes it's hot, sometimes it's not."[33]

Jurisdictions are loose enough to leave presiding officers room for some discretion in referring bills, if they want to use it. In Texas the state affairs committee of the house has jurisdiction over the "administration of state government," which is almost boundless. It not only receives a high proportion of the legislation introduced, but also the most difficult issues.[34] In Florida the senate commerce committee became a favorite place of second reference when Pat Thomas was presiding officer. The reason was that his ally, W. D. Childers, presided as chair, and the senate president could therefore trust the committee's action.[35] On the house side, judiciary was divided into three separate committees: Judiciary A, Judiciary B, and Judiciary C. When the speaker wanted a bill to be reported out favorably, he had it referred to A; when the speaker did not care, the bill went to B; and when he did not want to see it again, it went to C.[36]

The Distribution of Authority

In many respects, the chairperson *is* the committee. This is because participation by other members is often sporadic; they may have their own committees to chair or are spread thin among many assignments. Increasingly, practically all returning majority-party members have a committee or subcommittee to call their own; that is where they focus their energies while playing a more nominal role in the affairs of other units on which they sit. The more important the committee, the likelier it is that its members will be involved.

A chairman's power depends partly on whether or not other members choose to participate. It also depends on the rules and norms of the chamber. At one extreme, in some chambers a chairman has broad authority and can determine when the committee meets, which bills will be taken up for consideration, which bills will receive public hearings and who the witnesses will be, and when amendments might be offered. At the other extreme, in some chambers the chairman's authority is more circumscribed because all bills must be heard and all must be reported out—favorably, unfavorably, or without recommendation. Several years ago, a national survey showed that four out of five legislators believed the chairman had almost full control over the agenda.[37] In most states that was largely, if not entirely, the case.

Nevertheless, restrictions are now being placed on chairmen. Take Ohio's house as an example. Although chairmen were once quite powerful, house rules have recently deprived them of some of their clout. Now, every bill is entitled to one hearing.[38] Even more commonly, two hearings are held—one for proponents and the other for opponents. Each issue has to be confronted; the chairman can no longer simply push a matter aside.

Control of the agenda affords chairmen negative rather than positive power. Although they cannot ensure passage of a bill, they can usually sidetrack it if they so desire. As a chairman in Michigan described his role, "If something doesn't have my approval, it doesn't happen."[39] Even control over the sequence in which bills are taken up, as in Colorado, can allow for the delay and effective killing of the bill. In Kentucky, too, the decision by a chairman to delay posting a bill (that is, bringing it up for committee consideration) for a few weeks can kill it.[40]

In the face of a chairman's opposition, the sponsor has a very difficult time. If chairmen want to derail a measure, they are rarely overridden within committee. Rarer still is when nonmembers override the committee chairman. One California senator reflected that the worst thing to see is a member who fails to comprehend the chairman's opposition to his bill. The member will keep plugging away, and the result will be his embarrassment.[41] A chairman's opposition may be based on personal or political grounds, but it may also come about for other reasons. The bill may have no chance of passage. A majority of members may be against the bill, but they may not want to go on record. Or party leaders may request that the bill be buried. Under such circumstances the chairman will exercise a leadership role, despite the unhappiness of a sponsor.

Even where a chairman has no discretion about whether a bill receives consideration and/or a hearing, he or she still has the upper hand. The California assembly illustrates the chairman's advantage, albeit one that is constrained. The chairman has the authority to "set" bills—that is, to schedule them for a hearing. But in practice the chairman usually defers to the author of a bill, who decides when a bill should come up. The author may not want the bill heard early, or heard late, or may not want the bill to come up the same day as another bill. That an author gets a hearing when he or she wants it is a deeply ingrained tradition.[42] A system like this benefits junior legislators as well as members of the minority party. The chairman still controls the committee staff, however, and the staff finds witnesses for hearings and prepares an analysis of the bill.

Bills in California, and in many other states, are subject to serious analysis by staff.[43] In the words of one participant in the process, "every bill is analyzed to death"—by the executive departments, the legislative analyst, the department of finance, the legislative fiscal committee, and the policy committee. The policy committee consultant's analysis is seldom ignored by either the chairman, committee members, or the bill's author. The assembly judiciary committee, for instance, requests authors to fill out a worksheet ahead of the hearing. It asks for the following information: a statement of purpose, including the problem the bill seeks to remedy; studies and facts that support the assertion that a problem exists and that the proposal will address it; identification of similar bills introduced to address the problem; fiscal input; and the positions on the bill of the department of finance, affected state agencies, and interest groups. In preparing its analysis, judiciary committee staff works from this document.

Members of a committee put stock in the consultant's analysis. The way the analysis is shaped and the questions raised afford the chairman power—albeit power that is subtly exercised. Such analyses cause authors to amend their own bills in order to respond to the criticism. The process in California works to catch defects, inconsistencies, and problems and to suggest improvements. The chairman is central to the process—surely first among equals.

A chairman's influence depends in part on his or her control of resources, such as professional staff. It also depends on the chairman's relationships with legislative leaders. Generally speaking, house chairmen are on a tighter rein than those in the senate. Having been appointed by the speaker, they can be removed or not reappointed. They tend to be loyal members of a leadership team out of both conviction and calculation. When necessary, house chairmen do the speaker's bidding, but for the most part they are entrusted to run their own committees. They have considerable autonomy, but are not as autonomous as senate committee chairmen. Senates tend to be more individualistic than houses, and committee chairmen may owe their appointments to several people rather than to one. Their loyalties are more diffuse. Although senate chairmen are rather free to run things as they wish, the leader will step in and redirect them if they create a problem for the senate or for their legislative party.

Occasionally chairmen break ranks and are disciplined. Every now and then one is relieved of his or her committee at mid-term. Yet punishment is typically disguised a bit and meted out in the assignment process when the legislature organizes for the next session. In the event of a dispute, leaders and chairmen are inclined to clash privately, with words rather than action being the weapon. One chairman in Ohio held a hearing on a bill he was not supposed to hear. His party leader reached him on his car telephone and yelled so loudly the chairman drove into a tree.[44]

In the end, a committee chairman's influence depends on committee members themselves. A chairman can lead only with their acquiescence, although the chairman can slow things down without members always realizing it. A former speaker of the Pennsylvania house, which is considered to have a strong leadership system, had this advice for chairmen. Take control; a firm hand is necessary. Raw power is out; support must be built. He also counseled them to be fair, to encourage members to participate, and to recognize the minority. But fairness, he concluded, has its limits; the committee has to get things done.[45]

Maryland's senate budget and taxation committee has a tradition of operating in this mode. The current chairman, Democrat Barbara Hoffman, encourages participation.[46] Indeed, she asked the senate president to appoint to her committee legislators who would work hard. Early in the session, she met with each committee member privately and gave each of them—including freshman Republicans—responsibility for managing a bill. She assured them that she would never hang them out on the limb. "I treated them the way I would have wanted to be treated," she said.[47]

Committee chairmen can be characterized in terms of three general styles: advocates, mediators, and facilitators. Whether they pursue one or another style depends on the case and the circumstances. Advocates generally promote a program, policy, or point of view. They place their objectives first and try to lead committee members in their direction. Advocates are apt to believe in and represent the interests of the principal groups under their committee's jurisdiction, such as education, banking, or insurance. Mediators, in contrast, try to bring various parties to the table, along with committee members, so that disagreements can be worked out and the committee can agree on a product. The chairman as mediator works to reduce the issues to the critical ones and then get things worked out by disputants before the committee even meets.[48] Facilitators make few independent judgments, seeing their role as that of moving legislators' bills through the committee to the floor for passage. That way committee members can be assured that their own bills will receive favorable treatment in committees where they are lodged. Sometimes the result, lamented a veteran committee chairman from New York, is that bad legislation "flows to the floor as through an opened dam."[49] It may be "bad" in the eyes of the beholder, but it is what members want.

In the view of legislative party leaders, today's chairmen have more autonomy than their predecessors. Except on a few issues, they are left to run their committees as they see fit. They have less discretion than their predecessors, however, concerning committee members. Whatever their authority and resources, they can rarely dictate terms; they have to bring members along. A former president of the Florida senate characterized the contemporary committee chairman in his state: "Fewer people are willing to kick ass anymore."[50] One reason for this is that they can no longer get away with it.

Committee Influence

Committees stand at the center of the lawmaking process. Unless leadership substitutes for committees, as it occasionally does because of the importance of the issue, bills have to run the committee gauntlet in one or both houses. A questionnaire to legislators in eighteen states found that regular committee meetings were selected most frequently as one of three places where the most significant decisions were being made.[51] In another survey, of 330 veteran legislators in states across the country, 43 percent of the respondents reported that the influence of committees had increased, while only 17 percent reported a decrease.[52]

As important as standing committee systems are, they vary from state to state and chamber to chamber. Maryland and Ohio, on the one hand, are examples of strong-committee states, where decision-making authority is delegated to committees and exercised responsibly by committees. Leadership makes appointments, but then allows the chairman and the committees to work their will. Illinois, on the other, is a weak-committee state. Here, the practice has been for committees to ratify decisions made by the leadership and majority-party caucus, instead of the other way around. In fact, following the 1982 elections, the Democratic majority began to instruct members how to vote in committee. After the 1994 elections, with Republicans controlling both houses (as well as the governorship), important legislation was sent to a committee dominated by the house leadership, rather than to a standing committee. This "fast track" legislation then sailed through in a display of party government.[53]

The strength of standing committees systems can be assessed in terms of their functions performed in the legislative process: exercising jurisdiction, screening, modifying, and directing.[54]

EXERCISING JURISDICTION. The first dimension of performance involves the extent to which the jurisdiction of committees is respected and committees are referred bills. If many bills, or the most important ones, bypass committees, then the strength of a committee system is in doubt. The eighteen-state study found it was rare for more than a few proposals to bypass the committee system,[55] although some were screened only by committees in one house rather than by committees in both houses. Most bills in most places, then, are dealt with by standing committees.

SCREENING. The second dimension of performance involves the job done by committees on the bills that come within their jurisdiction. If committees positively report out all, or practically all, of the bills that come before them, we can probably infer that they are not exercising much of a role in screening legislation. In four out of five chambers, committees retain considerable discretion as to whether they report out bills. They have the option of just letting a bill die in committee without taking any action. Out of some three thousand bills introduced in Oregon, for example, half never receive consideration. In some states, like New Jersey and New York, a bill will languish in committee unless a sponsor requests action. This permits legislators to introduce bills on behalf of groups and constituents, even though they believe these measures are short on merit and should not move. Without the sponsor's prodding, they do not move. There are occasions, moreover, when sponsors publicly request a vote on specific bills they have introduced while privately imploring committee members to sit on the same bills.

Where the number of bills members can introduce is limited, legislators will not introduce legislation just for show. Each bill counts, as far as the sponsor is concerned. In California, for example, before a bill limit was imposed, about 25 percent of the referred bills were not pushed to a hearing. With a limit, however, sponsors are serious about having their bills considered, reported out, and passed.[56]

Rhode Island and Ohio serve as examples of states where the committee stage of bill consideration is very important. Rhode Island house committees have the choice of approving a bill and reporting it out for placement on the house calendar; approving it with amendments; approving a substitute bill; or failing to consider or approve a bill, thus killing it. Ohio house committees have the choice of reporting a bill favorably with no changes; adopting amendments and reporting it as an amended bill; redrafting the bill or adopting numerous amendments and reporting it as a substitute bill; combining two or more bills into one amended or substitute bill; indefinitely postponing action; or taking no action at all.

In contrast to states where committees can let a bill die without any formal action, both houses in Colorado, Maine, Massachusetts, New Hampshire, North Dakota, and South Dakota, and one house in Arkansas, California, Idaho, Illinois, Indiana, Maryland, and North Carolina, require that committees report out all bills, whether positively or negatively. For instance, committee reports in the North Carolina house may be favorable; favorable as amended; favorable as a committee substitute; without prejudice; or unfavorable. Even in these states, ways exist to dispose of legislation in committee. In Massachusetts, for example, citizens have "the right of free petition," which is the right to have bills introduced on their behalf. And the rules of the senate and house require that every bill receive action. Committees can, and do, gather individual bills in an omnibus bill for study, which is referred to the ways and means committee, but not directly to the floor.[57]

Where committees do have discretion, the proportion of bills that die in committee varies considerably. In strong-committee states, about two out of three bills are screened out, while one moves forward. From 1965 through 1986, for instance, the Michigan house reported 33.9 percent, and the senate 38.2 percent, of the bills that had been referred.[58] In contrast, in the 1986 session the Kentucky senate reported 58 percent of senate-initiated bills and 72 percent of those initiated in the house, and the house reported 54.4 percent of house-initiated bills and 81.9 percent of bills initiated in the senate.[59] In the 1960s Illinois committees reported four out of five bills to the floor; by 1993 only two out of five were being reported. Even with the dramatic change in the proportion of legislation that failed to clear the committee hurdle, the assessment was that committees in the Illinois legislature were almost meaningless.[60]

When bills are reported out of committee, they tend to be recommended for passage. Extraordinarily few emerge with a negative recommendation. In many legislatures the tendency is to say yes rather than no, and that tendency appears to have been growing stronger in recent years. In Florida, for instance, it has become relatively easy to move things out of committee. "Nobody wants to be a son of a bitch anymore," was the assessment of a former legislative leader.[61] Oklahoma's committees raise few obstacles to the passage of legislation. Here, members have "shell bills," which are reported out and receive structure afterwards when legislators and interest-group allies get together to draft provisions.[62] The New Mexico legislature is another one in which committees have become more benign. No longer are there killer committees. Most bills are reported favorably. Yet even some tabled bills eventually find their way to the floor. If the tabled bill is in the hands of the chairman willing to make a deal with the sponsor, the bill will get to the floor. Or the bill may be tabled with others that are referred to the judiciary and rules committees, which then negotiate with members and often give them the bills they want.[63]

A legislator in California described the reaction of committee members to bills as a knee-jerk "yes" vote (except, sometimes, with regard to the bills of freshman legislators). Why not support one's colleagues and in return receive their support?[64] The assembly judiciary committee typifies a system in which the emphasis is on reporting out legislation that can be enacted. Of all the policy committees, assembly judiciary has the third-heaviest volume of referred bills—four hundred or more bills each two-year session. Of the 449 bills assigned during 1992–1994, only 6.0 percent died in committee, 16.9 percent were dropped by the author, 3.1 percent were re-referred, and 5.3 percent failed. The other 68.7 percent were reported out of judiciary, with 12.7 percent passing (but not being enacted), 6.2 percent being vetoed, and 49.7 percent becoming law. In summary two-thirds of the assembly judiciary's bills are reported favorably and about half are chaptered in law.[65]

MODIFYING. The third dimension of performance relates to the role that committees play in shaping the legislation they report. Committees that merely say yes (and occasionally no) function differently from those that put their own stamp on bills within their jurisdiction. In most places committees have the prerogative to make whatever changes they desire, and in a number of places they take their prerogative seriously. The eighteen-state survey, mentioned earlier, found that the committees play a substantial role in shaping legislation in the Ohio house and senate and in the Arizona and Florida houses; the committee role is much more modest in the two houses of Massachusetts, North Dakota, and Pennsylvania, and the California senate.[66] About two-fifths of the chambers allow standing committees to put forward committee-sponsored bills, which normally consolidate several bills into one piece of legislation.[67] In Florida, bills produced by a committee, which usually reflect concern by the leaders or chairman, have a much higher probability of passing both houses than do member bills, which can lose momentum along the route.[68]

Omnibus bills also enable a committee to consolidate numbers of relatively noncontroversial proposals into a single legislative vehicle, thus facilitating the building of consensus. California's assembly judiciary committee circulates individual proposals to concerned groups for review. Those that get through without opposition go to committee members for review. Those without objection are included in an omnibus bill that has excellent prospects for enactment.

DIRECTING. The fourth dimension of performance relates to the parent house's respect for the authority of standing committees in their areas of jurisdiction. Committees whose jurisdictional control is overridden or whose recommendations are rejected fail the strength test. Virtually every chamber makes provision for discharging a bill from committee. Voting to pull a bill out of committee is considered an act of mutiny not only against the chairman but also against the leadership in most places. It compromises the committee system and the power of the majority.[69] Discharge rarely happens, although it may serve as a threat to arbitrary committee behavior. In the Rhode Island house, as part of 1993 reforms, a measure was adopted allowing the majority of the whole body to bring any bill to the floor even though it had been defeated in committee. If that measure were used with any frequency, it could overwhelm the house. But in its first year of existence, it was employed to bring only six relatively insignificant measures to the floor.

A positive committee recommendation predisposes a chamber to favor a proposal. But because this is no guarantee, the bill's sponsor and lobbyists for friendly interests try to line up commitments of support from noncommittee members. They seek the firm "yes"—not "probably," not "leaning," not "if needed."[70]

Most bills reported out pass in their house of origin, and somewhat lower proportions pass in the other chamber as well. Committee recommendations are generally followed,[71] although some proposals are amended before passage. Roughly eight out of ten bills reported by committees in Michigan are accepted by their parent chambers; roughly nine out of ten are accepted in Kentucky.[72] Oregon has especially strong committee systems. Of the more than 1,100 bills that reached the house floor in the 1989 session, only 14 failed to pass the house, and 90 percent had five or fewer dissenting votes. Divisive issues were either modified beforehand or sidetracked to spare members from having to vote on them.[73]

Another case of strong committees is Maryland, where the house has what is referred to as a "second-reading rule." This is an informal practice whereby all members of a committee are expected to vote with the committee on second reading. Exceptions are made for issues of conscience, like abortion, which are not subject to the rule. Since Maryland house committees are few in number and large in size, about one-sixth of the entire membership sits on each committee. If these legislators are added to the leadership structure, any committee bill starts out with a hard core of support on the floor. Rarely is a bill lost at second reading or amended on the floor.[74]

ACTION ON THE FLOOR

Specialized and technical issues, group interest issues, and major policy issues all make it to the floor of the house and senate for deliberation and decision. The overwhelming majority of bills reported by committees will go through relatively unscathed. Very few are lost on the floor, although some may be amended. Still, enough issues remain to be fought over and to keep members on their toes. A Michigan legislator, who listened one day to the case made by various interests on medical malpractice insurance, the human costs of closing hospital emergency rooms, and the service consequences of having fewer obstetricians, had this to say about the deliberative process: "Just a typical day of opposing views in Michigan. No rights and no wrongs—just lots of points to ponder. This job is a lot harder than I ever thought possible."[75]

CALENDARING. The route to passage is not without stumbling blocks. Bills have to be put on the house or senate calendars for disposition. This is the job of a rules or calendar committee or of the presiding officers and their staffs. Noncontroversial bills go on a consent calendar and can be voted on in bloc and routinely pass unless a member objects. If an objection is made, the bill will follow normal procedure on the floor. Bills that might arouse some controversy have to be scheduled for a floor session. Several legislative bodies take up bills in the basic order in which they have been reported out by committee. In the California senate, for instance, although members can request a special order, this is rarely done. Bills are taken up in the order in which they arrive, by what one member calls "a remarkably undirected body."[76]

Most legislatures have agencies that screen what committees report out. Especially in an era when committees in many states do not make tough decisions, but instead report all sorts of legislation favorably, leadership takes on the job of saying no. Rules committees serve leadership purposes when they take no action on bills or refuse to put them on the special-order calendar. Florida rules committees operate in this manner, making tough decisions that standing committees are unwilling to make. During the final weeks of the sixty-day session, sponsors will appeal to the chairman of rules to put their bill on the special-order calendar so that it will be heard, and presumably passed. If they receive no satisfaction, their recourse is to introduce the bill as an amendment to another bill on the calendar.

In New Jersey the presiding officers of the two chambers play the calendaring role. They decide whether and when a bill is put on the board, which gives them substantial power over bills sponsored by individual members. After the board list is prepared, the majority-party caucus meets to discuss each bill. A bill is pulled if it is too controversial and has insufficient support among majority-party members to pass on the floor.

The calendaring stage of the legislative process is where hard judgments are made as to what goes forward and what does not. Standing committees are, or have become, agencies of reciprocity, with members realizing that if they stand in the way of their colleagues' bills, then their colleagues may stand in the way of theirs. So, why not be tolerant? Thus, it is up to leadership to take responsibility for decisions that might irk members of their flock. In most chambers leaders still exercise such responsibility, although it would appear that today they are willing to make fewer of these hard decisions.

FLOOR CONSIDERATION. Legislators ordinarily have the opportunity to study bills on the calendar before they have to vote. Some chambers have established time requirements for how long a bill must lie on a member's desk before it can be considered on the floor. Typically, a member has a day or two. But relatively few members read all the bills and decide independently of other factors at play (as we shall discuss below). Debate is often irrelevant to decision and only infrequently wins over votes. Most people's votes have already been committed. Debate does make a difference, however, on amendments to bills, particularly where advance notice has not been given. In some states, like California, if members do not have prior notification and information, amendments can be referred to the rules committee to see if they have to be reviewed by a policy committee.[77] Elsewhere, however, floor amendments are made with little warning to the entire membership. Legislators look to their colleagues for cues.

Some floor amendments are products of committee work. In Colorado, for example, when bills are amended in committee, amendments have to be reported to the full house or senate, along with the bill itself.[78] Others are proposed by members who want to strengthen or weaken or extend or constrict a bill. The only requirement is that they be germane to the substance within the reported bill. In a few legislatures, such as Oregon's, only committees can amend their own bills. In most legislatures, anyone can propose an amendment. It is easier now to challenge a committee's work through the amendatory process than it used to be. Take the Minnesota house, where committee bills used to be virtually unamendable on the floor. Now, with the respect for the authority and work of the committee and the power of the chair diminished, floor amendments are a more common practice.[79]

In competitive, two-party legislative bodies, the minority party is a principal source of floor amendments, especially on the budget bill. Ohio typifies a state where the majority-party leadership rarely allowed floor amendments, until most recently, when the procedure was liberalized. Democrat Vern Riffe, who was speaker for twenty years, was willing to accept only a few amendments on the floor. When he did, he managed to avert roll-call votes on the substance of the amendment. He wanted to avoid putting members of his party on record against a budget increase, tax cut, or some other popular proposal. Instead votes were taken on procedural motions to table the amendment and, thus, were more difficult for outsiders to interpret. Under the old system in the Ohio house, everything went expeditiously and with as little public conflict as possible. When Republicans won control of the house in 1994, the new speaker, JoAnn Davidson, agreed to permit floor amendments. The new democracy in Ohio appeared to be more time-consuming, less efficient, more disruptive of committee authority, and not necessarily conducive to a better product; but it was fairer to individual members.[80]

END OF THE SESSION. Every session day is different from the ones that preceded it and those that follow. But no days are as different as those that come at the very end of the legislative session, especially in states with limited sessions. Whatever deadlines a legislature has installed, there is almost always a "log jam" as the session approaches its final days. Bills also pile up for political reasons. Some are held as bargaining chips in case a member's vote is needed for the budget (which is usually one of the last bills voted on), an administration measure, or some other project endorsed by a legislative leader.

Legislative log jams are nothing new. In the last half of the nineteenth century, the waning hours of the sessions in Illinois, Iowa, and Wisconsin witnessed a mad scramble as lawmakers tried to get their bills through.[81] A New Mexico lobbyist summed up: "In the last five days of the sixty-day session, that's where you earn your money."[82]

The end-of-the-session rush in Florida may be one of the most frenzied. In the final days, the senate and house each can pass 150 bills, including the budget. Some carry multiple amendments. Bills travel back and forth between the houses, seeking concurrence but being amended as they stop for consideration in each chamber. Known in Florida's legislative lingo as "trains," these bills pull amendment after amendment behind them. Some lug as many as thirty, many of which are bills that for strategic or tactical reasons are held back to be offered as amendments during the confusion of the session's close. "It's a damned train, but without an engineer" is the way one lobbyist described a process that leaves legislators baffled and glassy-eyed.[83]

Year after year, Florida's legislative leaders pledge to stop this end-of-the-session game. Under Senate Rule 7.1, any bill not heard or unfavorably reported by a committee of reference cannot be added as an amendment on the floor. In the last days, however, no one calls for a point of order if something rejected in committee reappears as an amendment. There may be an advantage in not even introducing a bill, but instead holding it back until the final rush. As long as it meets the germaneness requirement, or no one challenges its germaneness, it is in play.

Despite leadership pronouncements, legislators keep at the game because it suits the purposes of all involved. Lobbyists live or die by last-minute action. They appeal to leadership staff and to the presiding officers for favorable action, and the chances are that they will get it. Or lobbyists go it alone, exhilarated by the challenge of sneaking a provision through. For the most part, blatant abuse of the process does not occur, but items of concern to special-interest groups—what a lobbyist calls "nickel and dime" stuff—do go through amidst the confusion.

Legislators also take advantage of the end of the session to get many of their "cat-and-dog" bills enacted into law. These bills may not have made their way out of a standing committee or may not have been given a special order for floor consideration by the rules committee. Practically every member has an amendment to tack on somewhere, so the incentive to leave the procedure loose dominates. In the words of one senate staffer, "Everything passes but the kitchen sink."[84] Individual legislators may criticize the process publicly, but they do not want to surrender the benefits they derive from it.

Florida's legislative leaders, as expected, have the most to gain. They want to get as much good stuff into law as possible. That adds to their luster. They happily indulge members on the small items, and that adds to their popularity. They manage, however, to exercise control over the big items. In the rush to adjournment, they can accomplish things that they might otherwise find difficult to achieve. For example, with less then two days left in the 1994 session, the senate adopted an amendment to a Medicaid bill that sponsors described vaguely as cracking down on fraud in the program. By the time business lobbyists learned what had happened and members realized what they had voted on, the groundwork had been laid for Florida's $1.4 billion lawsuit against tobacco companies. By removing the major defense of tobacco companies, which has been that some of the blame for health problems falls on the smoker, the new law buttresses the case for reimbursement of tax money spent on treating tobacco-related diseases suffered by welfare recipients who smoke.[85] Many legislators felt hoodwinked, declaring that when they voted they had no idea of the full impact of the bill.

In the last-minute rush in Florida and in other states, individual interests prevail. Legislators have their needs met and interest groups and their lobbyists come away with something. Although the product may not always be pretty, the process maximizes participation, if not responsibility.

RECONCILING DIFFERENCES

The senate and house are normally rivals. Senators look down on representatives as upstarts and regard the house as a "zoo." Representatives resent it when the senate is called the "upper house" and theirs is described as the "lower house," convinced that they do most of the work while senators strut and claim credit. In many states rivalry has been continuous and especially intense. Florida exemplifies such a state, even though both houses were usually controlled by the same party. In other states, like Colorado and New Jersey, rivalry has been more restrained. It is always heightened when partisan control is divided, with Republicans a majority in the house and Democrats a majority in the senate, or vice versa.

Senates and houses, not surprisingly, do not always hold identical views on bills. Yet bills must pass each chamber in identical form in order to be signed into law. The two chambers have to reach agreement on the legislation. In about half the states companion bills are introduced in the two chambers and make their way through the process. In the other half, a bill will first be heard in one house and then be messaged to the other for consideration. In Connecticut, Maine, and Massachusetts, which have joint committees, the job of reconciliation is facilitated. Usually the same bill is reported to both chambers. If the bill is not amended on the floor, identical bills will be enacted by each body. In the seven states where appropriations or finance committees are joint, the same budget bill goes to the house and senate. The budget reported out of committee, however, is almost certain to be amended.[86]

It should be pointed out that when a bill passes the first chamber and moves on to the second, the response can vary. When bills are relatively noncontroversial, the second house may give it only a cursory review if the first has examined it carefully. The second may simply accede to the recommendation of the first, as is the practice in some places. Or the second can take a tougher attitude. Sometimes this results in stalemate, allowing each house to shift the blame to the other when legislation dies along the route. A member of the California assembly described the process by which legislators can indulge groups and individuals, but avoid the passage of what they consider to be bad bills: "We pass turkeys, assuming that they [the senate] will solve our problems, and the senate does the same."[87]

Concurrence comes naturally in many cases. When bills are noncontroversial, they will pass both houses unamended and in the same form. Then, there is no need for house and senate members to work to reach agreement on a single version. When bills arouse some controversy, disagreements within one chamber or between the chambers usually get worked out informally. Most decisions to reconcile differences are carried on continuously, in what Straayer refers to as "the thousands upon thousands of sidebar discussions among legislators of both parties and both houses, lobbyists, interested citizens, and others." Agreements are reached behind the scenes and brought to the committee or floor for ratification.[88]

Florida also works out disagreements between the houses along the way. The sixty-day session does not permit much time for formal conference committees, but informal negotiations are constantly under way. First, the house and the senate try to establish their positions on legislation. Then brokers for both chambers work on reconciling differences. The process churns on a continuous basis, with opportunities to influence the shape of legislation readily available.[89]

Usually, if the second house adopts a bill in any version other than that adopted by the originating house, the bill is returned for concurrence. By this time, in most instances, differences have been worked out and concurrence will be achieved. Take, as an example, Colorado. During the 1994 session, 620 bills passed both chambers, 239 without disagreement and another 277 with the first house concurring in an amendment of the second house.[90]

If the first house does not concur and the second house subsequently does not recede from its amendments, a conference committee is formed to get the job done in a more formal manner. In states such as Colorado and Minnesota, about one-sixth of the bills that pass both houses go to conference.[91] Conferees generally are appointed by the presiding officers (or sometimes by a committee on committees) in each house. Usually included in the conference committee are members of the standing committees that reported the bill and perhaps the bill's sponsor as well. In some states conferences are few. New York legislative leaders themselves confer on the major issues. Florida's conferences normally occur on the budget and a few major policy bills at each session.

Conference committees exhibit a great range of behaviors. In Illinois they may not even meet, but can still arrive at agreements by circulating language worked out by two or three key conferees.[92] On major issues, and in particular on the budget, conference committees stay in touch with the leadership, or conferees know what their legislative leaders and legislative parties want. If conference committees meet in open session, as they have since 1995 in Ohio, the critical negotiations will take place somewhere else, out of the eye of the press and public. Otherwise, settlements would be extremely difficult to reach.

A conference agreement requires the assent of a majority of the members of each house on the committee. A committee report is then submitted to the senate and house. The bill as reported cannot then be amended. It must be accepted, rejected, recommitted to the conference committee, or a new committee can be formed.

LEGISLATIVE DECISION MAKING

Legislators devote themselves to the legislation they themselves sponsor, but they are also obliged to make decisions on legislation sponsored by their colleagues. They have a huge number of voting decisions to make on bills, amendments, and procedural motions.

It is not unusual for a legislator during a single session to have to cast one thousand or fifteen hundred votes, including those in committee and on the floor. Four out of five chambers in the nation require roll-call votes on final passage. Most legislative houses enable one-fifth or so of the members to require a roll call on a vote. In earlier times record votes were fewer; nowadays they dominate.

Whatever the particular procedures in the state, it is not possible for legislators to avoid deciding—and deciding and deciding. They may miss some votes, but not many of the total. In a review of nearly 1,300 votes of the legislature in Florida, the *Tampa Tribune* found that the average lawmaker missed 35 votes apiece during the sixty-day session in 1994.[93] That still leaves about 1,265 votes cast, a formidable number by any standard.

Having to vote is a burden. Having to go on record is to risk being imprudent or mistaken. Frank Smallwood, a former Vermont legislator, describes the experience of voting: "No matter how complex the issue, no matter how much you know, or often don't know, the ultimate choice always boils down to a simple affirmation or rejection of the issue at hand. A roll call can be very rough. It's the moment of truth. There is no place to hide, no luxury of equivocation or vacillation. Every perplexity, ambiguity, and uncertainty must be frozen into one of two words: yes or no."[94]

Relatively few votes, however, are tough ones or on major issues. In Michigan, for example, fifty or so votes at a session—on the budget, taxes, auto insurance, ethics, or a comparable issue—cause the lawmaker concern. In California, a member described 95 percent of his votes as rather easy ones, while in New Mexico 95 percent of the issues on which members voted were said to be free from contention.[95]

Decisional Modes

Depending on the piece of legislation, legislators employ a number of decisional modes in determining their positions.

ACQUIESCENCE. Probably the dominant mode is that of *acquiescence,* or going along with the sponsor, committee, leadership, governor, or whomever. Where there is no conflict among interest groups, no cost to the state, no burdens on taxpayers, no controversy, there is no reason for members not to acquiesce. Most legislation is noncontroversial, so members go along.

Legislators want to vote for any worthy proposition, or for any proposition that is not unworthy. They want to say yes, not no, to constituents, lobbyists, and colleagues. Acquiescence works as a stance vis-à-vis constituents. Why make those seeking legislation unhappy if there is no compelling reason to do so? Acquiescence also works with one's colleagues. That is why Bill Richardson, a former California legislator, wrote some years ago that, "The prevailing rule of thumb nowadays is when in doubt, vote aye."[96] Acquiescence also works as far as the general public is concerned. When an "apple pie" or "motherhood" bill comes up, there is only one political option available. Vote yes. In Ohio, for example, a bill was introduced to require that a local impact statement accompany each piece of legislation. Such a statement was supposed to assess the effects a measure would have on localities throughout the state. The proposal had popular appeal but would have been almost impossible to implement effectively. Out of 132 legislators in the two houses, only one (who subsequently become senate president) voted nay.[97]

Withholding assent is difficult in California, and elsewhere too, if a colleague appeals for one's vote. The withholding of assent requires explanation and justification, which legislators would just as soon avoid.[98] Moreover, it can jeopardize friendships and lead to retaliation. That is why every bill in a California committee gets heard at the request of the author. The ethos is "Let him have his bill."[99] The ethos in Illinois is quite the same. "Bills are judged innocent till proven guilty," declares one Illinois legislator.[100]

If a bill receives approval along the way, members will be even more inclined to vote for it, unless there is a specific reason for not doing so. Legislators have a herd instinct, in part because in the midst of a herd there is greater safety. "Once the proponents of a measure gain a certain level of support," a former legislative staff member from California writes, "the burden of proof seems to shift, and instead of the proponents having to make an affirmative case, it is the opponents who must make a substantial showing why the bill should not be passed."[101] A legislator from Minnesota offers the insight that the most frequent decision legislators make is to go along with decisions made by others. This means supporting the committee recommendations—not offering amendments, not raising alternatives or questions—and accepting the consensus that has developed.[102] Going along generally makes sense in a process that relies on trust and reciprocity. It makes even greater sense where a legislator has neither cause to object nor knowledge to support an objection.

DEFLECTION. Another important mode of decision making might be termed *deflection*. Legislators often agree that a particular measure lacks merit and is simply bad legislation. They do not want to go on record against it, however, because of its popularity with a key interest group or its appeal to the public. Few legislators today feel they can afford to cast an unpopular vote. They can get blown away by a thirty-second television or radio commercial in the next campaign. A vote in favor of a tax increase, for example, can be used for years by opponents trying to unseat them. They refuse to take a bad but popular measure on directly, but instead use the process to let it expire along the way. There are many ways to kill legislation without leaving fingerprints. A bill can die in a standing committee, if no requirement exists to hear it or report it out. It can get lost in the rules committee and never find its way to a calendar. It can fall into a chasm between the two houses.

A wonderful illustration of the deflection process is the perennial bill to make "I'm from New Jersey" the state song. Although forty-seven municipalities and fifty-three organizations have endorsed the composition, the bill to enact the song never made it into law. Introduced session after session with a majority of members as sponsors, it has either not made it out of committee; not gotten to the floor; passed the assembly but not the senate; passed the senate but not the assembly; or passed both bodies, but with the expectation that the governor would veto it, which he did.[103]

After the committee hurdle, the chief barrier to unwanted legislation is the other house. In California, for instance, nearly any dog of a bill will pass if the sponsor wants it. But the assembly kills the senate's dogs, while the senate kills the assembly's, often by allowing them to starve at some point in the process.[104] Even in Arkansas, where 50 to 60 percent of bills introduced pass, the second chamber exerts something of a restraining influence. Although the dominant attitude in one's own chamber is to accommodate the wishes of colleagues, members of the other chamber are not quite as indulgent.[105] Deflection to the second chamber is tried and true, but occasionally something goes wrong. "Some of the bills that are supposed to die in the other house," said Maryland Speaker Ben Cardin, "wind up becoming laws."[106]

Some issues are simply too hot to handle. Whatever the outcome, virtually every member will suffer by having to cast a vote. On such matters legislators find themselves between a rock and a hard place, and do their best to choose neither. Often legislative leaders will protect members from unhappy choices and take responsibility for keeping such issues from a vote. Reformers want everyone to stand up and be counted on each item; the more votes the merrier. Legislators, who are on record from A to Z, try to avoid situations where nothing can be gained and a lot can be lost. In their control over the agenda, leaders do their best to prevent certain issues—particularly those that will leave members bloodied and in peril—from coming up for record votes. Those issues where prudence is the better part of valor are not taken head on.

BARGAINING. An important mode of decision making in legislative bodies is that of bargaining—negotiating, compromising, deal making, logrolling, and so forth. On most substantial issues, where matters are in contest and different interests in play, bargaining is the dominant way of resolving disagreements. Step by step, issues are negotiated. By the time votes are taken, whether in committee or on the floor, compromise agreements have already been reached. That is why so many roll-call votes are in the affirmative. Few bills get to the floor unless they are relatively noncontroversial or controversy has been worked out. By this time the tough decisions have already been made.

The lawmaking process is designed to produce compromise. As described by former Wisconsin speaker Tom Loftus: "Its many features—decision making by committee, amendments, the requirement that a proposed law pass both houses in identical form, the veto power of the governor— . . . are like machines on an assembly line, operating together to manufacture a consensus."[107] Negotiations proceed until all interested parties are satisfied and "sign off" on legislation. At that point, consensus has been built.

Only occasionally does bargaining take place in public, either at a meeting of a standing committee or in debate on the floor. It is seldom possible for lawmakers to patch together a compromise in public. Under such circumstances, prudence dictates that they take politically popular positions and hold to them, and this inhibits settlement. Only a degree of privacy affords them the political cover required in the give-and-take of bargaining.

Even in the most open legislatures, little gets solved publicly. A California legislator, in referring to the committee process, pointed out that the vital discussion takes place outside the committee room. "You always work out a deal before the public hearing," he said.[108] A former Maryland senator stated the case for negotiating behind closed doors as follows: "Behind every successful open meeting, there's a closed meeting somewhere."[109]

Bargaining goes on in practically every way. It may be delegated to interest groups that have a concern about a particular bill. If X wants a bill but Y objects, often the response of the legislature is to ask the groups to get together and try to reach a compromise. If X and Y both advocate legislation but disagree on provisions, the legislature (usually the committee with jurisdiction) is almost sure to ask them to get together and work things out. It is not unusual for a committee chair to request all health-care providers to get together and come back with a recommendation that the legislature can evaluate.[110]

In Illinois this practice, called the "agreed bill," finds the legislature delegating a decision to those whose interests are involved. If the groups arrive at an agreement satisfactory to all (or to most), the legislature ratifies that agreement.[111] For years Wisconsin has used a formal process to achieve consensus. During the interim period, the Legislative Council uses commissions composed of both citizens and legislators to conduct studies. If members can arrive at agreement, the legislation is nearly always enacted.[112]

Sometimes legislative leaders or committee chairmen participate in a bargaining process among groups. They serve as mediators or facilitators, pressing groups to arrive at a decision that each can live with. This was the pattern in New Mexico, when in a special session in 1990 the legislature enacted sweeping changes in the workers' compensation system. After a task force had made recommendations, the speaker brought business and labor, the major stakeholders, together. With legislators involved in the negotiating process, business and labor came up with a legislative package based on the task force effort to reduce litigation and lower the costs of the system. The agreement was backed by house and senate leaders, although a few legislators objected that the legislature had ceded its authority by ratifying a decision reached by organized interests.[113] For most legislators, however, agreement on legislation is preferable to stalemate, and preferable by far to combat.

FIGHTING IT OUT. Even though they try, legislators cannot avoid *fighting it out* periodically, still another mode of decision making. Not all controversial issues can be deflected or negotiated. A number of issues—such as abortion, gun control, and those with partisan electoral loading—do not lend themselves to the normal legislative process, geared as it is to compromise. Beliefs, ideologies, and political power are at stake, and the disputants—whether interest groups or legislative parties—insist on their positions. Compromise is not the purpose of their game. Only a small proportion of the issues dealt with and the votes cast fall into this category. But votes on these issues are more than sufficient to roil the waters and put everyone at risk.

Deliberation

Another way of examining the decisional process is by attending to the sources of information and cues that inform legislators, as they figure out their positions and engage in action. Here the focus is the individual legislator rather than the mode of decision making.

Legislators base their decisions on information and cues that come from many sources. Closest to home and of longest standing are their own beliefs. They bring commitments to a variety of public policies into office (and develop others while there). These core beliefs shape their behavior on many of the major public policy issues, although on specifics and details they can move one way or the other. Loftus of Wisconsin, for instance, always voted against changing the state constitution to allow a lottery. When he arrived at the legislature, he brought with him the belief that promoting gambling was not a legitimate function of government. "Even though 60 percent of my constituents favored a state lottery, I would not." It was, in his view, too regressive in its impact on the poor. "Better," he concluded, "that every Lutheran, Progressive, Norwegian, Dane County, *Capital Times* bone in my body crumble to dust than I vote for a lottery."[114]

Not far from these more basic beliefs are the views legislators acquire from members of their immediate family and close friends and, from time to time, personal experience. I recall a legislator in Florida imploring Gov. Bob Graham to veto a bill giving optometrists more license to use drugs for diagnostic purposes because, he told the governor, of eye problems his mother had some years before as a result of an optometrist prescribing a faulty lens. Another Florida legislator, in line to be speaker of the house, pushed for legislation requiring that restaurants serving the public be equipped with chairs for infants. This initiative was that of his wife, and was based on her firsthand encounters with ill-equipped restaurants while traveling with a small child. Two members of the health committee in the New York senate said that their views cracking down on insurers and twenty-four-hour maternity-care stays were influenced by the birthing experience of their wives. The heaviest lobbying they got, they said, was at home.[115]

Legislators' occupational backgrounds and group memberships, by virtue of shaping perceptions and developing understanding, also help to shape their decisions on issues. Those who have worked in the fields of banking, insurance, medicine, and education, for example, are inclined to be more sympathetic to these groups' positions. Still, group members do not always vote the group line.

Campaign promises and commitments made to important interests and blocs cannot easily be abandoned. The dangers of losing vital support are too great. It is also difficult to escape entirely from one's past record, although zigs and zags (or what is currently called triangulation) are often permissible.

Within the legislature itself, leaders, colleagues, and staff all provide information and direction. One's colleagues—bill sponsors who are soliciting support and the subject experts on committees or elsewhere—are responsible for the bulk of cues that are given and received. To a significant extent legislatures operate through a system of specialization. In practically any legislative body one will hear, "There are only two people in the entire place who understand the education-aid formula" or "Only a handful of members know about toxic wastes." Some members have expertise stemming from their legislative experience (usually on a standing committee), some have expertise stemming from their nonlegislative experience (normally in their outside occupation), some have expertise stemming from both, and a number are not looked to for expertise at all.

Legislators turn to fellow members whom they respect and trust, whose legislative role and nonlegislative background are pertinent to the issue at hand. In California, for example, "Legislators will listen to Newt Russell on retirement. If Newt says it's not a good idea, it isn't."[116] When legislators develop a reputation for being knowledgeable, "members treat their opinion almost like gospel."[117]

Legislators may also hold certain colleagues in low esteem, perhaps because their ideas are too far out because they are perceived to be shilling for special interests, or for any number of personal reasons. Sponsorship or advocacy of a bill by these members may impel others to move in the opposite direction. Occasionally a legislator is motivated by the desire to pay back a colleague who had done him (or her) wrong.[118]

Legislative party leaders and party caucuses also are important cue givers. As consensus builders within their parties and/or within the legislative chamber and legislature, leaders frequently help steer members one way or another. They may be advancing the governor's agenda, rounding up support for a committee's recommendations, recruiting legislators to vote for an amendment, getting backing for a house-senate compromise, or whatever. Sometimes they are acting as independent agents, moving their own issues; most frequently, however, they are taking on the legislation of others and trying to steer it through the process.

The party caucus also ranks as an important decision-making mechanism in a number of places. According to responses to an eighteen-state questionnaire, party caucuses from 1971 to 1987 have been consistently strong in both houses in Arizona, Iowa, Maine, North Dakota, Pennsylvania, South Dakota, Washington, and Wisconsin, and in the Ohio senate. They are sometimes strong in both houses as in California, Tennessee, and West Virginia, as well as in the house in Ohio, Nevada, and North Carolina. They have not been strong in Florida, Georgia, Massachusetts, and Texas, nor in the North Carolina and Nevada senates.[119] In short, where the legislative parties are competitive, the caucus is a key mechanism in building party consensus. Where parties are less competitive, the caucus tends to be a vehicle for organizing the chamber and possibly for informing members on bills.[120]

The caucus is especially significant in Colorado, where it is used to discuss major issues, come to a position of consensus, and mobilize as many votes for its position as possible. On the budget bill in Colorado, the so-called long bill, the caucus plays a critical role. After its formulation by the joint budget committee, the bill goes to the appropriations committee, to the floor, and then to the other house. But the majority party caucus works the bill over before the appropriations committee sees it. This enables the majority party to maintain control of the process and not have to rely on the minority for any votes.[121]

Within the capital community, the governor and executive officers, lobbyists and interest groups, and the statehouse press all feed information to legislators. The governor's views about his administration's initiatives are very influential, especially for members of the governor's legislative party. On administrative and housekeeping issues, executive officials at top and middle-management levels provide information that legislators take into account. Lobbyists and interest groups, as discussed in chapter 6, offer their positions on practically every issue that the legislature takes at all seriously.

The constituency and constituents are also heeded. Normally represented through interest groups, they also make their individual views known in person or by fax or mail.

Information, analysis, and substantive arguments also play a role. On many issues legislators have little predisposition and no set views. The policy justifications of both sides then come into play. As Thomas Birmingham, the president of the Massachusetts senate, said: "On the majority of matters that come before the legislature, I can go either way. I can see the legitimate arguments either way."[122] If the claims balance out, other factors will weigh on the scales of decision.

Different kinds of cues and information count in different stages of the legislative process. Preparing a bill, reviewing a bill in committee, or considering a bill on the floor normally requires information of various sorts.[123] In the first endeavor, documentary information and staff research and analysis are valuable. Similar materials, and information furnished by testimony, are useful in the second endeavor. By the time a bill has been reported to the floor, it has been researched, analyzed, and assessed and has a head of steam. At this stage, political information and cues from respected and reliable sources are primarily what counts. Members have access to documentary and analytical data, but this kind of information is less helpful as the process proceeds. Legislators have limited time and can attend to just so much.

This is why legislators read few of the bills on which they vote. They rely on what people say, which is the only way to make the workload a manageable one. Former president Jimmy Carter said that when he was a member of the Georgia senate, he read every bill before voting on it. It is not surprising that Carter did so, but many legislators would regard his behavior as foolish. Reading a bill may not be the best way to find out what is in it. As Harvey Dueholm of Wisconsin said wryly: "Read the bills? It's bad enough to have to vote on them."[124] Or according to a veteran senator in California: "Reading the bill isn't part of the procedure, and listening to a debate on the bill's merits certainly isn't either."[125]

The legislative process cannot be nailed down. It is not simply one that moves from introduction to committee to the floor of one chamber and then on to the other, as diagrams of "a bill becomes a law" depict it. It is more like a three-ring circus, with action occurring everywhere and at the same time. What one sees is not necessarily what is actually going on. A person in the visitor's gallery above the floor of the Florida house would watch the speaker presiding, running through a calendar of bills on special order. She would hear perfunctory debate, with a committee chairman explaining the bill and its rationale. Meanwhile, house members move about the floor, leaning over a desk or conferring with a colleague standing in the aisle or at the rear of the chamber. They are paying scant attention to the proceedings, except to rush to their desks to press a green (or occasionally a red) button casting their votes on a measure. For the most part, this is the formal business being decided. But members have already made up their minds, so they can use their time on the floor to attend to other business. And they do—negotiating with one another, planning strategy, and lobbying their own agendas.

It is not possible to specify precisely why members vote as they do. The process does not appear to be deliberative, not if a criterion for deliberation is that participants have to be open to one another.[126] It is not the case that participants are open to one another on strictly intellectual grounds; yet they are open to one another politically. They are normally willing to engage in negotiation, bargaining, and compromise that produce majorities (and most often substantial majorities) in favor of measures. The reasoning that goes on is rarely confined to the policy merits of a proposal, although policy merits are almost always part of the debate. Justification on the merits is virtually required for a proposal to receive serious consideration. The deliberative process in the legislature may not be highly rational nor primarily analytical. But it does allow for different sides to make their case, opposing voices to be heard, and a settlement to be achieved.

Enactments

The legislative process has been likened to an obstacle course, where good ideas have to leap hurdles in order to become law. The obstacle-course metaphor applies. Almost every member and many groups can cite a bill they devised or endorsed that failed to overcome a hurdle. Other members and other groups, however, might feel differently about the bill and thus would see, not a hurdle blocking a meritorious idea, but rather a way station where a fair assessment of the measure caused its demise.

Another apposite metaphor for the process is the assembly line, in which legislation mechanically and routinely passes through each workstation on its way to final product. Many measures move from introduction to enactment without much dissent. Many others get through after differences are worked out.

There is no lack of laws being made in state legislatures. Table 4.1, which reports for 1984–1985 and 1994–1995, shows the numbers of bills enacted, as well as the numbers introduced. In a few states more than two thousand bills became law in a biennium: Louisiana (1984–1985 and 1995–1996); New York and Rhode Island (1984–1985); and California (1994–1995). In seventeen states in 1984–1985 and eleven in 1994–1995, more than a thousand enactments were produced by legislatures. In some states the numbers of enactments are modest by comparison: five hundred or fewer in both periods in Alaska, Delaware, Indiana, Kentucky, Missouri, Ohio, Pennsylvania, Vermont, and Wyoming. Not only smaller states, but also larger ones like Ohio and Pennsylvania, are very conservative as compared with California and New York. Some laws are simple and some noncontroversial, others are complex, and still others controversial. Legislatures cannot be faulted for not producing law; they probably produce more law than can be effectively administered and absorbed.

Naturally, not every bill that is introduced passes. What is striking is that a sizable proportion of what goes in does come out, in one form or another. The fifty-state average is roughly 20 percent; that is, one out of every five bills in a biennium manages its way through both houses. In sixteen states more than one-third of those bills introduced passes. These states include Arkansas, Colorado, Idaho, Montana, Nevada, North Dakota, and South Dakota, where more than half pass. In some of the states only one bill out of ten is enacted. Massachusetts and New York have low enactment rates, mainly because the numbers of introductions are so high. But Minnesota and Pennsylvania also have low rates, without an inflation of introductions.[127]

A MORE DEMOCRATIC PROCESS

Some people think that too few bills make their way into law; other people think that too many bills are enacted. No one is entirely happy with the total product of the legislature after each session. Yet many people benefit in one way or another. Certainly, organized groups, if not ordinarily isolated individuals, have ample opportunities to engage in the process and (depending on who they are, the nature of their demands, and the politics of the day) come out with something. The process is open, but not as open as reformers would like. It is democratic, but not perfectly so. Numbers are not all that count. Yet during recent years the legislative process in the states has been becoming more democratic, not less so. Pluralities that show concern and engage in the process usually come out ahead, but no one group always wins the race. Meanwhile, elected representatives try to keep as many groups in their coalition as possible satisfied with what they are doing. They defer to their colleagues in the hope that their colleagues will defer to them when they have pet bills to advance. Much of what they do is open to public view and communicated to their constituents by candidates who challenge them for their seats and by interests who are dissatisfied with their positions.

NOTES

1. H. L. Richardson, *What Makes You Think We Read the Bills?* (Ottawa, Ill.: Green Hill, 1978), 70.

2. Data provided by Council of State Governments.

3. Frank Smallwood, *Free and Independent* (Brattleboro, Vt.: Stephen Greene, 1976), 81.

4. Interview with the author, March 16, 1995.

5. Ibid., March 15, 1995.

6. In addition to the New Mexico legislature, forty-six other legislatures have instituted deadlines for bill introductions to expedite the process. About half the states also have deadlines for committee and chamber action. Just about every legislative chamber also allows for the prefiling of bills, so that legislation is drafted early and the legislature can get off to a quicker start when it formally convenes.

7. Interview with the author, May 5, 1995.

8. Ibid., March 16, 1995.

9. Ibid.

10. Ibid.

11. Royce Hanson, *Tribune of the People* (Minneapolis: University of Minnesota Press, 1989), 123.

12. Interview with the author, March 14, 1995.

13. Wayne L. Francis, "Floor Procedures and Conference Committees in State Legislatures," in *Encyclopedia of the American Legislative System*, ed. Joel H. Silbey (New York: Scribner's, 1994), 722.

14. John A. Straayer, *The Colorado General Assembly* (Niwot: University Press of Colorado, 1990), 117.

15. Wayne L. Francis, *The Legislative Committee Game: A Comparative Analysis of Fifty States* (Columbus: Ohio State University Press, 1989), 27–28, 31, 32.

16. Interview with the author, March 16, 1995.

17. Apparently this is not very different from what it used to be. In the 1880s and 1890s Iowa, Illinois, and Wisconsin considered about 1,250 items per session. Most of them also were noncontroversial. Ballard C. Campbell, *Representative Democracy: Public Policy and Midwestern Legislatures in the Late Nineteenth Century* (Cambridge: Harvard University Press, 1980), 54.

18. Interview with the author, March 16, 1995.

19. From the *Helena Independent Record*, as reported in *State Capitols Report*, February 24, 1995.

20. Interview with the author, March 29, 1995.

21. Keith E. Hamm and Ronald D. Hedlund, "Committees in State Legislatures," in *Encyclopedia of the American Legislative System*, ed. Joel H. Silbey (New York: Scribner's, 1994), 672.

22. William P. Browne and Kenneth Ver Burg, *Michigan Politics and Government* (Lincoln: University of Nebraska Press, 1995), 121.

23. Council of State Governments, *The Book of the States, 1996–1997* (Lexington, Ky.: the Council, 1996), 113–114.

24. Interview with the author, March 27, 1995.

25. Ibid., February 23, 1995.

26. Ronald D. Hedlund and Keith E. Hamm, "Leader Accommodation to Members' Requests" (paper prepared for delivery at the annual meeting of the American Political Science Association, Chicago, September 3-6, 1992), 15.

27. See Hamm and Hedlund, "Committees in State Legislatures," 680–681.

28. Ibid., 682.

29. Jack D. Fleer, *North Carolina Government and Politics* (Lincoln: University of Nebraska Press, 1994), 75.

30. A. G. Block, "The Reality of Willie Brown Jr.," *California Journal,* August 1995, 9.

31. Interview with the author, June 6, 1995.

32. Hamm and Hedlund, "Committees in State Legislatures," 678.

33. Interview with the author, February 22, 1995.

34. Gregory S. Thielmann and Donald R. Dixon, "Explaining Contributions: Rational Contributors and the Elections for the 71st Texas House," *Legislative Studies Quarterly* 19 (November 1994): 498.

35. Interview with the author, March 29, 1995.

36. Ibid.

37. Francis, *Legislative Committee Game,* 39.

38. Interview with the author, February 24, 1995.

39. Browne and Ver Burg, *Michigan Politics and Government,* 118–119.

40. Malcolm E. Jewell and Penny M. Miller, *The Kentucky Legislature* (Lexington: University Press of Kentucky, 1988), 116–117.

41. Interview with the author, March 15, 1995.

42. Ibid.

43. This section is based on interviews with two members of the California legislature, March 15 and 16, 1995.

44. Interview with the author, February 22, 1995.

45. Bob O'Donnell, "How to Be an Effective Committee Chair," *State Legislatures,* January 1996, 28.

46. It should be noted that Senator Hoffman herself prefers the designation "chairman" to the alternatives "chair," "chairperson," or "chairwoman."

47. Interview with the author, June 6, 1995.

48. Ibid., March 15, 1995.

49. Alan Rosenthal, *Legislative Life: People, Process, and Performance in the States* (New York: Harper and Row, 1981), 194.

50. Interview with the author, March 31, 1995.

51. Hamm and Hedlund, "Committees in State Legislatures," 670–672.

52. Gary F. Moncrief, Joel A. Thompson, and Karl T. Kurtz, "The Old Statehouse, It Ain't What It Used to Be," *Legislative Studies Quarterly* 21 (February 1996): 61.

53. David Everson, "COOGA Redux?" *Comparative State Politics* 17 (April 1996): 9, 13, 14–15.

54. See Alan Rosenthal, *Legislative Performance in the States: Exploration in Committee Behavior* (New York: Free Press, 1974), 18–35; also Hamm and Hedlund, "Committees in State Legislatures," 692–695.

55. Hamm and Hedlund, "Committees in State Legislatures," 693.

56. Interview with the author, March 17, 1995.

57. Ibid., November 29, 1995.

58. Browne and Ver Burg, *Michigan Politics and Government*, 119.

59. Jewell and Miller, *Kentucky Legislature*, 124.

60. Samuel K. Gove and James D. Nowlan, *Illinois Politics and Government: The Expanding Metropolitan Frontier* (Lincoln: University of Nebraska Press, 1996), 87–88.

61. Interview with the author, March 31, 1995.

62. Information provided by Cindy Simon-Rosenthal, February 22, 1995.

63. Interviews with the author, May 15 and 17, 1995.

64. Interview with the author, March 15, 1995.

65. Files of Assembly Judiciary Committees, California; interview with the author, March 15, 1995.

66. Hamm and Hedlund, "Committees in State Legislatures," 693.

67. Wayne L. Francis, "Floor Procedures and Conference Committees in State Legislatures," in *Encyclopedia of the American Legislative System*, ed. Joel H. Silbey (New York: Scribner's, 1994), 723.

68. Interview with the author, March 29, 1995.

69. Tom Loftus, *The Art of Legislative Politics* (Washington, D.C.: CQ Press, 1994), 79–80.

70. Phil Keisling, "Thrills, Spills, and Bills," *Washington Monthly,* October 1990, 10.

71. Hamm and Hedlund, "Committees in State Legislatures," 695.

72. Browne and Ver Burg, *Michigan Politics and Government*, 119; Jewell and Miller, *Kentucky Legislature*, 124.

73. Keisling, "Thrills, Spills, and Bills," 16.

74. Interviews with the author, June 5, 1995.

75. Browne and Ver Burg, *Michigan Politics and Government*, 15.

76. Interview with the author, March 15, 1995.

77. Ibid., March 17, 1995.

78. Straayer, *Colorado General Assembly*, 110–111.

79. Hanson, *Tribune of the People*, 93.

80. Interviews with the author, January 26, 1995.

81. Campbell, *Representative Democracy*, 49.

82. Interview with the author, May 16, 1995.

83. Ibid., March 31, 1995.

84. Ibid., March 27, 1995.

85. *Tallahassee Democrat*, March 29, 1995, and *Palm Beach Post*, April 30, 1995.

86. Francis, "Floor Procedures and Conference Committees," 726–727.

87. Interview with the author, March 15, 1995.

88. John A. Straayer, "How Prevalent Are State Legislative Conference Committees?" *Comparative State Politics* 17 (April 1996): 6.

89. Interview with the author, March 29, 1995.

90. Straayer, "How Prevalent Are State Legislative Conference Committees?" 7.

91. Ibid.; also Hanson, *Tribune of the People*, 123–124.

92. Gove and Nowlan, *Illinois Politics and Government*, 79.

93. As reported by Louis Lavelle, *Tampa Tribune*, May 8, 1994. The speaker of the house missed 229 votes because instead of voting on bills that already had overwhelming support, the speaker was working behind the scenes in to negotiate settlements. Other legislators also missed a number of votes because they were engaged in critical negotiations during the final days of the session.

94. Smallwood, *Free and Independent*, 91.

95. Interviews with the author, March 16 and May 16, 1995.

96. Richardson, *What Makes You Think We Read the Bills?* 40.

97. Interview with the author, February 24, 1995.

98. William K. Muir Jr., *Legislature: California's School for Politics* (Chicago: University of Chicago Press, 1982), 42.

99. Interview with the author, March 17, 1995.

100. Gove and Nowlan, *Illinois Politics and Government*, 97.

101. Interview with the author, March 18, 1995.

102. Interview with the author.

103. Alan Rosenthal, "The Fine Art of Saying 'No'," *State Legislatures*, January 1986, 24.

104. Interview with the author, March 16, 1995.

105. Diane D. Blair, *Arkansas Politics and Government* (Lincoln: University of Nebraska Press, 1988), 105.

106. Rosenthal, "Fine Art of Saying 'No'," 24.

107. Loftus, *Art of Legislative Politics*, 76.

108. Interview with the author, March 16, 1995.

109. Ibid., March 7, 1996.

110. Interview with Sen. Robert Gorton for Pfizer tape, July 24, 1996.

111. David H. Everson and Samuel K. Gove, "Illinois: Political Microcosm of the Nation," in *Interest Group Politics in the Midwestern States*, ed. Ronald J. Hrebenar and Clive S. Thomas (Ames: Iowa State University Press, 1993), 35-40.

112. Interview with Rep. Scott Jensen for Pfizer tape, July 24, 1996.

113. Interview with the author, May 16, 1995.

114. Loftus, *Art of Legislative Politics*, 7.

115. *New York Times*, June 6, 1995.

116. Interview with the author, March 15, 1995.

117. Rich Jones et al., "Review of Legislative Operations in the Wisconsin Legislature," *National Conference of State Legislatures*, May 1994.

118. Richardson, *What Makes You Think We Read the Bills?* 44–45.

119. Keith E. Hamm, Ronald D. Hedlund, and R. Bruce Anderson, "Political Parties in State Legislatures," in *Encyclopedia of the American Legislative System*, ed. Joel H. Silbey (New York: Scribner's, 1994), 968–969.

120. Malcolm E. Jewell and Marcia Lynn Whicker, *Legislative Leadership in the American States* (Ann Arbor: University of Michigan Press, 1994), 99.

121. Straayer, *Colorado General Assembly*, 156–159.

122. Mark Leccese, "A Beacon in Boston," *State Legislatures,* July–August 1996, 23.

123. See Christopher Z. Mooney, "Information Sources in State Legislative Decision Making," *Legislative Studies Quarterly* 16 (August 1991): 445–455.

124. Cited in Tom Loftus, "Art of Legislative Politics," prepublication manuscript, 1992. The quote did not appear in Tom Loftus, *The Art of Legislative Politics* (Washington, D.C.: CQ Press, 1994).

125. Richardson, *What Makes You Think We Read the Bills?* 38.

126. Joseph M. Bessette, *The Mild Voice of Reason: Deliberative Democracy and American National Government* (Chicago: University of Chicago Press, 1994), 46.

127. A few states have been unstable in their enactment rates between 1984–1985 and 1994–1995. California's rate shot up, while rates in Illinois, North Carolina, Oklahoma, Rhode Island, and Utah declined.

CHAPTER 5

Competition for Legislative Control

It is only natural for legislators to want to retain their jobs.[1] For careerists, who devote nearly all their time to politics, defeat means the loss not only of status and equanimity but also of livelihood. "After all," as two scholars write, "for the old breed, electoral defeat was a disappointment; for the new breed, it may be the end of a career."[2] Even noncareerists want to remain in office— at least until they themselves decide to get out.

The election is always just around the corner, particularly for members of the house in forty-six states and senators in twelve who have to run every two years. House members in four states (and as of 1998, in North Dakota as well) and senate members in thirty-eight have a longer lease on life, having to run only every four years. (In three of these states, however, every third senate term is two years long because of the ten-year redistricting cycle.) Legislative terms are relatively short, enabling citizens to change their minds rather frequently as to who will represent them. But if two- and four-year cycles are not frequent enough, about one-third of the states allow citizens, if they are particularly disgruntled, to recall their elected officials through a petition process and then a referendum.

INDIVIDUAL COMPETITION

With occupational risk so high in elective politics, one can appreciate the electoral preoccupations of legislators. "They start running the day they take their oath of office," explained one observer in New Jersey. "Everything they do is geared toward the election," said another in Illinois. "The thought of reelection may not occur to a first-term legislator within the first five minutes after winning the election," writes a Michigan legislator, "but I would not count on that."[3] A national survey of 330 veteran legislators found that 67 percent of them agreed with the proposition that legislators were more likely today to give their reelection priority.[4]

Why do state legislators feel so vulnerable? In view of the advantages incumbents are thought to possess, the overriding concern with reelection may seem exaggerated. Overall, the incumbent reelection rate in state houses was very high in the 1970s and 1980s.[5] Roughly 90 percent of incumbents were returned to office in the professionalized legislatures of the large states—California, Illinois, Michigan, New York, Ohio, and Pennsylvania. But incumbent reelection rates were also high in smaller states with less-professionalized legislatures.

Many districts have been relatively safe not only for incumbents, who build a strong base for themselves, but also for one political party or the other.[6] National demographic patterns are one reason for this. Urban areas are inevitably Democratic, and suburban areas are typically Republican. In addition, decennial reapportionments normally protect as many incumbents as possible by giving them a comfortable margin of partisan voters. Over the course of a decade the demography of districts may change, reducing the incumbent's initial partisan advantage. But in most places, one or the other party will probably maintain the advantage, even ten years after redistricting.

Whatever the demographics, incumbents marshal their resources to keep the edge as wide as possible and to discourage serious challengers. Incumbents have advantages in addition to demography. They are more visible than challengers in their districts. In low-visibility elections, such as those for the legislature, incumbency has usually been an asset. Incumbents also have a media edge that goes with holding public office. In addition, incumbents have devoted a good deal of their time, and more staff time (if they are fortunate enough to be in states that provide legislators with personal staff or staff allowances), to constituent service. This allows them to respond to the problems posed by constituents, intervene on behalf of constituents with administrative agencies of government, and "bring home the bacon" in the form of public works and other projects. Incumbents also possess campaign organizations, donor lists, and, in all likelihood, more campaign experience.

All these advantages add up to a statistical picture of many "safe" or "relatively safe" legislative seats, at least by objective standards. One study of the lower houses of twenty legislatures, over the period from 1950 to 1986, found a decline in the proportions of marginal seats. In less than half the states examined were more than 50 percent of the seats competitive, as defined by the winner previously garnering less than 60 percent of the vote. In Tennessee only one out of five house seats was competitive; in Massachusetts it was one out of four. One out of three seats was competitive in California and New York.[7]

Yet for legislators running for reelection, subjective—not objective—standards are the ones that count. Statistics regarding the electoral success rates of incumbents do not matter, concludes Anthony King, a British political scientist, in a book about the vulnerability of American politicians. What matters to legislators is their subjective awareness of the uncertainties attending the world of politics and how much they personally stand to lose if they are defeated.[8] There is no such thing as a "safe" district for any legislator running for reelection. To an observer, the possibility of an incumbent losing may appear remote, and it may in fact be remote. But losing a reelection bid is always a possibility, whatever the statistical history of the district. Lightning can always strike, and it does strike on occasion. Legislators have seen colleagues relax their reelection efforts and subsequently lose their seats. They have seen seemingly entrenched legislators go down to defeat because they cast a vote that upset their constituency or caused a key group to mobilize against them. They have seen incumbents who could not survive a national tide, an unpopular candidate at the top of their ticket, or a scandal.

Incumbents in the large states—where media campaigns count for so much and money is the means to media—are ever alert to the emergence of a well-heeled, previously unknown opponent. So, whatever their previous margins, most incumbents go to prodigious lengths to avoid defeat. For incumbents, the campaign never ends; they begin to position themselves for their next race as soon as they are elected.

From the voter's point of view, the system is not competitive enough. In most districts, voters who normally identify with the district's partisan minority rarely have the opportunity to prevail. Majority-party voters can exert their will in the primary—at least in theory.

Reformers advocate greater district-by-district competition, their objective a "level playing field" across the state. In their view, the way to achieve this is through decennial redistricting, which could be designed to balance current partisan registrations or past partisan voting to create more competitive situations all over. Instead, the common practice is quite the opposite (except in a state like Iowa, where incumbency plays no role in the drawing of district lines). Incumbents tend to be protected with as substantial a partisan edge as is practicable. In some districts, the playing field could not be leveled very much in any case, not without flagrant gerrymandering. These districts are so homogeneous that one party or the other has comfortable majorities.

Reducing the power of incumbents is the only other way to increase competitiveness in noncompetitive districts. This would require placing limits on the resources legislators have at their disposal—namely, personal staff; subsidized communications with constituents; advantages in fund-raising; and channels for free publicity. All this, of course, would have to be accomplished over the objections of incumbent legislators; furthermore, it would inevitably have unintended consequences.

Particularly in those places with a lopsided partisan balance, a substantial proportion of citizens will not feel efficacious. These are people who identify with the minority party. Such a situation is inevitable under a single-member electoral system. It also partly explains the low voter turnouts in legislative elections. Even voters who identify with the majority party may feel frustrated if they do not want to see the incumbent reelected. Their turnout, too, may be rather low.

Despite these limitations on popular control, legislators seldom forget their electorates when anything controversial comes their way. They continuously calculate how their decision or action will play out at the next election. They look more to the reaction of their own partisans than to their adversaries. But in the attempt to be reelected, few interests and few people are completely written off. For representatives who want to stay in office, the pressures of popular democracy are unrelenting.

PARTISAN COMPETITION

Even though many legislative districts are not very competitive, competition is quite healthy at the state level. Nowadays, either party can win control of the senate or the house, or both chambers of the legislature, in about two-thirds of the states, while about one-third still remain comparatively safe for either the Democrats or the Republicans. Since the 1960s, and until very recently, Republicans could do no better than minority-party status in most places. The Democrats habitually won about three-fifths of the governors' races and the same proportion of the ninety-eight legislative bodies (excluding Nebraska, which has a unicameral, nonpartisan legislature). Democrats also retained approximately 60 percent of the 7,424 seats in the nation's legislatures. The distribution of partisan control, reported by region for the period 1960–1996, is shown in table 5.1.

TABLE 5.1
Party Control of State Legislatures, 1960–1996

| Year | Partisan Control by Number of States | | |
	Democratic	Republican	Split
1960	27	15	6
1962	25	17	6
1964	32	6	10
1966	23	16	9
1968	20	20	8
1970	23	16	9
1972	26	16	7
1974	37	4	8
1976	35	4	10
1978	31	11	7
1980	29	15	5
1982	43	11	4
1984	26	11	12
1986	28	9	12
1988	29	8	12
1990	30	6	13
1992	25	8	16
1994	18	19	12
1996	20	18	11

Source: Alan Rosenthal, "The Legislature: Unraveling of Institutional Fabric,"
in *The State of the States,* 3d ed., ed. Carl Van Horn (Washington, D.C.: CQ
Press, 1996), 122.

The picture before the 1994 elections was one of Democratic domination.
As many as twenty-four legislatures had long been under Democratic control,
while Republicans could manage a similar reign only in New Hampshire
(although in a few other states they came close). By 1995, however, only
Massachusetts, Rhode Island, and Hawaii (in addition to thirteen southern
states) remained Democratic. The other thirty-two states had mixed partisan
control of their legislatures. After a while, enough Democrats switched to the
Republican Party to give South Carolina to the GOP, so that two-thirds of
the states had elected Democratic *and* Republican legislative majorities. Even
though Democrats picked up seats and chambers in the 1996 elections, two-
party politics continued to be the dominant pattern in the states.

The increasingly competitive nature of legislative politics is measured by the Ranney Index of Interparty Competition, which has been calculated since 1948. The mean level of interparty competition (on an index ranging from .5, the least competitive, to 1.0, the most competitive) has been rising as follows:[9] 1948–1960: .78; 1962–1973: .83; 1974–1980: .81; 1981–1988: .84; 1989–1994: .87.

Hawaii, Arkansas, Rhode Island, Massachusetts, Louisiana, West Virginia, Maryland, Mississippi, Alabama, and Oklahoma have overwhelmingly Democratic legislatures. The overwhelmingly Republican legislatures are in Idaho, Wyoming, Utah, North Dakota, New Hampshire, and Montana. The rest of the states are quite competitive.

The Republican surge may have hit a high point with the elections of 1994, which also found the GOP taking control of the U.S. Senate and the U.S. House—the latter body for the first time in almost fifty years. Nevertheless, Republican gains in previously solid Democratic states may be here to stay. In the South, Florida presents the starkest shift toward the GOP. Republicans made steady legislative gains there throughout the 1980s and into the 1990s, ultimately capturing both the senate and the house. In the West, although New Mexico is still a predominantly Democratic state, Republicans have been adding to their ranks. In the East, Maryland is no longer the Democratic bastion it used to be. The party was traditionally a combination of old-line southerners, yellow-dog types, ethnic and Jewish voters from Baltimore and the Washington suburbs, and African Americans. Lately, the party has been losing the southern and even yellow-dog types, who are becoming Republicans. Rural Maryland is becoming Republican, and once-complacent Democratic candidates in Howard County have begun knocking on doors to solicit votes they can no longer count on. Republicans had never been elected at the county level, but they now have a majority on the county councils of the state.[10] Democrats still hold a 100-41 majority in the Maryland house, but the GOP has targeted twenty of these seats. The picture is even rosier for Republicans in the Maryland senate. Although they hold only fifteen of forty-seven seats, they are only nine seats short of a majority.

THE RISE OF LEGISLATIVE PARTIES

Political scientists have drawn a distinction between three types of political party: the party-as-organization, the party-in-government, and the party-in-the-electorate. The latter continues, but in attenuated form as partisan loyalties weaken. The party-as-organization was once thought to be the state, county, and local groups that managed recruitment, nomination, and election campaigns. Party organizations continue, but they are now dominated by officeholders, not traditional party leaders. The party-in-government continues to refer to the party of the governor and the legislative caucuses.

The major organizational change in the state party system in recent years has been the increasing role of the legislative party in campaigns. In the old days, state party organizations were patronage-based groups that controlled the nominating process and played a key role in state and local campaigns. With their passing, a vacuum was created. The legislative parties moved into this vacuum, no longer content with making laws and governing. The lines between campaigning and governance thus became blurred as the party-in-government took on responsibility for both.

State and county parties lost influence because of changes in nominating processes, campaigns, and voter loyalties. The influence of the Democratic and Republican party hierarchies was eroded even further as direct primaries began replacing conventions as the principal method of selecting candidates for the party's line on the general-election ballot. Over time, even primaries have been diluted. Only seventeen states have "closed primaries," meaning that voters must be registered Democrats or Republicans in order to vote in the party's primary. In ten other states the primaries are semiclosed, permitting voters to switch registration on election day. Another eleven states have semiopen primaries in which voters can publicly request a party ballot and vote in either primary. The other twelve states have open primaries, in which voters need not declare partisan preference to vote.[11] The direction has been toward a system in which voters of either party can cross over and participate in the other party's nominating election, weakening the little control left to parties and enhancing the power of individual voters.

California has never had strong parties, but in 1996 it sapped its party system even further when voters approved Proposition 198. The so-called single-ballot initiative was condemned by Democratic and Republican leaders as a threat to the institutional integrity of their parties. As in Alaska and Washington, all candidates for partisan positions in California are now listed on a single primary ballot. Voters can pick whomever they want in either party. The person from each party with the most votes then appears on the November ballot. The effect of this change is to thwart extremist candidates and assist those who appeal to the middle of the two-party spectrum.[12]

State and local party organizations were once key campaign mechanisms in places where parties, partisanship, and patronage counted. Around election time, parties made a difference in states like New Jersey, New York, Ohio,

Connecticut, Pennsylvania, Illinois, Michigan, Minnesota, and Wisconsin. Chosen by party leaders, candidates were largely dependent on party organizations for campaign workers and campaign funds. This is no longer the case. For several decades now, legislative campaigns, like congressional ones, have become "candidate centered" instead of "party centered." Candidates have taken it on their own to run, putting together personal organizations, war chests, and campaign management.

Eight or nine out of ten voters used to identify as Democrat or Republican, with only a small proportion identifying as Independent. This pattern began to break down years ago as partisan affiliations weakened. Currently one-quarter to one-third of the voters consider themselves Independents, and the other two-thirds divide among the two parties in varying proportions depending on the state (see table 5.2).

TABLE 5.2

Party Identifications for Selected States (percentages of respondents)

State	Democratic	Independent	Republican
Alabama (1994)	31	29	22
Arizona (1995)	26	25	33
California (1995)	37	17	36
Florida (1995)	27	34	39
Illinois (1994)	25	36	29
Indiana* (1994)	31	37	25
Minnesota (1994)	28	44	27
New Jersey (1995)	27	32	29
North Carolina (1995)	32	26	31
South Carolina (1994)	25	30	31
Tennessee (1994)	34	31	30
Wisconsin (1994)	27	33	28

Source: These data have been provided by the Louis Harris Data Center, Institute for Research in Social Science, University of North Carolina. Sources of data are: Florida, Survey Research Laboratory, Policy Sciences Center, Florida State University, Florida Annual Survey 1995, p. 25; Alabama, Capital Poll, Institute for Social Science Research, University of Alabama, 1994; Social Research Laboratory, Northern Arizona University, Spring 1995; Illinois Policy Survey, Center for Government Studies, Northern Illinois University, 1994; Center for Survey Research, Indiana University, 1994; Center for Survey Research, University of Minnesota, 1994; Eagleton Institute, Rutgers University, 1995; Institute for Research in Social Science, School of Journalism, University of North Carolina, 1995; Survey Research Laboratory, Institute of Public Affairs, University of South Carolina, 1994; Social Science Research Laboratory, University of Wisconsin, 1994. California data are from the Field Poll, September 18, 1995.

* Choice here is Democrat, Republican, something else, or "do you have no party identification?" The latter is reported in the "Independent" column.

Despite the decline of partisanship, party strength remains an important factor in legislative election outcomes. A study of elections in California and Iowa suggests that, on average, a 10 percent increase in the proportion of voters registered for a party in legislative districts yields a 5 to 6 percent increase in the vote for that party's legislative candidates.[13]

The distribution of partisan affiliations still matters, albeit less than formerly. Furthermore, voters today are more likely to split their tickets—favoring a Republican for governor and a Democrat for the legislature or vice versa. Neither party, therefore, can sit back and rely heavily on prior affiliations in the district. There are too many Independents, too many switch-hitters, and too great a risk that an advantage in registration or affiliation will not prevail at the polls.

LEGISLATIVE PARTY CAMPAIGN LEADERSHIP

In 1988, shortly after he became speaker of the assembly in New Jersey, Chuck Hardwick was addressing a group at Princeton University's Woodrow Wilson School. His subject was the speakership of the assembly and its many tasks. Reelecting members was the first task he discussed. That the reelection of legislative party members came before the rest is not accidental. Without a majority, Hardwick would have no other tasks—he would no longer be speaker. Seven years later, Ken Maddy, the Republican senate minority leader in California, was ousted by the more conservative and aggressive Rob Hurtt. The new minority leader was quick to declare that he thought his primary responsibility was "to support his incumbents and get new people elected to his caucus."[14] That is where he had been putting his energies, and it paid off for him.

For the legislative party as well as the individual legislator, the election has assumed overriding importance. As leaders of the legislative party, the speaker and minority leader of the house and the president (or president pro tem) and minority leader of the senate are expected, first, to help get members of their caucus reelected and, second, to help defeat vulnerable incumbents of the opposition party. In many states nowadays, the personal prospects of legislative leaders are tied to the number of seats won or lost by their party in the election.

A leader who loses a majority naturally loses the presiding-officer position. And a leader who loses members, even while retaining majority status, encourages a challenge from a colleague within the caucus. A leader who converts a minority into a majority is ordinarily awarded the speakership in the house or presidency in the senate. If a leader simply gains some seats, his or her position becomes more secure. Thomas Ritter, the Democratic speaker of the Connecticut house, had the good fortune to pick up seats in 1994 and win recognition for his achievement. His chamber was the only one in the nation where Democrats made substantial gains. Out of the eight seats Democrats picked up nationwide, four were in the Connecticut house.

With the demise of the old state parties and their replacement by those that neither control nominations nor run campaigns, legislative leaders and campaign committees faced a vacuum. They were prompted to fill that vacuum with intensified partisan competition for control of legislative chambers. Legislative campaign committees—under the direction of legislative party leaders—are now the major source of party assistance to legislative candidates. They are particularly helpful to viable candidates who are most in need of assistance. They have become full-service organizations, involved in recruitment, training, research, press, polling, strategy, and phone banks.

Leaders have a stake in recruiting the most attractive candidates possible. Some leaders recruit with a special eye to building support within their caucus. Since the 1980 battle between Speaker Leo McCarthy and challenger Howard Berman, the assembly speaker in California has become involved in the recruitment process. As speaker, Willie Brown put campaign funds into primary as well as general elections. He supported candidates who were likely to win and who would, in turn, support him for speaker.[15]

Other legislative leaders have also made it their business to cultivate candidates, but most have distanced themselves and the party campaign committees from primary races. Informal recruitment has probably gone on for years, but it has become more organized as elections became more competitive. In Ohio, legislative parties have been recruiting candidates since the late 1970s. Vern Riffe, who was speaker of the house for twenty years, would target six or seven seats for capture and then collaborate with county party leaders in a search for candidates. In return for identifying the most promising candidates, Riffe agreed to pay for polling, mailing, and media and provide staff and money for their campaigns.[16] JoAnn Davidson, Ohio's Republican minority leader and Riffe's successor as speaker, also recruited, although she had fewer resources at her disposal. Her special talent was attracting women candidates. On the senate side Stanley Aronoff, a moderate Republican who served as president, made a pitch to potential candidates, less on philosophical than on public service grounds. His priority was open seats. Aronoff would solicit county chairs, civic leaders, and business and labor leaders for lists of potentials. The top criterion for endorsement by senate Republicans was viability—could the candidate win? Their public service record was also important, as were gender and other demographic considerations.[17]

Legislative leaders' campaign committees and legislative parties in some places also deliver training to candidates. In the Maryland house, Republican leaders Ellen Sauerbrey and Robert Kittleman started raising money and identifying candidates as early as 1986. They put in a lot of effort training candidates—through techniques of playacting and simulation—in workshops held around the state. These activities were instrumental in producing impressive GOP gains—in 1990 Republicans in the house increased from sixteen to twenty-five and from twenty-five to forty-one in 1994.[18]

Some campaign committees take on the bulk purchase of campaign technologies—consultants, polling, and media production. They spend money "on behalf of" candidates for mailings, brochures, and advertising in the print and electronic media.[19] Coordinated campaigns have been conducted in Arizona, California, Florida, Illinois, Michigan, New Jersey, New York, Ohio, Pennsylvania, and Virginia. In 1992, for instance, Ohio's Riffe hired a consulting firm that undertook a statewide survey, district benchmark surveys, and shorter-trend polls, testing the movement of the electorate as direct mail, radio, and television began to hit; during the final three weeks, the firm conducted tracking polls in targeted districts.

Legislative party efforts appear to be paying off. One study suggests that focusing party resources has resulted in increasing margins for members of the New York senate.[20] It is also thought that Democrats took the Vermont house in 1992 largely because Speaker Ralph Wright spent several years recruiting and coaching candidates and kept watch over his party's campaigns. Republicans in Kansas also started to take on a campaign function in 1992, managing well enough to take back control of the house and make gains in the senate. Kansas Democrats had been organized and aggressive, but the Republicans began to match them blow for blow. "It's almost scary how this is evolving," said the chief of staff to the Kansas senate president, "we're a part-time legislature, but running for office is becoming a near full-time job."[21]

FINANCING CAMPAIGNS

Raising and allocating funds is perhaps the key campaign role of legislative leaders and legislative parties. Jesse Unruh immortalized the line, "Money is the mother's milk of politics," in the 1960s. It is no less apposite today. Cam-

paigns cost money, and the expenses incurred are unavoidable and even meritorious. They enable candidates to get their messages across to the public.
Campaigns provide most of the political education that Americans receive.
And the higher the levels of spending in state legislative elections, the higher
the levels of voter turnout.[22]

The Costs of Campaigns

A former legislator, like Sandy D'Alemberte of Florida, can recall the old days
of the 1960s when his campaign in Dade County cost $12,000, making it one
of the most expensive legislative campaigns in Florida at the time. He recalled
a colleague who ran in Dade for a mere $350, relying, as did so many others,
on appearances at civic clubs and organizations. Tom Loftus, the former speaker
of the Wisconsin assembly, remembers spending $11,000 on his first cam-
paign in 1976—the most expensive race that year.[23] Today in Florida and
Wisconsin competitive races cost much, much more—not all of which is due
to inflation.

Campaign spending in California ranks the highest, but California also has
the largest senate and house district populations. Tom Hayden once spent a
record $2 million on an assembly seat, and Cecil Green spent $1.4 million in
a special election for a senate seat. In 1992, five senate candidates spent more
than $350,000 in the general elections, while forty-three assembly candidates
spent over $225,000. In nine of twenty senate races in 1994, the candidates
raised more than $1 million between them. In a 1994 Ohio race, the Demo-
crat spent $350,000 to narrowly win a house seat, while the Republican spent
nearly $1 million in losing the seat.

Not every state has the expensive campaigns of the targeted districts in
California, Ohio, Illinois, Michigan, New Jersey, New York, and Pennsylvania.
An examination of data for house contests in sixteen states from 1988 to 1990
shows a low average of $7,153 in Maine and averages of about $10,000 in
Idaho, Montana, and Utah.[24] Rhode Island races range from $1,000 for an
uncontested seat to $10,000 for a contested one. Even in Massachusetts, with
its professional legislature, candidates for the house can mount a campaign for
$40,000, with about twice that needed for the senate. The highest amount
spent on a house race in Vermont in 1992 was $11,880. In 1994 the Repub-
licans spent $17,000 to oust Ralph Wright, the Democratic speaker of the
Vermont house. A study of the 1994 elections in five states indicates that an
Illinois senate race generally costs $156,000, while a house race in Wyoming
typically costs $4,000. In 1996 four candidates for the Illinois senate each

spent more than $1 million. Although there are great variations, these diminish substantially when cost is controlled for population.[25]

The general perception, however, is that campaigns—even at the state legislative level—are extremely expensive and becoming more so at a tremendous rate. Critics of campaign finance systems again hold California out as an example. About $1.4 million was spent in legislative contests in 1958. By 1978 the amount had grown to $20 million, and by 1988 it had reached $68 million, dipping to $54 million in 1990. The falloff in 1990 does not signify a decreased reliance on campaign money in California. Rather, it largely results from two factors specific to 1990. First, Proposition 73 put contribution limits in place, before the state supreme court overruled them; and, second, the gubernatorial race that year was extremely costly and diverted funds from legislative campaigns. In 1994, despite the fact that statewide candidates were also competing for dollars, California's legislative fund-raising climbed from the $71.9 million of two years before to $78.4 million—a 9 percent increase.[26]

Generally speaking, inflation and population growth have something to do with rising expenditures. A study of California found that, after adjusting for these two factors, the amount spent actually decreased from 1980 to 1992. Another study, of campaign costs in ten states from 1986 to 1994, does show increases. But adjusting for inflation eliminates the increases in eight of the ten, with higher costs incurred in the first election after redistricting and where control of the legislative body is in contest.[27]

Raising Funds

Whatever the increase in campaign expenditures, campaign fund-raising activity is on the rise. In a national survey of 330 veteran legislators, 79 percent attested to this.[28] It is on the rise in part because laws limiting the size of campaign contributions have forced candidates to work harder to raise as much. It is on the rise, too, because of the expanded role of legislative leaders and legislative parties in fund-raising.

As Democratic speaker of the California assembly, Unruh was a pioneer in this area, raising money from interest groups and dividing it among Democratic assembly candidates. Soon, assembly Democrats took it for granted that their leaders would to raise money for them. When Speaker Leo McCarthy neglected to do so, because he was fund-raising for the gubernatorial campaign he had in mind, his caucus forced him out of the speakership.

Democratic and Republican leaders in California have been careful to follow in Unruh's footsteps. Willie Brown holds legislative fund-raising records that are unlikely to be surpassed. As Democratic assembly speaker during 1993–1994, he raised $6.8 million, while Jim Brulte, the Republican assembly minority leader, raised $2.2 million. Bill Lockyer, the Democratic senate president pro tem, raised $3.9 million during the 1993–1994 cycle, while Ken Maddy, the Republican senate minority leader, raised $1.3 million.[29] As mentioned above, Maddy was unseated by a conservative colleague, Rob Hurtt, who had personally given $1.22 million to Republican candidates for the legislature in 1993 and 1994. Senator Hurtt, by himself, was second only to the California Teachers Association in contributions. Third place went to Allied Business Political Action Committee, which was formed and financed by five businessmen, one of whom was Hurtt.[30]

Yet California isn't the only state where party leaders and their party caucuses are heavily involved in campaign finance. Leadership political action committees (PACs) and caucus campaign committees began developing in the 1970s in the legislatures of Illinois, Minnesota, New York, Washington, and Wisconsin. They spread further in the 1980s, and such committees now exist in about thirty-five states. According to one study, they exist in all four legislative parties in twenty-two states and in one to three legislative parties in thirteen other states.[31]

These committees were formed for a number of reasons: first, no other party organization existed; second, legislators—especially legislative leaders—preferred not to rely on the state parties, which might have been under control of the governor, or on county parties, which also were not in their hands; third, increasing competition between the parties for legislative seats inspired greater effort by the legislative party committees; and, fourth, running campaigns out of the legislature itself afforded a more efficient way to raise and allocate funds.[32]

A distinction can be made between a leadership PAC and a legislative party campaign committee.[33] The former is under the complete control of the leader; the latter is governed by several members. Whatever the precise distinction, however, leaders tend to run both shows. Caucus committees, as well as their personal PACs, are largely in the hands of leaders. They are the chairmen, the chief fund-raisers, and the strategists.[34] The distinction, without very much of a difference, is illustrated by Ohio's house Democrats.

During his speakership, Vern Riffe started caucus fund-raising. The money was in Columbus, held by interest groups and lobbyists with offices there. It was Riffe's idea that one huge fund-raiser would achieve an economy of scale. This fund-raiser coincided with the speaker's birthday. At his first birthday party reception in 1973, tickets sold for $100, netting a total of $165,000. At his party in 1993 tickets sold for $500, netting around $1.5 million. Because he was probusiness, as well as prolabor, Riffe managed to attract money that otherwise might have gone to Republicans. "I never had an organization turn me down," he recalled when he was leaving the speakership. Not only did Riffe demonstrate personal political skill in the fund-raising enterprise, but "he created an illusion of invulnerability," convincing just about everyone that the Republicans could not win. In any case, it is much more difficult for a lobbyist or interest group to turn down a request for funds from a legislative leader than from a rank-and-file member.[35]

The overriding objective of leaders and their parties is to win or maintain a majority, gaining as many seats as possible along the way. The money they raise must therefore go to candidates who can put it to best use. These are incumbents from marginal districts who are targeted by the opposition and challengers running for open seats or against incumbents who are beatable. Thus, party resources are concentrated where they will make the greatest difference—in close races.[36] The resources are more likely to be given to challengers and newcomers and not to veterans, since "very few candidates can win on their own the first time out." Indeed, party resources may be the principal sources of money for a few of the new members. Certain districts, however, may be so evenly balanced for the parties that they will always need extra help, no matter how long a member has held office.[37] In the 1992 elections, for example, Democratic leaders in Illinois gave to twenty-one targeted districts more money than the candidates could raise for themselves.[38]

Legislative leaders may control the allocation of funds, but they actually have little discretion. They must produce results, or they risk displeasing their caucus. Willie Brown, despite his political power, was not free to distribute money to whomever he pleased. He had to consider his followers' interests when deciding which candidates to fund and to what extent.[39] The same held true in Minnesota. Bob Vanasek, the assembly speaker, commented: "I can't give some dissident out there some money to shut him up, because it means we're not funding a race somewhere else that we can win. We can't give money to incumbents in safe seats."[40] The bottom line is too vital for leaders to play around with campaign funds.

The dollar value of resources distributed by legislative campaign committees represents a small proportion of total funds. But targeted, they have had important effects.[41] They have strengthened the legislative parties as campaign organizations. Targeted resources have also encouraged a distribution of funds based on party need rather than on individual power or other factors. Party organizations, furthermore, distribute a larger proportion of their money to candidates in close races than do nonparty organizations. Willie Brown, for instance, channeled about three-quarters of his funds to open-seat races and to challengers in marginal districts, while political action committees contributed mainly to candidates in safe seats.[42] The increasing role of the party tends to reduce the gap between the revenues of incumbents and challengers.

A few legislators relax their own fund-raising efforts, knowing the caucus will do much of their heavy lifting for them. A number, however, chafe at the system's restraints, which they feel hinder their own fund-raising. Leadership PACs simply exert a stronger pull on potential contributors, thus siphoning off money that might otherwise have gone to the campaigns of relatively safe rank-and-file members.

Leadership and caucus campaign committees also have the effect of insulating members from contributors. Leaders serve as a buffer between interest groups and legislators. This tends to diminish any sense of obligation to the interest group on the legislator's part. Lobbyists and interest groups, who feel they ought not to refuse leadership requests, would prefer to give directly to candidates of their choice. They would rather have control over the flow of their funds than risk the very real possibility that their funds will wind up helping candidates who oppose them.[43]

Those who see the dire need for reform of campaign finance call for the abolition of leadership PACs. Whatever their party-building merits, the fear is that they confer too much power on too few people—namely, the leaders. The drive to curb leadership and legislative party campaign committees has achieved some success. In recent years, transfers of funds from such PACs have been restricted or prohibited in Arizona, Connecticut, Florida, Iowa, Kansas, Kentucky, Michigan, and South Carolina—and in California, until the prohibition was overturned by the courts. But, not surprisingly, leaders still exert influence over campaign-funding operations. Take New York, for example. Prior to 1989 each of the four legislative party caucuses had a leadership fund-raising effort. In response to public objections, these units were eliminated in 1990. The structures have not really disappeared, however. Both state party committees now have groups specifically geared to house and senate elections. They are not, in a legal sense, separate organizations, but elements of the state parties. Legislative leaders maintain control, nonetheless.[44]

PARTISANSHIP WITHIN THE LEGISLATURE

Although party has played an important role in most legislative bodies outside the South, partisanship has usually been constrained. It has been in the interests of both parties to try to work things out whenever possible. But as competition for control of legislative bodies became more balanced and intense, partisanship assumed greater salience both in those legislative bodies where it already mattered and in those where it had never mattered much at all.

The Importance of Party

One simple indication of the partisan nature of legislative bodies is the way in which members are seated on the floor of the chamber. An examination several years ago of seating arrangements in eighty-seven chambers in forty-four states found that in only twenty of the forty-four senates and twenty-three of the forty-three houses were members seated according to their party. In a few states—Minnesota is an example—party members tend to cluster, although seating is not along formal partisan lines.[45]

Perhaps the best indication of the importance of party, however, is the partisan organization of the legislature. Normally, the majority party succeeds in organizing the legislative body. The majority caucus selects its candidate for the position of presiding officer. Then, in an election of the entire chamber, majority caucus members coalesce in support of their candidate, beating back the minority party's candidate. In addition, majority party members are generally appointed to chair the standing committees and special committees. Positions of power are for the majority to dispense and exploit.

There are departures from the norm, however. On occasion a minority member will be appointed to chair a major committee or subcommittee by the presiding officer. This happens with greatest frequency where bipartisan coalitions have engineered the selection of the presiding officer, and members of the minority wind up sharing committee chairmanships with members of the majority. Bipartisan coalitions may have become more common nowadays, but they are not unprecedented. Some years ago they were a constant feature of New Mexico politics, with its "cowboy coalition" and loyalist Democrats. They occurred in the California assembly on several occasions, notably when Jesse Unruh turned to the Republicans to retain control and Willie Brown turned to them to gain control.

In the New York assembly, New Jersey assembly, Oregon senate, Vermont house, and Florida senate, Democratic-Republican coalitions selected the presiding officer. In three notable instances during 1989, leaders were ousted by bipartisan coalitions. Irv Stolberg, the Democratic speaker of the Connecticut house, Liston Ramsey, the Democratic speaker of the North Carolina house, and Jim Barker, Oklahoma's Democratic speaker, were all overthrown. Most recently, in 1996, the practically unthinkable took place: The Democratic caucus's candidate for speaker in Massachusetts was defeated by his competitor, who signed up the entire Republican caucus along with his Democratic allies.

As state legislatures become competitive, the minority grows more frustrated, more partisan, and more disposed to welcome majority members who offer a coalition candidate. They may or may not be awarded chairmanships or rules changes, but they do create political mischief by sowing seeds of rebellion and rancor in the majority. In Connecticut, for example, it took a while for the breach between Stolberg's liberal Democrats and his successor's more conservative Democrats to heal, and during that period Republicans assumed a more pivotal position.

As in so many other areas of political life, California is on the cutting edge of legislative party development. Party loyalty and disloyalty exist side by side, as was demonstrated by the assembly speakership battle that ran for about a year and involved a succession of defections, recall elections, and shifts in power.[46] The story is worth telling in some detail.

In the 1994 elections Republicans succeeded in electing their first majority to the California assembly in twenty-five years, but it was a slim one of 41–39. Democrat Willie Brown, who had been speaker for fourteen years, was not yet ready to surrender the office. He managed to win over one Republican defector and neutralize one Republican loyalist to hold onto the speakership. Republican Paul Horcher, who supported Brown, had been given a key committee assignment by Brown two years earlier and, as a consequence, had been ostracized by his Republican colleagues. In the 1994 organization of the assembly, he quit the GOP, turned Independent, and voted with the Democrats, leading to a 40-40 tie vote between Brown and the Republican assembly leader, Jim Brulte.

With that, the Republicans started a drive to recall Horcher from office, while Brown tried to figure out how to get a forty-first vote. Republican Richard Mountjoy had been elected to both the senate and the assembly by winning a special election to replace a senator who went to prison while being reelected to the assembly seat he had been contesting. With Brown presiding over the assembly (he presided as the senior member, not as speaker, when the chief clerk who had been presiding called in sick and was unable to return to work for a while), the assembly voted, along party lines, 40-39 to exclude Mountjoy, who himself was not allowed to vote on the motion.

Outraged, the Republicans boycotted assembly sessions, denying Brown a quorum of forty-one. Within a short time, Horcher was recalled by the voters, and Brown, seeing the handwriting on the wall, stepped down from the speakership. In doing so, however, he lined up all thirty-nine Democrats behind another renegade Republican, Doris Allen, who won the speakership 40-39; Brown became minority leader. Ironically, he moved into Jim Brulte's old suite, while Brulte was assigned to the office of the ousted assemblyman, Horcher.

The Republicans then aimed a recall petition at their colleague and new speaker, Doris Allen. She could not withstand the pressure and resigned her speakership after several months—before she was recalled in the November election. On the next-to-last-day of the 1995 session, the assembly elected its third speaker of the year—Republican Brian Setencich. He commanded forty-one votes—all thirty-nine Democrats, in addition to Allen and himself. But when Brown left the assembly in December 1995 to become the mayor of San Francisco, the Republican majority finally elected to the speakership its own choice, and not that of the Democrats. With the help of the state GOP and Gov. Pete Wilson, Curt Pringle in January 1996 became the first real Republican speaker in twenty-five years. He could not serve long in that position, however, because under term limits he had only one more term of eligibility for the assembly. In any case, the Republicans lost control of the assembly in the elections of 1996 and the Democrats regained the speakership in 1997.

Despite the coalitions that form and threaten in the background and the peculiar behavior in California, parties do exert a great deal of control over organizing the legislative chambers. They also influence how members vote, both indirectly and directly. Normally, Democrats and Republicans differ ideologically and philosophically. Although not every Democrat is to the left of every Republican, the party caucuses do occupy different points on the political spectrum. These differences are more apparent in two-party states like Ohio, where during the 1988 legislative sessions most Democrats classified themselves as "moderate," while most Republicans classified themselves as "conservative."[47]

Not every issue on which legislators act, however, is relevant to their ideological or philosophical beliefs. Relatively few are. Therefore, party voting is the exception rather than the rule, occurring on less than 10 percent of the matters that come up for decision. Still, party votes do take place in states like California, Colorado, Connecticut, Illinois, Massachusetts, and New York, and especially on tax and appropriations bills. Differences between Democrats and Republicans are also manifest on welfare, health, and employment and on the overall role of government versus that of the marketplace.

But in many states, party voting has been rare, either because one party overwhelmed the other or because party affiliations meant little to legislators. In some places, party voting is extremely rare. "In my ten years in the House," Tennessee's Bill Purcell said, "there were only two issues that broke down along party lines."[48] Alabama, Arkansas, Louisiana, and Mississippi are also among these states. A recent study demonstrates that among contested votes a higher percentage are partisan in competitive senates—that is, 68.6 percent in Ohio but 38.3 percent in Maryland. Partisan-support scores are 62.1 in Maryland, in the 70s in North Carolina, Delaware, and Virginia, but 93.7 in Ohio.[49]

Although the two parties hang together and oppose one another for certain purposes, nowadays it is more out of a sense of common need than feelings of party loyalty. Legislators as individuals do not conceive of party as having much influence on how they vote on bills. Nor are they inclined to go along with a party position at the risk of losing some support in their districts. In 1988 among Ohio legislators 55 percent disagreed, while 37 percent agreed, with the following statement: "If a bill is important for his or her party's record, a member should vote with the party even if it costs some support in the district." In 1969 the percentages were reversed—53 percent agreed and 26 percent disagreed.[50]

Single-issue, factional politics are also splitting parties internally. When veteran legislators were surveyed about what they perceived to be changes in their job, 52 percent of them said they saw an increase in ideological conflict in the caucus, while only 11 percent reported a decrease.[51] Democratic splits have been more pronounced than those among Republicans. Democrats range in ideology from liberal to conservative, with the latter often an unhappy minority within the party. In Wisconsin, conservative Democrats in the assembly tried to oust their liberal speaker, and in New Mexico conservative Democrats in the house looked for an opportunity to form a coalition with Republicans. The Republican ideological range is narrower, from moderate to conservative. In 1994, moreover, Republican conservatives, united under the banner of Newt Gingrich, were ascendant. Their legislative candidates signed contracts (like Gingrich's "Contract with America") with Ohio, Maryland, and other places. Republican moderates are by no means extinct, but philosophically they took a back seat after the November elections. But even Republican conservatives were being challenged by Republicans of a more rightist orientation.

Democrats were demoralized by the 1994 defeats. One member of the Ohio house described the "humiliating anger" felt among the caucus members because they lost their long-held majority. The response of Wisconsin's

assembly Democrats was not terribly different. They were "divided and resentful, pointing fingers at one another," is how a senior staff member characterized the mood after Republicans won control. Florida Republicans won
the senate, having achieved a tie two years earlier. They had been making
steady gains in the 120-member house—from 46 in 1990 to 49 in 1992 and
to 57 in 1994. Democratic members reacted with fear that the Republicans
would pick up the four seats they needed to achieve a house majority. In
1996, their fears proved to be justified.

The Rise of the Minority Party

Legislative bodies that traditionally pursued a bipartisan approach also began
to change. The Maryland legislature, for example, had never been a partisan
place. Although a partisan pattern eventually developed in the house following some Republican gains, this was not true of the senate. The senate Republicans continued to stress cooperation with the Democrats largely because
of Minority Leader John Cade, a moderate who stressed conciliation, coalition building, and compromise in order to get things done. For him, legislative progress was made by working things out. He believed that if issues cut
along party lines, Democrats in Maryland would have always outvoted Republicans. Under the system of cooperation, Republican members of the
senate got a good proportion of their legislation through, because whether or
not a bill passed depended on the issue and the argument, and not on the
sponsor's party. Cade was interested in governance, problem solving through
legislation, and in achieving policy results. He rejected the idea that the only
way for the minority to pick up seats is by confrontation; he believed that,
instead, Republicans could make gains in the senate even if they cooperated
with the Democrats.[52]

When Ellen Sauerbrey became minority leader, the Republicans in the
Maryland house were the third-weakest minority in the country. House politics were almost totally nonpartisan. But Sauerbrey had a different game plan
from the one employed by her predecessors. She led her party in a more
partisan direction in an effort to increase its membership. "How will Maryland ever become a two-party system," she asked, "if Republicans are content
to sit back and do our little individual things and feel good when we get a bill
passed?"[53] She made a conscious decision to fume, fuss, and toss bombs in
order to throw the Democrats off stride and make them sit up and take notice
of the Republican caucus. She was less concerned with legislative results than
with electoral victory. According to one of her colleagues, she "couldn't get a

bill passed if she bought votes." But she and Robert Kittleman, her successor as minority leader, adopted a confrontational, no-compromise approach and made headway, picking up seats and gaining recognition.[54]

Democratic leaders in Maryland have treated the minority with consideration, trying to bring them into the tent. Senate President Mike Miller was "very good" to Cade, giving him the chair of a major subcommittee of senate finance. House Speaker Cass Taylor appointed Kittleman to a committee of fiscal leaders, and the minority leader serves on the house policy committee by statute. A member of the nonpartisan fiscal staff was also appointed to work with the Republican caucus, and the caucus was given a larger room in which to meet.[55] The speaker also agreed to allow minority-party requests for roll-call votes, enabling Republicans to make their positions distinct from those of the Democrats.

Despite the nonpartisan traditions of the Maryland General Assembly and the willingness of the Democratic leadership to respond to minority concerns, Republicans have been becoming more combative. A more conservative group of senators grew recalcitrant under the leadership of a moderate like Cade, and when Cade passed away in 1996, a strong force for bipartisanship left the scene. Democratic leaders no longer can treat Republicans as individual legislators, but have to take into account minority-party members and think about where they might stand and what they might do.[56]

The Virginia General Assembly used to be known as a bastion of southern civility. No longer. Its 1995 session has been called the "ugliest, meanest, and most partisan" in decades. Traditionally, each session day the legislature would begin with the "Morning Hour," a custom that affords lawmakers a chance to introduce hometown guests and schoolchildren sitting in the gallery. In a recent session, however, nearly every day for six weeks, both Democrats and Republicans took the floor of the house and, invoking personal privilege, delivered angry speeches attacking one another.[57] The sea change in Virginia can be attributed in large part to increasing party competition in the state. The "Virginia way" of bipartisanship began eroding when Republicans started to capture seats in the house and senate. As of early 1995, with elections in November, the GOP needed to pick up three seats in each chamber to gain control for the first time. Thus, almost everything that went on in the legislature itself had a partisan cast and electoral ramifications.

The New Mexico legislature is another place where Republicans have been a small minority and where members of both parties have worked well together. Even though important legislation was carried by the Democrats, Republicans did not feel like a minority. There were only a few party votes, mainly on the budget, and a relatively equal division of capital outlay money to members of both parties. The majority leadership has been fair, but partisanship in New Mexico is on the rise, with the attitude of the house Republican caucus being, "How can we stick them?"[58]

A minority, even if it is well treated by the majority, becomes more organized and more partisan as it gains members. This explains changes in minority behavior in states like Florida, Maryland, and Texas. Ideology also feeds partisanship, in that policy differences between the parties foster conflict more than cooperation. Legislative districting tends to enhance such differences. Where three or four out of five districts are relatively safe, the caucuses of the parties are dominated by the ideologically purer members, making compromise in the legislature tougher to achieve. "Legislative politics," according to an observer of the California scene, "becomes much more expressive—much less instrumental."[59] This trend toward "expressiveness" may bias the system toward what critics call "gridlock." When gridlock sets in, it is usually because fundamental philosophical or policy differences are involved. What has transpired is that the function of the legislature has been shifting toward crystalizing, rather than resolving, divergent partisan views. This trend renders the traditional legislative process of deliberation and negotiation less important, making more important the exploitation of issues for the purpose of partisan gain in election campaigns.[60]

Partisan Struggle

Ideological differences are not trivial, and they have grown more pronounced in recent years. This shift is partly attributable to the conservatizing of the Republican Party. In a number of states, as well as the nation as a whole, conservatives have been replacing moderates in the GOP. The California senate illustrates the change. That body had traditionally evidenced a bipartisan spirit, but the moderate Ken Maddy was recently ousted as minority leader by the much more conservative Rob Hurtt. Similarly, in the assembly, Jim Brulte was succeeded as the Republican leader by Curt Pringle, who carries a more conservative banner.[61]

Add to all this the increasingly negative and nasty election campaigns—at the legislative level as well as at congressional, state, and national levels. Attack ads, whether delivered by the electronic media or by direct mail, are thought to be effective by campaign professionals, and that is why they are used. Studies have shown that people remember the negative better than the positive, so negative messages are usually more powerful campaign tools than positive ones. Challengers see attack ads as their best, or only, chance of upsetting entrenched incumbents; candidates in competitive races cannot permit their opponents to land most of the negative punches, so they, too, go negative.

Legislative leaders and rank-and-file members regret that the negativism of their campaigns feeds public cynicism and befouls the legislative atmosphere. A member of the Florida house observes that this kind of campaigning has escalated "to the point where people from out of state are now in control of the things that we say to and about each other. They are only interested in the notch on the gun. They have absolutely no interest in what is left [in the legislature] when the smoke clears."[62] When Republicans took control of the Florida house in 1997, Democrats challenged the credentials of six GOP legislators while Republicans challenged those of two Democratic legislators.[63] Some legislators, however, do refrain from engaging in the mean-spirited campaigns that have come into vogue. Washington house Republicans, for example, will not allow legislative party funds to be used for negative ads. Speaker Ray Sanchez of New Mexico insists: "I will not cross that line, nor will my campaign people."[64] For Sanchez, the line is drawn in cement; for others it is drawn in sand. But many legislators do not feel inclined to draw it at all; they feel they have to use what works.

The attacks on legislators and legislatures come from incumbents and challengers alike. The challenger will attack the incumbent and the system itself, which he portrays as controlled by the interests and as not responsive to the people. In Minnesota, one observer found that "all sense of collegiality had vanished" from the house.[65] Nowadays, challengers of both parties make an issue of state-funded travel by legislators who attend meetings of legislative associations in different parts of the country. Even veteran legislators blame the system, maintaining that while they are doing the job the voters sent them to do, many of their colleagues are failing in their responsibilities.

Legislators run against their opponents, the other party, and the institutions in which they serve. All of this has the effect of crippling the legislature, undermining public confidence in its legitimacy, and destroying whatever legislative community is left. "Our campaigns not only leave you defeated," commented a legislator in Florida, "they leave you absolutely destroyed where you live."[66] A survey of veteran legislators from across the country found that 65 percent of those responding believed legislators nowadays were more likely to campaign against the legislature.[67]

The campaign pervades the legislative process, even when partisanship can be contained. The legislature, as well as the terrain outside, is the arena for contesting elections. Legislatures have never been sanctuaries from electoral politics, but now they are electoral battlegrounds.

Electoral considerations help shape the way the majority manages the legislative process. It will ensure that new and vulnerable members are given assignments on key standing committees—positions that make it easier for them to raise campaign funds from affected interest groups or to bring the bacon home to their constituents. The majority can also provide targeted members with bills to carry or with items for their district in the appropriations act, giving them accomplishments to tout to their constituents. Although the majority is burdened with the responsibility of governing, the minority can direct virtually all its attention to its electoral objectives—and minority parties with the hope of winning majority status will do just that.[68]

During the stage of enactment on the floor, each party attempts to put the other on the wrong side of a vote on a popular issue.[69] The minority, in particular, will raise issues with electoral fallout in mind. It introduces amendments designed to force a roll call that will embarrass the majority, rather than accomplish a legislative purpose. In the Maryland house, for instance, Republicans forced Democrats to go on record against a tax cut. Then, the Republican state party put out a "hit piece" targeting about twenty Democrats from suburban and rural districts. Later on, Republicans took a partisan position on the Democratic governor's budget, introducing a number of amendments proposing cuts. Virginia Republicans employed similar tactics, using Democratic votes on the budget and downsizing government in the 1995 elections, trying to capture control of both houses of a legislature in which they had been steadily gaining. They ultimately managed to win a tie in the senate. The minority Democrats in the 1995 Ohio house succeeded in offering nine amendments to the budget, including one that would have taken workers' compensation out of the general state budget and earmarked it as a special fund. Although all but a single Democrat supported the earmarking, most Republicans stood with their governor and legislative party voting against it. Thus, the next Democratic campaign could portray the Republicans as "against workers' compensation" and as "not caring about common folks."[70]

The majority party uses all its power to avoid being put on the downside of an issue. It knows its marginal members feel they cannot afford to cast even one very unpopular vote. A vote for a tax increase can be used against them for years in the future, and a thirty-second advertisement on television can help unseat them at any time. One defense of the majority is to refuse to recognize the minority for amendments that may be mischievous. Kansas

Republicans, angry after the 1988 campaigns produced Democratic gains, pushed through a rules change that made it almost impossible for the minority to force a roll-call vote on amendments, thus saving themselves the substantial embarrassment that could accompany recording a position on a controversial issue.[71]

In a legislative body up for grabs, members do not want to have to cast tough votes if they can help it. And their leaders do whatever they can to take their people off the hook. It is possible to cushion the shock by enabling members to vote *for* rather than against something through the use of substitute amendments. This may only be "slight comfort," according to a legislative leader in Florida, "but it prevents a head-on vote against a popular issue." The neediest members are allowed to vote against the party. New York's legislative leaders see how many votes they can spare and then excuse as many members as possible. Who is let off depends on their margin of victory in recent elections, the political landscape of their districts, their fund-raising capacity, their poll numbers, and the presumed strength of their opponents.[72]

Partisan Staff

Over the years the legislative parties in many states have hired staff to support their cause. Partisan staffing, which was relatively unknown thirty years ago, is now the mainstay of legislatures in the large, two-party states. Illinois, Pennsylvania, Michigan, and New Jersey are among the nation's leaders in this respect. Growth has been marked. Connecticut exemplifies one way in which partisan staff can mushroom. Until the early 1970s, the Connecticut general assembly had little professional staffing. Then, its nonpartisan central staff—research, fiscal, bill drafting, and program review—became firmly established.

Somewhat later, the party caucuses added a few of their own professionals. But after the Republicans took control of the legislature in 1984 and the Democrats regained their majorities in 1986, the staffing pattern in Connecticut changed dramatically. In 1987, one hundred partisan staff positions were added to the fewer than three dozen already in existence. These jobs were divided up among the four legislative parties for allocation to their members. In the early 1980s, Connecticut's small caucus staffs were oriented mainly toward legislation. Now the orientation of larger caucus staffs is toward constituencies and campaigns.

In California, the politicization of staff has spread beyond the caucuses and to standing committees. Earlier a distinction could be made between political and policy staff. The former worked for individual members, caucuses, and leaders. The latter were the committee consultants and on the staffs of the legislative analyst and legislative counsel. Over the years the balance has shifted from policy to political staffing.[73] In the words of a longtime observer of the California scene, "The policy experts have been replaced by political hired guns whose main job is to get their bosses elected."[74]

The campaign activities of legislative staff have sometimes gone too far and have been challenged in several states. In 1987 the Manhattan district attorney brought an indictment for grand larceny and conspiracy against the New York senate minority leader and one of his colleagues. The charge was that public funds were being used for campaigns, with eight Democratic candidates, of whom six were challengers, receiving the services of workers on the senate minority's payroll. The minority leader was acquitted, but only after a period of painful publicity.

A few years later, New Jersey endured its own staff-campaigning scandal. Called into question were the incidental campaign activities of partisan staff on legislative time and the use of public resources, such as office computers and telephones, for campaign purposes. Perhaps the most dramatic case of illegal staff involvement in political campaigns occurred in Washington in 1992. After a lengthy investigation there, the state Public Disclosure Commission found that the four party caucuses had used state equipment, time, and personnel to plan and run campaigns. The caucuses admitted responsibility, agreed to desist from such practices, and paid fines for having violated the law. But public resentment ran high and the legislature was badly scarred as a result.

Officially, partisan staff will not get involved in campaigns (unless individual staff members take leaves of absence). Unofficially, one of their jobs is to advance the electoral fortunes of their masters. As one New Jersey staffer described their electoral connection: "We don't do anything *on* a campaign, but everything we do is *for* the campaign." Whatever their direct involvement in campaigns, partisan staff members approach issues in a partisan way, emphasize partisan differences, and seize on opportunities to score partisan points.

THE EFFECTS OF COMPETITIVE POLITICS

Certainly as far as the legislative candidates and legislative parties are concerned, elections today are more competitive than before. Individual incumbents cannot afford to take their reelection for granted, except in scattered cases. The parties, as collectivities, are competitive in more states and more legislative chambers than in the past thirty years. This competition has been an important democratizing force.

Legislators are more responsive to their districts, to important voting blocs, and to the few mandates that may exist. Nowadays they keep a close eye on the next election, which always seems to be approaching. Thanks to term limits, the legislature has more lame ducks than before; yet, overall, legislators are demonstrating a greater propensity to respond to the needs, requests, and mandates of their districts.

The legislative parties' stakes in having their members win are as high as the stakes of the legislators themselves. In order to govern—to exercise power and advance policy—they have to maintain or win control of the senate or of the house. The parties have adjusted to these incentives, becoming campaign organizations as well as governing blocs. An increasing amount of what they do is influenced by the forthcoming election. They, too, are responsive to the voters, constantly calculating on which issues they might win net votes and on which they might lose them. They struggle to position themselves advantageously vis-à-vis their competitors.

Competitive politics is no longer strictly confined to campaigns outside the legislature, if they ever were. Partisanship and partisan jockeying have become integral to some aspects of the legislative process (and several salient issues), but by no means on all. The negative nature of many campaigns has had repercussions within legislative halls. The transformation of legislative parties and legislative leaders into campaign organizations and campaign managers has had further repercussions. Bipartisanship is more difficult to achieve where each party is trying to score points off the other. Nonpartisan motivations are neither credited nor trusted. Collegiality across party lines is more difficult when those in the other camp are striving to capture your prerogatives as a member of the majority or even to defeat you. Sometimes civility, as well as collegiality, suffers.

Although legislative leaders may appear to have acquired more power as a consequence of their campaign-manager roles, in fact, their positions are less secure than earlier. Their members expect them now to raise funds diligently, distribute them strategically, and win elections continuously. Despite the heightened partisanship in legislative bodies, leaders cannot always rely on their own caucuses for support. The instances of bipartisan coalitions in the selection of leaders have been increasing.

The effects of competitive politics have promoted democracy in the legislative institution and the legislative process. Members are more responsive to their constituencies, parties are more attuned to voters' decisions at elections, and legislative leaders are more dependent on the satisfaction of their members. The center of gravity no longer resides in the legislature itself, but has moved outside, to the state and districts and among the interest groups.

NOTES

1. Portions of this chapter draw on Alan Rosenthal "The Legislature: Unraveling of Institutional Fabric," in *The State of the States*, 3d ed., ed. Carl E. Van Horn (Washington, D.C.: CQ Press, 1996), 108–142.

2. Joel A. Thompson and Gary F. Moncrief, "The Evolution of the State Legislature: Institutional Change and Legislative Careers," in *Changing Patterns in State Legislative Careers*, ed. Gary F. Moncrief and Joel A. Thompson (Ann Arbor: University of Michigan Press, 1992), 203.

3. William R. Bryant Jr., *Quantum Politics: Greening State Legislatures for the New Millennium* (Kalamazoo: New Issues Press, Western Michigan University, 1993), 126.

4. Karl T. Kurtz, ed., "The Old Statehouse, She Ain't What She Used to Be," National Conference of State Legislatures, July 26, 1993. Photocopy.

5. John F. Bibby and Thomas M. Holbrook, "Partisan Elections," in *Politics in the American System: A Comparative Analysis*, 6th ed., ed. Virginia Gray and Herbert Jacob (Washington, D.C.: CQ Press, 1996), 115.

6. Malcolm E. Jewell, "State Legislative Elections: What We Know and Don't Know," *American Politics Quarterly* 22 (October 1994): 488.

7. Harvey J. Tucker and Ronald E. Weber, "Electoral Change in the U.S. States: System Versus Constituency Competition," in *Changing Patterns in State Legislative Careers*, ed. Gary F. Moncrief and Joel A. Thompson (Ann Arbor: University of Michigan Press, 1992), 75–86.

8. Anthony King, *Running Scared* (New York: Free Press, 1997), 51. See also Thomas E. Mann, *Unsafe at Any Margin: Interpreting Congressional Elections* (Washington, D.C.: American Enterprise Institute, 1978)

9. Bibby and Holbrook, "Partisan Elections," 106–107.

10. Interview with the author, June 7, 1995.

11. Bibby and Holbrook, "Partisan Elections," 99–102.

12. David Broder, "California Quietly Alters the U.S. Political System," *Newark Star-Ledger*, April 3, 1996.

13. Samuel C. Patterson, "Legislative Politics in the States," in *Politics in the American States*, 6th ed., ed. Virginia Gray and Herbert Jacob (Washington, D.C.: CQ Press, 1996), 172.

14. Steve Scott, "Changing of the Right Guard," *California Journal*, October 1995, 10.

15. Richard A. Clucas, *The Speaker's Electoral Connection: Willie Brown and the California Assembly* (Berkeley: Institute of Governmental Studies Press, University of California, 1995), 98–100, 102–103.

16. Interview with the author, February 23, 1995.

17. Ibid., February 22, 1995.

18. Ibid., June 7, 1995.

19. Jeffrey M. Stonecash, "Campaign Finance in New York Senate Elections," *Legislative Studies Quarterly* 15 (May 1990): 254.

20. Chao-Chi Shan and Jeffrey M. Stonecash, "Legislative Research and Electoral Margins: New York State Senate, 1950–1990," *Legislative Studies Quarterly* 19 (February 1994): 79–93.

21. Rob Gurwitt, "Legislatures: The Faces of Change," *Governing,* February 1993, 32.

22. Anthony Gierzynski, "Elections to State Legislatures," in *Encyclopedia of the American Legislative System,* ed. Joel Silbey (New York: Scribner's, 1994), 435–449.

23. Collins Center for Public Policy, "The Nature of Representation: An Overview" (discussion by members of the Florida house, Tallahassee, November 6, 1995), 1: 16–17. Transcript. See also Tom Loftus, *The Art of Legislative Politics* (Washington, D.C.: CQ Press, 1994), 27.

24. Keith E. Hamm and Robert E. Hogan, "Explaining Differences in State Legislative Spending Patterns" (paper prepared for delivery at the annual meeting of the Western Political Science Association, San Francisco, March 14–16, 1996), 3.

25. Robert E. Hogan, "Campaigning for the State Legislature: Factors Influencing Strategy and Use of Techniques" (paper prepared for delivery at the annual meeting of the American Political Science Association, San Francisco, August 28–September 1, 1996), 20–21.

26. California Common Cause, April 1995.

27. Corey Cook, *Campaign Finance Reform* (Sacramento: California Research Bureau, California State Library, 1994), 25; Gary F. Moncrief, "The Rise in State Legislative Campaign Costs" (paper prepared for delivery at the annual meeting of the Western Political Science Association, San Francisco, March 14–16, 1996).

28. Gary F. Moncrief, Joel A. Thompson, and Karl T. Kurtz, "The Old Statehouse, It Ain't What It Used to Be," *Legislative Studies Quarterly* 21 (February 1996): 64.

29. California Common Cause.

30. *State Net Capitols Report,* October 6, 1995.

31. Malcolm E. Jewell and Marcia Lynn Whicker, *Legislative Leadership in the American States* (Ann Arbor: University of Michigan Press, 1994), 107. A recent estimate is that legislative leadership or party PACs exist in as many as forty-one states. Cindy Simon Rosenthal, "New Party or Campaign Bank Account?" *Legislative Studies Quarterly* 20 (May 1995): 249–268.

32. Anthony Gierzynski, *Legislative Party Campaign Committees in the American States* (Lexington: University Press of Kentucky, 1992).

33. Daniel M. Shea, *Transforming Democracy* (Albany: State University of New York Press, 1995), 19–20.

34. Loftus, *Art of Legislative Politics*, 37.

35. Interviews with the author, February 22 and 23, 1995.

36. Gierzynski, *Legislative Party Campaign Committees in the American States*, 71–92; Jewell and Whicker, *Legislative Leadership*, 112.

37. Interview with the author, February 22, 1995.

38. Samuel K. Gove and James D. Nowlan, *Illinois Politics and Government: The Expanding Metropolitan Frontier* (Lincoln: University of Nebraska Press, 1996), 94.

39. Clucas, *Speaker's Electoral Connection*, 6.

40. Quoted in Loftus, *Art of Legislative Politics*, 37–38.

41. Gierzynski, *Legislative Party Campaign Committees*, 115.

42. Clucas, *Speaker's Electoral Connection*, 76–82.

43. Alan Rosenthal, *Drawing the Line: Legislative Ethics in the States* (Lincoln: University of Nebraska Press, 1996), 171–177.

44. Shea, *Transforming Democracy*, 143–144.

45. Alan Rosenthal, "Where Do You Sit?" *State Legislatures*, March 1984, 22–24.

46. This account is based on William Schneider, "Old Politics Hangs On in California," *National Journal*, December 17, 1994, 3004; Steve Scott, "Willie Brown's Magic Act," *California Journal*, January 1995, 8–11; and items in *State Net Capitols Report*.

47. Samuel C. Patterson, "Legislative Politics in Ohio," in *Ohio Politics*, ed. Alexander P. Lamis (Kent, Ohio: Kent State University Press, 1994), 241–242. See also Gove and Nowlan, *Illinois Politics and Government*, 100.

48. Charles Mahtesian, "The Sick Legislature Syndrome," *Governing*, February 1997, 20.

49. Thomas H. Little, "Electoral Competition and Legislative Minority Parties: Schlesinger's Parties in a Legislative Setting," *American Review of Politics* 16 (fall–winter 1995): 311–312.

50. Patterson, "Legislative Politics in Ohio," 249–250; also Keith E. Hamm, Ronald D. Hedlund, and R. Bruce Anderson, "Political Parties in State Legislatures," in *Encyclopedia of the American Legislative System*, ed. Joel H. Silbey (New York: Scribner's, 1994), 947–981.

51. Gary F. Moncrief, Joel A. Thompson, and Karl T. Kurtz, "The Old Statehouse Ain't What It Used to Be: Veteran State Legislators' Perceptions of Institutional Change" (paper prepared for delivery at the annual meeting of the American Political Science Association, Washington, D.C., September 2–5, 1993).

52. Interview with the author, June 6, 1995.

53. Quoted in Sharon Randall, "Out of Power: Struggling for Influence," *State Legislatures,* February 1990, 22.

54. Interview with the author, June 6, 1995.

55. Ibid., June 7, 1995.

56. Ibid., June 5, 1995.

57. *Washington Post,* February 27, 1995.

58. Interviews with the author, May 15 and 17, 1995.

59. Ken DeBow, "Decline of the California Legislature: Why New Faces Won't Help" (paper prepared for delivery at the annual meeting of the Western Political Science Association, San Francisco, March 14–16, 1996).

60. Royce Hanson, *Tribune of the People* (Minneapolis: University of Minnesota Press, 1989), 65, 96.

61. Scott, "Changing of the Right Guard," 9–10.

62. Collins Center, "Nature of Representation," 1:100–101.

63. Mahtesian, "Sick Legislature Syndrome," 18.

64. Interview with the author, May 16, 1995.

65. Mahtesian, "Sick Legislature Syndrome," 16.

66. Collins Center, "Nature of Representation," 1:100.

67. Kurtz, "Old Statehouse," 3.

68. Little, "Electoral Competition," 301, 305–308.

69. The following paragraphs are based on Rosenthal, "Legislature," 121–126.

70. Interview with the author, February 23, 1995.

71. Burdett A. Loomis, *Time, Politics, and Policies: A Legislative Year* (Lawrence: University Press of Kansas, 1994), 54–55.

72. Kevin Sack, "The Great Incumbency Machine," *New York Times Magazine,* September 27, 1992, 54.

73. DeBow, "Decline of the California Legislature."

74. Sherry Bebitch Jeffe, "For Legislative Staff, Policy Takes a Back Seat to Politics," *California Journal,* January 1987, 42.

CHAPTER 6

The Dispersion of Interest Group Influence

Interest groups have been on the American political scene for some time now. In the Federalist Papers James Madison recognized the dangers of such groups—or "factions," as he called them—and the founding fathers designed a republic that they hoped would hold factions in check. A half-century later, on his travels through the country, Alexis de Tocqueville noted how disposed Americans were to organize into interest groups. If anything, the group phenomenon, notable in the early nineteenth century, has been gaining in strength since then. Currently, interest groups are fundamental units, and their lobbyists key actors, in the national and state political systems. They are vilified but also accepted as part of America's pluralistic political landscape.

The First Amendment to the U.S. Constitution guarantees the people the right "to petition the government for redress of grievances." On that clause hangs the critical role of interest groups in capitals of the fifty states. The right to petition enables groups (and individuals) to appeal to government for their share of resources that government controls by means of its powers to tax, spend, and regulate. When petitioning government is guaranteed, the presence of lobbyists is assured.

The inevitable presence of lobbyists raises the question of their role and influence in the legislative process. In this chapter we shall explore the interest-group environment in which legislatures are situated, and the strategies, tactics, and effects of lobbying—attending to the location and exercise of their influence in the legislative system and on legislative outputs.

THE GROUP STRUGGLE

State legislatures are besieged by groups and lobbyists, all of whom want something that government can grant or deny them.[1] These petitioners have

200

an ideology or point of view that they are trying to have enshrined in policy, as is the case with pro-choice and pro-life (or pro-abortion and anti-abortion) forces, gun enthusiasts and gun regulators, the get-tough-on criminals contingent and the civil libertarians, and scores of other single-issue groups. Alternatively, these petitioners have an economic stake, as is the case with businesses, professions, occupations, and other groupings in our society.

Interest groups participate in practically all the issues that come before a legislature. Taxes, education, transportation, criminal justice, health, economic development, welfare, and job training are domains about which state government makes major public policy decisions and in which many groups and coalitions have a concern. More emotional and morally loaded issues (such as abortion, gun control, sex education, pornography, and the death penalty) arouse different constellations of groups.

Although the issues mentioned above constitute the major agenda items of governors and legislatures, somewhere between one-third to one-half the bills addressed by a legislature can be considered rather minor, at least from an overall public-policy perspective.[2] These bills on the "special interest" agendas have only indirect relevance to statewide policy, but they are of considerable import to one group or another or, more likely, to several of them. They primarily affect the pocketbooks of business, professional, or occupational groups, which are seeking either a benefit from government or an advantage over their competitors, or are trying not to be taken advantage of by government or by their competitors in the private sector.

A public utility, such as gas and electricity, is affected by almost anything state government does. It is a big taxpayer, so a change in tax policy can be critical. Environmental legislation has important ramifications for its operations and its balance sheet. Currently, the electric power industry is being deregulated, having been a monopoly protected from competition and guaranteed rates that yielded profits. The legislative impact on the industry will be enormous. The agenda for large companies of every type is expanding. In the early 1980s, for example, Unilever had only two state issues on its agenda. By 1994 it had seventeen, each of which was in play in fifteen to twenty states.[3]

A primary objective for some groups is the state budget. "The real action is in the budget," remarked a California lobbyist for a nonprofit association. Pro-choice groups lobby to make funds available to family-planning clinics. State universities and colleges want to expand or, at least, maintain their share of the budgetary pie. The pharmaceutical industry works to ensure that sufficient funds are set aside for Medicaid, particularly to pay for the drugs that the industry markets. Teacher organizations concentrate on the state budget as the main way to promote the interests of the schools and their members.

Another objective, especially for business groups, is to avoid paying more in taxes or fees. A Florida legislator, addressed a gathering of state government relations representatives of large companies and associations with the admonition, "When the state needs money, you are all at risk." Although raising income and sales taxes is not in political vogue in the 1990s, the so-called sin taxes on alcohol and tobacco continue to be viable. The affected industries have to be wary in defending their purses. Just as groups seek to avoid tax burdens, they also look for tax benefits. It may be a tax break for art collectors, or a tax credit for solar-electricity producers, or one for the families with children attending college.

Businesses and professional groups, on their parts, engage in an ongoing contest to pull even with or gain ground on their competitors or to maintain the edge they have. The legislature has to decide between competing private interests, taking into account the merits of opposing arguments, questions of equity, the public interest, and the play of politics. In recent years, tort reform, product liability, and workers' compensation have provoked the biggest running battles in the states, with the trial lawyers and consumer advocates on one side, and business, the insurance industry, and doctors on the other.

Many issues split industries. One significant local battle was between Steve Wynn and Donald Trump, who were competing for casino business in Atlantic City. Wynn had persuaded the New Jersey senate to pass a bill that would have given him a tax break for cleaning up a landfill where he was going to build a huge casino. Trump, with four casinos, felt threatened by Wynn's entry into the market and waged battle in the legislature. He lost, however. The commercial fishing industry in Massachusetts was split when lobstermen wanted to ban the sale of trawled lobsters and fishing-vessel owners wanted no limits whatsoever—each side reflecting their group's economic interests.

Car rental companies waged a classic contest, with Hertz and Avis versus Alamo and some of the smaller firms. Known to the lobbying profession as "Car Wars," the dispute centered on the collision damage waiver (CDW), a contract provision in which the rent-a-car company for a fee waives its right to recover damages against the renter in case of an accident. A source of profit to Alamo, which rented mainly to individuals rather than self-insured companies, the CDW was assailed by Hertz and Avis as not in the renter's interest. It was also, parenthetically, not in their own interest.

Another classic contest matches optometrists against ophthalmologists in what has come to be known as "Eye Wars." The first shots were fired about twenty years ago when optometrists, who were limited to eye examinations and prescriptions for glasses, sought permission to use drugs for diagnostic purposes. Since then, optometrists have won legal authority to do this in almost every state, despite the opposition of the ophthalmologists. In thirty-four states, at the present time, optometrists can use drugs for diagnosing eye diseases like glaucoma. In trying to become the primary health care provider for eye problems, optometrists have been seeking laws allowing them to perform laser surgery to correct nearsightedness. Millions of dollars in fees are at stake, and ophthalmologists are fighting such proposals on the grounds that the procedure is invasive surgery, and as such should not be performed by individuals who have no medical training. Optometrists have already won in Idaho and are lobbying for it in Alaska, Colorado, New Jersey, California, and Virginia.[4]

A similar struggle finds chiropractors on one side and physicians' groups, insurance companies, and business associations on the other. Chiropractors in New York succeeded in getting the legislature to pass a bill requiring health insurance companies to pay for unlimited chiropractic services, despite the intensive campaign against it. The chiropractors argued that the care they provided was cheaper and just as successful as that provided by orthopedists and other doctors. Opponents argued that reimbursing chiropractors would raise the cost of health insurance and induce more people to seek treatment from a fringe medical specialty.[5]

Competition between interests is also illustrated by the contest between G-Tech and Automated Wagering, two computer firms going after Florida's electronic gaming contract. Automated Wagering has had the contract since the state lottery began in 1987, grossing about $40 million a year from the business. G-Tech made a run at the contract not only with its bid but also in seeking legislation that would take away its competitor's incumbency advantage by moving the administration of the contract from the lottery department to the department of management services. In its campaign, G-Tech charged that Automated Wagering had grown too friendly with the lottery department and asked that another department be given jurisdiction.[6]

Despite these battles, many bills introduced in a legislature are uncontested. Some of them, which are advocated by interests, stimulate no opposition. These measures are likely to concentrate benefits but distribute costs. They may help one interest, but they impose no visible costs on others or are simply too minor to matter.[7] If no one objects, the legislature's tendency is to go along and satisfy the group and its lobbyist. Occasionally, but only occasionally, something with significant public policy implications sneaks through or catches the opposition completely off guard.

The system is a highly competitive one, with conflict among groups the norm. The incidence of conflictual issues seems to have increased since the 1960s and 1970s, as legislatures have professionalized and taken on more responsibilities and as more groups have mobilized to fight for their interests. Contemporary lobbyists handle relatively few uncontested issues, so they can seldom take things for granted. Rather, they have to make as strong a case as possible, practically all the time. It is up to the legislature, then, to judge the merits—both substantive and political—of the contenders, and to bring the sides together in fashioning an acceptable compromise. Balancing interests, while taking into account other and broader values, is no easy task. Yet it defines much of what the legislature and the legislative process are about.

THE BASES OF GROUP POWER

A few years ago Clive Thomas and Ronald Hrebenar concluded in their study of interest groups that the number of organizations active in the fifty state capitals had substantially increased and the diversity or types of groups that attempt to affect public policy had similarly expanded. In the 1960s and 1970s fewer groups, representing a much narrower range of interests, were active at the state level.[8] Another study found that the number of interest groups per state on average had increased from 342 in 1980 to 617 in 1990, almost doubling.[9] Growth apparently continued into the 1990s, as suggested by the 35.7 percent increase of interest groups in California during the period from 1989 to 1995.[10]

What happened at the state level is not unusual; the same expansion has been taking place at the federal level, substantially changing the interest-group environment in Washington, D.C. Jonathan Rauch refers to the system—with its proliferation and professionalization of interest groups and lobbies and the explosion of advocacy—as "hyperpluralism."[11] Hyperpluralism has ranged widely across the states. Take Texas, for example. Group power in the Lone Star state used to be shared by cotton growers and cattle raisers, who were later joined by oil producers. Now the influence structure is far less monolithic and includes doctors, trial lawyers, realtors, teachers, truckers, chemicals, and labor.[12] Maine's interest groups developed in similar fashion, from the 1960s when three interests—power, timber, and the manufacturing of textiles and shoes—dominated until today, when many more groups have acquired substantial influence. The pluralistic direction of group development is also illustrated by Kentucky, which once was dominated by coal, horse racing, liquor, and agriculture. No longer are they the only major players; others have joined the lineup.

The rise of groups in Washington, D.C., is also reflected in the states. Most notable in the broadening of interests, conclude Thomas and Hrebenar, are the public employees and teachers, local governments, and public-interest and citizens' groups. Overlapping the citizens-group category are the single-issue groups, such as advocates on both sides of the abortion issue, the religious right and the agnostic left, and others that have acquired significant clout on those matters that concern them. These groups normally have no commercial, material, or governmental interests—rather, they are philosophically and ideologically grounded, appealing to moral principle rather than self-interest or pragmatism.

Because of the many groups and players competing in the legislative game, the power of most groups vis-à-vis each other has diminished. As additional groups join the political process, the configuration of group power changes further. Thus, with the emergence of public-employee, education, environmental, women's, single-issue, and public-interest groups, business, labor, and agriculture no longer have the legislative arena to themselves.[13]

Still, certain groups are reputed to have more influence than others. In Pennsylvania, the top five groups are business and industry, labor, trial lawyers, insurance, and education.[14] In North Carolina, the most influential are business, lawyers, local governments, banking, state employees, and teachers.[15] Maine's top groups are labor, utilities, paper companies, environmentalists, and teachers.[16] In Ohio the groups with most influence are business, banking and finance, labor, insurance, medicine, realtors, and education.[17] Nevada's most powerful groups are reputed to be the gaming industry and the teachers.[18]

Teachers make virtually every list of the most powerful groups. The fifty-state study of interest groups, by Thomas and Hrebenar and their colleagues, produced a ranking of the most influential interest groups in the early 1990s (see table 6.1). Teacher organizations were considered more effective than any other group, ranking as "most effective" in forty-three states and as "moderately effective" in five others.[19] The teachers in New Jersey are typical. The New Jersey Education Association (NJEA) has developed markedly over recent years: its grassroots activity has increased; its PAC has become larger; and its campaign activities have become more effective.

Although the association has grown stronger internally, its overall influence has probably declined. That is because the NJEA now operates in a more pluralistic environment. State revenues have also not kept pace with state expenditures, so education has had to struggle for its share of the state budget. It is difficult nowadays for the NJEA to achieve a number of its goals, but it maintains impressive veto power. Although it cannot get everything it wants,

TABLE 6.1

Ranking of the Twenty-Five Most Influential Interests in the Fifty States in the Early 1990s

		Ranking in states		
Rank	Interest group	Most effective (no. of states)	Moderately effective (no. of states)	Less effective (no. of states)
1	Schoolteachers' organizations (predominantly NEA)	43	5	2
2	General business organizations (chambers of commerce and the like)	37	16	1
3	Utility companies and associations (electric, gas, water, telephone, cable TV)	23	24	7
4	Lawyers (predominantly trial lawyers and state bar associations)	26	14	14
5	Traditional labor associations (predominantly the AFL-CIO)	22	13	15
6	Physicians and state medical associations	22	12	16
7	Insurance: general and medical (companies and associations)	21	15	16
8	Manufacturers (companies and associations)	20	15	21
9	Health care organizations (mainly hospital associations)	15	24	14
10	Bankers' associations (includes savings and loan associations)	21	11	18
11	General local government organizations (municipal leagues, county organizations, and so forth)	16	21	15
12	State and local government employees (other than teachers)	18	14	21
13	General farm organizations (mainly state farm bureaus)	14	20	17
14	Individual banks and financial institutions	14	8	28

Rank	Interest group	Ranking in states		
		Most effective (no. of states)	Moderately effective (no. of states)	Less effective (no. of states)
15	Environmentalists	9	16	26
16	Universities and colleges (institutions and personnel)	7	16	28
17	Realtors' associations	8	12	30
18	Individual cities and towns	8	12	32
19	Gaming interests (racetracks, casinos, lotteries)	7	11	33
20	Contractors, builders, developers	7	10	34
21	Liquor, wine, and beer interests	7	10	35
	K–12 education interests (other than teachers)	7	10	35
22	Retailers (companies and trade associations)	6	11	34
23	Senior citizens	1	19	30
24	Mining companies and associations	6	7	38
25	Truckers and private transport interests (excluding railroads)	5	8	37

Source: Clive S. Thomas and Ronald J. Hrebehar, "Interest Groups in the States," in *Politics in the American States,* 6th ed., ed. Virginia Gray and Herbert Jacob (Washington, D.C.: CQ Press, 1996), 149–150.

the NJEA can stop what it does not want. Like the New Jersey association, teacher organizations elsewhere may now exercise less influence than in past years, but they cannot be dismissed.

Group Characteristics and Resources

The proliferation of groups is one reason for the greater dispersion of group power. Another is that the bases of group strength are also more dispersed. Different groups have different resources, and each of them can be converted into influence in the legislature.

Money is popularly considered to be the major resource at an interest group's disposal. It pays for organization, buys skilled lobbyists, underwrites political campaigns, and subsidizes a style of socializing that appeals to legislators. There is no question that wealthier groups have an advantage over poorer ones. Yet the influence of money goes only so far. Richer groups do not always prevail; other factors come into play on major issues. But the less important the issue and/or the less central the action, the more of an edge monetary resources have. In other words, if there is a difference in wealth between two sides, if other factors are about the same, and if the issue is peripheral or marginal, then the better-endowed group will have the upper hand.

Political, organizational, and managerial skill, along with the quality of representation, count over the longer run, if not on each and every issue. An example of an organization extremely well endowed to express its interests is the Associated Industries of Florida (AIF), which is headquartered in Tallahassee and represents business in the state. It has twelve lobbyists—four on the association's payroll and eight outside consultants. Its corporate members also have another one hundred lobbyists promoting their individual agendas. Beyond lobbyists themselves, the AIF has a computer communication system that reports on legislation; a fax network, which permits the AIF to communicate quickly with thousands of members; video and audio production services; departments that furnish the organization with interactive telephone, satellite communications, and publications. Money, of course, funds operations such as the AIF.

Size and geographical distribution probably count more than any other group-related factor. The larger the group's membership, and the more legislative districts in which its members live or do business, the more influential that group is likely to be. That is because the group can affect the outcome of elections through the political activity of its members. As mentioned earlier, legislators feel unsafe at almost any margin and do not want to alienate an interest that is organized in their district. Size alone is not sufficient, or public employees would be less threatened by downsizing and layoffs than they are. The problem is that a large proportion of public employees reside in just a few legislative districts, usually in the capital city and its environs. Most legislators can write off public employees as far as their own reelections are concerned, while only a few are beholden to them for votes.

In contrast, teachers have both size and geography in their favor and therefore constitute a potent electoral force. Wisconsin's Tom Loftus writes that "teachers are influential in legislative races because they come already apportioned for political power." Every legislator's district has at least one school; and where there is a school there are teachers. Loftus notes that in Wisconsin the electoral influence of teachers tends to be greatest in rural and suburban areas, where they are best organized and where marginal seats are more likely to be. This gives teachers additional clout statewide.[20]

A group's *image* or *standing* also has to be factored into the equation. Individual companies in a state have a corporate identity, as well as an impact on the economy. A state government relations professional for a large pharmaceutical company expressed the view of many of those who lobby for large corporations. He noted that his company "has an outstanding record in the quality of its products, in the way it treats its employees, and in its contribution to the community in a social-investment way." All of this, in his opinion, is of far greater import than the company's lobbying per se.[21]

Image, especially as conveyed by the media, has been a major resource of a number of environmental and public-interest groups. Although these groups seldom occupy the top ranks of influential interests, they cannot be discounted. Groups like the Sierra Club, the Audubon Society, Common Cause, and the PIRGs (public interest research groups) are not generally perceived as advocating special interests. And this perception helps them promote their agendas. Other groups fare less well. Oil is suspect, and a rise in the price of gasoline—during a long period during which gasoline prices have risen hardly at all—occasions public outcry and governmental investigation. In the states the image people have is of Big Oil. Yet, outside of a few states where it has a local refining base, oil is not a major force. An oil lobbyist from one state commented, "Breaking even is a victory; if we don't lose ground, it's a win." Anyone can pick a fight with oil because it is such an easy target, and oil backs off, figuring it cannot win.[22]

The image of Big Tobacco is that of the evil empire. Arrayed against the "Merchants of Death" are the American Heart Association, American Lung Association, American Cancer Society, American Medical Association, victims, and taxpayers. Since 1964, when the first surgeon general's report warned of health dangers from smoking and especially since 1982 when "secondhand smoking" was labeled a risk, the antismoking movement has been making steady progress. Tobacco has won some victories, but its overall posture has been defensive and its movement has been in reverse, although it is one of the biggest contributors to legislative campaigns. To add to the rough handling the industry is receiving in the legislatures, twenty-three state attorneys general filed lawsuits against the companies, advancing a new legal theory that because the states incur Medicaid expenses for smoking-related illnesses, they should be reimbursed by the industry responsible.[23] The attorneys general and negotiators for the industry reached a settlement, which at the time of this writing is awaiting congressional action.

The *cohesiveness of a group's membership* is also critical. Business probably suffers as much from lack of cohesion as any other group. Associations, such as the Louisiana Association of Business and Industry or New Jersey Business and Industry Association, rarely speak with a single voice. The Colorado Association of Commerce and Industry (CACI) is influential. But it is often divided: large banks compete with small banks and savings and loan associations differ with banks over banking and lending policy.[24] The horse racing industry of Kentucky might seem monolithic; yet it too is deeply divided among the major horse breeders, owners, and trainers and the smaller horse owners and trainers.[25]

Other groups stand in sharp contrast. Teachers are united on most issues, and they are adept at developing cohesion within their organizations when they have to do so. In those situations where there are irreconcilable membership divisions, the associations will not engage on an issue. Narrow occupational groups manage to maintain cohesion, even with members who diverge in their interests. Take the Wisconsin Chiropractic Association, for example. It has one overriding issue—a statutory provision that would require insurance providers to cover chiropractic services on a basis comparable to the one covering physician and hospital fees. Despite opposition by doctors and hospitals, after years the single-minded effort of the chiropractors paid off.[26]

Groups that can form *coalitions with other groups* are better off than those that go it alone. Nowadays organizations seldom act in isolation from like-minded groups. The greater and more broad-based the support, the more inclined legislators are to see the wisdom of a particular policy direction. The creation of a large coalition, according to one observer, "provides the comfort level necessary to make it easier for politicians to endorse your group's goal."[27] Coalitions, however, are by no means easily maintained. The interests of member groups can easily diverge, just as the interests of a group's own members diverge. Yet manufacturing companies manage on occasional issues to recruit environmental and consumer groups. Business and labor can also cooperate to create a formidable political force.

A group whose members are *dedicated to the cause* has a lot going for it. Sportsmen and National Rifle Association members are resolute in their positions. In contrast, antigun groups are less fervent or inspired. An example of a group that is particularly hard-hitting is the police. The activity of the police association in New York is reported by the *New York Times* (February 6, 1996): "When the Assembly voted on a bill recently that would strengthen the hand of New York City police officers in contract disputes, a group of burly men sat stiffly in the back of the chamber, taking down the names of the wayward.

They said little, but everyone knew who they were: the leaders of the Patrolmen's Benevolent Association, a union that often seems to work the State Capitol like a legislative battering ram." The bill passed the assembly by a vote of 141-1, having already passed the senate by an overwhelming margin. The union represents 29,000 police officers, contributes tens of thousands of dollars to election campaigns, and intimidates legislators who fear that opposition might lead to accusations that they are hostile to the police.

Not only dedication, but also a *willingness to compromise* can be an asset. Settling for less than a whole loaf need not necessarily conflict with a group's goal or its tough stance. Legislators are ordinarily disposed to look more favorably on groups that are willing to split the difference than on those that insist on going to the mat. They do not want to get caught in the middle of a bloody battle and have to choose sides. That is why legislators try to avoid confronting certain issues and the uncompromising groups promoting them. Abortion typifies the kind of issue that all legislators, except for those who are solidly in one camp or the other, prefer to avoid.

The *nature of the opposition* has much to do with whether a group can achieve its legislative goals. The stronger the opposition, the more difficult it is for a group to win. Many groups face tough opposition. Business has to face the environmentalists; nurses have to beat back doctors; and casinos and race-tracks battle over gambling spoils. In contrast, state societies of public accountants have little opposition. Few legislators or scholars would consider them to be at all powerful, but they do well legislatively, nonetheless. Nearly every legislator can support them on most issues. It helps to have little opposition and also to possess a group agenda that arouses little controversy.

A *narrow agenda* works in a group's favor. As a rule, groups that can exercise influence over a broad range of policies are considered more powerful than groups that are influential in only one policy area.[28] Group power, however, can also refer to the ability of a group to achieve its goals, even if they are limited in scope. Legislators try, whenever possible, to look favorably on limited demands, particularly ones that cost nothing and arouse no one.

The *nature of the issue* makes a difference. Some issues appear to legislators to have more merit than others. Environmental issues, such as pollution abatement, natural resources management, and coastal protection, have appeal. The needs of people with developmental disabilities, represented by an organization called Arc, with chapters in forty-six states, are difficult for legislators to resist. In New Jersey, for example, Arc has been concerned with tight state budgets, particularly funds for the operation of community residences. The organization adopted a strategy of getting a bond referendum passed in 1994, and successfully appealed to the legislature to have the issue put on the ballot.[29]

Whether a group is on the *offense or defense* counts. A defensive strategy, trying to defeat or water down legislation, is easier to accomplish. Given a competitive situation, it is harder to push a bill through the legislative process than to stop one. To move forward, a bill requires a majority at a number of steps along the way, from committee to caucus to floor in one house and then through the other.[30]

Timing cannot be overlooked as a factor related to a group's influence. If on the one hand the economy is in recession and the state budget is tight, groups laying claim to funds for their causes will be hard-pressed. If, on the other, the economy is developing healthily, chances are better that claimants will be able to share a piece of an expanding pie.

The *composition of the legislature* weighs heavily in the group struggle. Some groups are more apt to prosper when Democrats are in control, other groups fare better with Republican majorities. In many states the trial lawyers are almost an extension of the Democratic party, while business is closer to Republicans. When the Democrats controlled New Jersey's legislative and executive branches, environmental groups made gains in regulating business. When the Republicans took control of the legislature in 1992, and then the governorship in 1994, the balance shifted, with business highly successful in achieving its agenda of deregulation. Since then (and through 1995) thirty-two probusiness measures have been signed into law. In the 1995 session alone, a dozen probusiness laws were enacted, including tort reform, tax incentives, and the easing of regulations. Colorado's Republican legislature, despite a Democratic governor, has blocked proposals adverse to business, kept taxes down, and prevented government's role from being more than minimal.[31]

Republicans are less sympathetic to unions than Democrats, teachers unions included. The Republican legislative majorities in Illinois, Michigan, Indiana, Pennsylvania, Wisconsin, and other states have advanced proposals designed to limit tenure, reduce bargaining power, promote school choice, and curtail the ability of teachers to strike. When Republicans took over the Illinois legislature, they joined with Gov. Jim Edgar to outlaw a strike for eighteen months, eliminate the right to bargain over issues such as class size, and give principals broader authority to dismiss teachers.[32]

Not only does party control matter to various constellations of interests, but the personnel composition of the legislature matters as well. Education interests look to teachers serving in the legislature for a sympathetic ear; attorneys look to lawyer legislators; and African Americans to black legislators. Other groups, too, ordinarily have an edge with legislators who share memberships with them. A group with special ties to legislative leaders, to those who chair the committees with jurisdiction over their concerns, or to other influential legislators will be a step ahead in the process.

Interest Representation and the Public

These very varied bases of power suggest that almost any group has resources with which to exercise influence in the legislature. Group resources, of course, are not equal; but they are not as unequal as is popularly portrayed. Still, where is the public interest amidst these contending special interests? Nearly every group will make the argument that its case promotes the public interest or, at the very least, does it no harm. These arguments are obviously self-serving, but not without some justification.

Given the multiplicity of groups, almost every member of the public is represented directly or indirectly on selected issues by one or another of them. It is estimated that seven out of ten Americans are members of at least one association, and one out of four Americans belongs to four or more associations.[33] Today everyone is part of what in academic parlance are called "intermediary institutions," ranging from the Girl Scouts to General Motors. Nearly all these institutions have a lobbyist; many make political contributions; and a number have phone banks at their disposal.[34] California lobbyist Dennis Carpenter described the contemporary state of affairs: "The media call us special interests, but there isn't a person in the state who isn't represented by some lobbyist in Sacramento."[35] Some years ago a Texas senator expressed the same idea in more graphic terms. "They call me a tool of the special interests," he said. "Damned right, I'm a tool of the special interests. Every son of a bitch in my district has some special interest or another." More recently a Florida legislator explained: "To me, there's no such thing as a special interest." In her view, "Everything is a special interest, until it's yours. Then it's a vitally important issue."[36]

Legislators are responsive to special interests not only because of their clout but also because through their organization, citizen needs and desires get communicated to the legislature. The problem is not that legislatures defy the principle of democratic responsiveness; quite the contrary. Legislatures are extraordinarily responsive to demands made of them by citizens, but often by citizens acting through a multiplicity of interest groups. Responsiveness and indulgence is surely the path of expediency. As Wisconsin's Loftus explains it, giving in to a powerful interest group with a narrow agenda is almost a natural instinct of legislators. It is not worth the pain to fight, to risk one's political career. After all, how much harm can be done by going along?[37]

Interest-group systems, as they operate in the state capitals, are criticized on several grounds. One criticism is that the proliferation and strength of special interests have led legislators to lose sight of a more general interest, that is the public interest. This is not the case, however. On the big issues of the day, the notion of "the public interest" plays a part in the decisions legislators make. Legislators, for the most part, believe there is a public interest. They pay more than lip service to it, and they sometimes pay a political price for trying to promote what they think the public interest is.

Another criticism is that the interest-group system offers some citizens greater access to the arena of decision making. This is true. Although no one is completely shut out, some are advantaged. Yet participants disagree about which specific groups come out ahead. A survey of Kansas legislators asked whether some groups were underrepresented or overrepresented in the legislative process. Three-quarters of the legislators responded that, yes, some groups were underrepresented. Half of them named the "average citizen" and one out of five mentioned the poor. Three-fifths of the legislators said that, yes, some groups were overrepresented; but they did not agree on which specific groups. Hence, the researchers concluded that legislators shared "no general perception that any particular groups are disproportionately influential."[38]

It is believed that interests with money have disproportionate influence. Although this is true, this is partly because those groups normally have more at stake and engage fully in the legislative process. Furthermore, they have some of the best lobbyists, with ample resources at their disposal, advocating their case. In many cases, it is likely that even if they did not have money, they would be influential for other reasons.

Yet not every well-endowed group is successful. Tobacco has been on the defense for more than a decade, and it has steadily lost ground in the states. For example, during the 1992 election cycle, the tobacco industry contributed $240,000 to Illinois legislators. The very next year, a major increase in the cigarette tax, backed by the governor and legislative leaders, was enacted.[38] In Florida, under its tobacco liability law, the state filed a $1.4 billion lawsuit against cigarette manufacturers seeking to recoup the costs of treating Medicaid patients with smoking-related ailments. In the 1996 session the tobacco industry, employing dozens of the top lobbyists in Tallahassee, made a huge effort to repeal the liability law. It failed. One can infer that more important than the lobbyists at work were the views of citizens. A 1996 survey by the Pew Center for the People and the Press indicated that only 20 percent of the

American public has a favorable opinion of tobacco companies, while 75 percent do not. "That makes them," in the words of the center director, Andrew Kohut, "a pretty big target for politicians."[39]

THE ROLE OF LOBBYING

Just about every interest group is represented by one or more lobbyists. At the high end, 3,500 interest groups are registered in Illinois, 2,100 in Florida, 1,800 in California, and 1,200 in Minnesota. At the low end, 200 groups are registered in Hawaii, 250 in Iowa, 290 in Maine, and 325 in Mississippi.[40] These figures give only an approximation of the number of interest groups that lobby. The comparisons from state to state must be treated cautiously because the number of groups registered depends on how state law defines a lobbyist and a lobbyist's principal (or client).

In states where the definition is very narrow and does not include part-time volunteers, fewer individuals have to register. In places where any person having relatively few contacts with legislators is legally defined as a lobbyist, the registration lists tend to swell. At the high end, the numbers of lobbyists are 3,500 in Illinois, 2,000 in Florida, Missouri, New York, and Ohio, 1,600 in Virginia, and 1,300 in Michigan and Minnesota. At the low end, the numbers are 265 in Alaska, 275 in Maine, 350 in Nebraska, and 360 in South Carolina.[41] Just as the number of groups employing lobbyists has increased, so has the number of lobbyists employed by groups. In California, for example, from 1989 to 1995, registered interest groups rose by 35.7 percent, while registered lobbyists rose by 31.6 percent and lobbying firms rose by 28.9 percent. Most recently, the growth of lobbying appears to have slowed. Of 264 companies surveyed on their public affairs offices and practices, the number of full-time professionals engaged in government relations increased in 25 percent, decreased in 20 percent, and stayed the same in the rest.[42]

Of the hundreds of people signed up to lobby, relatively few are featured players in the processes of lawmaking. Out of about six hundred lobbyists registered in New Jersey, only sixty to seventy spend a good deal of time in Trenton, and fewer still are involved in either a small number of important issues or a large number of trivial issues.

Lobbyists have as their job trying to advance or protect the interests of their clients. They represent legitimate ideological, social, and economic concerns and attempt to persuade legislators of the substantive and political merits of their cases. They accomplish this through a variety of techniques: drafting bills and amendments; planning strategies and tactics; providing information to legislators and testifying before committees; building coalitions; coordinating grassroots and media campaigns; providing campaign contributions and campaign assistance; and participating in negotiations leading to compromise and settlement. Few groups with anything at stake can afford to be without a lobbyist at the capital. If they lack professional representation, they run the risk of a higher tax bite than otherwise or of a competitor getting an advantage over them.[43]

When legislators are asked about the business of lobbying, they overwhelmingly acknowledge the essential role of lobbyists in providing them with the information they need in lawmaking. The fact is that no one can be expected to make the case better than lobbyists. They can explain why a group needs legislation; how it serves the state's broader interests; what it will cost; its likely utility; who favors the measure and who opposes it; where other legislators and executive-branch officials stand; the opposition's position and strategy; and the political effects of the legislator's support or opposition. A lobbyist will usually communicate both the upside and the downside for the legislator. Lobbyists on the other side of the issue will present a counter case. On the basis of lobbyist information, as well as other factors, legislators make their decisions.

Although legislators may be critical of the methods employed by some lobbyists and the influence of campaign contributions, hardly any feel that they themselves are corrupted by lobbyists. They may point a finger at a colleague or colleagues (most often ones from the opposite party), but they do not see themselves as victims or tools of the system. This does not prevent them from running against lobbyists during their campaigns and then turning to them for information, assistance, and understanding when they reassemble in the capital.

One safeguard that currently prevents legislators and lobbyists from becoming too chummy is the disdain in which they are jointly held by the media and the public. The popular image of the lobbyist is still that of wheeler-dealer Artie Samish, who operated in California during the 1930s and 1940s, representing the liquor, cigarette, railroad, racetrack, banking, and chemical industries. Samish was a newspaper cartoonist's dream, with his straw hat, large cigar, big paunch, and loud tie. He was memorialized by an article in a 1949 issue of *Collier's* magazine titled "THE SECRET BOSS OF CALIFORNIA." On the cover was a color photo of Samish posed with a ventriloquist's dummy, "Mr. Legislature," on his lap. Samish had a good run until 1953, when he was convicted of tax evasion.[44]

The contemporary belief as demonstrated by information derived from public opinion polls and focus groups, is that lobbyists have their way with legislators, always at the public's expense. Focus groups that we conducted in California, Minnesota, and New Jersey revealed that people felt that lobbyists wine and dine legislators to excess and have access that is denied ordinary citizens. It is unfair, according to a focus-group participant from New Jersey, that while people cannot get their views heard, the lobbyists are "down there in Trenton talking to the right people, knowing how to get to the right channel."[45] A poll by the *Hartford Courant* found that 40 percent of the citizens of Connecticut said that the state would "be better off in all respects if there were no lobbyists."[46]

It is not surprising that the attitudes of citizens toward lobbyists and state legislatures parallel their attitudes toward lobbyists and Congress. People believe the "Washington system" is evil incarnate, and runs on greed and special privilege. It seduces members of Congress and allows them to be corrupted by special interests and lobbyists. Legislators and lobbyists form a "deadly mix" in the public mind, contributing greatly to American dissatisfaction with elected public officials.[47]

The press is relentless in its condemnation of the lobbying system. Every so often one or another of a state's dailies is likely to wage a crusade against lobbyists and lobbying. Not atypical is the following invective from the *Pensacola Journal:* "The Florida Legislature is a wide-open play land for lobbyists armed with unlimited expense accounts. And so many of their playmates—who in their spare time make this state's laws—have become so openly greedy that it's not clear that they even recognize greed anymore" (July 1, 1990). The implication of many of the editorials and analyses that appear in the press is that lobbyists are trying to buy legislators' votes with campaign contributions, gifts, entertainment, and other blandishments.[48]

THE WEAKENING OF RELATIONSHIPS

Traditionally, lobbying has been an "inside game" of relationships. Without credibility and trust in the dealings among individuals, the process of lobbying would not work. The development of relationships is the way in which lobbyists develop their credibility and trustworthiness in the eyes of legislators. Only if legislators have confidence in the veracity of the messenger will they give the message itself a full hearing, and perhaps also—other things being relatively equal—the benefit of doubt. A good relationship does not result in acquiescence, but it does predispose a legislator in the lobbyist's direction. If, through a relationship, a lobbyist proves to be a credible, reliable, loyal, empathetic, generous, and likable person, the path of direct lobbying will have been made smoother.

The optimal way for a lobbyist to earn the trust of lawmakers is by working with them on legislation. It takes more than an issue or two; it takes a while. Some relationships predate the interaction between legislator and lobbyist in the legislative process. A friendship may go way back. Or the lobbyist and legislator may have served in the legislature together. In a few states lobbyists have come from the ranks of legislative staff. About one out of five of the principal lobbyists in Sacramento were on the senate, assembly, or central staff. Several of the contract lobbyists in Trenton also came the same route. A few Florida committee staff directors or leadership aides followed their legislator bosses who opened up lobbying shops near the capitol. All of them brought to their new craft convictions from their old craft. An example of a staffer-turned-lobbyist is John Stierhoff of Maryland, a top aide to the senate president who left that position at the end of 1994 and joined a law firm. Stierhoff explains that legislators will take his call mainly because they trust him to provide credible, straightforward, accurate information. They trust his information because they trust him. "Look, I'm not going to kid you, my twelve years of working with Mike [Mike Miller, the senate president] and my years of working with the General Assembly . . . count for something, no doubt about it."[49]

The most trustworthy relationships are those forged between members themselves. So when a legislator leaves office and hangs out a lobbyist shingle, chances are that good relationships will already be in place. There is no better way to demonstrate credibility than to have been with legislators in the legislative trenches. If members trusted an individual when he or she was in office, they will continue to trust that individual as a lobbyist.

After defeat or retirement a number of legislators become lobbyists. This happens for several reasons. They have neglected their outside jobs or professions, particularly if they were full-time legislators and have little to go back to. Outside of legislating and politicking, they have little experience and their prospects in other fields on the outside are not bright. Lobbying, however, is a field in which they can use their skills and draw on their experience as legislators. They need not depart from the capitol scene and the legislative process, which they undoubtedly enjoy. And they can make a good living from lobbying, the kind of living that they deferred while serving.

Just about everywhere, a few or even a number of legislators turn to careers in lobbying. Don Tucker, Ralph Haben, Lee Moffet, and James Harold Thompson, all speakers of the Florida house, became lobbyists, as did Sam Bell and Herb Morgan, former chairmen of the house appropriations committee. In Maryland about ten legislators entered the lobbying ranks in 1995, including Melvin Steinberg, former president of the senate (and lieutenant governor), Clay Mitchell, the speaker, and Lawrence Levitan, chairman of the senate budget and taxation committee. Levitan acknowledges that his earlier service in the legislature gave him a step up, but it is because of *how* he served, not only *that* he served. "Over the years, I've been pretty fair and up-front with my colleagues, and that comes back to help you," he says.[50]

The phenomenon of legislators becoming lobbyists is not viewed favorably by the media or by reform groups. They charge that legislators use their current positions to set up future jobs. That is to say, they can throw what influence they presently have to certain interests in return for a future commission or retainer when they become lobbyists. It is also charged that these legislators have an unfair advantage as lobbyists because of the relationships they bring to the job. Largely because of the insistence of the media and the appearance conveyed to the public, a number of states have enacted revolving-door provisions to keep legislators from lobbying for one or two years after leaving office. This makes the adjustment for some legislators from public to private life more painful than otherwise. By requiring a cooling-off period, it also militates against reliance on relationships. The message of such regulations is that relationships between legislators and lobbyists are suspect.

To develop and maintain relationships, lobbyists used to rely on entertaining legislators and socializing with them. The lobbyist's objective was to spend quality time with a legislator so they could establish or strengthen their relationship. The lobbyist would thus pick up the tab for a dinner, a basketball game, or a trip during which lobbyist and legislator could get to know one another better. Socializing, and particularly socializing in pleasant surroundings, fosters a sense of familiarity, commonality, trust, all of which frequently leads to friendships.

The old days of lobbyist-provided entertainment are not completely gone, at least not everywhere. One can still read about the excursion taken by Georgia legislators, where they played golf, smoked cigars, watched baseball, drank whiskey, and conversed with strippers.[51] But in all but a few places, this style of lobbying is virtually nonexistent. In chapter 3, we described how capital cultures had changed and how both legislators and lobbyists are a different breed today. Many of the newer lobbyists entertain little, except for an occasional reception at which members of one or another group can get together with legislators. Both the big parties and intimate dinners and, of course, the hunting, fishing, and related pleasure trips are pretty much a relic of the past. Maryland's Alan Riffkind, for example, in the 1995 session spent about $3,000 entertaining legislators—a very small proportion of his total fees of almost $450,000.[52]

Add to the natural inclinations of legislators and lobbyists the new reality of ethics law. In the past few years, some thirty states have tightened restrictions on legislator-lobbyist interaction. Today's laws prohibit or limit the amounts lobbyists can bestow on legislators in gifts and meals and require the public disclosure of who is taking how much in what form. These limitations have taken their toll on the pleasures of legislative life and, more important, on legislator-lobbyist relationships. The stings and ethics laws in California, South Carolina, and Kentucky have created a gulf between lobbyists and law-makers. "The two are now waltzing at arm's length in these states instead of dancing cheek-to-cheek," writes one observer.[54] In Massachusetts, where a lobbyist and legislators have crossed the line, the state ethics commission is now on the alert for illicit perks. Both lobbyists and legislators are now thinking twice about being seen with one another.[55] In still other states, where limits have been imposed and disclosure is required, legislators are fearful of taking any gift lest it be misinterpreted by the media and by constituents. In Kentucky, for instance, many lobbyists and their clients adopted an informal no-cup-of-coffee rule for themselves, just to have some breathing room.[56] According to a former speaker of the Oregon house, who is now a lobbyist, the new ethics laws "are really putting a lot of honest people at risk of doing something criminal because they may have made an honest mistake."[57] To avert this, legislators take nothing at all rather than chance failing to disclose or disclosing improperly. The benefit is not worth the risk.

Without lobbyists picking up the tab, socializing declines. Although this is likely to weed out relationships based on the ability of one party to foot the bill for the other, it also reduces the total time legislators and lobbyists spend with one another. Trust now has to be developed on the job and over time. But there may not be as much time as there has been in the past, certainly not in the states that now are term limited.

Legislators who can serve no longer than six, eight, or even twelve years in their office view relationships differently from their predecessors who could achieve veteran status. They do not have time for apprenticeship or learning; they insist on hitting the ground running. Given the pressures on term-limited legislators, relationships have little bearing on how they do their jobs. Lobbyists are concerned about having to redevelop relationships with each new class of members in those states that have enacted term limits. A number in Sacramento are reportedly retiring because of the change in the relationships game.[58] In the opinion of Bill Lockyer, California's senate president pro tem, lobbying is "essentially about credibility and relationships," with relationships conferring credibility over time.[59] If time is curtailed, credibility suffers and lobbyists have to rely on other strategies and techniques in laying the groundwork for their specific case.

THE ASSAULT ON CAMPAIGN CONTRIBUTIONS

For some time now, campaign contributions have been a prominent means by which lobbyists worked to establish a connection to legislators, and, for twenty years political action committees have been a principal device for political giving. A Maryland lobbyist, emphasizing the significance of reelection for legislators, remarked that "relationship lobbying is a dinosaur" because it produces neither contributions nor votes.[60] But for the press and the public, money is the root of evil (perhaps not *all* evil, but nonetheless a goodly amount), so campaign contributions by lobbyists, their clients, and PACs are under continuous fire.

The Purposes of Contributions

Money given by interest groups, the so-called special-interest money, is assumed to be contributed to candidates with the idea of getting something in return. Much of the money that supports the campaign system comes from special interests—interests that range widely and include labor unions, large corporations and small businesses, professional and occupational associations, and many others. A large part of this money is channeled through PACs. In California and Washington, in fact, these committees are responsible for over half the total contributions.[61]

In Massachusetts, for example, the *Boston Globe* (May 23, 1993) analyzed more than forty thousand contributions made from 1991 to 1992. The newspaper found that three-fourths of the $8.8 million total was donated by thirty interest groups, with lobbyists and PACs accounting for nearly 30 percent of donations over $50. The *Globe* pointed out that Francis G. Mara, the chairman of the house insurance committee, received more than half his money from PACs and 97.1 percent from special interests. His total war chest, however, was only $34,500.

The prevailing belief is that for every campaign contribution there is a quid pro quo, an agreement by the legislator to do something in return for the donor. Although the explicit agreement is rare and would legally constitute a bribe, special interests do not give for nothing. The Josephson Institute, in surveying California legislators and legislative staff, found that 92 percent of the respondents thought that contributors expected special advantages. There is no question that interest groups and lobbyists give for strategic reasons and not simply out of the goodness of their hearts. Their objective is to promote group interests, and campaign contributions are intended, in one way or another, to accomplish that objective.

One of the purposes is to elect and reelect friends—incumbents and candidates who see eye to eye with the group on its issues. In such situations, money follows votes rather than votes following money. Take, for instance, the campaign activities of Florida Business United (FBU), an affiliate of Associated Industries of Florida. In 1994 the FBU distributed a fourteen-page candidate questionnaire covering thirty-nine issues such as health care, minimum wage, attorney fees, tort liability, tax policy, environmental policy, and so forth. The FBU decided whom to support on the basis of the incumbents' key-vote record, the candidates' views on the issues, and personal interviews with 237 individuals conducted by the FBU's political operations department. It contributed to 16 candidates in the 40-member senate, all of whom won, and to 47 candidates in the 120-member house, of whom 37 won. Were candidates catering to business in order to get contributions, or was business contributing to candidates who shared their views? The answer is yes in some cases to the former, and yes in many cases to the latter.

Another purpose of a campaign contribution is to spur friendly legislators to greater activity on a group's behalf, inducing them to take a leadership role. A contribution may also help to predispose the open-minded to a group's position. Seldom intended to convert opponents, a contribution may nevertheless soften them up so that their opposition is less intense and vocal.

Groups usually pursue a conservative strategy, contributing primarily to incumbents. Given incumbency reelection rates, these are the people most likely to be around to advance or derail a group's agenda. A minimal-risk strategy suggests that groups seeking to make friends or keep from making enemies had best invest in incumbents' campaigns. That is why PACs favor incumbents, contributing one-third to half of incumbents' war chests but only about one-fifth or less to the funding of challengers, with a larger proportion going to candidates in races for open seats.[63] When New York's senate majority leader, Ralph Marino, was asked during a 1989 hearing why

PACs gave so heavily to incumbents, he responded: "Because the incumbents generally win 99 percent of the time, and why give to a loser? . . . Why not be friendly with the winner?"[64]

What Money Buys

Reformers allege that even if money does not actually buy votes, it buys access. It gives the contributor the chance not only to speak with a legislator, but to be listened to as well. That is the least that contributors get. Those who do not give or, worse, give to one's opponent are also entitled to a hearing, but static may make the communication somewhat less audible.

Bill Lockyer of California is remarkably candid in describing how difficult it is for legislators to overlook how money distinguishes friends from enemies: "In a campaign contest what happens is, especially the first time you run, there are indelible impressions left of who supported you and who opposed you. It sometimes takes years to be able to sever that sense of connectedness, responsibility, obligation, whatever you might call it."

Probably the most indelible impressions are made by those who opposed the legislator. Lockyer remembers the largest contributor against him in his first race was the realtors. "It took a while for me to look at a bill sponsored by the realtors fairly," he recalls. "I'd try, but I'd have this little feeling that these were my enemies."[65] It should be mentioned that with limited terms in California and elsewhere, legislators will have less time to outgrow initial feelings about their funding friends and their nonfunding enemies.

A campaign contribution, by offering support to a legislator in his or her time of need, creates an "attitudinal tendency," in the words of a former Ohio legislator, on the part of a receiver toward a donor: "I'll support you unless I can find or be given a strong reason not to."[66] Rep. Leslie Johnson of Arizona describes how she came to feel a sense of obligation: "I had a lobbyist host a fund-raiser. After that I realized I felt differently about him. I regarded him as a friend. That made me uncomfortable."[67] The sense of obligation that develops with respect to campaigns contributions operates at either a conscious or less than fully conscious level.

It operates in the interstices of the process or at the margins. Under most circumstances, a sense of obligation does not sway votes, but it probably earns from legislators the willingness to consider a case or even some slight change in their behavior. They will try to help out a contributor if they can, but not at the cost of conscience, constituency, or other values the legislator prizes.

Campaign contributions are given not only to foster good will but also to avert bad. Legislators expect business lobbyists and their clients to give. They count on economic interests to support the electoral system; otherwise, where would campaign funds come from? Thus, lobbyists and groups feel pressure to contribute as generously as possible. They may not know what giving buys, but they are reluctant to find out what *not* giving costs. Moreover, if their competitors are contributing to campaign coffers, they feel they had better contribute as well. Why be at a competitive disadvantage? The money donated for fear that certain interests must "pay to play"—or ante up in order to have a seat at the table—is known as "self-preservation" money. Usually, it goes to both parties, with special allotments for legislative leaders and those who chair committees with jurisdiction over a group's affairs.

On their parts, legislators cannot help but take cognizance of their bene-factors. The more senior and better-positioned legislators are, the more independent they can afford to be. They do not have to worry about any individual contributor; there are others to take that one's place. But legislators with less tenure and less clout are apt to be in a more precarious financial situation, and cannot help but be concerned. They may not be able to readily replace a contribution. Mindful of the positions of big donors, they will try not to make them angry and certainly not angry enough to fund an opponent.

Money is not without some influence. But its influence is less than commonly portrayed by the press. Raising money furnishes an occasion—perhaps the main one in more and more states—for lobbyists and legislators to get together. In California, for instance, the $500–$1,000 fund-raiser has become the most common way for lobbyists to meet legislators, although little social-izing can take place at such events. Money also functions as a resource that creates a sense of obligation and feelings of uncertainty on the parts of legis-lators and interest groups. And money matters on issues of lesser import or narrower concern or on legislator behaviors that are peripheral rather than central to the process.

Neither lobbyists nor legislators are entirely comfortable with the issue of campaign finance. The former get the feeling that they are constantly being shaken down while the latter think that begging for bucks puts them at ethi-cal and political risk. A Maryland legislator, Leon Billings, stated the problem from the perspective of the public official: "All of us in politics tend to want to look the other way when it comes to money. None of us likes the implica-tion of obligations, the potential of a relationship between how we vote and where the money comes from."[68] Yet both parties to campaign finance ar-rangements have little choice. Campaigns have to be funded and, therefore, those who can afford it must give and those who need it must take.

Regulating Campaign Finance

Almost everyone pays deference to campaign-finance reform, at least reform of some sort. The status quo has few defenders. Reformers advocate removing the pernicious effects of money in politics and leveling the playing field. Most of them would agree with one academic who sums up: "It is a commonplace of political analysis that the United States does not have effective political equality because of the operation of PACs, the campaign finance system, and the role of organized interests."[69] Common Cause and other public interest groups champion changes in the campaign finance system. The media condemn the status quo, whatever it is, and beat an editorial drum for change. The public wants to see private money eliminated from campaigns but is ambivalent about whether it wants to see public money in its place.

In the legislature a few members lead the charge for reform. Republican and Democratic members are willing to go along, but only if their parties' interests are safeguarded. The minority is more inclined than the majority to back change. Under continued pressure, legislatures tinker with the system and adopt so-called reforms, rarely with a sense that they will bring substantial improvement. They simply want to move on to other matters.

Where the voters have the initiative, limits tend to be more restrictive. Sometimes the electorate itself enacts a dramatic change, such as the extraordinarily low contribution limits in Missouri, which were later declared unconstitutional in the courts. Sometimes, under threat of an initiative, legislatures are forced to adopt something, and what they adopt is usually less draconian than what is being proposed for the ballot. Ohio's legislature moved when Ohioans for Campaign Reform had almost enough signatures collected, and the Massachusetts legislature acted when Common Cause had gathered enough signatures to put campaign finance reform on the ballot.

For at least twenty years, campaign finance systems have been under assault and practically everywhere the flow of money from contributor to candidate has been regulated and restricted. The most ambitious reform schemes have involved public financing, which is designed to limit expenditures, help individuals who want to challenge incumbents, and reduce the reliance of legislators on special interests for funding. Until an initiative brought public financing to Maine in 1996, only four states had enacted public financing for legislative elections. Of the four, only Minnesota and Wisconsin have provided anywhere near realistic financial support for the enterprise. The Minnesota system has succeeded in reducing the amount of special interest money in campaigns, while the Wisconsin system has not. Candidates in Minnesota may not accept more than $500 from any source except a political party unit, which can give $5,000. No more than 20 percent of a candidate's total of somewhat more than $20,000 for house candidates and twice that much for senate candidates can come from PACs, lobbyists, and "big givers" (defined as those who give a total of over $250 in a year to that candidate). To qualify for public subsidies, all candidates have to do is demonstrate that they have raised at least a total of $1,500 from thirty or more people. That is not difficult to do, in particular because the state refunds up to $50 that an individual contributes, or up to $100 for a couple. In 1993 changes were made in the law to allow challengers to spend 10 percent more than incumbents or people seeking legislative office from another elected job.[70]

Lobbyists in Minnesota have more money to give than there are candidates who can take it, since expenditures are capped, large gifts are restricted, and direct and indirect public funds accounted (in 1994) for 59 percent of total campaign spending. Special interests, however, have been able to direct their money to legislative party caucuses, which are not limited as to the amounts or percentages from PACs, lobbyists, or big givers. The caucuses, in turn, contribute to candidates in targeted races.[71] Whereas in Minnesota 95 percent of candidates participate in the public financing system, in Wisconsin only half the incumbents and two-thirds of challengers do. This is because Wisconsin's expenditure limits have been kept so low that many candidates decline to participate. Here, the general tendency is for candidates in competitive races to pass up public funding because of the unrealistic spending limits that go with it. An incumbent, who feels safe and does not need to spend a lot, can afford to accept public funding. A challenger in a relatively hopeless race cannot raise much outside of public financing.[72] The parties take public monies to fund "nuisance" challengers to harass incumbents. Overall, however, analysis in Wisconsin shows that the availability of public money has not encouraged many challengers to emerge. Meanwhile, private funds are channeled into independent expenditures by groups that used to contribute generously to candidate campaigns, but now find themselves capped. Independent expenditures have grown from $225,000 in 1987–1988 to more than $1 million in 1993–1994.[73]

The number of states with limits on contributions from individuals, corporations, and PACs has been growing and the size of the limits coming down. In effect, in thirty-four states, contribution limits are the most popular means employed to curb the flow of money to candidates. In some states the limits are quite low—$100 in Montana, $250 in South Dakota, $500 for a senate race and $250 for a house race in Connecticut, and $500 in Florida. In ten states, aggregate limits also exist. In Georgia, individuals can give a total of only $2,000 to non-statewide candidates, in Arizona only $2,560 per calendar year, in Maryland $10,000 in a four-year cycle, in Massachusetts $12,500 per year, and in New York as much as $150,000 per year.[74]

Campaign finance reformers are constantly striving to reduce contribution limits further. Take New Jersey, for example, where limits of $1,500 for individuals and $5,000 for PACs were enacted in 1993. Even before the announcement that more than $10.7 million had been spent on the assembly elections of 1995, several groups—New Jersey Public Interest Research Group, Hands Across New Jersey, New Jersey Common Cause, United We Stand America, and the League of Women Voters—had coalesced and called for capping all donations at $250 (as well as setting an expenditure limitation of $100,000 per candidate in legislative races). The $250 cap would apply to both individual donors and PACs.[75]

As of 1996, however, stringent contribution limits were being challenged by the courts. In *Carver v. Nixon* (1995), which struck down $100 limits for the house in Missouri, the Eighth U.S. Circuit Court of Appeals said the state had failed to show that the previously higher contributions were corrupting enough to justify restricting the constitutional rights of donors.

Although individual contributions are acknowledged to be legitimate as long as they are not too high, reformers believe PAC contributions to be corrupting. Many of the critics of the status quo want to abolish PACs or place severe limits on what they can donate to candidates. Where PAC contributions are severely restricted, special-interest money still manages to flow into the system, albeit by different routes. In Arizona, for example, the PAC run by U.S. West Corp. gave its maximum contributions, which accounted for only half the money it had raised. It used the other half in independent campaigns it mounted in a number of key races.[76] Wisconsin law limits PACs to $500 for assembly candidates, with each candidate able to take only a total of about $8,000 from all PACs. Yet the money still gets through by means of independent expenditures and bundling, a method of collection whereby individuals with similar interests are solicited and represented through the same channel. The irony is that when states clamp down too hard on candidates' fund-raising, the money flows elsewhere—to independent expenditures or to "issue ad" campaigns by groups that claim to be promoting causes, not candidates. These campaigns tend to be more aggressive and negative than candidate-sponsored ads.[77]

Minnesota legislators have also been limited in what they can take from PACs. Only 20 percent of their total funds can come from lobbyists, PACs, and contributions of over $50. The result here is that more monies have been flowing into independent expenditures in Minnesota. In *Day v. Holahan,* however, the Eighth U.S. Circuit Court of Appeals concluded that Minnesota went too far in prohibiting PACs from giving more than $100. That low a limit, according to the court, significantly impaired the free-speech rights of contributors.

Legislatures have also begun to prohibit lobbyists themselves from making contributions to campaigns. As of 1994, twelve states had banned lobbyist giving. In Massachusetts lobbyists are limited to $200. All of this makes it more difficult for candidates to raise funds, but easier for lobbyists who now have an excuse for not providing them. In most places lobbyists can still advise their clients on contributions, but in Maryland they are not permitted to directly solicit clients for campaign contributions.[78] In California Common Cause asked all lawmakers to sign a pledge promising that they would not ask lobbyists for contributions from the lobbyist's employer. Instead of using lobbyists as collectors, they would have to go directly to the clients.[79]

After twenty years of campaign finance reform, there has been considerable change. Efforts to limit campaign contributions from the special interests have generally achieved their objectives. As a recent study reports, most interest groups—and even those in highly regulated states—have shown little interest in getting around the limits. (Indeed, many like caps on contribution, because it gives them an excuse for saying no.) But a few groups in each state find loopholes and manage to get around the limits. A few channel their funds into independent expenditures, although this process makes sense only to the small number of aggressive groups that are by nature oriented toward stirring up the pot. Thus, the rise in IEs, or independent expenditures, can be seen in states like Washington and Wisconsin. A few groups resort to "issue" advocacy, which, unlike IEs, does not even have to be reported. Others engage in bundling or make soft-money contributions. Some set up separate committees or conduits and still others prod their members into giving as individuals.[80] In Wisconsin, for example, in recent years interest groups have been spending substantial amounts directly. The money is used for attack ads against candidates whom the groups oppose. But since the advertisements do not specifically urge voters to cast their ballots for or against a candidate, the advertisements are claimed to be educational and not political.

Where there is imagination or legal counsel, there are always ways of contributing to legislative campaigns. The money continues to be raised and spent. As a staff member of Washington's Public Disclosure Commission said: "Money is like water. It will find its way no matter."[81] Whether it finds its way to legislative leaders and then to candidates, directly to candidates, or instead to independent committees acting to promote candidates is the question. How the campaign-finance system works may be less important than the fact that it has been so thoroughly discredited. Few citizens believe much good can come of it. While they may have been skeptical with regard to special-interest money in the past, they are even more skeptical today.

THE OUTSIDE GAME OF LOBBYING

Serge Garrison, now a lobbyist but formerly director of the Iowa Legislative Council, describes how lobbying had been changing in his state: "We're probably driving a lot of legislators crazy both at home and at the statehouse because of our phone banks and other grassroots campaigns. We use those techniques because many legislators don't necessarily want to see us at the statehouse. It's partly the ethics issue. Our new Iowa ethics law has changed the whole lobbying procedure. . . . We have about forty new members in the legislature this year, and we don't know them very well. They are being taught not to trust us, which makes lobbying extremely difficult."[82]

With relationships more difficult to cultivate and campaign contributions highly suspect, lobbying by interest groups is no longer a game played almost exclusively by insiders. Today an outside lobbying game has grown up alongside the old inside one.[83] The new environment of term limits, angry voters, partisan competition, and institutional instability demands more than warm relationships and campaign contributions (although relationships and campaign contributions are still in play). It demands the involvement, or what can appear to be the involvement, of voters. No longer is it enough to communicate with legislators; now, interest groups communicate with the public, who in turn tell it to lawmakers.[84]

The Rise of Grassroots

The objective of a grassroots, public relations, or advertising campaign is to show legislators that their constituents, and perhaps a broader public as well, are concerned about a particular issue. This kind of lobbying has been called "the constituency connection" or "farming the membership." The legislator's district is where political power resides, and grassroots and media campaigns put legislators in touch with constituents who hold that power. The idea of grassroots is for constituents to tell legislators how they feel about things instead of relying on lobbyists to do it. Such a campaign can demonstrate tangible support for (or opposition to) a measure, and at a greater level of intensity than a lobbyist would convey. The idea of lobbying through the media is to mold public opinion, perhaps mobilize the public, and certainly to make legislators think that the public is on the group's side.

Grassroots lobbying is not a new phenomenon, although it has become a more fashionable one. As early as the 1960s, labor, civil rights groups, and the peace movement directed their efforts at mobilizing members and/or building support. Environmental and public interest groups pioneered at the state level and demonstrated the effectiveness of new techniques. Currently groups with many members, particularly if they are distributed throughout a state's legislative districts, see it in their strategic interest to organize for such campaigning. Teacher organizations in California, Texas, Minnesota, and New Jersey—indeed, in most states—rely heavily on grassroots techniques. So do single-issue groups, like the National Rifle Association and the National Abortion Rights League. The professional and trade associations and individual corporations have been building their grassroots capacity for over a decade now, with impressive results. The beer industry, for example, spawned the establishment of Beer Drinkers of America, a citizens' group with 750,000 members in all fifty states which advocates "the freedom of Americans to drink beer responsibly, without excessive governmental regulations or unfair taxation."

The prime power of many of these groups, particularly those with a dedicated membership or following, is not the campaign contributions they make. Campaign contributions are a resource that legislators try to convert into votes back home. The power of groups like those made up of teachers, senior citizens, and sportsmen is in mobilizing members and nonmembers, first on specific issues and then on the reelection of legislators. When it comes to reelection, legislators are risk averse; and that is why they take grassroots campaigns very seriously.

When they are surveyed, legislators claim to respond to constituents and citizens more than to any other force. Asked why they backed legislation supported by an interest group, 97.4 percent said that it was because their constituents favored it, 71.1 percent said because the general public favored it, and 57.9 percent said because it was in tune with their own views.[85] In another survey, legislators reported that their own votes were influenced by environmentalists and grassroots citizens' groups, while they perceived that business and labor (i.e., "special interests") had the most influence over the votes of their colleagues.[86] Given the prevalence of consultants and their "boiler room" operations in Washington, D.C., signing on to manufacture "grassroots" opinion, legislators have become skeptical as to the true nature of some campaigns. They are skeptical about the numbers who write or call in to express views and doubtful that these people will vote according to their legislator's responsiveness on the issue in contention. But they do not know for sure what the grassroots expression means or where it will lead. They may not be convinced, but they cannot afford to dismiss communications that come—or might have come—from constituents. Not with an election ahead of them. And, at the very least, such communications make it easier for lawmakers already predisposed in a group's direction to vote for (or against) a measure by citing support for (or opposition to) it in their districts.[87]

Practically every type of interest group in practically every state now has grassroots in their repertoire of campaigning techniques. One recent study of lobbyists in California, South Carolina, and Wisconsin found that grassroots lobbying efforts were mounted by 80 percent of the corporations, 94 percent of trade and professional groups, 97 percent of labor groups, and 96 percent of citizens' groups. Large percentages of these groups also inspired letter-writing campaigns and had influential constituents contact legislators. Another study of the governmental relations offices and practices of 264 companies found that grassroots programs were the fastest-growing areas of public affairs activity.[88]

Although grassroots lobbying may be ubiquitous, it has not yet become the dominant technique in lobbying legislatures everywhere. Not at least in Ohio. According to a lobbyist there, grassroots techniques are less effective than maintaining friendly relations, providing reliable information, contributing to campaigns, and wining and dining. Ohio legislators agree; they do not rate letter-writing campaigns or using the media high in terms of effectiveness. Information, personal persuasion, and contributions rank higher.[89]

Grassroots Techniques

The outside game of lobbying depends on citizen involvement. The numbers involved can range from a few to many. Maryland is an example of a state where grassroots lobbying is still a relatively modest enterprise. Contract lobbyists who use it rely most heavily on "key contacts." These are group members who have some tie to a legislator in whose district they live. A Maryland lobbyist who recognizes the efficacy of being able to mobilize six or eight opinion leaders in a district refers to this as "grass tops" lobbying—there being no attempt to get as far down as the roots. These local leaders are drawn on by a group or lobbyist to testify at a committee hearing or to visit with legislators they know in their capital or district offices. A campaign can be rather narrowly focused, as was that by the automobile-leasing coalition in Maryland in 1995. The objective of the coalition was to have taxes removed from leasing arrangements, on the ground that it was unfair and harmful to the industry. Whereas the bill advocated by the industry had been dubbed by opponents the "Cadillac Relief Act" because it was portrayed as helping the wealthy, the campaign was designed to change this image by showing a lessor was no different from an ordinary purchaser of an automobile. The coalition relied heavily on automobile dealerships to contact legislators and framed the issue as one of cutting taxes. Legislators perceived that people favored the removal of the lease tax and that support for the position had reelectoral value.[90]

Expansive grassroots techniques mobilize as many members as possible. Corporations count on their employees, their stockholders, suppliers, distributors, and so on. Anheuser-Busch, the manufacturer of Budweiser and Michelob beers among other products, has a well-developed grassroots organization that it keeps in a state of readiness and can activate whenever necessary. Anheuser-Busch employs more than forty thousand individuals who are assigned to legislative districts through a computer matching system. They can be directed to contact their own legislators. In addition to its immediate employees, its family includes 960 wholesalers (who deal with almost 500,000 outlets nationwide). Every two weeks each person who holds a liquor license is visited by an Anheuser-Busch wholesaler, and these wholesalers receive the company's action alerts with support and briefing materials, as well as notification by phone.[91]

Writing letters, sending faxes, and making phone calls are now commonplace features of grassroots campaigns. The sheer weight of communications can make an impression on legislators. The Texas Civic Justice League, a coalition whose focus is product liability and tort reform, has had forty phone-bank operators in a special facility in Austin to support its grassroots operation. During one of its major campaigns, the league's staff made calls to 35,000 businesses that presumably had an interest in its issue. These businesses were then mailed materials and asked to write legislators.[92]

An example of grassroots lobbying in action is provided by Associated Industries of Florida. The issue was "joint and several liability," which business had been trying to overturn.[93] In 1993 Florida's supreme court in *Fabre v. Marion* interpreted the section of the statute to mean that liability would be apportioned on the basis of fault rather than on the basis of who could afford to pay. The trial lawyers then tried to override the court decision through legislation. The AIF went on the defensive, activating the business community and targeting members of the house judiciary committee. The organization sent faxes to its board of directors, its corporate members' lobbyists, and others, urging recipients to contact members of the committee and ask them to vote no. The AIF listed committee members and their phone numbers in Tallahassee and included a tally of how members were inclined to vote based on the previous year's voting records and the group's own interviews and questionnaire. With 8 yeas and 7 nays likely, and 2 undecided committee members, the AIF targeted those who were most in doubt. During a two-week period in the 1995 session, 444, 228, 197, 55, and 40 telephone calls were made to five key legislators from representatives of business in their districts.[94]

Grassroots has taken on new dimensions in recent years, with persuasive efforts aimed at many, many more people. These new dimensions are most notable at the federal level, where the strategists, pollsters, and media experts who shape political campaigns now play a prominent part in campaigns for nonpolitical clients—corporations, trade associations, and advocacy groups. The success of the "Harry and Louise" advertising campaign against President Clinton's health-care reform plan gave great impetus to mass-mobilization campaigns in general.[95]

"The winning edge," write two political scientists in their study of Texas, "now comes with sophisticated studies, public opinion polls, and computerized mailings."[96] Technological advances in direct mail, computer databases, telemarketing, cellular phones, faxes, and the Internet have speeded up communications and facilitated targeting. The media have offered a means of reaching large populations, while polls and focus groups have provided strategic and substantive grist for the campaign mill.

The Efficacy of Grassroots

On many issues, at the state as well as the federal level, the economic or policy stakes are not high enough to warrant expenditures on polling, public relations, advertising, and a bevy of consultants. In New Mexico, for instance, such lobbying is almost unheard of—no issue in contest is worth it. Yet in California, campaigns of this sort are most likely to be waged over health care and tort reform. But other issues are also fought out on statewide terrain. In 1993 manufacturers pushing to repeal a sales tax on equipment hired a public relations firm to make its case. When lawyers in 1994 fought over the regulation of television advertising by attorneys, both sides advertised. In 1995 on issues from electric cars to antismoking to HMOs, sophisticated campaigns were waged. In New York multimillion-dollar advertising campaigns opposing Gov. George Pataki's budget and employing TV and radio commercials, subway posters, and direct mailings, were engaged in by unions of hospital workers, teachers, and state employees.[97] Another campaign, a year later, by the City University of New York (CUNY), also was directed at Governor Pataki's cuts in the budget for higher education. Not only did about 80,000 alumni send letters to Albany, but CUNY also produced television commercials in its own studios and got television stations to run them as public service announcements.[98] Turf battles, such as the previously discussed contest between optometrists and ophthalmologists, may justify hefty expenditures. Although both sides hired major lobbying firms in a 1995 battle in Connecticut, the optometrists ran full-page newspaper and radio advertisements, in addition to sending stacks of letters to lawmakers.[99]

The efficacy of the outside approach to lobbying can be illustrated by several recent campaigns. The hard-liquor industry, through the Distilled Spirits Council of the U.S. (DISCUS), has been engaged in a national public relations and advertising campaign to reduce disproportionate state taxes on hard liquors as compared with wine and beer. Tax increases have led to a decline of about 4 percent in industry revenues because consumers of alcohol substituted beer or wine for distilled spirits. The council is advancing the "equivalency concept," which is that distilled spirits are no more alcoholic than beer and wine in comparable amounts: one beer = one glass of wine = one drink of liquor. In its campaign DISCUS is endeavoring to overcome the idea that beer is the drink of moderation with its own theme that there is no beverage of moderation, but rather people of moderation. If faced with a bill to increase sin taxes in the states, the first objective of the distilled-spirits industry is to defeat it. If it cannot be defeated, the next objective is to achieve tax equity, paying its fair share along with beer and wine. According to DISCUS, it is unsound public policy to tax distilled spirits at a higher rate, for among other things it will send the message that some forms of alcohol are better than others, whereas alcohol is alcohol is alcohol.[100]

Another DISCUS campaign took place during a six-month period in 1994 at the state level, focusing specifically on defeating a price increase on distilled spirits sold in state stores in Alabama. The legislature was about to pass a resolution, SGR 5, calling for the Alcoholic Beverages Commission to raise retail prices by 35 percent. Legislators were under pressure from state employees who wanted an 8 percent pay raise. The increase in liquor prices would raise $18 million and, thus, fund most of the pay raise. The battle, then, was between the distilled-spirits industry and the state employees association.

In terms of grassroots strength, state employees were strongly embedded in the political terrain, while alcoholic beverages had little grass and even fewer roots.

DISCUS was fighting an uphill battle. No organized groups in Alabama stood in opposition to SGR 5. But DISCUS managed to wage an effective media campaign, with its president's press conference covered by television, radio, and every major newspaper in the state. The argument put forth was that a price increase would result in people going out of state to purchase liquor. Not only would the price increase fail to raise what was expected of it, but it would lead to a loss of business and jobs. DISCUS's president ended up charging that the process had been unfair because the resolution had been passed in the "dead of night."

Thanks in part to the attention paid by the media to the issue, a grassroots coalition took shape. It included restaurants, hotels and motels, and local governments concerned that Alabama might lose convention business because of liquor prices that were out of line with those in other states. Phone calls were made to targeted legislators and the process was slowed up, as DISCUS intended. A study was done of the impact of the price increase, and the ABC (Alcoholic Beverage Commission) scheduled hearings. Local groups, not national companies or out-of-state people, provided testimony against the price increase, and they were given good coverage by the media.

Liquor was up against politics, however. It was an election year and the governor and legislators were seeking the endorsement of the state employees association. DISCUS hoped to slow up the price increase, so no action would be taken until after the endorsements were made. Because of its grassroots coalition and activities and its media strategy, it succeeded in its efforts and finally managed to beat the price increase that had originally been proposed.[101]

When grassroots and media campaigns are employed, the business of lobbying undergoes a metamorphosis. Although the statehouse press corps continues to focus on how much lobbyists spend on entertaining legislators, by far the largest amounts of money are expended on issue campaigns and not on gifts. However, such expenditures by PR or advertising firms need not be disclosed. The question facing legislatures today is whether to require reporting by those who are paid to persuade others to contact lawmakers on behalf of legislation.

The Ethics of the Outside Game

Despite—or because of—lobbying going public, additional ethical issues arise. Inside lobbying, resting partly on relationships, is essentially an honest game.

It has to be. Lobbyists cannot afford to jeopardize their credibility by communicating anything but truthful, useful information to legislators. If they mislead or deceive, or even omit to tell legislators the downside of a proposal they are advocating, they risk losing friends or making enemies. Lobbyists are in it for the long run, so no single issue is worth the sacrifice of a potential ally. Not only can a lobbyist suffer at the hands of an aggrieved legislator, but a lobbyist's reputation can also be tarnished with the entire legislative membership. That is why, even allowing for the obligations incurred in return for gifts, the inside game of lobbying is essentially one of integrity. The incentive system ensures that it will be so.

The outside game, in which constituencies and publics are mobilized, has a very different basis. The objective is to exert pressure on legislators (or support for legislators, if they already agree with a group's position). To do this, members of legislators' constituencies or of the broader public are engaged in order to mobilize support, or the appearance of support, for the groups's position. The purpose of the manager of the enterprise is to shape public opinion, or at least the perception legislators have of it. Grassroots lobbying, as it is often practiced, is known as "Astroturf lobbying" because the target group extends well beyond an organization's core or membership, so that the "grass" is artificial and not rooted naturally in the ground.

Astroturf lobbying campaigns leave considerable room for manipulation, as is illustrated by the Casino Association of New Jersey's attempt to place sports betting on the ballot as a constitutional amendment. The legislature had to act by August 3, 1993, or the possibility of betting on sporting events in casinos would have expired forever because of a federal law that had been passed the previous year. The constitutional amendment to legalize sports betting had been approved by the New Jersey senate and was waiting action in the assembly. In its campaign, the Casino Association targeted thirteen legislative districts, represented by twenty-six members of the assembly, a number of whom were possible swing votes. The association commissioned a poll by a major survey research firm. The questions were introduced by the following statement, one that could only have been designed to encourage positive responses: "Estimates are that legalized sports betting would generate an additional 50–150 million dollars in added revenues to fund utility and prescription-drug assistance for senior citizens." Of those surveyed, an overwhelming majority answered that the proposal should be put on the ballot, with 55.8 percent of the total also saying they were in favor of sports betting. Those in favor were asked if they would authorize the Casino Association to send a letter on their behalf to their legislators urging them to vote for the constitutional amendment. Of the 12, 612 expressing themselves in favor, 10,928 agreed.[102] Thereupon, the association made its calls to the targeted legislators. Despite the casino industry's efforts, however, the sports betting amendment was killed in the assembly appropriations committee. Reportedly, the reason was that the Republican assembly majority did not want on the ballot an item that might increase turnout in Democratic areas, giving an advantage to Gov. Jim Florio in his race for reelection.

A candid description of how a grassroots campaign is conducted is provided by Neal M. Cohen of Apco Associates, a Washington firm. Cohen addressed a gathering of lobbyists about his efforts on behalf of tort reform in Mississippi. In 1993, he said, he began a public attack on "greedy" trial lawyers, on behalf of a coalition called "Mississippians for a Fair Legal System." He commissioned a study of the costs of the tort system in the state, which were found to be higher than those of education. The public relations and advertising campaign began to pay off. Within four weeks the coalition had 1,200 members, including nonprofit agencies, schools, and business and had apparently won the media to its side. What was most important in this campaign was the recruitment of many individual citizens to lend cover to the insurance, industrial, and business initiators, so that broad-based membership was what the public and legislators would see.[103]

The labeling of grassroots coalitions also raises ethical issues. A coalition's name is a function of what sponsors of a measure wish to communicate about their proposal and its intent. The nomenclature in use is less than completely truthful about the composition of a group. In the 1993–1994 session of the California legislature, for example, the following coalitions were active: Crime Victims United (prison guards); Californians for Schools (the building industry); Californians for Fair Business Policy (tobacco companies); and Californians Allied for Patient Protection (doctors, hospitals, insurance companies).[104] In the environmental area, the organization named Northwesterners for More Fish was founded by utilities and other companies in the region that are under attack by environmentalists for depleting the fish population.[105]

RESTRICTION AND EXPANSION

The contemporary public images of special interests and generous lobbyists belie what has actually been happening in the states. Over recent years more groups have organized and entered the political and policy fray at state capitols. For every group or coalition of groups, a group or coalition ordinarily exists on the other side. There is usually a balance, but it is rarely perfect. The system is pluralistic, but not one of equality. Some interests are better-endowed than others.

The representation of interests is changing dramatically. Lobbying was once almost exclusively an inside game, depending largely on relationships. A group's policy arguments and ideas always mattered, but they matter even more now. Information counts more in the lobbying equation. A current Kentucky lobbyist and former legislator put it this way: "No longer do you have the opportunity to cultivate a relationship, . . . so you have to rely on facts and data when you are trying to convince them that you are right."[106] Legislators require justification in policy as well as political terms. A leading lobbyist in Massachusetts, who is highly regarded by members of the legislature, acknowledged that "They want to be helpful to me, but not unless I can build a case for which they won't be criticized."[107]

Electoral politics is now becoming integral to many lobbying efforts, as lobbying has become an outside game. This relatively new game is designed to engage group members, legislators' constituents, and sometimes also the public at large. It relies ultimately on numbers—the numbers of people who can be recruited, or appear to be recruited, to a cause. Maximizing the numbers may require the investment of substantial funds on the part of a group or coalition. Informal referendums on issues—such as tort reform, health care, and the environment—are becoming periodic as grassroots, public relations, and media campaigns become more commonplace. Meanwhile, the enactment of legislation restricting gifts by lobbyists to legislators, the adoption of term limits, and the dispositions of younger generations of legislators and lobbyists have all led to a decline in the impact of relationships in lobbying.

Lobbyists and legislators continue to connect through campaign contributions, but this nexus is perpetually under attack. The public is distrustful of the motives of those who contribute and of those who receive. Large contributions, if permitted at all, arouse grave suspicion. The campaign-finance system is unlikely to wither away. But those who engage in financial transactions must be alert and on guard in today's environment. Given statutory restrictions, disclosure requirements, and scrutiny by the press and the opposition, legislators are always at risk of misstep in raising funds for their campaigns.

The comfort level of legislators is lower than it used to be. New generations of legislators will not be entertained by friendly lobbyists as their predecessors had been. They will not have lobbyists as friends, as their predecessors had. Instead, they are more apt to be pressured by insistent groups and grassroots campaigns. The mode is becoming less that of the *club* of colleagues, of insiders and more that of the *campaign* of adversaries, of outsiders. Legislative walls are almost completely down, and democracy is a more striking feature of interest-group struggles in the legislature than ever before.

Lobbying is becoming more and more an effort to demonstrate public support for a group's position. That involves not only lobbyists of yore, but different cadres of professionals with "outside" rather than "inside" skills. As an observer of the California lobbying scene wrote: "If you view politicians as people who lick their fingers and hold them to the wind, political public-relations practitioners are the wind makers."[108]

NOTES

1.The following paragraphs are based in part on Alan Rosenthal, *The Third House: Lobbyists and Lobbying in the States* (Washington, D.C.: CQ Press, 1993), 155.

2. Many of the remaining issues are even less consequential. Some are introduced on behalf of individuals and apply narrowly; some are noncontroversial amendments designed to repair glitches in existing law; and some have to do with the nitty-gritty of governmental housekeeping.

3. Interview with the author, May 1, 1996.

4. *New York Times*, April 8, 1996.

5. Ibid., June 19, 1996.

6. *Tallahassee Democrat*, March 29, 1995.

7. James Q. Wilson, *Political Organizations* (New York: Basic Books, 1973), 333–334.

8. Clive S. Thomas and Ronald J. Hrebenar, "Interest Groups in the States," in *Politics in the American States*, 6th ed., ed. Virginia Gray and Herbert Jacob (Washington, D.C.: CQ Press, 1996), 122–158.

9. Virginia Gray and David Lowery, "Reflections on the Study of Interest Groups in the States," in *Representing Interests and Interest Group Representation*, ed. William Crotty, Mildred A. Schwartz, and John C. Green (Lanham, Md.: University Press of America, 1994).

10. *Sacramento Bee*, July 16, 1995.

11. Jonathan Rauch, *Demosclerosis: The Silent Killer of American Government* (New York: Times Books, 1994), 38.

12. Keith E. Hamm and Charles Wiggins, "Texas: The Transformation From Personal to Informational Lobbying," in *Interest Group Politics in the Southern States*, ed. Ronald J. Hrebenar and Clive S. Thomas (Tuscaloosa: University of Alabama Press, 1992), 174–175.

13. Clive S. Thomas, "Conclusion: The Changing Pattern of Interest Group Politics

in the Western States," in *Interest Group Politics in the American West*, ed. Ronald J. Hrebenar and Clive S. Thomas (Salt Lake City: University of Utah Press, 1987), 146.

14. Patricia McGee Crotty, "Pennsylvania Individualism Writ Large," in *Interest Group Politics in the Northeastern States*, ed. Ronald J. Hrebenar and Clive S. Thomas (University Park: Pennsylvania State University Press, 1993), 290.

15. Jack D. Fleer, *North Carolina Government and Politics* (Lincoln: University of Nebraska Press, 1994), 183.

16. Kenneth T. Palmer, G. Thomas Taylor, and Marcus A. Librizzi, *Maine Politics and Government* (Lincoln: University of Nebraska Press, 1992), 44.

17. Frederic N. Bolotin, "Ohio: A Plethora of Pluralism," in *Interest Group Politics in the Midwestern States*, ed. Ronald J. Hrebenar and Clive S. Thomas (Ames: Iowa State University Press, 1993), 258–259. For a similar listing, see Charles Funderburk and Robert W. Adams, "Interest Groups in Ohio Politics," in *Ohio Politics*, ed. Alexander P. Lamis (Kent, Ohio: Kent State University Press, 1994), 303–330.

18. Don W. Driggs and Leonard E. Goodall, *Nevada Politics and Government: Conservatism in an Open Society* (Lincoln: University of Nebraska Press, 1996), 147.

19. Thomas and Hrebenar, "Interest Groups in the States," 144–145.

20. Tom Loftus, *The Art of Legislative Politics* (Washington, D.C.: CQ Press, 1994), 131.

21. Quoted in Rosenthal, *Third House*, 210.

22. Rosenthal, *Third House*, 217.

23. The argument is a popular one. Some economists maintain, however, that the economic costs of illnesses related to smoking are less than the economic benefits (in the form of savings on nursing homes and unpaid pensions and social security) from the earlier demise of smokers.

24. Paul Brace and John A. Straayer, "Colorado: PACs, Political Candidates, and Conservation," in *Interest Group Politics in the American West*, ed. Ronald J. Hrebenar and Clive S. Thomas (Salt Lake City: University of Utah Press, 1987), 56.

25. Malcolm Jewell and Penny M. Miller, *The Kentucky Legislature* (Lexington: University Press of Kentucky, 1988), 264–266.

26. Ronald Hedlund, "Wisconsin: Pressure Politics and a Lingering Progressive Tradition," in *Interest Group Politics in the Midwestern States*, ed. Ronald J. Hrebenar and Clive S. Thomas (Ames: Iowa State University Press, 1993), 317–318.

27. Bruce C. Wolpe, *Lobbying Congress: How the System Works* (Washington, D.C.: CQ Press, 1990), 35.

28. See David L. Cingranelli, "New York: Powerful Groups and Powerful Parties," in *Interest Group Politics in the Northeastern States*, ed. Ronald J. Hrebenar and Clive S. Thomas (University Park: Pennsylvania State University Press, 1993), 268–269.

29. Based on information in an independent study conducted by Robin Cincotta, Eagleton Institute of Politics, Rutgers University. May 3, 1996. Photocopy.

30. Rosenthal, *Third House*, 178–182.

31. Brace and Straayer, "Colorado," 56.

32. *New York Times*, September 4, 1995.

33. Rauch, *Demosclerosis*, 48.

34. Sigrid Bathen, "Clay Jackson in Prison," *California Journal,* November 1995, 13.

35. Christopher Schwarz, "Remodeling the Lobby," *State Government News*, May 1994, 31.

36. Collins Center for Public Policy, "The Nature of Representation: An Overview" (discussion by members of the Florida house, Tallahassee, November 6, 1995), 1:205–206. Transcript.

37. Loftus, *Art of Legislative Politics*, 93.

38. Allan J. Cigler and Dwight C. Kiel, *The Changing Nature of Interest Group Politics in Kansas* (Topeka: Capitol Complex Center, University of Kansas, June 1988), 16–18.

39. Quoted in *New York Times*, May 9, 1996.

40. Council of State Governments and American Society for Public Administration, *Public Integrity Annual* (Lexington, Ky.: the Council, 1996), 327–330.

41. Ibid.

42. *Sacramento Bee*, July 16, 1995; James E. Post and Jennifer J. Griffin, *The State of Corporate Public Affairs: 1996 Survey Results* (Boston: Foundation for Public Affairs/Boston University School of Management, Public Affairs Research Group, 1997), fig. 7.0.

43. To put the job of lobbying in full light, it is necessary to point out that much of a lobbyist's efforts are directed internally toward the client, the association, or company represented. One of Massachusetts' leading contract lobbyists explains: "I spend 90 percent of my time lobbying my clients and 10 percent on legislators." His biggest hurdle is convincing his clients that they cannot get everything they feel entitled to. Interview with the author, November 28, 1995.

44. Rosenthal, *Third House*, 7.

45. Cited in Alan Rosenthal, *Drawing the Line: Legislative Ethics in the States* (Lincoln: University of Nebraska Press, 1996), 104.

46. *New York Times*, May 5, 1996.

47. John R. Hibbing and Elizabeth Theiss-Morse, *Congress as Public Enemy: Public Attitudes Toward American Political Institutions* (New York: Cambridge University Press, 1995), 105, 107.

48. Rosenthal, *Drawing the Line*, 105.

49. Quoted in *Baltimore Sun*, December 19, 1994.

50. *Washington Post*, March 17, 1995.

51. Story from *Atlanta Journal and Constitution*, as summarized in *State Capitols Report*, August 25, 1995.

52. Interview with the author, June 5, 1995.

53. Rosenthal, *Drawing the Line*, 112–113.

54. Schwarz, "Remodeling the Lobby," 28.

55. John Powers, "Altered State: It's a New Era on Beacon Hill, With New Players, New Rules, and New Attitudes," *Boston Globe Magazine,* June 16, 1996, 35.

56. Schwarz, "Remodeling the Lobby," 30.

57. Garry Boulard, "Lobbyists or Outlaws?" *State Legislatures,* February 1996, 22.

58. Ibid., 20.

59. Daniel M. Weintraub, "California Leaders Look at Limits," *State Legislatures,* July 1994, 42.

60. Interview with the author, June 7, 1995.

61. This section uses material in Rosenthal, *Drawing the Line,* 138–182.

62. Information furnished by Associated Industries of Florida, dated January 23, 1995.

63. William E. Cassie, Joel A. Thompson, and Malcolm E. Jewell, "The Patterns of PAC Contributions in Legislative Elections: An Eleven-State Analysis" (paper prepared for delivery at the annual meeting of the American Political Science Association, Chicago, 1992), 8.

64. Kevin Sack, "The Great Incumbency Machine," *New York Times Magazine,* September 27, 1992, 48.

65. Weintraub, "California Leaders Look at Limits," 41.

66. Newsletter written by Dean Conley, February 9, 1994.

67. Eagleton Institute of Politics, Rutgers University, ethics conference, Phoenix, Arizona, October 23–24, 1993.

68. Quoted in *Baltimore Sun,* April 16, 1995.

69. James Fishkin, *Democracy and Deliberation* (New Haven: Yale University Press, 1991), 45.

70. Virginia Gray and Wy Spano, "The Minnesota Legislature: Pretty Good and Now Purer Than the Rest" (paper prepared for delivery at the annual meeting of the American Political Science Association, San Francisco, August 29–September 1, 1996).

71. Ibid.

72. Ruth S. Jones and Thomas J. Borris, "Strategic Contributing in Legislative Campaigns: The Case of Minnesota," *Legislative Studies Quarterly* 10 (February 1985): 89–105.

73. Kenneth R. Meyer and John M. Wood, "The Impact of Public Financing on Electoral Competitiveness: Evidence for Wisconsin, 1964–1990," *Legislative Studies Quarterly* 20 (February 1995): 69–88; Eiza Newlin Carney, "Taking on the Fat Cats," *National Journal,* January 18, 1997, 113.

74. Council of State Governments and American Society for Public Administration, *Public Integrity Annual, 1996,* 347–358; also Thomas L. Gais and Michael J. Malbin, "Administering Campaign Finance Reform: What Happens After the Law Is Signed?"

Rockefeller Institute Bulletin 1996 (Albany: Nelson A. Rockefeller Institute of Government, 1996), 58–60.

75. If contribution limits are too low, they create inequalities among groups. The most powerful groups become the only ones with the needed infrastructure to get around them. Thomas L. Gais and Michael J. Malbin, "The Day After Reform: Sobering Campaign Finance Lessons From the American States," chapter 7, p. 33. Manuscript prepared for publication.

76. Rob Gurwitt, "The Mirage of Campaign Reform," *Governing*, August 1992, 51.

77. Dave Travis, "Opinion: Public Campaign Financing Could Work but It Doesn't," *State Legislatures,* September 1991, 40; Carney, "Taking on the Fat Cats," 111–113.

78. Interview with the author, June 5, 1995. Four years earlier Maryland lobbyists had been prohibited from running PACs.

79. Schwarz, "Remodeling the Lobby," 29.

80. Gais and Malbin, "Administering Campaign Finance Reform: What Happens After the Law Is Signed?" 57–69.

81. Quoted in Gurwitt, "Mirage of Campaign Reform," 51. See also Alan Rosenthal, "Why It's Hard to Fix Campaign Finance," *State Government News,* June–July 1997, 9–11, 38.

82. Karl T. Kurtz, ed., "The Old Statehouse, She Ain't What She Used to Be," National Conference of State Legislatures, July 26, 1993. Photocopy.

83. Mark P. Petracca, "A Legislature in Transition: The California Experience With Term Limits" (paper prepared for delivery at the annual meeting of the American Political Science Association, San Francisco, August 29–September 1, 1996).

84. Laureen Lazarovici, "The Rise of the Wind-Makers," *California Journal,* June 1995, 16.

85. Janet B. Johnson and Joseph A. Pika, "Delaware: Friends and Neighbors Politics," in *Interest Group Politics in the Northeastern States,* ed. Ronald J. Hrebenar and Clive S. Thomas (University Park: Pennsylvania State University Press, 1993), 69.

86. John C. Berg, "Massachusetts: Citizen Power and Corporate Power," in *Interest Group Politics in the Northeastern States,* ed. Ronald J. Hrebenar and Clive S. Thomas (University Park: Pennsylvania State University Press, 1993), 194–195.

87. Hamm and Wiggins, "Texas," 171.

88. Anthony J. Nownes and Patricia Freeman, "Interest Group Activity in the States" (paper prepared for delivery at the annual meeting of the American Political Science Association, San Francisco, August 29–September 1, 1996); and Post and Griffin, *State of Corporate Public Affairs,* fig. 3.2.

89. Funderburk and Adams, "Interest Groups in Ohio Politics," 323, 329–330.

90. Interview with the author, June 7, 1995.

91. Rosenthal, *Third House,* 158–159.

92. Ibid., 160.

93. "The joint and several liability" doctrine requires that any person responsible for any part of an accident, no matter how small that portion of fault, is responsible for paying for the entire damage award. For example, Walt Disney World had to pay 86 percent of a punitive damages award for an injury for which they bore 1 percent responsibility.

94. Information provided author by Association Industries of Florida.

95. James A. Barnes, "Privatizing Politics," *National Journal,* June 3, 1995, 1330–1334.

96. Hamm and Wiggins, "Texas," 172.

97. *New York Times*, March 21, 1995.

98. Ibid., May 23, 1996.

99. Ibid., April 8, 1996.

100. Presentation of Fred Meiser, DISCUS conference, October 22, 1994.

101. Presentation of Elizabeth Board, DISCUS conference, October 22, 1994.

102. Casino Association of New Jersey, Release 93-017, June 30, 1993.

103. *New York Times,* March 19, 1996.

104. *San Jose Mercury News,* January 9, 1995.

105. *New York Times,* March 25, 1996.

106. Schwarz, "Remodeling the Lobby," 30.

107. Interview with the author, November 28, 1995.

108. Lazarovici, "Rise of the Wind-Makers," 16.

CHAPTER 7

The Job of Leadership

"You bring thirty to one hundred people together, each having a different viewpoint. To make matters worse, each legislator represents his own unique legislative district and pays attention to that. On top of this, almost every member thinks he is more important than almost everyone else and wants things on his own terms." That is how one legislative leader described his job—a challenging job indeed.[1] The leader's fundamental challenge is to achieve common ends by mobilizing individuals who hold different values, represent different interests and constituencies, and pursue different objectives.

From one perspective, the legislature is a body—or rather two bodies (except for Nebraska, with its unicameral legislature)—of individuals representing both their own values and the interests of their constituencies. From another perspective, the legislature is an institution composed of separate houses, competing parties, and diverse members with an overarching responsibility to fashion policy and budgets for the entire state and to promote the overall welfare of its population. Without leadership from within the legislature and from the governor (as discussed in chapter 8), the first perspective would be more pronounced and the second more subdued than is currently the case. As much as anything else, it is up to leadership to take a statewide perspective and to concern itself with the legislature's institutional well-being.

The job of leadership has never been easy. Tom Loftus recalls typical times during his eight-year stint as speaker of the assembly in Wisconsin: "On some days I was like the teacher in front of the classroom. I was the font of real knowledge, and I decided what we did during the day, including when we took recess. On other days I was like someone in front of a firing squad who is fumbling with his blindfold and last cigarette in order to buy time. If leaders are lucky, they will have more days like the former than the latter."[2] The job is harder today than in earlier times, and it appears to be getting harder all the time.

The resurgence of state legislatures and the reascendancy of state governments have increased leadership burdens. The organizational reforms discussed in chapter 2 not only enhanced the overall capacity of the legislature but also energized the role of rank-and-file members. Legislators began to spend more time on the job, acquire information that had previously been tightly held, and develop subject-matter expertise by serving on standing committees, which were now playing a central part in the process. Meanwhile, the pendulum of American federalism was starting to swing back to the states.

As a consequence of movement within and outside the institution, citizens now demand more from state legislatures. This translates into higher expectations of what legislative leadership has to deliver. Yet as our expectations of leaders have been increasing, their control has been decreasing. By the 1980s, the democratization of legislatures had markedly changed the way legislative leaders did their business. Resources became more broadly distributed, and the time, staff, and information gap narrowed between leaders and other legislators. Leaders came to need the support (i.e., votes) of their members as much or more than members needed the favors (i.e., committee assignments) that their leaders could bestow. Nor has the independence of members diminished in the past decade. Instead, partisanship has been on the rise, further adding to the leaders' problems and responsibilities. A principal job of legislative leaders today is to protect incumbents and win additional seats in legislative elections. Meanwhile, organized interest groups have multiplied and the pressures they exert have intensified. Conflict among them is continuing. Fragmentation is characteristic of the environment in which legislatures function; it is also characteristic of legislatures themselves. Leaders have to try to put the pieces together.

THE SELECTION OF LEADERSHIP

Leadership in a legislature is not restricted to one or two or three or four persons. Anyone can exercise leadership. Rank-and-file members with experience or substantive knowledge provide leadership on various issues. Those who chair committees are leaders in their areas of expertise. Although formal leadership is relatively stable during the legislative term, informal leadership shifts from issue to issue and from one point to another.

Leadership Positions

Formal leadership is specific; it accompanies a particular position; it is titular. Normally, house leadership positions include speaker, majority leader, assistant majority leader, and minority leader and assistant minority leader. Some houses also have a speaker pro tem and majority and minority whips. A few go even further, designating deputy speakers, a conference leader, assistant whip, associate minority leader, and even minority budget officer. Normally, senate leadership includes president and/or president pro tem, and majority and minority leaders. Positions may extend further to deputy majority leader, senior assistant majority leader, assistant majority leader on conference operations, and so forth. In some legislative bodies committee chairs are formally designated as leaders and in some committee vice-chairs are so designated.

The number of positions that confer leadership standing varies greatly by legislature. At one extreme are states that abound in leadership positions. In New York the senate has 28 party leadership positions for the 61 members, while the assembly has 33 party leadership positions for its 150 members, not to mention committee chairmanships and vice-chairmanships. Every member of the senate and most members of the assembly has some sort of leadership title and an extra payment (called a "lulu" in New York) for leadership duties. Michigan's senate has 21 leadership positions for 38 members and its house has 38 positions for 110 members. Thus, 40 percent of Michigan legislators have leadership titles, and even more qualify if committee positions are also included. At the other extreme are states, like Louisiana and Mississippi, where leadership positions are scarce. In these places the senate has a president and president pro tem and the house a speaker and speaker pro tem, but no others are designated as leadership.

The tendency has been to create new slots and distribute them to members for a variety of reasons, not least of which is membership desire for inclusion, titular recognition, or extra compensation. Leaders have both anticipated the demand and responded to it.[3] At first glance, it might appear that the greater the number of leadership positions, the more dispersed leadership power. This would be true if power actually inhered in many of these positions. It does not, because many leadership positions are only nominal. Their objective is to confer on members letterhead recognition and salary supplements. Despite the number of positions in New York, power is highly concentrated in both the senate and the assembly. It is concentrated in Michigan, too, although many members of the senate and house have leadership posts.

The focus of the discussion in this chapter is not on leadership broadly defined but on the top leadership of the majority party. It is the majority party that, for most intents and purposes, has major responsibility for the chamber and the process. In the house the principal leader in nearly all the states is the speaker, whom the membership of the entire house officially elects. Most frequently, the majority-party caucus selects a member whom it nominates and has sufficient votes to elect. On occasion, a bloc of majority-party members coalesces with a minority-party bloc to elect the choice of a minority of the majority party. This occurred in April 1996 with a contest to succeed the speaker in Massachusetts after Democrat Charles Flaherty resigned from the post in midterm. The choice of most Democrats was Richard Voke, the majority leader. But Thomas Finneran, chairman of the ways and means committee, added the support of all thirty-five Republicans to that of a number of Democrats and won election to the speakership.

In the senate, top leadership designations vary to a greater extent. The principal leader is either the president, president pro tempore, or occasionally the majority leader. In twenty-six states the role of the lieutenant governor complicates the picture because this official of the executive branch also serves ex officio as president of the senate and presides over the body. But only in Texas and Georgia does the lieutenant governor have significant power in the legislature. Texas's lieutenant governor—at least since the late 1940s—has exercised substantial control over the senate, making committee assignments and affecting the flow of bills, and presiding over the body. Where lieutenant governors are also senate presidents, the principal legislative leadership position is that of president pro tem. In states where lieutenant governors have no legislative role, the principal leadership position is that of president. In Minnesota, North Dakota, Washington, and Wisconsin the majority leader wields predominant power. In New York the positions of president pro tem and majority leader are combined; the same individual holds both.

Qualifications for Leadership

Any member is eligible to be elected to the top leadership position. All it takes is the backing of a majority of one's colleagues, which normally means support from a majority of the majority-party caucus. What does it take to gain that support? Personality, skills, energy, and work. Although anyone is eligible, until recently women and African Americans—in part because of their small numbers in legislative chambers—have been shut out of leadership ranks. That is the case no longer. Women still account for a smaller proportion of top leaders than the size of their legislative membership nationwide, but they have made gains. In 1996 Alaska, Ohio, and Oregon had women speakers, and the Alaska senate had a woman president. Even fewer African Americans have held top leadership positions. Most notable among them is Willie Brown, California's assembly speaker who, facing the end of his term-limited term, in 1995 ran for and was elected mayor of San Francisco.

Experience in legislative office helps one to enter the ranks of leadership. It enables members to demonstrate their abilities, build alliances and friendships, and win over colleagues. But the tenure of members prior to being selected speaker or president or president pro tem has never been great. As of 1991, the average tenure of speakers before their selection was only 7.8 years, up from 4.4 years in 1975.[4] With term limits, average tenure prior to top leadership will decrease substantially. If they are limited to six, eight, or even twelve years, senators and representatives will not have time to prove themselves. Nor will they be disposed simply to wait around, allowing a colleague to serve for a number of years while their legislative lives expire. Members in term-limited states can be expected to succeed to leadership in their second or third terms. Tom Birmingham, with only five years in the Massachusetts senate in 1995, succeeded a veteran member as president. Term limits was an important factor in his decision to run immediately rather than wait until he was more seasoned. Today it is possible, although still not likely, for a freshman to become speaker.

The patterns of succession to top leadership range widely. In some chambers, members move up through the chairs. That is, they hold subleadership posts before reaching the top. In New Jersey and New Mexico the majority floor leader has the inside track to the speakership. A minority leader who helps his or her party win control of the chamber can also expect to be awarded the top position, as was Republican David Prosser of the Wisconsin assembly, who led his party to victory after having been in the minority for twenty-five years. The launching pad may be a committee chairmanship— often appropriations or ways and means. In California, Bill Lockyer progressed to the pro tem position by virtue of ten years of solid work as chairman of judiciary, probably the most difficult policy committee in the senate.[5]

The selection process is anything but automatic. Individual members do not have a common view of what they want in a leader. Some line up beyond an individual mainly on the basis of gender or race, while others favor ideological soul mates. Those from the northern part of the state may back a candidate from their region, while those from the southern part may back a candidate from theirs. Urban legislators may pull for one of their own, while suburban legislators may pull for one of theirs. Past favors, especially help in raising campaign funds, count with nearly everyone. The prospect of future favors, especially a committee chairmanship, counts even more. As important as anything else in determining votes is friendship,[6] which incorporates or is a surrogate for a number of the factors already mentioned.

It is not enough for candidates to be qualified or available for leadership. They must make their interests known before the party caucus and organizational session of the chamber. That means running for the office, campaigning with colleagues, persuading them, and getting commitments. Sometimes the campaigns begin a year or more in advance. It helps, moreover, to have no strong opponent. Take the effort to succeed David Roberti as president pro tem of the California senate. Among those with leadership skills and ambitions, one candidate resigned, another never really focused his energies, and a third waited for someone to ask him to run. In contrast, Bill Lockyer went to work and spent more than six months consulting with each senator, Republicans as well as Democrats, and rounding up votes.[7]

The Florida house offers an example of early candidacy. Here, the speakership rotates biennially, everyone knows when a vacancy will occur, and candidates declare years in advance. Formal selection, which is specified in caucus rules, begins two weeks after the election. Candidates can declare for speaker for the biennium after the one immediately ahead. Then, during the first year of the session, the majority-party caucus designates its candidate, although formal selection does not occur until after the next election. Sixty days thereafter, members can begin gathering pledges from colleagues for the following term, almost four years in the future. Informally, however, announcing candidacies and rounding up support gets under way even earlier.[8]

The 1995–1996 speaker of the Florida house, Peter Wallace, was elected to the house in 1982. He became an informal candidate for the speakership in the summer of 1988. At that time, Tom Gustafson was about to take office as speaker, to be followed, respectively, by Sam Bell and Carl Carpenter—both of whom had the requisite number of pledges for the future. Two other legislators had already made known their candidacies, and one of them managed to put together a coalition of Democrats to be named speaker. Wallace had to wait, but in the spring of 1989 he announced his candidacy for the next speakership. This time, with none of his colleagues competing, he lined up sufficient support, which he managed to hold until he was formally designated by the Democratic caucus in 1993. Wallace still was not home free. The conservatives in the Democratic caucus threatened to withdraw their support and, in fact, did so right after the 1994 election. At the November caucus, Democrat George Grady nominated himself, but Wallace prevailed. Thereupon, Grady tried to put together a coalition with Republicans but failed to best Wallace for the speakership. It had been a tough journey for Peter Wallace.

Despite the rotation of speakers, the Florida selection process has had elements of continuity. Future speakers have been identified years in advance and (unless they were defeated in a general election, as was Sam Bell, or made a run at someone slotted ahead of them, as did Carl Carpenter) they assumed the top position after chairing the appropriations or rules committees as "speakers-in-waiting." With their speakership approaching, the power of the speakers-in-waiting increased, eclipsing that of the sitting speaker halfway through his tenure. Leadership teams also provide continuity, as members succeed one another as speaker. Hyatt Brown's tenure as speaker of the Florida house, for example, was followed by the speakerships of Ralph Haben and Lee Moffett, both of whom were on his leadership team. Even when successive speakers were not close allies, they felt a responsibility to their successors and even passed unfinished issues along to them. T. K. Wetherall, for instance, did not complete his affordable-housing agenda, and discussed the issue with the two speakers-in-waiting, Bo Johnson and Peter Wallace. Although Johnson was less interested in the subject, Wallace agreed that if it were postponed two years, he would take it up during his term.[9]

The predictability and continuity of Florida's speaker selection process depended in large part on one-party control of the house, which prevailed until the 1990s. The minority Republicans were always out of contention. But in the 1990s the Republicans gained ground, and in the election of 1996 they won control and elected Dan Webster, one of their own, to be speaker, while Buzz Ritchie, the Democrats' speaker-designate, was left at the gate. The process of selecting a speaker in Florida will be different in the future.

Continuity and Turnover

Obviously, where a state has a system of rotating leadership, as in Florida, the presiding officers have limited tenure in office. In the 1950s speakers were rotated every two years in as many as one-third of the house and senate chambers. During that time the New Jersey assembly speaker and senate president could look forward to only a single year in office. More recently, such rigid limits have been relaxed. By the early 1990s the two-year tradition remained only in both chambers in Arkansas (but was abandoned here when term limits was instituted), Florida, and North Dakota, and the house in South Dakota. A number of other states, such as Connecticut and New Jersey, observed as a matter of custom a four-year rotation (although Donald

DiFrancesco won a fifth and sixth year as president of the New Jersey senate). In an analysis of tenure norms for president officers from 1947 to 1992, Jewell and Whicker point out that the number of houses and senates where all or most top leaders served one or two terms diminished from twenty-eight to thirteen and thirty-three to seventeen respectively. The number of houses and senates where some served five terms or more increased from eight to twelve and ten to eighteen respectively.[10]

Most recently, however, presiding officers may be turning over at a somewhat more rapid rate. Some depart because the opposition party wins control. Republican victories in statehouses in the 1994 elections are responsible for the departure of a number of house speakers and senate presidents. A few, targeted by the opposition or by an interest group, are defeated in their bids for reelection. Sam Bell was in line to be Florida's next speaker, but he was upset by a Republican opponent in his district. Bell explained the perils of a speaker-designate: "When you are a leader and you make tough decisions, you are going to make enemies. . . . That is why you are elected, to make the tough decisions and then take what comes when you make enough of them."[11] Democrat Ralph Wright of Vermont was defeated in 1994 after being targeted by the Republican party.

A number of leaders give up their positions to run for higher office, such as Tennessee's Ned McWherter, Wisconsin's Tom Loftus, and Iowa's Don Avenson—all of whom ran for governor. (McWherter succeeded, but Loftus, Avenson, and most other leaders who run for governor fail in their election bids.) Six of the top leaders in the Arizona legislature by 1996 had announced their candidacies for governor in 2000.[12] Some run for lesser statewide offices or for congressional seats. A few are forced out of office after being indicted or convicted, as was Mel Miller of New York (whose conviction was later overturned by the courts) and Kentucky's Don Blandford. Some are defeated for reelection after being involved in a scandal, as was Sammy Nunez of Louisiana. Some are touched by scandal and, though they bear no culpability, are forced to relinquish their leadership positions. A few leaders became exhausted, and others got frustrated; these just walk away.

Increasingly, leaders are pressed by members of their own party who want their turn at the top. After a while the rank-and-file becomes impatient, and leaders will feel their hot breath. This encourages leaders to leave public life or run for another office, perhaps before they are ready to do so. The alternative is to risk challenge and possible ouster. Some leaders are accused by their colleagues of being too liberal or too conservative or too weak or too strong. Others have been rejected by their colleagues when they ran for reelection to the house speakership or senate presidency. Jim Kennelly and Irv Stolberg in Connecticut; Kentucky's Bobby Richardson, Joe Clarke, and Eck Rose; John Martin in Maine; Tommy McGee in Massachusetts, Minnesota's Irv Anderson; New York's Ralph Marino; Liston Ramsey and Victor Mavretic in North Carolina; and Jim Barker in Oklahoma are among them. Buddy Newman of Mississippi chose to step down when, as he presided, the house membership reduced his powers.

Term limits will surely have effects on the tenure of leaders. David Roberti left his position as president pro tem of the California senate, Paul Hillegonds departed as speaker of the Michigan house (two years before his term expired because, as he put it, he did not want to serve with eighty lame ducks), and Dan Gwadosky of the Maine house exited as term limits kicked in. In the term-limited states, leaders will have little or no chance of serving more than one or two terms. Curiously, perhaps, Arkansas moved in the other direction. In part because of the imposition of term limits, Speaker Bobby Hogue broke the tradition of the rotating speakership. Since 1940 no Arkansas speaker had succeeded himself. Hogue, however, was reelected to the post.[13] When members have a tenure in the legislature of twelve, eight, or six years, they will insist on having the opportunity to go through the chairs—from committee leader to chamber leader. No one will be able to hold a position in such assemblies for very long.

The decline of leadership tenure has not occurred overnight. In four out of five of the states, the speaker in 1977 was different from the one in 1973, and the speaker was different in three out of four states with no change in party control. In considering both senate presidents (or pro tems) and house speakers, nearly half of them were new to their positions in 1979, with only one out of four of the changes attributable to the alteration of party control.[14] In 1995 only four out of forty-nine speakers and only three of fifty presidents (or pro tems) had also been serving in their positions a decade earlier.[15]

We can expect to see few top leaders hold their positions as long as South Carolina's Edgar Brown, who had thirty years as senate president pro tem, and Solomon Blatt, who had thirty-two years as speaker. We cannot expect to see those with the staying power of John Martin of Maine, William Bulger of Massachusetts, or Tom Murphy of Georgia, all of whom achieved remarkable tenure records in their states. Few leadership stints equal that of Vern Riffe of Ohio, who served twenty years as speaker and virtually ran things for two years previously when a friend was speaker. He stood for the speakership ten times and never had opposition. "I must have been doing something right," he recalled at the end of his career.[16] For two or three years before his retirement, Riffe's health was a problem, which led to speculation that he might soon leave. This led to jockeying by members of his party. When he announced he was retiring at the end of his 1993–1994 term, he began to lose the control he had exerted for so many years.[17] The Riffe era was over, and nothing quite like it will be returning to Ohio.

THE RESPONSIBILITIES AND POWERS OF LEADERSHIP

A legislator's responsibilities are substantial indeed, but they seem trifling in comparison with those of senate and house leaders. The president or president pro tem and the speaker must not only deal with everything that concerns the average member—constituency needs and desires, interest group demands, and the upcoming election—but also perform additional roles dictated by a legislature's history and culture and the expectations of their legislative colleagues. Along with the responsibilities of leadership go certain powers. Responsibilities and powers are interwoven. What leaders are supposed or expected to do—such as appointing legislators to committees—also affords them power.

Making Appointments

The business of managing the institution and the legislative process requires that, at the outset, the presiding officers assemble a leadership group to assist them. This group of individuals ordinarily includes members of the top leader's party—typically the majority leader, assistant majority leader, and chairs of the major standing committees. In most states, top leaders are not completely free to decide on all the people in leadership. The majority-party caucus usually decides who the majority leader will be. This may mean that the candidate who lost the election for speaker or president (or president pro tem) becomes the majority leader, and thus different party factions, different philosophies, different styles, or different personalities are represented in leadership ranks. The results may be better representation of the legislative party in leadership on the one hand and internal friction and conflict among leaders on the other. Only in both houses in Florida, Maryland, Massachusetts, and West Virginia, and in the house (but not the senate) in Illinois, New Hampshire, and New York is the majority leader chosen by the presiding officer and not the caucus. In most instances in these states the caucuses also select assistant leaders and whips, but the presiding officers are more apt to have authority here than in the appointment of the majority leaders.

The major organizational task with regard to personnel is assigning the members and, in particular, naming the chairs of the standing committees.[18] Top leaders have primary authority in this process. In forty-four states the power to appoint members to standing committees on the house side is that of the speaker. In some of these places, however, several leaders share the appointments process. In Ohio, all six Republican leaders shared in making assignments for 1995–1996.[19] When Curt Pringle became Republican speaker in California, he turned committee appointments over to the rules committee, but the power reverted to the speaker when the Democrats regained control of the assembly in 1997. In three states a committee on committees makes assignments, and in one assignments are made by the rules committee. Although the speaker appoints majority members in Massachusetts, Iowa, Colorado, and Arizona, the minority leadership appoints all minority members. In most other states the speaker consults with the minority leadership and accepts most of its recommendations. But the presiding officer can turn down the minority's slate. California's Willie Brown in 1993 appointed a Republican maverick as vice-chair of the ways and means committee, ignoring the minority leader's designee. In Vermont, Maryland, Oregon, and North Carolina consultation is not the customary practice.

On the senate side the formal power to appoint is more dispersed. It resides with the president or president pro tem in thirty states. When the lieutenant governor constitutionally presides—as in Alabama, Georgia, Mississippi, and Texas—that official enjoys the power to appoint senators to standing committees. In Ohio, Iowa, Colorado, Washington, and Kentucky the minority leadership appoints minority members and in other places the president or president pro tem has the authority, but consults with the minority leadership. In Colorado and Iowa the majority and minority leaders appoint majority and minority members respectively and in Nevada the majority and minority party caucuses have authority. In nine states a committee on committees, rules committee, or committee on senate organization makes appointments. In Minnesota the rules and administration committee, composed of the majority leader and senior members, makes appointments, although the majority leader has the most influence. In South Carolina seniority governs committee assignments, and in Virginia committee members are elected by the body.

The appointments process is less centralized than the location of official authority would lead one to believe. Top leaders have a big say, but they operate under constraints. Very important in the process of assigning members to committees is what legislators want. Indeed, the rules of the New Mexico senate prescribe that members shall be assigned "on the basis of the member's preference wherever possible." Different legislators want different committees. Many would like to be on appropriations and revenue, the most influential committees. Some seek a committee that can serve their district's needs, such as agriculture or natural resources. Others want to go where they have interest, experience, or knowledge. Teachers may opt for education and bankers for banking, while lawyers frequently choose judiciary.

As far as all but one or two key committees are concerned, a member's preferences weigh heavily. Leaders solicit assignment requests after an election and before the legislature meets to organize. They ask members to list two or three assignments, sometimes in preferred order. "I often told the members of the caucus," reported speaker Loftus of Wisconsin, "to think carefully about what committee assignment they asked me for because they might get it."[20] Leaders usually are able to give their members one out of the two or three committees they request.[21]

Other constraints also limit leadership discretion. First, leaders have to observe partisan ratios, which they largely determine. Normally, the proportion of Democrats and Republicans on committees mirrors the proportions in the chamber, although the majority may have a disproportionate share of seats on key committees, such as appropriations. Second, they have little discretion when rules specify that each member of the house and senate serve on appropriations, as they do in Iowa, or that each member serve on either appropriations or finance, as they do in North Carolina. Third, the custom is to reappoint members who have already been on a committee, if that is what the members want. Fourth, leaders are obliged to consider seniority, at least to some degree. In South Carolina's senate, seniority is binding. It used to govern in Arkansas, too, but with term limits, the house has revised its rules so that committee members no longer get chosen by seniority. Elsewhere, seniority is one factor that counts in deciding among candidates for the most sought-after committees.

Other factors are also at work. Many leaders feel they have to achieve a balance on key committees. Maryland's committees are diversified geographically and by gender and race. A balance between wings of the party may be sought, as is the case with Ohio's senate Republicans. Electoral considerations are seldom overlooked. In a competitive state, if an assignment to a particular committee would help a majority-party legislator's reelection, appointment is practically assured. After the 1994 elections, the Democratic leaders of the assembly in California assigned members facing tough reelections to the "juice committees"—agriculture, environmental safety, and ways and means—so that they could fatten their campaign war chests with contributions from affected interest groups.[22] In New Jersey freshman members of the assembly majority who have won close elections pretty much wind up with their choice of assignments.

With the election of 1994, particularly with the advent of term limits, another criterion for appointment achieved prominence. Newly elected members were purposely given key committee slots. Republican classes, who had run on state variations of U.S. House Speaker Newt Gingrich's "Contract with America," insisted on being assigned to budget committees so they could downsize government as they had promised. Republican leaders could not deny them. Term-limited freshmen did not feel like marking time, and leaders were responsive to their desires. Consequently, first-termers were appointed to appropriations and finance committees in Michigan, Montana, Ohio, and Washington.[23]

Factors such as a member's position on a leadership contest, background and ability, and personality also come into play at one point or another. The leader ordinarily wants to utilize membership skills as much as possible. The appointments process is complicated. Although the leader often makes assignments, the process is by no means autocratic, as is often portrayed. It works, at least in terms of satisfying legislators (who are not easy to satisfy). A national survey found that 83.5 percent of the legislators polled were pleased with their assignments, while only 2.3 percent were displeased. Perhaps this is partly because these "satisfied" members did not ask for positions they believed they could not get. But leaders also like to accommodate members whenever they can.[24] It bolsters morale, encourages work, and increases the leaders' chances to continue in their coveted leadership positions.

The selection of committee chairs is much more important than the assignment of rank-and-file members, but the process follows similar lines. Appointing authority is held by the speaker of the house in forty-four states and by the presiding office of the senate in twenty-nine. In other places, a rules committee or a committee on committees holds appointing authority. In the Rhode Island house, committees elect their own chairs (although the speaker's influence is certainly felt in the process). A member of the majority party holds a chairmanship in more than two-thirds of the states. Minority-party chairmanships have been most common in southern states where, until recently, the few Republicans did not constitute much of an organized opposition. Vermont has a tradition of bipartisan chairs. The minority also has been awarded chairmanships when it has helped to select the presiding officer as part of a bipartisan coalition.[25] Occasionally, an extremely able minority member is sufficiently bipartisan to merit a chairmanship. Jack Cade, the Republican minority leader of the Maryland senate, was appointed by the Democratic senate president to chair the subcommittee on health, education, and human resources of the budget committee—the first such appointment in almost fifty years. More frequently, minority members are appointed to be committee vice-chairs.

In appointing chairmen, especially of key committees, leaders give weight to all sorts of factors—support and loyalty being among the most important. In Colorado, speakers have generally appointed close friends or political allies to three or four major committees, which can then be trusted to carry out leadership wishes. If the speaker wanted to kill a bill, he would send it to one of these committees.[26] For a while Ralph Wright of Vermont generously appointed his opponents for the speakership to chairmanships, but then stopped that practice because he felt it might encourage other members to take him on.[27] In Minnesota, the various speakers have looked for different qualities in making chairmanship assignments. Martin Sabo was interested in leadership potential. Irv Anderson wanted to reward friends and punish enemies. David Jennings wanted to put close allies in key spots. Fred Norton had to worry about maintaining his party's fragile consensus among metropolitan and rural members.[28]

Top leaders prefer to have committee chairs upon whom they can rely politically. They expect the team will pull together on those few occasions when it is necessary. But leaders are not always free to appoint trusted allies. They have to consider some of the factors that govern the appointment of committee members: seniority, geography, other committee service, and qualifications. If those whom they appoint cannot run a committee, leaders will surely hear from the committee's members. Ralph Wright had to endure complaints about chairmen whom members did not find competent.[29] On occasion, interest-groups endorsements have to be factored in.[30] Leaders, like Bill Lockyer in California, in anticipation of term limits, are elevating less-tenured members to chairmanships.[31] Where parties are divided ideologically between conservatives and liberals, leaders must try to name chairs that represent both blocs. In the Florida house, where the rules committee sets the calendar, the Democratic speaker named cochairs to head the committee in order to satisfy both conservatives and liberals.[32]

Presiding

Among their managerial responsibilities, leaders have to preside over floor sessions of their houses. This allows them to steer debate, if not control it.

Presiding officers recognize members who want to speak on an issue and determine the order in which they speak. They are expected to be even-handed, permitting both sides to express their views; and to keep the session moving along. Presiding officers can determine which amendments are germane and which are not. But leaders must make their calls objectively so that their behavior seems fair and is acceptable to members of the other party as well as members of their own. Often they rely on the secretary of the senate or the clerk of the house for parliamentary advice. Although some leaders preside in autocratic fashion, with an "I-have-the-gavel" approach, most are fair.

Some leaders choose to hand the gavel over to other members so they can engage in backroom negotiations. Most leaders, however, spend considerable time at the dais. The very act of presiding can contribute to the strength of their leadership. They are judged by the way they handle themselves, their knowledge of rules and precedents, their decisions, the clarity of their actions, and their ability to maintain control without being arbitrary. A former presiding officer in Ohio was a firm believer in not giving up the gavel. "If I gave up the gavel," he said, "it would be interpreted as a sign of weakness." Just as in the schoolroom, where the teacher at the podium is an authority figure, so is the speaker or president (or president pro tem) on the dais of the house or senate chamber.[33]

Referring and Calendaring Bills

The power to refer bills to standing committees usually resides with top leaders, although sometimes a rules committee or a reference committee of the senate or house is allowed to make these decisions. Either way, the leaders can, and occasionally do, steer a bill to one committee or another in order to get the type of action they want. They can send a sponsor's bill to a committee that will give it a cool reception, or one where it will be treated with favor. They can give it "dual" or "consecutive" referrals, so that a proposal has to clear hurdles set up by two committees, instead of just one. But if assignments show a pattern of capriciousness, or if recommendations of bill sponsors are repeatedly ignored, a leader can get into trouble with members.[34] For the most part, bills are directed to the committees that should receive them. Jurisdiction is predictable, even though it is stretched on occasion for overriding political or policy purposes.

The leaders have greater discretion over the calendaring of bills. In many places, calendaring is their principal power—both over members inside and interests outside the legislature. In a few states, bills go directly to the calendar in the order in which standing committees report them. More often they go to the calendar by way of a rules committee. No matter who has formal authority, however, leaders can get bills on, or off, the day's agenda. "Posting" bills is a formidable weapon in New Jersey, and the speaker's ability to keep a bill off the board encourages members to cooperate. The assembly speaker and senate majority leader in New York have equivalent power. Even if a bill finds its way onto the calendar, they can "star" it, thereby preventing it from reaching the floor. Florida's leaders operate through rules committees; but they themselves can hasten a bill's passage or keep it off the "special order calendar." In the final days of the session, amidst the frenzy of activity, their control over the destiny of bills is probably at its height.

In exercising their calendaring power, leaders sometimes appear to be acting unilaterally and arbitrarily when, in fact, they are responding to the expressed needs of members. Some bills arouse emotion and controversy, and no one wants to vote on them. A vote would produce more losers than winners. Leaders consider it their job to protect members—usually members of their own party, but sometimes members on the other side of the aisle too.

Taking the Heat

The leader's role as flak-catcher—providing cover or taking the heat for members—extends well beyond scheduling authority. Vern Riffe, Ohio's speaker, stopped bills at the committee stage of the process. He would not allow a gun bill to be reported out because he regarded it as a "no winner"—that is, almost every member would lose whichever way he or she had to vote on the floor.[35] JoAnn Davidson, his successor as speaker, operated differently. She did not protect members from tough votes in part because she had less control over the Republican caucus than Riffe had over the Democratic caucus.[36]

Many people outside the legislature, and especially the *Boston Globe*, criticized William Bulger, president of the Massachusetts senate, for his rigid rule. But what might have appeared to be unilateral action on his part was frequently a reflection of what his members wanted. Bulger took the lead in opposing term limits and keeping the measure from coming to a vote, which earned him the gratitude of a number of senators who opposed the measure but did not want to appear at odds with their constituents. He was also willing to take the lead in advocating a legislative pay raise that, although very unpopular with the Massachusetts electorate, was acclaimed by members. His members wanted as much cover as they could get on the issue; they wanted their pay raise but did not want to have to pay for it. Bulger, even more than leaders elsewhere, took the blame for unpopular items and the heat for a lot of people.[37] California's Willie Brown is another leader who believed that part of his job was shielding members. In battles over the state budget—with Republican governors George Deukmejian and Pete Wilson—Brown fronted for assembly Democrats and allowed them to blame him for the stalemate, the mess, and the state's failure to pay its bills. Meanwhile, his colleagues were afforded time to hold out for more concessions from the governor before they agreed to a compromise.[38]

Maintaining Intercameral Relationships

As representatives of their respective chambers, another task of top leaders is to maintain relationships with each other. Rivalry between the senate and house is almost endemic, even when the same party has control. If the two bodies are under the control of different parties, cooperation becomes more difficult. Yet the two chambers are expected to produce a budget and both major and minor legislation for the state, and it is the job of the leaders to ensure that this is accomplished. They are the chief negotiators of both process and policy. It helps if their relationships are cordial, and even more if they are friends.

Some senate and house leaders, although of the same party persuasion, have a hard time getting along. They behave more as rivals than collaborators. Virginia's C. Richard Cramwell, the majority leader and principal power in the house, and Hunter Andrews, the senate's majority leader and principal power, had their difficulties.[39] In Maryland Speaker Clay Mitchell and President Mike Miller found it tough to work together, while Speaker Ben Cardin and President Mickey Steinberg found it easy. David Roberti and Willie Brown did not get along well.[40]

A most unlikely combination was Ohio's Riffe and Aronoff, the former a Democrat and the latter a Republican, who became friends when they both were in the house and grew to respect one another during their service as top leaders in their respective chambers. Throughout their leadership tenures, they helped each other on numerous occasions.[41] The two men came from completely dissimilar backgrounds and possessed quite different personalities. Riffe was keen on possum hunting, Aronoff on ballet. Although of opposing political parties, they were alike in some crucial ways: both had moderate views. They were pragmatists, not ideologues, and saw the legislature not as a battleground but as a ground for problem-solving. Neither cared about scoring political points; each wanted to get things accomplished.[42] Because of their joint leadership, the Ohio legislature proved to be a most effective institution during the 1980s and into the 1990s.

Leaders of opposing parties are able to work together because they are not rivals but rather opponents. They will not be competing for the same nomination for statewide office; they have entirely different bases and career paths. Leaders from the same party have greater incentive to outshine one another. They are competitors, like brothers within the same family. Yet friendship can overcome even rivalry. It enables leaders to trust each other and play by the rules. For Tom Loftus and Tim Cullen, Wisconsin's assembly and senate leaders and good friends, the rules that enabled them to negotiate productively were simple: (1) no surprises; (2) pretend in public that it wasn't a surprise, even if it was; and (3) defend each other in their respective caucuses.[43] As a consequence, the individual leaders benefited, and so did the legislature.

Ministering to Members

Institutionally, leaders also have a responsibility for ministering to members. Their doors have to be open and their empathy forthcoming. Legislators will come to them with problems that run the gamut—from the highly political to the intensely personal. One member needs an appointment for a constituent, and pleads with the leader to intervene with the governor. Another member is having marital difficulties and needs a sympathetic ear. For the most part, leaders just have to listen; sometimes they also have to act to help their member address a problem.

Handling Ethical Issues

Especially today, when the climate for politicians is hostile, leaders have to set an ethical example for other legislators and counsel them if they are straying. The penalties to both legislators and the legislature from unethical behavior are too high for leaders to ignore the subject. One of their tasks is to try, insofar as possible, to prevent a scandal from occurring, rather than to put out the fire after it starts. Until recently, only a few leaders considered it their role to set an ethical tone or to involve their offices in the ethical lives of legislators.

California offers an example of what can happen when leaders evade responsibility in this domain. In the 1960s and 1970s shakedowns occurred in the legislature when members wrote proposals harmful to interest groups, but dropped them in return for compensation. These incidents brought discredit to the legislature; it had to be the job of leaders to see that they did not take place. Speaker Leo McCarthy intervened on one occasion, but the affected member, in retaliation, withheld his vote on an important bill until the speaker relented.[44] Senate President Pro Tem David Roberti believed intervention was futile. Although he sensed that three of his Democratic members were overstepping the bounds, he took the view that it was not his job to rein them in; moreover, he believed he could not do so anyway. In addition, he needed their support and felt he could not afford to alienate them. "There are only so many people you can treat as pariahs," he said. If he could not get the votes of the three, he would not be able to put majorities together. Among other things, Roberti would lose his leadership position. Even worse, if a leader bangs heads, it will affect his prospects on many future bills. It can produce an enemy who will badmouth him in the press. Thus, trying to clean up a mess can lead to a bigger mess.

In retrospect, Roberti may have wished that he acted to avert scandal before it occurred. His three allies were indicted and convicted in the Shrimpgate sting, Roberti was embarrassed, and the California legislature suffered severe damage.[45] The culture of the California assembly was not terribly different from that in the senate. The primary example set by Speaker Willie Brown was in special-interest fund-raising, encouraging an "arms race" whereby other legislators sought out contributions to enhance their own power. Brown, according to one journalist, "set an ethical tone for his house, a tone that seemed to condone the selling of access."[46]

Current leaders are coming to the realization that they are obliged to deal with members who may be getting out of line, however difficult intervention may be. In the Mississippi house, Speaker Buddy Newman took the conduct of members seriously and had his lieutenants deliver his message to errant members: "This is something you can't do."[47] A number of senate leaders take the same approach. Mike Miller of Maryland attributes some ethics infractions to new members simply not knowing statutory provisions. "I feel like a camp counselor," he said. Pennsylvania's Robert Jubelirer described his ethics responsibility as a serious business. "As chief administrative officer," he declared, "I must protect the senate against suit or loss of public trust." His duty in this respect extended beyond party or friendship.[48]

Ethics leadership is particularly touchy in a collegial body, where friendships and loyalties count almost as much as votes. This is illustrated by Riffe's way with the Ohio house. He had no problem advising members if he thought they were too far off course. He would call a member into his office and, behind closed doors, confront him: "I have it from a source that this is going on. If you're doing it, stop." But Riffe was also there to go to bat for them if they got into trouble. One Democratic representative, for example, was picked up for drunk driving. The speaker helped to get the charges dismissed.[49] The speaker developed loyalties to those who were loyal to him. As described by a colleague, "Vern puts his arm around you and he stays that way." Rep. Paul Jones, who chaired the health committee, was one of his protégés, but "he grew too big for his britches," shaking down interest groups for speaking engagements and honoraria. Riffe, however, did not discipline Jones until it was too late.[50] Other members of the caucus questioned the speaker's loyalty to his health committee chairman. They wanted to know, "Just how far are you going to go with this guy?"[51] Apparently Riffe went too far, and at some cost to the Ohio house.

Managing the Institution

Legislative leaders have little spare time and slight inclination to devote to the management of the legislature as an institution. Management is usually at the bottom of their priority list. Although legislative leaders are responsible for staff, facilities, and the activities of their own chamber, these are supervised de facto by secretaries of the senate, clerks of the house, directors of legislative service bureaus, and partisan staff heads. The presiding officers generally shy away from administrative details because they are so busy with the legislative agenda and with partisan and campaign politics.

A committee of leaders from the two chambers is usually entrusted with managing and operating joint senate and house agencies and operations. New Mexico's Legislative Council, for instance, has sixteen members, including the speaker and minority leader of the house and the senate president and minority leader. The council sets policies for staff and facilities. The Joint Legislative Management Committee in Connecticut, the Joint Committee on Legislative Organization in Wisconsin, and the Legislative Services Commission in New Jersey are other leadership units entrusted with overall management. Here, too, much of the work is done by top staff in accord with the general intent of the leaders.

Most of the larger states have partisan and nonpartisan staffing. Connecticut, Michigan, California, Illinois, New Jersey, Pennsylvania, and Iowa are examples of states where each legislative party caucus has its own partisan staff providing support. In these states, leaders may rely on their top partisan aides to represent their interests on matters of legislative management. In Connecticut, leaders at one time involved themselves in management issues, giving guidance to the executive director of the Joint Committee on Legislative

Management. Now leaders operate through their partisan aides and are thus further removed from the administration of the legislature. Leadership engagement in this domain falls short, and whatever problems that beset legislative staff services in the states can be attributed in part to the neglect of legislative leaders, who are overwhelmed with other duties and rarely inclined to exercise whatever managerial skills they may have.

Helping Members Get Elected

The leaders' principal responsibility, as far as their legislative party colleagues are concerned, is to help them get elected and retain or win a majority in the senate or house. We have already discussed in chapter 5 the leadership role in this respect, so it is unnecessary to elaborate further here except to point out that these electoral responsibilities sometimes clash with the leaders' other responsibilities.

ACHIEVING LEGISLATIVE OBJECTIVES

The jobs of presiding officer and majority-party leader in the chamber cannot be disentangled. The fusion and overlap are considerable. As partisan and bipartisan leaders, the speaker and president (or president pro tem) have to ensure that the house and senate work their will on legislation. Thus, they have as a major role that of considering and enacting legislation generally, and more particularly legislation advanced by the governor, especially if the governor is of their own party, and by majority-party legislators.

Depending on the state, the partisan lineups, and the circumstances surrounding the issues, leaders either have to build a majority for legislation out of a consensus within their own party or reach across party lines to fashion a bipartisan majority or consensus. Every coalition is different and gets built a different way, most frequently on an ad hoc basis. "You invent the strategy for each situation," observes Scott Jensen, the majority leader in the Wisconsin assembly.[52] Coalition building is very much an art, not a science, that depends heavily on the leader's style, nature of the membership, and the ways in which consensus is built.

Styles of Leadership

In their study of legislative leadership, Malcolm Jewell and Marcia Lynn Whicker distinguish among three leadership styles. The first is the "command" style.

Leaders in this category need to control the behavior of others, minimize participation by rank-and-file, and suppress conflict. They limit debate and rarely consult the minority. The second is the "coordinating" style, which includes leaders who are more consultative, willing to deal with various groups, and seeking control through negotiations. The third is the "consensus" style, where leaders have less of a need to control the behavior of others; instead, they encourage participation and try to resolve conflict. These consensus leaders rarely reward or punish members.[53]

Although the notions of command and consensus are generally useful in thinking about legislative leaders, it is extraordinarily difficult to assign individual leaders to particular categories. It is more manageable, albeit less precise, to imagine leaders on a continuum ranging from command at one end to consultation at the other. Relatively few contemporary leaders rely on command; even those that resort to command consult as well. Most contemporary leaders are consultative, but they, too, employ punishment from time to time.

Some legislative systems endow leaders with more authority than do others. Some systems have traditions that run in a strong-leadership direction and some have systems where weaker leadership is expected. Practically everywhere the powers of the speaker of the house are greater than those of the president (or president pro tem) of the senate; the latter have to share power more. But the variation from state to state is great. One study found that, according to members' perceptions, the strongest leadership was found in the Massachusetts house and senate, and in the Ohio, Pennsylvania, and Tennessee houses, while the weakest was found in the Arizona, South Dakota, and Texas senates and houses and in the North Dakota, Tennessee, and Wisconsin senates.[54]

Although some places allow for command and others discourage it, individual leaders have ample choice. Leadership style is as much personal as systemic. Despite the overall pattern, some senate leaders are deemed more powerful than their counterparts in the house. Both of New Mexico's leaders are considered strong, but Manny Aragon, president of the senate, employs a harder fist than Raymond Sanchez, speaker of the New Mexico house. Aragon tries to control as much as possible, intimidates his colleagues, and has been called a "bulldozer" by some. Sanchez is less emotional, is good at prodding and coaxing, and knows how to proceed by indirection.[55] Even within the same house, successive leaders display very different styles. Maryland is a case in point. Marvin Mandel, although a strong and effective leader, was diligent in stroking members, taking care of their needs, and consulting with them. His successor, Thomas Hunter Lowe, ruled more firmly, while Lowe's successor, John Briscoe, held the reins more loosely. Ben Cardin's speakership was of a consultative and consensus-building nature. His successor, Clayton Mitchell, reverted to Lowe's style, while Mitchell's successor, Cass Taylor adopted the Cardin mold. Little consistency or pattern can be discovered here; leaders simply did what came most naturally to them.

Jewell and Whicker suggest that John Martin and Ralph Wright, speakers of Maine and Vermont respectively, were of the command type.[56] Martin's tenure lasted twenty years, and by the end of his reign he was known to his detractors as "the Imperial Speaker." Certainly a strong leader, and perhaps at times dictatorial, Martin could not deal well with the new generation of Democrats who evidenced little party loyalty. He would use his position and power to advance the caucus agenda, but that raised the hackles of some. At one point, after the chairman of the appropriations committee was killed in an automobile accident, Martin appointed himself to the vacancy. The budget was a major issue, and the Republicans had a strong member on the appropriations committee. The speaker believed he was the only Democrat who had enough knowledge of the process to take her on. But the assumption of so much power gravely damaged Martin. He was finally overthrown after an election-rigging scandal involving one of his top aides. The *Maine Times* (January 21, 1994) celebrated his fall with an editorial entitled, "THE KING IS DEAD," in which it criticized house members for delegating to leaders the power to set the agenda and control how issues would be decided.

Ralph Wright brought modern political techniques to the old-fashioned house in Vermont. He was a strong house speaker who got into more than his share of fights and confrontations.[57] On the one hand he could be amiable and warm, on the other intimidating; it depended on the situation. His special skill was in how he played people. "He knew everyone's hand"—what someone would need in return for going along. Wright would not hesitate to bend the rules to reach the results he wanted. He liked the exercise of power, and wrote in his memoirs: "I satisfied my need for love and acceptance by accruing power. It was power to do good things as I saw it, but nevertheless it was there for all to see."[58] Members began to chafe under Wright's leadership. After he was defeated for reelection in his district, his successor as speaker— Michael Obuchowski—operated in an entirely different manner. He was more interested in the process than in results; he went by the book instead of using the rules to accomplish his purposes.[59]

However impressive their use of power, neither Martin nor Wright was a pure type. Nor was Vern Riffe, who probably came closer to the mark. Riffe stated his philosophy: "If you're the leader, you're the leader. If you're strong, everyone wins, and if you're weak, they all lose."[60] Although Riffe had a few trusted lieutenants, they got the word from the speaker and carried out his commands. His style was to deal with members one-on-one and thus never be outnumbered. New members, in particular, could easily feel intimidated. But Riffe prided himself on being honest and fair with his colleagues, bound by his commitments and his loyalty. The senate was very different from the house in Ohio, with senate Democratic leaders nearer to the command style than the Republican leader. No one, however, approached Riffe in terms of authority. Although highly effective, Republican leader Stan Aronoff could never exercise control. Democracy reigned in his caucus meetings, and Aronoff "always had to have his finger in the wind" in order to know where to lead his flock.[61]

Willie Brown is credited with having been one of the more powerful legislative leaders in the country. He even called himself the "ayatollah" of the assembly.[62] He was forceful, even threatening to some; but above all he was a "member's speaker," a leader who gave his colleagues leeway to push their own policy agendas. He did not stand in the way of the creative energies of Democratic assembly members and their staffs.[63] As a members' speaker, Brown met the needs of his colleagues, and they met his need for the speakership. He helped them achieve their legislative objectives and provided them with funding for their campaigns. After leaving the assembly and being elected mayor of San Francisco, Willie Brown looked back on his years of catering on a daily basis to legislators. In a moment of obvious distemper, he referred to his former colleagues as "pantywaist politicians" and claimed he held on to the speakership because he "understood the smallness of them," "lived with the smallness of them," and "fed the smallness of them!"[64]

Neither David Roberti nor William Lockyer, as senate presidents pro tem, could be likened stylistically to Willie Brown. Moreover, Roberti and Lockyer differed from one another. Roberti was a big-picture person and did not involve himself in detail. He delegated much of the landscape to staff. In contrast, Lockyer was more engaged in the process and more policy oriented. He would insert himself into the budget process early on, whereas Roberti would not enter negotiations until the end, when the so-called Big Five were meeting.[65] Both pro tems were accessible and effective in working with their colleagues; Roberti, though, was especially generous—willing to give practically whatever senators wanted,[66] while Lockyer was more restrained. Leo McCarthy probably came as near to being an autocrat as any one legislative leader in California. He was stern, tough, and intrusive. One member felt "schoolmarmed" by him, suffering "a thousand razor nicks of humiliation" at his hands.[67]

Whether leaders command or consult, their principal responsibility is to help laws get passed. Relatively few leaders can afford to advocate and promote their own policies rather than work to achieve a consensus within their caucus and/or chamber. Jewell and Whicker cite Irv Stolberg, the speaker of the Connecticut house, as one who did not put his own agenda aside. Stolberg characterized his leadership style as "strong and directive" and took pride in using his power to advance a progressive agenda, despite a caucus divided between liberal and conservative Democrats.[68] On the other side of the political spectrum, a number of conservative legislative leaders pushed their own agendas, which incidentally did not run counter to the dominant views in their caucuses. For example, David Jennings of Minnesota kept house Republicans on a short leash and had them help in developing legislation to rein in government.[69]

Curt Pringle, who took over the speakership of the California assembly in 1996, was a staunch social and economic conservative. His agenda was faithful to that of most of his caucus colleagues. But if he wanted to get as much of it as possible through a house where he had no votes to spare and a Democratic senate with which to contend, he had to moderate his own positions. "There are people here on both sides that I consider 100 percenters," he said. "They want to get all or nothing." Pringle wanted to get something rather than nothing.[70]

Probably no other system has spawned more in the way of policy advanced by leadership than the Florida house. For the past thirty years, it has been customary for speaker after speaker to promote his own legislative agenda, in addition to the governor's agenda and whatever bills had to be moved. The speaker's lieutenants, who chaired standing committees, would generally be expected to sign onto his agenda and do their part to advance it. A few speakers along the way had modest policy goals, but most sought to enact broad-ranging programs. Hyatt Brown, one of the most effective modern speakers, had fifty-three issues he wanted passed in his two-year tenure, and he succeeded with all but one.[71] Even Florida's senate leaders had their own agendas, although they were usually more limited than those of their counterparts in the house.[72] The heyday of Florida's legislative programmatic leadership may be over because it is now more difficult for the house speaker and the senate president to get ambitious proposals passed.

Florida has been an anomaly among the states. In most places leaders have been happy to settle for extra benefits for their districts, while on other issues they have worked to build consensus and forge majorities from their caucuses or the chamber as a whole. Ohio is typical in this regard. The house's program for years was generated by the Democratic caucus. Speaker Riffe was moderate in his outlook and not committed to particular policies per se. He just wanted to get the job done to the satisfaction of as many of his colleagues as possible.[73] Yet he did not neglect his district in southern Ohio, accomplishing much for the area, including the establishment of a state college. On the senate side, Republican leader Aronoff fashioned a program that his caucus favored and that helped members in their negotiations with the Democratic house. Aronoff, too, looked out for his district, to the extent of opposing his own governor on taxes that would hurt retailers in Cincinnati.[74]

Another leader who showed relatively little concern with policy was Willie Brown. He was especially reluctant to embrace an issue that was visible or salient; he did not want his views to disrupt the caucus. So his approach was to allow the caucus consensus free rein. There was no point in making his colleagues unhappy, for unhappy caucus members might breed challenges to his leadership. Yet, contrary to criticisms, he did exercise influence on policy, although his efforts in shaping legislation were circumscribed.[75] David Roberti was of a similar mind; he would work for agreement, even if he did not himself agree with the results.[76]

Legislative leaders occasionally have to set aside their own strongly held views in service to their caucuses. JoAnn Davidson, the Republican who succeeded Riffe as speaker in Ohio, would not bottle up an anti-abortion bill that had fifty sponsors even though she was pro-choice. She only went so far as trying to discourage her caucus from taking a party position. Maryland's Clay Mitchell was anything but happy helping to enact a large tax increase, which he opposed. Unable to win over his leadership team to his position, he had to go along with theirs.[77]

The Nature of the Membership

Every legislator has a set of principles, policy preferences, and political needs. They all want something, and it is seldom the same thing, out of the legislative process. "There are ninety-nine members in the Wisconsin assembly," said Jensen, "and ninety-nine bottom lines."[78] Jensen's main concerns, of course, were the fifty-one Republicans who had a bare majority at the time he commented on the bottom line. Members maintain their independence, and senators especially so. Since independence is a tradition in senates, leaders have had to be respectful of the interests of each of their colleagues. The trend has been toward more and more independence. As described by Harry Meshel of the Ohio senate: "There is a different breed of members today. They are on stage all the time, and we are all prima donnas around here; if you are secure in your district, the hell with the leaders."[79] Today's legislators consider themselves to be neither apprentices nor followers. They have little or no inclination to learn their trade slowly and gradually. Where they are term-limited, they have little choice but to get a running start. Add to this their belief that their constituents did not send them to the capitol to take marching orders from anyone else—leaders or otherwise. They are there to do the bidding of their districts. Thus, practically every legislator conceives of himself or herself as a leader in the legislature (and a follower of district sentiment, when there is such a thing).

Compounding this is the heterogeneity within the ranks of both parties, not only because members hail from diverse constituencies but also because they bring various philosophies with them. The more ideological they are, the greater their insistence on their agendas, no matter what the repercussions. The California assembly illustrates the transformation of a pragmatic membership to a more hard-line one, which began with the "Proposition 13 babies" of the 1970s, a group of conservatives who were agenda-driven instead of consensus driven.[80] The Democratic, and Republican, caucus changed markedly through the 1980s. But Willie Brown, according to a former staffer, was always able to keep the "screwballs and crazies" in his ranks on a short leash.[81] The number of legislators who bring heavy-issue baggage to the legislature appears to be increasing, while the number of problem-solving members seems to be in decline. Ideological or pragmatic, the agendas are there.

Despite their independence and insistence on their agendas, members acknowledge their need for leaders, but not leaders who try to tell them what to do. Their need is for leaders who bite the bullet when a decision can no longer be deferred and for leaders who take risks on their behalf. They also realize that the whole process is held together by glue, and that leaders provide that glue. They know they need leadership, even though they are not always ready to follow it.

Despite their diversity, members of the leader's party will go along whenever they feel they can. Often it is in their interests to do so. Majority status in the chamber may be contingent on their party's ability to deliver a program or enact specified bills in the legislature. Without majority status, individuals lose clout and benefits as members of the legislature. Their loyalties do predispose them to give the benefit of doubt to those they elected to preside. Occasionally circumstances, such as the flush of electoral victory, help to unify party members behind leadership, at least for a while. For example, David Prosser, the speaker of the Wisconsin assembly, whose Republicans had just taken control after many years in the wilderness, took advantage of the momentum to enact choice for parochial schools, a program championed by a Democratic chairwoman. The speaker staked his leadership on achieving that goal and won the support of his entire caucus.[82]

If a leader's party has a large majority, individual members may be more inclined to stray from the fold. The predominant attitude is, "You can get their votes, so you don't need mine." By contrast, if the majority is slim, the leader can argue to his caucus that every vote counts, so that no one can be let off the hook. It is difficult for a member to hold out when he is the only dissident or one of two or three. But, still, some do.

A principal obligation to the leadership is incurred when members feel they owe their elections to campaign funds or other assistance provided by the leaders. As discussed in chapter 5, leaders have come to be principal actors in their legislative party's campaigns. Although they have very limited power over decisions about the allocation of funds, the leaders benefit from the members' sense of obligation because of their efforts. Some members, it is true, feel no gratitude at all, believing they are entitled to whatever the leader provides. Minnesota's speaker, Robert Vanasek, pointed out that "the ones who are getting it [funding] don't bother to thank you because there is now an expectation that they are going to get it."[83] Most, particularly those who continue to rely on leaders for help, do feel some sense of obligation. But obligations erode over time, as the fund-raising abilities and the independence of members grow.

The experience of Willie Brown illustrates how benefits accrue to the beneficent leader. Brown's financial support earned him membership support in his reelections to the speakership. His ability to raise money was thought to be an asset that assembly Democrats did not want to be without. Those who profited directly may have felt their gratitude diminish, but it never vanished entirely.[84] New Jersey's tradition has been to rotate presiding officers every two terms (or four years). Donald DiFrancesco broke this tradition in 1996, when he began his third term as senate president. His achievement can be attributed in part to his contributions to the campaigns of his Republican colleagues. Yet DiFrancesco's affability, interpersonal skills, and the dearth of Republican challengers are also responsible.

Although leaders undoubtedly reap personal benefits, they get few votes on critical issues in return for their efforts. They cannot turn around legislators whose constituency and/or conscience point in the opposite direction. They rarely try. An analysis of roll-call votes in the California assembly suggests that members who received the most from Speaker Brown gave back little by way of votes.[85] It is likely, however, that on the more peripheral aspects of the process, members who have enjoyed leaders' largess will do what they can, if called on, to repay their benefactors.

The Ways in Which Consensus Is Built

Most legislative leaders subscribe to the view that their major role in the lawmaking process is that of building consensus—searching for common ground and encouraging people to come together and cooperate. Initially, leaders must develop consensus within their own chamber. That task may entail securing agreement either among members of one's own party or across party lines. The closer to unanimity, the better; the more divisive, the worse (except when the principal objective is to score partisan points by forcing the opposition to cast an unpopular vote on an issue). Secondarily, they must help manage the quest after agreement with the other chamber. Finally, they must ensure that the legislative consensus, signified by the enactment of a bill by both chambers, is ratified by the governor.

LEADERSHIP TEAMS. Consensus-building is the task not only of the top leaders themselves but also of their leadership teams. Each house speaker and each senate president (or president pro tem) relies on a leadership team, a group of lieutenants, who play key roles in the lawmaking process. The team can be rather formally or informally constituted. Usually, it consists of the majority leader, assistant leaders, and the chairs of the key standing committees. Occasionally, a few of a leader's trusted lieutenants have no official status, but even in those cases most team members have formal legislative assignments regarded as important.

Leaders feel free to assemble their teams as they wish. Maryland's senate and house leadership teams have always been relatively large. On the senate side, Mike Miller is essentially a consensus builder who consults with his leadership team of about twenty people, listens to what they say, and then tries to bring other members into the fold as he works from the bottom up. Only where there is a possible breakdown or where a divisive issue threatens the senate community does Miller step in to exercise control.[86]

On the house side in Maryland leadership, teams have varied in size. Marvin Mandel had a team of thirty-five, but Thomas Hunter Lowe employed an eight-person leadership group. John Briscoe expanded the group's size, and then Ben Cardin in the 1980s built it up to about thirty-five. Cardin consulted regularly with his leadership group, also dealing with legislators one-on-one in order to reach consensus positions. Clay Mitchell relied on only a few key leaders, was far less consultative, and insisted on discipline.[87]

Not every member of a leader's team has the same influence. Maryland's full house leadership in 1996 numbered about fifty people (out of a total membership of 141). It can barely fit into a meeting room. But Speaker Taylor's senior leaders amount to fourteen people, including the minority leader and committee chairs. Within that smaller group is an even smaller "kitchen cabinet" of a few trusted lieutenants. This is the inner circle—the legislators who "are in the room when the door gets closed."[88]

Leaders rely on members of their teams, and delegate policy-making authority to those of them who chair committees. Some leaders delegate substantial authority, others try to retain as much as possible for themselves. The former appears to be the dominant pattern. Wisconsin's Tom Loftus operated in this manner. In his view, although leaders have to keep their goals in mind, they cannot worry too much about how to achieve them. Instead, they must rely on their committee chairs, which entails letting go of some power and giving it to others.[89] According to this pattern, the speaker or president would choose able and trustworthy chairs for the major committees and permit them to chart their course. Only when they got far out of line with the legislative party would top leadership rein them in.

The delegation of power can be seen in the approach of Peter Wallace, speaker of the Florida house in 1995–1996. The practice previously had been to micromanage committees from the speaker's office. Wallace rejected that practice and took a hands-off approach. Some of his chairs put bills on their agendas for which the speaker had little enthusiasm; some reported out bills that he preferred not to bring to the floor. But he did not exercise control and, instead, insisted on decentralizing power. Too much control, too much centralization, according to him, did not allow members to use their talents and did not yield the best results.[90]

Temperament has something to do with just how much control leaders try to exercise over committees. New Mexico's speaker and president are both hands-on leaders who have to be involved in most of the big decisions. Speaker Sanchez serves on several standing committees, which helps him stay on top of their operations. Senate President Aragon is even more involved. In 1994, for instance, he sat on about ten interim committees. As a member of the Legislative Finance Committee, he often dominated the questioning of executive witnesses. He engaged in floor debates, speaking on nearly every significant bill, and he appointed himself a member of the budget conference committee almost without fail.[91]

THE USE OF DISCIPLINE. In return for being delegated some power, members of the leadership team are expected to support collective decisions. So are members of the caucus. If they do not, they may be subject to discipline. Leaders rarely resort to the use of discipline. Most are likely to withhold rewards from (or even punish) legislators who make a run at them for the top leadership post or who are core supporters of their opponent in a leadership race. Frequently, these people wind up with a minor committee chairmanship instead of a major one. Occasionally they lose a preferred office or parking space. Years ago, when Willie Brown did not vote for Jesse Unruh for speaker, Unruh retaliated by giving him a poor committee assignment and a small office he had to share with another member. "He shat all over me," is the way Brown recalls it years later.[92] But, still, punishment is relatively rare.

Even in New York, where leadership is highly centralized, there are occasions when the majority leader of the senate and the speaker of the assembly release members from party discipline. Where conscience or district dictates a position, the leaders are inclined to let the member off the reservation. One senator, for example, fought Joseph Bruno, the majority leader, on two significant issues in the 1997 session. He helped kill a measure to legalize casino gambling that Bruno had championed, and then he allied himself with senate Democrats in upholding rent-control laws. The majority leader explained publicly that punishment would be coming. "Members know that when they take a position that isn't reflective of the leadership, that there is a downside," he said. "He [the member in question] knows it might make his life less comfortable."[93]

Punishment is the exception, even when members refuse to go along with their legislative party on an issue. Vern Riffe was a strict disciplinarian, although he was an understanding and compassionate one. According to him, "If you haven't got discipline, you don't get the job done." In return for the authority delegated to his committee chairs, he demanded loyalty. They were expected to go along with the legislative party program. If they did not, retribution was a distinct possibility. But over the course of twenty years, Riffe dealt with no more than a half-dozen instances of apostasy. A few chairmen were relieved during their terms of office; a few others were not reappointed at the next organization of the legislature. Riffe recalls that after one Democratic caucus, the African American delegation (minus one notable member) boycotted the floor session, and the Democrats lost their issue by one or two votes. Riffe thereupon met with the delegation and dressed members down, and he threatened to remove from the budget items they wanted. The next day the bill passed and there were no further problems.[94]

· Riffe hated surprises. He insisted on being notified in advance by members who felt they could not go along. If a legislator had to oppose the caucus because of his or her district, Riffe would ordinarily allow the legislator to leave the fold. One observer characterized the system under Riffe: "You only vote against the will of the leadership with permission."[95] With Riffe's retirement, discipline is no longer the threat it once was. In the 1996 session, Republicans brought up a major tort reform on the house floor (after it had passed the senate) but had trouble getting the required votes. It was initially defeated and had to be brought up again two weeks later. A few committee chairmen voted against it, but they were permitted to go their way without any retribution.[96]

Elsewhere, discipline is invoked, but not frequently. Even in a state like Massachusetts, where leadership control used to be strict, nowadays sanctions for disloyalty are rare. Voting "off," or against the leadership, once carried a price—loss of a budgetary plum for one's district. Now opposition is simply accepted.[97]

Leaders reserve sanctions for very special situations. Florida's speakers have removed committee or subcommittee chairs who opposed them on particular issues. Gwen Margolis, who served as senate president, thanks to the support she received from a bipartisan coalition, took punitive action when senate Republicans and one of her Democratic colleagues threatened to sabotage the budget. She removed all of the Republicans and the one wayward Democrat from their chairmanships of committees and subcommittees. Although she got the budget approved, she incurred the enmity of the Republicans. New Mexico's Raymond Sanchez normally avoided exercising discipline. But one Democrat, who crossed the aisle to uphold the Republican governor's veto of an education-budget item, incurred the speaker's wrath. Sanchez felt he had to do something, so he took the renegade off the Legislative Council and saw to it that the senate amended out items of his in the capital budget bill.[98]

The newer generation of leaders is even less inclined to punish than the older ones. Since members are less apt to accept discipline, its exercise may boomerang. In more philosophical terms, many of today's leaders agree with Robert Garton of Indiana, who maintains that "You cannot manage the legislative process by fear, but only with respect and trust."[99] In more practical terms, many of today's leaders subscribe to the dictum, "If you punish them today, they'll punish you tomorrow." When the Republicans took control of the Wisconsin assembly, there was talk in their caucus of doling out punishment to members who deserted the team in a crisis. Speaker David Prosser refused to do so, however; it was out of character for him and would not, in his judgment, be good for the team. Moreover, with a close margin in the assembly, a punished member would be embittered and could very well defect to the other side.[100]

PARTICIPATIVE MANAGEMENT. Leaders encourage participation well beyond their leadership team. They are in continuous touch with members of their party, and sometimes with members of the opposition as well. Garton exemplifies this style of participative management. As president of the Indiana senate (and a management consultant in his occupation outside the legislature), he is a firm believer in face-to-face communications, building personal relationships, and establishing an open and fair climate. "Everyone knows," he maintains, "that they will get their say in the legislative process." Before a decision is made, he brings in as many senators as possible to make them part of the process. If in the process mutual respect is engendered, then negotiations will proceed and compromise will result.[101]

Talking to members individually and continuously is at the core of consensus building. Few leaders remain aloof or isolated. Some, of course, are less convivial than others. David Roberti was not particularly sociable, and senate Democrats had to make an effort by going through leadership staff to see him. Most leaders, in contrast, have an open-door policy for their colleagues.[102] They visit with their colleagues regularly either to discuss problems or just to chat.[103] In Ohio, Stanley Aronoff made it his business to talk to members one-on-one and to know what was on their minds. JoAnn Davidson began her tenure as speaker by taking ten legislators at a time out for lunch.[104] A more partisan leader like Vermont's Wright finds it fruitless to consult with members of the other party. He would not even talk to any Republicans because it was, in his judgment, a waste of time. "They did not like me, and I didn't like them."[105]

Leaders draw on different interpersonal skills that serve their styles and purposes. Riffe played it straight and prided himself on his candor. "If I couldn't do something, I told them," he said. His operating principles were: "Tell it like it is" and "Don't bullshit people."[106] He could be personally charming, exhibiting an almost southern gentility. Underneath he was as tough as steel.[107] Riffe's personality worked for him, just as Aronoff's and Davidson's worked for them.

Ben Cardin, speaker of the Maryland house, had the advantage of being likable and knowing how to humor people. His charm seldom failed him. He could arrive late for a meeting, flash his boyish ("Who me?") grin, and not miss a beat as everyone forgot that they had been kept waiting.[108] Mike Miller also played the interpersonal game extremely well. Sometimes he would be serious, sometimes funny, and sometimes outrageous, but he appeared to know when and with whom to be each.[109]

Leaders are prepared for dissent. They do not expect every member of the caucus to be with them on each and every issue. Even the strongest leaders of the most disciplined parties recognize that the political and philosophical interests of their members come first, even before party loyalty. Riffe rarely demanded that members walk the plank. On the rare occasion that he did, his gratitude for member loyalty was noteworthy. For example, on one bill he succeeded in getting a vote from a legislator who had tried to beg off because he could not afford to cross the Ohio Education Association. Riffe needed the vote and persisted until he got it. When the legislator was targeted for defeat in a primary by the association, Riffe went into his district with a substantial war chest and helped beat back the onslaught.[110]

"I have never asked anyone to vote either against their conscience or their constituents" is the way Garton expressed his approach. Leaders have to understand the pressures both on and within each legislator. They have to be sensitive to the political climate in members' districts. If they ask legislators to vote against major blocs in their district, they may sacrifice these members and consequently lose their majority. Members in marginal seats have to be protected, and to be properly protected, their political needs must be indulged. Nor do leaders normally insist that members act contrary to their convictions or to their public records. "You don't make people for political reasons do something that hurts their self-image," said a Maryland senator, referring to Speaker Mitchell, whose insistence on loyalty had embarrassed a number of house Democrats.[111] With rare exceptions, even the strongest legislative leaders make allowances for dissension, and without recrimination.

THE USE OF REWARDS. In trying to develop consensus, leaders must be able to persuade legislators whenever they can. This entails knowing their colleagues' strengths and weaknesses and which of their buttons to push. Brown of California was a master in these respects.[112] So was Wright of Vermont.[113] Consensus building requires intimate knowledge and consummate skill, upon which is built the ability to persuade. It also requires the employment of inducements. "Sticks" are used only in rare instances, although some leaders are more inclined to punish than others. Wright was one of them. He would make sure his opponents' bills never saw the light of day—and he wanted members to know it.[114]

The use of carrots is the conventional approach. If leaders know, or are made aware of, what members want, they generally try to make them happy. Sometimes they make them very happy, requiring little in return. Florida's Peter Wallace simply did not believe in dealing. A house member came to Speaker Wallace's chief of staff to ask for x, y, and z. When the chief turned him down, he reduced his request to only x. The chief of staff still refused, told the legislator to see the speaker, and rushed to brief the speaker in advance. "He'll ask for x, y, and z. You might give him x," the staffer advised his boss, "but be sure to get something in return." After the legislator left the speaker's office, the staffer went in and asked the speaker, "What did you give him?" "X, y, and z," the speaker said. "What did you get?" "Nothing," the speaker replied.[115]

Most leaders try to take care of everybody. Particularly where partisan margins are close, leaders cannot afford to annoy anyone, so they have to spread the goodies around. Often this means moving members' bills through the process, helping their constituents find employment, getting their key supporters appointed to state boards and commissions, providing them extra staffing assistance, funding their travel to attend conferences, and making sure they have a new desk or computer.

Favors do not always result in gratitude, however; sometimes they simply result in complaints. Rod Searle, who had a brief stint as speaker of the house in Minnesota, describes how even benefits can boomerang. After Searle assigned members office space, one veteran lost his composure upon learning that his office was not on the side that faced the capitol. Another became upset because his office was not as close to the speaker's office as he thought it should be. Another member was insulted because his desk was metal rather than wood. One member was unhappy because his office did not have a credenza and another because his office had no drapes.[116]

Unless they satisfy members, leaders can forget about holding their leadership positions for very long. Even Vermont's Wright went out of his way to cater to his colleagues. He wrote: "My criteria to judge how far I would go to help a member was simple and straightforward. As long as it wasn't against the law, didn't require that I go to confession, or wouldn't break up my marriage, I did it."[117] Willie Brown operated in a similar manner. His whole edifice, Brown's biographer writes, was built on a simple principle: Keep members happy. As long as he could keep forty-one members happy (there were eighty in the assembly), he knew he would remain speaker.[118]

ENCOURAGING COMPROMISE. In their efforts to develop consensus, legislative leaders stress the need for the various sides and parties to compromise in order to resolve their differences. For Indiana's Garton, "the name of the game is compromise."[119] That is the principal business of many leaders. Compromises are made at several stages of the process: among interest groups, among committee members, in caucus, between the house and the senate, and perhaps with the governor as well. Leaders are responsible for bringing disputants together and encouraging them to find common ground and settle. In doing this, a test of their skill is how they communicate to the disputants and structure the conditions of the contest. According to Loftus, the leader must direct the group, state the obvious, and know when to put the question. "If you keep people in a room long enough," he writes, "they will eventually make a decision."[120]

One theory to which many leaders subscribe is that compromise and consensus emerge out of discomfort. That is why leaders occasionally keep their meetings going or their chambers in session until the legislators' will to hold out is worn down. Consensus develops, according to Scott Jensen of Wisconsin, "when the members are grumpy and tired and want the issue to be over."[121] House and senate chambers in Rhode Island have not been air-conditioned, it is believed, because of the need to resolve budget disputes at the end of the session in June or July. Legislative leaders feel that if they air-condition the capitol, members would not mind hanging around, and they would never be able to reach agreement on a budget.[122]

THE PARTY CAUCUS. When leaders are trying to build consensus, probably the most important agency at their disposal is the party caucus. The caucus is often the formal setting in which the most extensive discussions and negotiations take place. In some states caucuses meet only for purposes of organizing the chamber at the outset of a session. In other states, caucuses take real shape as two-party politics gain vigor. In Maryland, for example, the Republicans established caucuses in the house and senate as their numbers in each chamber increased. The Democrats, on the other hand, with super majorities, felt no need to caucus. Senate Democrats in Maryland had not caucused in a quarter-century.[123]

When the minority party begins to gain in numbers, it is likely to caucus more frequently. Then, the majority party responds by forming its own caucus. This has been the recent experience of Florida, South Carolina, and Virginia. Mississippi, in contrast, still has no caucuses because the minority party has not reached a critical mass. In Texas the election of a Republican governor stimulated the Republicans in the legislature to develop a caucus to support their chief executive. As partisan competition persists, caucuses tend to become more frequent and more structured.[124]

In competitive, two-party states caucuses usually meet regularly, unless the leader is in such firm control that no caucus is desired. Rarely did Democrats get together in the Ohio house. Riffe chose not to convene them on a regular basis because bringing members together could only cause problems for leadership. When he did call a caucus meeting, it was to have a "pep rally" or on occasion a "gripe session."[125] Ohio's other legislative parties, however, met regularly and dealt with controversial legislation.[126]

If leaders could rely on cohesive caucuses, they would be less reluctant to have them meet. Many caucuses are sharply split, however, between liberals and moderates among the Democrats and moderates and conservatives among the GOP. Generally, today's leaders do not stand in the way of caucus meetings. They have no recourse but to play the hand dealt them. They regularly confer with their members, state the position of leadership on legislation, receive support from committee chairs, and determine whether everyone is comfortable with the position. Leaders deal with policy and strategy. On critical issues, such as the budget, they try to get as many votes as they require for passage. When it comes to voting on the budget, in Garton's words, "We know where we are before we get to the floor."[127] Controversial and partisan issues are not brought to the floor unless leaders know they have enough votes in their own caucus. Leaders rarely flout this principle, as Paul Gillmore of the Ohio senate once did, bringing a divisive bill to the floor and letting the chips fall where they may.[128]

Few caucuses, however, take binding votes. New Mexico's Democrats do so on budget and tax bills, while New Mexico's Republicans do so on procedural matters. In Oklahoma a binding vote may occasionally be taken on an issue. Binding or not, leaders come away from a caucus with a fair idea of how many votes they have.

Sometimes the majority has to rely on minority votes, even on critical matters. On less important matters, where partisan loyalties are not in play, minority members may be as important in the process as majority members. And leaders deal with them as well.

RELATIONS WITH THE MINORITY. Most bills processed by the legislature are nonpartisan or bipartisan, so whether one is a Democrat or a Republican does not count in the decision. Majority-party members, however, are likely to have more of the bills they sponsor reported out of committee, calendared, and enacted by their chamber than are their minority colleagues. They are likely to get a bit more for their districts in the appropriations act. They also acquire superior office space and larger staff allotments. Generally, the leader of the majority tries to be fair, which means giving the minority what it wants "within reason."[129]

At times, the leader will make a special effort to bring the minority into the process. With Republicans growing in numbers and threatening to win control of the house, Florida's Peter Wallace gave the minority a larger role on standing committees than it had before. He did this partly because of his own political needs, but partly to improve the process. Wallace gave Republican representatives vice-chairmanships of all committees (except appropriations and rules), and he appointed a few Republicans to chairmanship positions. Moreover, he counseled his Democratic chairmen to involve their Republican vice-chairmen in the actual leadership of the committees. The speaker wanted Republicans to be prepared to govern in the event they won the 1996 election, which they then did.[130]

The relationship between majority and minority depends mainly on the size of the minority and its electoral threat to the majority, the ideological disposition and cohesiveness of the minority caucus, and the way in which majority and minority leaders work together. The minority has a basic choice: it can either cooperate with the majority and reap the benefits; or it can stand in opposition, creating issues that can be used against the majority in the next election. The closer the minority comes to parity with the majority, the more inclined it will be to engage in skirmishes as a phase in the war to topple the majority. Also, one can expect less negotiation, compromise, and acquiescence from a minority dominated by an extreme wing of the party.

Partisan conflict on major issues is the norm in a number of legislative bodies. It occurs more frequently in houses than in senates. It is most likely to occur on the budget and taxes. Today conflict typifies relationships in California, New Jersey, and Pennsylvania houses, for example. One political scientist describes the Minnesota house as a legislative body whose major function has become one of crystalizing the partisan issues in legislation, not resolving them, except in the most formal sense of taking a vote. This combative pattern, according to him, may sharpen issues in the election, but it is harmful to the democratic processes of deliberation and legitimation.[131]

Partisan accommodation may be on the decline, but it still exists, particularly when one side has an overwhelming majority or where majority and minority leaders get along with one another. The Maryland senate is illustrative. Mike Miller included the minority leader and two other Republicans in his leadership team of eighteen senators; he appointed the minority leader to chair an important appropriations subcommittee.[132] The minority leader on his part, worked to inject his and his caucus's views into the majority agenda, with some success. Other senate presidents or pro tems have also maintained good relationships with their minority leaders. Jim Scott worked well with Ken Jenne in Florida, and David Roberti had a good relationship with Ken Maddy in California. In Massachusetts William Bulger and David Locke got along. Indeed, upon his defeat in 1992, Locke commented on Senate President Bulger: "Despite the fact I've probably given him more trouble than any other member in his career, underlying it all is respect and appreciation on a personal basis."[133]

One of the closer personal relationships was that existing between Speaker Vern Riffe and Corwin Nixon, the minority leader, in the Ohio house. They were good friends, and went off on trips together. In fact, Riffe had helped Nixon become minority leader.[134] Nixon had a sense of obligation toward Riffe, and it was not difficult for him to set aside partisan politics in much of his dealing with the speaker. Moreover, he believed the minority Republicans had more to gain by cooperating with Riffe than by engaging in partisan conflict.[135] Because trust existed, compromise across party lines was possible. In Ohio cooperation characterized both Republican dealings with the Democrats and the senate's relations with the house. But such cooperation probably depended on the pragmatism of the leaders.[136]

THE POWER OF LEADERSHIP

The principal question is not whether legislative leaders have power, but whether they possess too much or not enough. Leaders have weighty responsibilities that range from advancing the interests of their members to overseeing the management of the house in which they serve. Not least among their responsibilities is that of finding common ground, facilitating compromise, forging consensus and enabling the legislature to locate and work its will. It is normally a bipartisan will, although on some matters—critical ones, including the state budget—the will may be that of the majority party.

The speaker of the house and the senate president or president pro tem have substantial authority. Leaders control the assignments of members to standing committees and can name and remove chairmen. They can facilitate passage of a member's bill or to block it entirely. They can help mightily with pork for the district, as well as with appointments and jobs for a member's supporters and constituents.

Tom Loftus describes the speaker's power as "near dictatorial," but he learned from experience that "it was wisest not to use it."[137] Others rarely wield their power demonstrably, and few use it arbitrarily or vindictively. Occasionally, they feel compelled to punish errant legislators, but the penalty is often applied in response to the wishes of the caucus. For the most part leaders rely on their strategic and tactical skills, their persuasive abilities, the indulgences they can grant, and the support they have within the caucus rather than on intimidation and punishment.

The chamber membership, but especially the caucus membership, is key. Legislators today are independent agents. They run their own campaigns, although those who are most threatened still have to depend on leadership help. (But leaders really cannot afford *not* to help these swing-district members.) They relate to their own constituencies, have their own agendas, and pursue their own ambitions. If anything unites them, it is the caucus. Caucus members share partisan affiliations and orientations, and their individual prosperity is seen to hinge on the party's fortunes. They are disposed to go along with their legislative party, if they feel they can, which is much of the time. But sometimes they feel they cannot.

Leaders elected by their caucuses have to be responsive to their colleagues, or they will not be leaders for long. Even New York's assembly speaker and senate majority leader, considered among the most powerful leadership positions in the country, cannot risk displeasing their caucuses.[138] In Connecticut, too, leaders are strong; they get to write important parts of the legislative budget. But they also have to sell what they have done, persuading members not to exercise the personal vetoes they believe they are empowered to cast.[139]

Even the legendary Willie Brown ruled at the pleasure of the Democratic assembly caucus. His biographer, James Richardson, recounts the many times Brown would assert he had forty-one votes, and that with forty-one he could continue as speaker. During one period a group of dissident Democrats, called "the Gang of Five," tried to dethrone him. Even if he could not round up sufficient Democratic votes, Brown could count on two or three Republicans who were in his debt.[140]

The caucus, or the membership as a whole, determines the leader's positions on a policy or sets parameters within which the leadership can try to establish positions with members. Either way, issue-by-issue consultation, compromise, and persuasion are the leader's stock in trade. He or she consults with members, responds to their views, and respects their judgments. This is not the stuff of a New England town meeting, but neither is it the stuff of autocracy.

It is true that some leaders consult more, others less. The consultative leaders delegate responsibilities to their leadership team and even to rank-and-file members. The others hold power more closely, but there are fewer of them. New York may have the strongest legislative leadership in the nation. One critic of the system here has written that "it is no exaggeration to say that the speaker of the Assembly and the majority leader of the Senate are the legislative branch in Albany."[141] Yet it *is* an exaggeration; there are limits on leadership powers even in New York.

Leadership has been losing power. Legislators are now more individualistic and their perspectives more diversified. As Jewell and Whicker report, members want to have input into decision making, so leaders now have to negotiate a wider range of matters.[142] A survey of 330 veteran legislators asked about the influence of different groups over the years. While most responded that the media, lobbyists, standing committees, and legislative staff now had more influence, only 24 percent responded that the legislative leadership had increased its influence, while 47 percent said its influence had decreased.[143]

The decline of leadership power is evidenced by the number of leaders who have seen their tenure cut short by their caucus colleagues or by bipartisan coalitions. Even with the weapons at their disposal, leaders who have lost the support of their colleagues have also lost their positions. Events in California, Oklahoma, Massachusetts, Connecticut, Minnesota, New York, Kentucky, and North Carolina have been somberly noted by legislative leaders elsewhere. Where term limits exist, leadership will be short-lived—no more than two or four years—and less powerful. Experience in the legislature and in leadership enables individuals to learn how to be effective. There is no substitute for time on the job. Art Hamilton of Arizona is one of many who doubt that leadership can be taught, as it may have to be with term limits reducing tenure so markedly. "There are certain things you can't learn in training sessions," he says.[144] Leadership is one of them.

The decline of leadership power is also evidenced by the diminution of the formal authority of the office of speakership and the presidency. In revolting against incumbent leadership, rank-and-file members have made a run at the leaders' authority to manage legislative personnel and the legislative process. They have eroded top leadership's control over the appointment of assistant leaders, the naming of conference committee members, the referral and calendaring of bills, and the selection of chairs and members of standing committees. And they have limited the terms of top-leadership office. Efforts along these lines have been successful in North Carolina, Massachusetts, Mississippi, Rhode Island, and Kansas among other places.

Some leaders, moreover, are quick to surrender formal power, feeling they have to respond to the will of the caucus. After the Democratic speaker was forced out in Minnesota, Phil Carruthers, his successor in 1997, announced that the house would become more participative and less top-down.[145] Other leaders do whatever they have to do to retain any power at all. To get elected speaker, Willie Brown needed Republican votes. In return, he not only gave Republicans chairmanships and vice-chairmanships, but he also changed assembly rules, authorizing the rules committee instead of the speaker to assign legislation to committees.[146] When the Republicans finally took control in 1996, the power of the speakership was eroded further. Under Curt Pringle, the right to allocate internal budgets and name members of committees was transferred to the rules committee, whose members would be selected by the majority and minority caucuses.[147] When the Democrats regained control of the assembly after the 1996 elections, the speaker took back this authority.

Legislative leadership is not what it used to be. The likes of Jesse Unruh of California are not apt to be duplicated. Vern Riffe in Ohio, Bev Bledsoe in Colorado, and John Martin in Maine were all strong leaders. "You think of a big rock, you think of Gibraltar," says Massachusetts speaker Thomas Finneran." "You think of a senate president, you think of Bulger."[148] Leaders have little time nowadays to grow in office or to accrue power. What power remains will probably be depleted because of the legislature's expanding responsibilities, interest groups' increasing demands, and members' growing needs.

With weaker leadership, the legislature will be less able to withstand the pressures from outside. Responsibilities for the legislature as an institution and for the state as a whole will be given shorter shrift, while special and parochial interests and populist demands will carry greater weight.

NOTES

1. This section is based on Alan Rosenthal, "Challenges to Legislative Leadership," *Journal of State Government* 60 (November–December 1987): 265–266.

2. Tom Loftus, *The Art of Legislative Politics* (Washington, D.C.: CQ Press, 1994), 47.

3. In the 1970s I was called by the newly chosen speaker of the New Jersey assembly, who said he wanted to meet with me to discuss some ideas he had for legislative reform. When we met, the speaker showed little interest in structural or procedural change. He really wanted to find out whether other states had leadership titles that he might adopt for New Jersey. From my knowledge of other states, I was able to contribute some new titles, which he was happy to accept. Others have been added in the decades since then.

4. Patricia K. Freeman, "A Comparative Analysis of Speaker Career Patterns in U.S. State Legislatures," *Legislative Studies Quarterly* 20 (August 1995): 369.

5. Interview with the author, March 17, 1995.

6. Loftus, *Art of Legislative Politics,* 52.

7. Interview with the author, March 17, 1995.

8. Timothy Hodson, Rich Jones, Karl T. Kurtz, and Gary Moncrief, "Leaders and Limits: Changing Patterns of State Legislative Leadership Under Term Limits" (paper prepared for delivery at the annual meeting of the Western Political Science Association, Portland, Oregon, March 1995).

9. Interview with the author, March 27, 1995.

10. Malcolm E. Jewell and Marcia Lynn Whicker, *Legislative Leadership in the American States* (Ann Arbor: University of Michigan Press, 1994), 64.

11. Collins Center for Public Policy, "The Nature of Representation: An Overview" (discussion by members of the Florida house, Tallahassee, November 6, 1995), 2:231. Transcript.

12. George Peery, "Transcending Term Limits," *State Legislatures,* June 1996, 25.

13. Robert S. McCord, "Revival in the Arkansas House," *State Legislatures,* July–August 1995, 43.

14. James R. Oxendale Jr., "The Impact of Membership Turnover on Internal Structures of State Legislative Lower Chambers" (paper prepared for delivery at the annual meeting of the American Political Science Association, Washington, D.C., August 31–September 3, 1979); Alan Rosenthal, "An Evaluation of the NCSL New Legislative Leaders Symposium," January 12–13, 1979, Dallas, Texas.

15. Nancy Rhyme, "Moving Up, On, Out, or Over," *State Legislatures,* July–August 1996, 46.

16. Interview with the author, February 23, 1995.

17. Interviews with the author, February 24, 1995.

18. As part of the appointments process, leaders play the major part in determining the number of committees that will exist and the ratio of majority to minority members on each of them. See chapter 4.

19. Interview with the author, February 23, 1995.

20. Loftus, *Art of Legislative Politics,* 59.

21. Ronald D. Hedlund and Keith E. Hamm, "Leader Accommodation to Members' Committee Requests" (paper prepared for delivery at the annual meeting of the American Political Science Association, Chicago, September 3–6, 1992).

22. *San Jose Mercury News,* January 8, 1995.

23. Peery, "Transcending Term Limits," 25.

24. Wayne L. Francis, *The Legislative Committee Game: A Comparative Analysis of Fifty States* (Columbus: Ohio State University Press, 1989), 26–27.

25. Keith E. Hamm, Ronald D. Hedlund, and R. Bruce Anderson, "Political Parties

in State Legislatures," in *Encyclopedia of the American Legislative System,* ed. Joel H. Silbey (New York: Scribner's, 1994), 971.

26. Thomas E. Cronin and Robert D. Loevy, *Colorado Politics and Government* (Lincoln: University of Nebraska Press, 1993), 181.

27. Ralph Wright, *All Politics Is Personal* (Manchester Center, Vt.: Marshall Jones Co., 1996), 168.

28. Theodore Rueter, *The Minnesota House of Representatives and the Professionalization of Politics* (Lanham, Md.: University Press of America, 1994), 116–118.

29. Wright, *All Politics Is Personal,* 170.

30. William P. Browne and Kenneth Ver Burg, *Michigan Politics and Government* (Lincoln: University of Nebraska Press, 1995), 114.

31. Steve Scott, "Transitional Pro Tem?" *California Journal,* November 1994, 8.

32. Interview with the author, March 27, 1995.

33. Ibid., February 22, 1995.

34. Robert Garton, "The Leader as Manager of People," *Journal of State Government* 60 (November–December 1987): 258.

35. Interview with the author, February 23, 1995.

36. Ibid., February 24, 1995.

37. Garry Boulard, "The Compleat Politician," *State Legislatures,* June 1996, 12.

38. James Richardson, *Willie Brown: A Biography* (Berkeley and Los Angeles: University of California Press, 1996), 302, 318.

39. *Richmond Times-Dispatch,* February 5, 1995.

40. Richardson tells the story that on the invitation to one of his galas Brown listed himself as "Speaker of the Legislature," not of the assembly. Roberti declined to attend. *Willie Brown,* 316.

41. Interview with the author, June 5, 1995.

42. Interviews with the author, February 22, 23, 24, 1995.

43. Loftus, *Art of Legislative Politics,* 64–65.

44. William K. Muir Jr., *Legislature: California's School for Politics* (Chicago: University of Chicago Press, 1982), 165–168.

45. Richard C. Paddock, "The Mixed Legacy of a Practical Politician," *California Journal,* March 1992, 144. Also interview with the author, March 16, 1995.

46. A. G. Block, "The Reality of Willie Brown Jr.," *California Journal,* August 1995, 11.

47. Interview with the author, March 16, 1996.

48. "Roundtable Discussion: Critical Institutional Issues Confronting Legislatures," Senate President's Forum, vol. 3, no. 1. Roundtable held at a conference, February 22–25, 1996, in Indian Wells, California.

49. Interview with the author, February 23, 1995.

50. Ibid., February 22, 1995.

51. Interviews with the author, February 24, 1995.

52. Interview with Scott Jensen for Pfizer tapes, July 24, 1996.

53. Jewell and Whicker, *Legislative Leadership in the American States,* 124–130.

54. Hamm, Hedlund, and Anderson, "Political Parties in State Legislatures," 966.

55. Interview with the author, May 16, 1995.

56. Jewell and Whicker, *Legislative Leadership in the American States,* 137–138.

57. Wright, *All Politics Is Personal,* 155.

58. Ibid., 201.

59. Interview with the author, October 17, 1996.

60. Ibid., February 23, 1996.

61. Interviews with the author, February 22, 23, 24, 1996.

62. Daniel M. Weintraub, "New Course in Sacramento," *State Legislatures,* July–August 1996, 29.

63. Block, "Reality of Willie Brown," 8–9.

64. Marshall Frady, "Profile: An American Political Fable," *New Yorker,* October 21–28, 1996, 216–217. Emphasis in original.

65. The governor, along with the speaker and minority leader of the assembly and the president pro tem and minority leader of the senate, constituted the Big Five.

66. Interview with the author, March 17, 1995.

67. The characterization is by Bill Lockyer, as reported in Richardson, *Willie Brown,* 245.

68. Jewell and Whicker, *Legislative Leadership in the American States,* 140.

69. Royce Hanson, *Tribune of the People* (Minneapolis: University of Minnesota Press, 1989), 76.

70. Boulard, "Compleat Politician," 13.

71. Interview with the author, March 29, 1995.

72. Ibid., March 27, 1995.

73. Ibid., February 23, 1995.

74. Thomas Suddes, "Panorama of Ohio Politics in the Voinovich Era, 1991–," in *Ohio Politics,* ed. Alexander P. Lamas (Kent, Ohio: Kent State University Press, 1994), 164.

75. Richard A. Clucas, *The Speaker's Electoral Connection: Willie Brown and the California Assembly* (Berkeley: University of California, Institute of Governmental Studies Press, 1995), 19–20; Richard A. Clucas, "Whither Legislative Leadership? Assessing the Tenure of California Assembly Speaker Willie Brown" (paper prepared for delivery at the annual meeting of the Western Political Science Association, San Francisco, March 14–16, 1996).

76. Paddock, "Mixed Legacy of a Practical Politician," 149.

77. Interview with the author, June 7, 1995.

78. Ibid.

79. Quoted in Jewell and Whicker, *Legislative Leadership in the American States,* 50.

80. Interview with the author, March 15, 1995.

81. Cited in Boulard, "Compleat Politician," 13.

82. Interview with Scott Jensen for Pfizer tapes, July 24, 1996.

83. Quoted in Loftus, *Art of Legislative Politics,* 37–38.

84. Clucas, *The Speaker's Electoral Connection,* 114–121, 126.

85. Ibid.

86. Interview with the author, June 5, 1995.

87. Interviews with the author, June 5 and 7, 1995.

88. Ibid.

89. Loftus, *Art of Legislative Politics,* 60.

90. Interview with the author, March 31, 1995.

91. Ibid., May 18, 1995.

92. Richardson, *Willie Brown,* 115; interview with the author, March 3, 1997.

93. Eric Lane, "Albany's Travesty of Democracy," *City Journal* 7 (spring 1997): 52; *New York Times,* June 8, 1997.

94. Interview with the author, February 23, 1995. See also Samuel C. Patterson, "Legislative Politics in Ohio," in *Ohio Politics,* ed. Alexander P. Lamis (Kent, Ohio: Kent State University Press, 1994), 247.

95. Interview with the author, October 24, 1996.

96. Ibid.

97. John Powers, "Altered State: It's a New Era on Beacon Hill, With New Players, New Rules, and New Attitudes," *Boston Globe Magazine,* June 16, 1996, 31.

98. Interview with the author, May 12, 1995.

99. Ibid., July 24, 1996.

100. Interview with Scott Jensen for Pfizer tapes, July 24, 1996.

101. Interview with the author, July 24, 1996.

102. Ibid., March 17, 1995.

103. Rod Searle, *Minnesota Standoff* (Waseca, Minn.: Alton Press, 1990), 88.

104. Interviews with the author, February 22, 24, 1995.

105. Wright, *All Politics Is Personal,* 178.

106. Interview with the author, February 23, 1995.

107. Ibid., February 24, 1995.

108. Ibid., June 5, 1995.

109. Ibid., June 6, 1995.

110. Interviews with the author, February 24, 1995.

111. Interview with the author, June 6, 1996.

112. Block, "Reality of Willie Brown," 9.

113. Interview with the author, October 17, 1996.

114. Ibid.

115. Interview with the author, March 31, 1995.

116. Searle, *Minnesota Standoff,* 89.

117. Wright, *All Politics Is Personal,* 24–25.

118. Richardson, *Willie Brown,* 317.

119. Interview with the author, July 24, 1996.

120. Loftus, *Art of Legislative Politics,* 49.

121. Interview with Scott Jensen for Pfizer tapes, July 24, 1996.

122. Maureen Moakley, "The Rhode Island Legislature: The Center Still Holds" (paper prepared for delivery at the annual meeting of the American Political Science Association, San Francisco, August 29–September 1, 1996).

123. Interview with the author, June 6, 1995.

124. R. Bruce Anderson, "Party Caucuses in Formerly One-Party Legislative Chambers: The Transformation of Internal Party Organization by External Forces" (Ph.D. diss., chap. 4, October 1996); Cole Blease Graham Jr. and William V. Moore, *South Carolina Politics and Government* (Lincoln: University of Nebraska Press, 1994), 134; and Clifton McCleskey, "Party Caucuses in the Virginia General Assembly: A Preliminary Report" (paper prepared for delivery at the annual meeting of the Southwestern Political Science Association, Houston, March 21–23, 1996).

125. Suddes, "Panorama of Ohio Politics," 164.

126. Interviews with the author, February 22, 24, 1995.

127. Interview with the author, July 24, 1996.

128. Ibid., February 23, 1995.

129. Ibid., March 30, 1995.

130. Ibid., March 31, 1995.

131. Hanson, *Tribune of the People,* 96.

132. Interview with the author, June 6, 1995.

133. *Boston Globe,* December 15, 1992.

134. Interview with the author, February 23, 24, 1995.

135. Patterson, "Legislative Politics in Ohio," 248.

136. Senate Democrats recognized the value to their own interests of Aronoff's majority-party leadership. They cooperated in order to make him effective, rather than see him lose control to conservative Republicans in his caucus. Interview with the author, February 22, 1995.

137. Loftus, *Art of Legislative Politics,* 81.

138. David L. Cingranelli, "New York: Powerful Groups and Powerful Parties," in *Interest Group Politics in the Northeastern States,* ed. Ronald J. Hrebenar and Clive S. Thomas (University Park: Pennsylvania State University Press, 1993), 176.

139. Alan Ehrenhalt, *The United States of Ambition* (New York: Times Books, 1991), 160.

140. Richardson, *Willie Brown,* 333–345.

141. Lane, "Albany's Travesty of Democracy," 49. See also "Fixing the Two-Man Legislature," editorial, *New York Times,* June 18, 1997.

142. Jewell and Whicker, *Legislative Leadership in the American States,* 51.

143. Gary F. Moncrief, Joel A. Thompson, and Karl T. Kurtz, "The Old Statehouse, It Ain't What It Used to Be," *Legislative Studies Quarterly* 21 (February 1996): 61.

144. Peery, "Transcending Term Limits," 25.

145. Charles Mahtesian, "The Sick Legislative Syndrome," *Governing,* February 1997, 20.

146. Richardson, *Willie Brown,* 277; Clucas, *Speaker's Electoral Connection,* 14–15, 17.

147. Weintraub, "New Course in Sacramento," 29.

148. Powers, "Altered State," 30.

CHAPTER 8

Balancing Executive Power

One of the democratic pillars of our political system is the constitutional principle of separated powers, whereby the executive, legislative, and judiciary are restricted in the power they can exercise independently of the other branches of government. Each one checks the other, with the major role of the legislature being to check the executive.

Our system is based on a fear of concentrated power in any one place. Early in the political history of the states, the people's specific experience with colonial governors, who acted as agents of the English Crown, led to a general distrust of the executive. Thus, the framing of state constitutions in the 1776–1787 period began with the weakening of executive power and the granting of power to the legislature and the people. Typically, under the original state constitutions, the legislature selected governors, who were limited to one term and denied veto power. Soon after such radical democratic origins, however, constitutional framers pulled back, concluding that in a republican form of government the legislative branch had a national tendency to exert control over other departments.[1] Subsequent to national independence, the executive role therefore increased and the governor began to act as a check on legislative power.

By the early nineteenth century, governors had become noticeably stronger. Authority to elect them was transferred from legislatures to the people; their terms were extended to two or four years; and they acquired veto authority. Executive power still was limited, but governors were gaining on legislatures. In the twentieth century, and specifically in the 1950s and 1960s, the executive succeeded in carving out a distinct advantage over the legislature.

The executive advantage—some would say executive dominance—continues today, in the view of most political scientists, journalists, and other observers. There are exceptions of course. Governors are constitutionally weak in states like Texas, South Carolina, Mississippi, and Florida; but in these states the recent trend has been toward more balanced power systems. Governors have dominated in states like Connecticut, Louisiana, Alabama, Maryland, Tennessee, New York, and New Mexico; but the trend has been toward more balanced power systems in these states as well.

THE GOVERNOR'S UPPER HAND

Popular lore distinguishes between the powers of the legislative and executive branches as follows: the legislature makes the laws and the executive administers them.[2] A neat division of labor, but one that is hardly the case in either theory or practice. Constitutionally and politically, governors have a lot to do with lawmaking, and statutorily and politically, legislatures have something to do with administration.

Indeed, governors are thought to have the principal role in the lawmaking process, although that would appear to be the legislature's bailiwick. The textbook stereotype of gubernatorial preeminence in lawmaking derives from the role of "chief legislator" attributed to chief executives. "The governor proposes, the legislature disposes" is how observers often describe the lawmaking relationship of the two branches.

Although such characterizations exaggerate executive dominance, in general, governors undoubtedly have the upper hand, and the choice is theirs as to whether to wield it or not. The bases of gubernatorial advantage vis-à-vis the legislature combine constitutional, statutory, institutional, and political elements and include the powers of initiation, rejection, provision, party, unity, and publicity, each of which shall be touched on below.

The Power of Initiation

State constitutions provide for the initiation of policy by governors. Article V, section 1 V of the New Jersey Constitution is illustrative. It states that "The Governor shall . . . recommend [to the legislature] such measures as he may deem desirable." Politically, custom dictates that governors fashion and present a program for the legislature to enact. By means of the "state of the state" address and special messages, governors offer their agendas and then have major items drafted and introduced as bills. In addition, as we shall discuss in greater detail later, governors in most states are the initiators of the budget.

Governors, therefore, have substantial influence on the legislature's law-making calendar. Their agenda tends also to be the legislature's agenda, at least in substantial part. In his study of a session of the Kansas legislature, for example, Burdett Loomis found little disagreement over what should be on the agenda. The governor and the legislature both saw school finance, highways, prisons, an income-tax windfall, and tort reform as among the top six issues. The legislature was less concerned about the death penalty than the governor, and the governor was less concerned with reapportionment than the legislature.[3]

Moreover, governors advance agenda items that tend to be limited to a few priorities. "Almost every governor," write two political scientists, "has a small number of issues or policy initiatives that define his or her term of office."[4] Ned McWherter of Tennessee, for example, had a few issues he wanted to advance but left the remaining ones to the legislature. "We let the legislature do their thing," said one of the governor's aides, "and they've been supportive of letting the governor do his thing." Gov. Zell Miller of Georgia operated similarly. Among all the issues, Miller would try to manage three or four—usually those that resonated with the public. For Carroll Campbell of South Carolina, the priorities were economic development, automobile insurance reform, and education.[5] In Texas George W. Bush concentrated on more local control over education, stricter provisions for people on welfare, tougher juvenile justice laws, and tort reform. He got much of what he wanted in one session of the legislature, but then lost on a proposal to restructure taxes in another.

Most contemporary governors see the wisdom in limiting themselves to a few legislative priorities for each legislative session, and perhaps one or two other items when a special session is deemed necessary. But there are exceptions. In Missouri John Ashcroft initiated thirty to thirty-five proposals per session, and in Iowa Terry Branstad advanced forty-four proposals in the 1988 session. Few, if any, governors were as legislatively ambitious as New York's Mario Cuomo. In 1988 he was responsible for about 100 program bills, and in 1989 his proposed measures amounted to about 150. Cuomo did not winnow out his preferences, as evidenced in his state of the state messages laying out his agenda. In 1982, the last year of Hugh Carey's administration, the state of the state was 24 pages; Cuomo's 1990 address ran 178 pages. With so many initiatives, it was virtually impossible for the governor to build much legislative support. Nor did Cuomo really try; his style was not that of courting and cajoling. From a legislative point of view, his political leadership was wanting. Cuomo laid out an agenda and then abandoned it.[6]

The governor has an important initiatory role, if he or she chooses to use it. But the legislature also has a role in initiating legislation. In fact, the chief executive's bills constitute a very small part of the legislative agenda. Depending on the state, five to ten issues may be the governor's, while many more are the legislature's. Various matters of broad scope and major import, as well as hundreds of special-interest items, are initiated by the legislature. Much of the legislative workload may seem trifling, but these bills are by no means minor to a number of people or to a variety of interest groups. They may not affect the public interest writ large, but they do confer benefits on some individuals and entail costs for others.

The Power of Rejection

If initiation allows governors an opening salvo, the power of rejection gives them the last, or practically the last, word. Although the governor has relatively few policy proposals, his or her veto has broader application. Theoretically, the governor can veto any bill the legislature passes, and in all but six states it takes an extraordinary majority by both houses to override. The veto of legislation is a potent weapon, and the nation's governors thus use it with varying frequency. Nelson Rockefeller of New York wielded the veto with abandon—on 20 to 35 percent of the bills passed by the legislature from 1965 to 1971. In recent years Gov. Pete Wilson, a Republican, vetoed about one out of five bills passed by California's Democratic legislature, and Gary Johnson, New Mexico's Republican governor, set a record by vetoing almost half (200 of 424) the bills passed by the Democratic legislature.

In the executive-veto arsenal, the regular veto is supplemented by the line-item and the conditional, or amendatory, veto. Governors in forty-three states have the power to veto sections or items of appropriations bills without having to reject the entire bill. In eleven states governors can also reduce the dollar amount of appropriations items.[7] Governors consider this an essential prerogative because some legislatures, like Mississippi's, appropriate lump sums to agencies. Such an appropriations strategy forces the governor to employ the line-item veto to strike out an entire agency budget.[8] Fifteen states give the governor additional leverage, which allows a veto unless certain conditions are met. In Illinois, a governor can return a bill to the legislature with specific recommendations for changes and language to amend the bill. If the legislature accepts the revisions by majority vote in each house, the governor certifies the bill and it becomes law as amended. Otherwise, it becomes a vetoed bill requiring a three-fifths vote in each house to override.[9]

Vetoes are occasionally overridden; many more, however, are sustained. In some places, like New Mexico, overriding the governor simply is not in keeping with state tradition. In 1997 Governor Johnson managed to anger lawmakers from both parties by vetoing legislation that would have allowed the early release of some nonviolent criminals. Legislative leaders objected because the veto violated an agreement they had with the governor, which conditioned passage of the inmate-release bill for one that shipped some inmates to Arizona. With help from some Republicans, the Democratic-controlled house voted to override. But the override failed in the senate, and New Mexico's tradition of the inviolate veto continued.[10]

But even more important to the governor than exercising the veto and prevailing is using the threat of the veto as a weapon in negotiations. A governor can often secure a member's support for legislation by threatening to veto a member's pet bill or item in the appropriations act. The veto power, in effect, allows the governor to take legislation and appropriations hostage. "Both the item veto and the simple veto," writes Muir with respect to executive-legislative relations in California, "could be used to break an individual legislator's resistance." Imagine the governor telling a legislator that he would kill his bill, a bill the legislator had worked for several years to have passed, unless the legislator helped him elsewhere.[11] The veto also allows the governor to discourage the enactment of bills that do not meet with his approval: "Make changes, or else I will veto the bill," or, "Recall the bill, or else I will embarrass you by vetoing it." Such threats are persuasive.

The veto is therefore a source of considerable power if the governor seeks to exercise control over the legislative process. It allows him or her to negotiate from a position of strength both with legislative leaders and with individual members.

The Power of Provision

The other side of the power of rejection is the power of provision. The governor can fulfill members' needs, just as he or she can deny them the benefits of legislation and appropriations. The governor may give them the appointments they desire, the projects their districts require, and the attention they seek. Over the course of their tenure in office, just about every member will contact the governor's office for something; and most members make repeated requests for jobs, roads, license plates, contracts, or visits.

Although atypical, the following case illustrates the governor's use of the power of provision. New Jersey's governor, Christine Whitman, proposed that the state sell $2.76 billion in bonds to cover unfunded liabilities in the pension fund and, incidentally, to help balance the budget. The plan was extremely controversial, with all the Democrats in the senate opposing it and the Republicans divided. The *Star-Ledger* reported (June 8, 1997) that, to win over reluctant Republicans, the governor either discussed, or agreed to, the closure of an outmoded juvenile facility in one senator's district and the construction of a new one elsewhere; finding a job for a lame-duck senator; supporting state funding for a hotel in Trenton; backing a bill that would provide money for debt service on school-construction bonds; and helping to get a state agency office moved out of a county building because the county wanted the space. Ten Republicans had been on the fence, and seven finally voted for the governor's plan.

What legislators probably want from the governor more than anything else are appointments for key supporters in their districts. Thus, the appointments at the governor's disposal are a critical stock in trade. Naming people to higher positions—such as cabinet offices—is the most visible appointive power. But what counts with legislators is who they can get named as judges and state attorneys and to the hundreds of positions on boards, commissions, authorities, and councils. Although many of these positions are unpaid, they confer prestige, and perhaps some influence, on the occupants. Most of them are political plums, albeit some are juicier than others. In the hands of a skillful governor, patronage can be an estimable tool in winning over legislators and keeping them in line. In his memoirs, Tom Kean, who served for eight years as governor of New Jersey, writes how a state senator approached him to say he might change his mind and vote for the budget, but one of his supporters wanted a judgeship, while another senator was willing to play ball, but had an uncle who needed a job. Kean turned them down, however. He did not trade jobs for votes.[12]

Governors may also convey recognition, something prized by all legislators. They do this by having their photographs taken together visiting a legislator's district, inviting legislators to a reception at the mansion, or commending them to the media. Few governors were as adept at working the egos of legislators as Nelson Rockefeller of New York, whose wealth made the recognition he accorded extra-special. He would invite legislative leaders and other legislators to his estate at Pocantico to view the modern sculpture on the grounds, to tour the collection of paintings in the house and its galleries, and to dine and take in the exquisite scenery on the Rockefeller spread. Legislators could not help but be impressed. They naturally wanted to be invited back to Pocantico, but this depended on their staying on good terms with the governor. Thus, though Rockefeller's invitations may not have bought any votes per se, they surely had a subtle effect: they softened members up, particularly the ones who remembered Pocantico fondly and wanted to return for another visit.

The Power of Party

The governor is the leader of his or her state political party. Although state party leadership is not what it used to be, neither is it inconsequential in terms of the executive-legislative relationship. It still confers substantial advantage.

Senate and house leaders of the governor's party serve, to some extent at least, as the governor's lieutenants in the legislature. The governor consults with them, and, if they have a majority in the legislature, they are expected to manage the governor's priorities through the process. Legislative leaders represent the governor to their colleagues and their colleagues to the governor. Sometimes they try to move legislators closer to the governor's position. Sometimes they have to bring the governor closer to the legislature. Often they go back and forth.

Governors used to control the choice of legislative leaders in several of the southern states. Prior to 1966, the Georgia governor handpicked the speaker and major committee chairs. In Kentucky, the governor, if a Democrat, selected the speaker, president pro tem, and floor leaders, but Gov. John Y. Brown abandoned that prerogative in 1979. Louisiana still follows the tradition of legislative leaders serving with the consent of the governor. Reportedly, not a single speaker has been elected over the governor's objections.[13] In other states, as well, governors influence the selection of their party's legislative leadership, although their role tends to be less obvious, as when Lawton Chiles provided behind-the-scenes help to Gwen Margolis in her drive to become president-designate of the Florida senate.

Under normal circumstances, governors can expect support from members of the legislative party with whom they share affiliations, associations, and policy preferences. Almost all legislators bring with them a set of party-favoring predispositions, so they will go along with "their" governor if they possibly can. All this is buttressed by political necessity, particularly if the governor will be at the head of the ticket on which they will be running at the next election. Even though legislators are less likely nowadays to be elected on a governor's coattails, they do not want to run the risk that those coattails will drag them down. They personally feel a stake in the governor's reelection and therefore in his or her success in the legislature. For a variety of reasons, from party loyalty to self-interest, it is better not to oppose your governor on legislation.

The Power of Unity

An enormous advantage of the governor over the legislature stems from the fact that he or she is one, while they are many. The governor has one, and usually a limited, agenda, while the legislature has as many agendas as there are members.

Compared with legislatures, governors are remarkably unitary, but some are more unitary than others, for some governors must share governance with other statewide-elected officials. In New Jersey, for instance, the governor is the only state official elected statewide. By contrast, forty-two states also have lieutenant governors (twenty of whom are elected separately from their governors). In most states other officials—the attorney general, education commissioner, secretary of state among them—are also elected statewide. Florida's cabinet system probably constitutes the extreme case of executive power-sharing, with each of several officials not only administering a department of state government but also serving equally with the governor on a number of boards that administer other departments.

Ordinarily, one is outnumbered by many. In the case of the governor and legislators, one has the upper hand over many. The governor has a much easier time arriving at a consensus. True, the governor has to be sensitive to various constituencies, and he or she consults others before fashioning a policy proposal. Still, the process is far more manageable than that in the legislature, where a number of legislators (each of whom has concern for interest groups and constituencies) must come together to get anything done. Given the centrifugal forces in politics today, it is becoming increasingly difficult for this coming-together to take place.

The Power of Publicity

Because the governor is a single person elected by all the people of the state, and the legislature is a collection of individuals, each elected from a small part of the state, governors are the ones who command the attention of the media. "The cacophony of legislator voices," writes a former member of the Washington legislature, "can rarely compete with a governor who can capitalize on his singular visibility in the media."[14]

The availability of television and other means of communication enables governors to speak to the public quickly and directly. Governors command the attention of both the print and electronic media whenever they respond to crisis or want to make news. The availability of the media affords governors a "bully pulpit," which they can use to drum up public support for what they want to achieve in the legislature. If they feel they have to, governors can go over the head of the legislature. Alternatively, they can take a constructive approach, supporting the direction the legislature appears to be taking.

The legislature is no match whatsoever in a media battle with the governor. Individual members attract little attention (unless they are involved in scandal or unusual behavior). Governors weigh in as heavyweights or light heavyweights, while legislatures can barely hope to make featherweight status. When governors and legislatures compete, the media tend to take the side of the executive, whose position appears more objective, more thoughtfully formulated, and more clearly communicated.

The media deal with governors' policy proposals, rather than with their political peccadilloes. When it comes to the legislature, however, the media probe for selfish or political interests, maverick behavior, and misfeasance or malfeasance. Individual members may manage a good press. The institution seldom does, partly because no one speaks for the legislature as the governor speaks for the executive. A leader speaks for his or her house only, and more likely only for the majority party, if that. Individual members speak for themselves—thus the clamor and the confusion of messages.

LEGISLATIVE ASSERTIVENESS

Gubernatorial advantage or not, legislatures today have a sense of their own independence. Their self-regard makes them sensitive about their constitutional status as the first branch of government, assertive in their use of power, and defensive about executive encroachment. Legislatures may not always prevail in contests with the governor, but they can no longer be taken for granted or expected simply to rubberstamp gubernatorial initiatives.

Legislative Capacity and Independence

Legislative independence vis-à-vis the executive branch is largely an outgrowth of the modernization movement of the late 1960s and 1970s. Before the building of capacity, governors had little difficulty with their legislatures. Coequality of the legislature was one tenet of the modernization movement;

one objective was greater legislative strength. As discussed in chapter 2, state legislatures markedly increased their capacity during this period of reform.

Because legislatures expanded their time spent on the job, they were around more and had the time and resources to examine and refashion the governor's program. Typically, governors looked forward to the day when legislatures adjourned *sine die* and the lawmakers left town. But, with the state legislature's modernization and professionalization, legislators spend more days in the capital each year, sharing in the affairs of state rather than turning everything over to the chief executive.

Capitols and legislative buildings were constructed and renovated, with rank-and-file members and legislative leaders acquiring ample workspaces. Private offices and even suites were not uncommon in many states. With comfortable and convenient facilities, legislators could be lured to the capital on days when the legislature was not in actual session. Interim committees, task forces, commissions, and standing committee meetings commanded their attention and became vehicles for the legislatures' expanding role in policy-making.

The professional staffing of legislatures grew rapidly into the 1980s. As much as anything else, staff drove legislatures to greater involvement. Non-partisan staff uncovers problems, offers options, and analyzes putative solutions. Little of an important policy nature is accepted without careful scrutiny. Partisan staff serves to safeguard the political position of its party, making sure that policy works to the advantage of most members of the caucus. Policy-making by the legislature increases as a consequence.

The attainment of greater capacity on the parts of legislatures probably fed the collective ego of the institution. Because they had the wherewithal, legislators began to feel they were up to the job. Perhaps lawmakers started believing their own rhetoric of legislative independence. In any event, they started acting as though it were true. In states where the executive had "owned" the legislatures, lawmakers took special pride in displays of independence in their dealings with the governor.

Kentucky may provide the best example in this regard. The legislature challenged the governor by undertaking its first serious review of his budget. It also pushed through an amendment to the constitution that took legislative elections out of the gubernatorial election year, thus reducing the governor's ability to determine the choice of legislative leaders. Over the past two decades, it shucked off its habit of acquiescence. Even today, years after its declaration of independence, veteran members take special pride in the legislature's hard-won coequality.

Strengthened egos combined with legislative assertiveness, further serving to stiffen resistance to the executive. Members are naturally envious of those who have achieved "higher office," something to which most legislators aspire but which most are denied. Few legislators of either party are uncritical of the incumbent governor; they think they could do as good a job or even better. (It is curious that a governor's job performance rating tends to decrease the nearer one gets to the statehouse.) The problem, as they see it, is that legislators have not been as fortunate—lucky, well-endowed, or strategically connected—and the opportunity has not come their way. Moreover, the struggle between the branches is an uneven one in legislators' eyes. They see the governor as one united against the many divided. The center of attention, the governor commands respect, while legislators do the hard work and suffer derision.[15]

When an opportunity arises, legislatures will put governors in their place. No opportunity, it would seem, is too insignificant. For example, in 1995 President Bill Clinton was scheduled to address a joint session of the Florida legislature, a historic occasion for the state. Gov. Lawton Chiles wanted to introduce the president, but the senate president objected, maintaining that it was a legislative function and the governor had no role to play. As it turned out, the senate president presided, the speaker of the house introduced the president, and the governor played no role at the joint session.[16]

Divided Government

Governors derive some advantage from being leaders of their parties, but they are obviously disadvantaged if their party is in the minority in the legislature. The legislative role vis-à-vis the governor differs when the legislative majority is controlled by the opposition party. When one or both houses are controlled by the party in opposition to the executive, the legislature is apt to be more cantankerous.

Divided government undoubtedly accounts for some of the aggressiveness of state legislatures in recent years. From 1946 to 1990 the incidence of unified government declined.[17] And as of 1997–1998 in thirty-one states at least one chamber was controlled by a different party from that of the governor. In some states, as a matter of fact, unity is rare. In Nevada, for example, from 1905 to 1995 the governor's party controlled both houses of the legislature less than one-fifth of the time.[18] In New York Democrats have had a lock on the assembly and Republicans on the senate. So, under a succession of both Republican and Democratic governors, control in New York has been split almost continually since the 1960s. In California government was divided in 1966–1968, 1970–1974, and 1982–1998—all told almost three-fourths of the time.

Divided government alters the process, and both the governor's and the legislature's respective roles in it. One recent study of Georgia, Tennessee, Mississippi, and South Carolina found that the two governors with party support in the legislature tended to emphasize an inside game, relying on their partisan allies. Where government was divided, in contrast, governors resorted more to an outside game, seeking public support.[19] At the least, partisan division fuels conflict between the governor and the legislature,[20] requiring accommodation on both sides if stalemate is to be avoided.

Often the executive and legislative parties can get together, even when government is divided. Under such conditions, however, the policy settlement may be less coherent than it would have been with one party in control of both branches. Nevertheless, both sides can claim achievement, and with justification. In his recent study on the subject at the national level, David Mayhew found nothing in the historical record to suggest that periods of divided government are less productive than periods of unified control. Moreover, there is some reason to believe that citizens prefer divided government.[21] The point, however, is that under divided government, the legislature (or one of its houses) has probably taken on a more aggressive role and has a larger impact on the policy produced.

Confrontational Relationships

Legislatures are provoked by governors who show them little respect, even if the governors share partisan affiliation with the legislative majority. Some governors insist on the supremacy of the executive and are disdainful of the legislature. They would prefer to use the legislature as a whipping boy rather than defer to its needs. These governors appear to be looking for trouble, and legislatures do what they can to oblige them.

William Donald Schaefer, as governor of Maryland, displayed as combative and confrontational a style as any contemporary governor. In most of his stint in office, he would not budge on his program; compromise was out of the question. He referred to the senate office building as a "war zone," and for a period of almost six months he suspended communications with the speaker of the house. For a time, Schaefer tried to undermine the senate president's authority with his own colleagues. It was a stormy period in Annapolis. Schaefer changed course in 1992–1994, improving his relations with the legislature and succeeding with his legislative program.

New York's Mario Cuomo had little respect for the legislature and was unwilling to stroke legislators in order to get their support. He chose instead to use the legislature as a foil, rallying the public to his cause and against the other branch of government. In the budget struggle of 1994, for instance, Cuomo hammered at the legislature, accusing members of "brutal conduct" and calling them "fools," "dummies," and "greedy." He even likened legislators to pigs, "working with two hands to feed themselves from the trough."[22] This is not customarily the way to win support.

Michigan's John Engler, unlike a predecessor Republican governor, William Milliken, emphasized politics. Legislative Democrats, in particular, criticized his leadership style, which they characterized as demanding capitulation, not cooperation, from the legislature. The politics of the middle ground, traditional to Michigan, had been replaced by what critics called "the politics of the middle finger."[23]

In New Mexico Gov. Gary Johnson took on the legislature not only with his two hundred vetoes one year but also with his disregard for the legislative branch and its leadership. Repeated meetings in 1995 between the governor and legislative leaders produced an agreement on the state budget. But according to the legislative leaders, Johnson subsequently cut $36 million out of the budget, violating their agreement.[24] The governor is said to have reneged on deals several times, resulting in frustration and anger on the parts of the leaders.[25] After the legislative session, the house speaker and senate president would usually meet three or four times with the governor, but these meetings were discontinued in 1995 because the governor and legislature were so angry at one another.

Virginia's Republican governor, George Allen, and the general assembly may have had as antagonistic a relationship as any executive and legislature in the country. As far as the legislature—and particularly the Democrats—were concerned, Allen made all the wrong moves. In 1994 he announced his budget for 1995–1996 before Christmas without consulting legislative leadership—a traditional courtesy in a traditionally courteous state. The senate Democratic leader, Hunter Andrews, recounted: "Well, that said volumes to me. Then I knew the game plan was going to be different."[26]

Andrews, the strong-willed, long-term majority leader, did not hide his feelings about the governor. Among other slights, the governor's director of appointments told the majority leader to fill out an application form to request an interview with Allen. At one point or another, the governor referred to the Democrats in the legislature as "fat cats," "dinosaurs," and "elitists." The Democrats gave as well as they took. On the first day of the 1995 session, a dispute over senate rules caused an adjournment without allowing the governor to deliver his state of the commonwealth address. Democrats, further-more, ignored much of his agenda and opposed the rest. On one occasion, Andrews reported saying when he was with Allen in his office: "'Governor, I want to shake your hand,' and he said, 'Why?' I said, 'I want to thank you because every time you criticized us, we became more united'."[27] Allen learned his lesson. The next year saw a kinder, gentler governor trying to build con-sensus in the legislature. This time around, he shared his budget with legisla-tive leaders, setting the tone for a different type of session. The governor's agenda was agreed to—in part and in modified form—and Allen could claim some success.[28]

BALANCE OF POWER: THE CASE OF THE BUDGET

As good a way as any to see how state legislatures balance the power of the executive is to examine the performance of the legislature's and the governor's budgetary role. The state budget—through which resources are allocated among functions, programs, and interests—is probably the most significant policy that the governor and the legislature promulgate. Budgets, in the view of an experienced budgeter, "are typically the most important legislative actions in a session."[29] Whereas the governor and the legislature may choose whether or not to place most policy issues on the state agenda, they have no choice in the case of the budget. Constitutionally, a budget must be enacted either annually (as in thirty states) or biennially (as in twenty others). Even those states with biennial budgets make adjustments in the off years, with corrective or supple-mental appropriation bills, so budgeting in one form or another goes on continually.

The budget is a contest over who gets how much. The claimants are many—the schools, universities, institutions, transportation, health, law enforcement, the young and the elderly, business and labor, environmentalists, and many others. Because the pie is always limited, the budget pits agency against agency, client group against client group, cities against suburbs, Democrats against Republicans. It also provides a major test in the struggle between the gover-nor and the legislature to determine who decides how much is spent on what for whose benefit.

Executive-legislative rivalry in the budget area can manifest itself in vari-ous ways—loudly or quietly, publicly or privately, confrontationally or diplo-matically. But just about everywhere, the two branches have to work out their differences and reach an agreement. A spokesman for the senate majority leader referred to the process by which New York's governor and legislature work things out as "the annual dance of the budget flamingoes," with an opening gambit "where the birds bow, then strut around flapping their wings."[30] By the end of the process, the birds will have squawked, pecked at one another, and perhaps got into a fierce fight, but they will also have settled on a budget that holds, at least for a time.

Budget Formulation

In most states the executive formulates the budget, and in thirty states it submits a budget bill or bills. Governors may not be intimately involved in shaping the budget, but their broad priorities and goals will be reflected in the budget they propose, and their budget will serve as the state's operational frame of reference.[31] Still, in a number of states, the legislature prepares its own budget and in other states the legislature drafts the initial budget bill.

The initial process in shaping a budget is that of setting budget targets, which limit the amount that executive agencies can request, and then reviewing agency requests. In May or June, the governor's budget agency—such as the Office of Budget and Management (OBM) in Ohio or the Department of Administration (DOA) in Wisconsin—prepares a set of budget guidelines and budget request forms that are sent to the agencies of the executive branch. These guidelines are basically instructions from the governor and usually indicate the administration's policy directions.

Even at this executive-centered stage, the legislature is often involved. In a number of states a legislative agency is consulted. In Ohio, for example, the Legislative Budget Office (LBO) consults OBM on budget guidelines and works with executive agencies on the requests they will be submitting. In Florida, too, the governor's budget staff, housed in the Office of Planning and Budgeting, jointly develops instructions to the agencies with the staffs of the senate and house appropriations committees. Similar procedures are followed in Kentucky, where the Interim Appropriations and Revenue Committee, using the initial draft of the Office of Planning and Management, issues the budget instructions that are circulated to all the agencies. The legislative committee, and not the executive, has the ultimate say over what goes out.[32]

In the next phase— from July to November—agencies submit their budget requests, often asking for more than the governor is proposing. The executive budget agency normally reviews their requests, and may also conduct budget hearings. The executive budget staff analyzes and evaluates agency requests, and then makes its recommendations to the governor. In thirty-seven states the legislature also receives agency budget requests, usually at the same time as the governor, well before the executive budget is prepared. Legislative staffs begin working the budget over in much the same way as executive staffs. Ohio's LBO holds budget hearings with the agencies, as does the OBM, and conducts its own analysis. Florida's appropriations committees receive agency requests at the same time as the governor, and staff analysis begins right away.

One of the executive staff's activities is that of revenue estimation. State spending decisions depend on the amount of revenues available (and on decisions to raise or lower taxes as well). If revenues are high, a larger pot can be shared; if revenues are low, then expenditures have to be held down or cut, taxes have to be raised, or other sources have to be found. Revenue estimates or projections will differ, depending on economic assumptions. If the economy grows, tax revenues will flow to the treasury; if the economy shrinks, tax revenues will decline, and there will be less to spend. Projections are part art, part science, and part politics. No one can know for certain where the economy will go. Whoever makes revenue estimates, however, has the edge in shaping the budget. Exaggerating revenues will allow for higher spending; minimizing revenues will require more scrimping. Revenue forecasts generally are made when budgets are being prepared and are then updated on a quarterly basis.

Until relatively recently, only the executive had the authority and/or ability to produce revenue estimations, thus giving the governor an advantage. Now, however, legislative fiscal staffs in three-fifths of the states prepare their own estimates, and these estimates provide grist for the legislature's budget review and negotiations with the governor. In a number of states now the executive and legislative staffs come together in formal sessions to reconcile the differences in their estimates. Mississippi and Florida are examples of states that use a consensus process. Mississippi reaches an informal agreement, whereas in Florida the law requires that consensus-estimating conferences develop revenue forecasts, as well as economic and demographic forecasts, caseloads, and the like. The purpose is to remove, insofar as possible, political factors and to get agreement on the numbers. This allows both sides to start with the same assumptions.[33]

On the basis of agency requests and the analysis and recommendations of executive budget staff, the governor makes final budget decisions in November or December. It is his or her budget to deliver to the legislature, which already is at work examining the requests made by agencies. Even in states where the governor dominates the budget-formulation stage, legislatures are not without early influence. Such influence is usually exercised by legislative leaders who are consulted informally, and whose priorities find their way into the budget document and budget bill. A governor's close allies will certainly have their pet projects included.[34] In Maryland, where the general assembly is constitutionally proscribed from increasing the budget, the legislature is skillful in influencing the governor up front, before the budget is delivered. Through a process referred to as "spending affordability," the legislature sets a spending target, to which governors normally adhere. In addition, legislative leaders meet with the governor and express individual and collective priorities that run the gamut from local matters to executive departments and agencies to statewide policies. Governors usually try to accommodate these requests so that legislative leaders feel ownership and will push the budget through.[35]

Though the overall pattern is executive-centered, governors share responsibility for budget formulation in Arizona, Arkansas, Colorado, Florida, Kentucky, Louisiana, Mississippi, New Mexico, North Carolina, Texas, and Utah. Texas has its Legislative Budget Board (LBB), which is composed of legislators and the lieutenant governor, who serves as senate president. Instructions to state departments and agencies are drafted jointly by the LBB and the Office of Budget and Planning. Requests are submitted simultaneously to the legislative board and to the governor's office. But it is the LBB, and not the governor's office, that presents the budget bill. While legislators have two budgets before them for consideration—one in bill form and the other a document—only rarely is the executive proposal seriously considered. Normally, the legislature responds to the LBB bill, so that in Texas budget formulation is truly a legislative function.[36]

As in Texas, in Mississippi the legislature receives two budget proposals—one from the governor and one from the Legislative Budget Committee (LBC). The committee is dominated by legislative leaders, who negotiate the budget with which the legislature deals, while it ignores the governor's proposal.[37] Elsewhere, too, the legislature refuses to settle for a reactive role. Colorado's executive budget is said to have about as much status as a child's letter to Santa Claus. Here, the Joint Budget Committee (composed of six legislators, three from each chamber, who also sit on the appropriation committees) assembles the budget after analyzing agency requests and hearing agency testimony.[38]

The two-budget model is also used elsewhere. In New Mexico the Legislative Finance Committee prepares its own budget, which competes in the legislative process with the governor's.[39] Although formally an executive-budget state, Utah's joint appropriations subcommittees can choose between the governor's budget and the legislative fiscal analyst's.[40] The governor submits a budget and a budget bill in Florida, but it is only a starting point. Within a few days it has been completely reworked by the staffs of the senate and house appropriations committees. "For major issues, we do what we want to do," is the way one staffer described the legislative role in shaping the budget.[41]

Legislative Review

In January the governor of Ohio presents his budget message to the public and releases the executive budget document, called the "blue book." Meanwhile the LBO, jointly with the Legislative Service Commission, prepares the budget bill, which is based on the document. Ohio's budget bill for 1993–1995 ran to 1,300 pages and weighed in at 13 lbs. In addition to its biennial operating budget (which includes all the agencies of state government, with the exception of the Department of Transportation and Highway Safety and the Bureau of Workers' Compensation and Industrial Commission), Ohio also has a biennial capital budget, as do many other states. In fact, the majority of states use more than a single budget bill for operating expenses.[42] Virginia and North Carolina have two or three. New Mexico has separate budget bills for highways, state fairs and parks, game and fish, public employee salaries, and education.[43] Illinois deals with 80 bills, one for each executive agency. Mississippi has about 250 and Arkansas about 350 budget bills. The more bills, the greater the fragmentation and the more difficult it is for legislative leaders to maintain control over the entire process.

The legislative budget review process is anything but centralized. Tasks are shared between the house and senate. In Illinois, for instance, half of the eighty budget bills start out in the house, and the other half begin in the senate.[44] They are shared in each house among a number of committees or subcommittees. In Minnesota, for instance, the budget is divided among the appropriations, revenue, and education committees on the house side and the finance, revenue, and education committees on the senate side. Appropriations and finance each have four subcommittees (or divisions, as they are called in the house), with jurisdiction over higher education, health, human services, and corrections, state departments and agencies, and agriculture and transportation.[45]

In all but six states, as a matter of fact, appropriations committees make use of subcommittees, which are organized along programmatic lines.[46] The key work goes on in subcommittees. They review staff analyses, hold hearings, deliberate, and arrive at recommendations. The full committees generally accept their subcommittees' work and recommendations.

While in some states the two houses divide up the budget, in others the budget begins in one chamber and then goes to the other. Take Ohio. In February the budget bill is heard in the House Finance-Appropriations committee. Then its subcommittees review the bill and recommend changes to the full committee. From March until early April, House Finance-Appropriations acts on subcommittee recommendations and amends the appropriations bill. The house then passes the bill and sends it to the senate. During April, May, and early June the Senate Finance Committee and its subcommittees review the agency budget requests and changes. The senate passes the appropriations bill, with senate changes, and it is sent to conference committee.

The legislative role in the budget process hinges largely on the performance of the appropriations committees. These committees are those most sought after by members seeking assignments, and leaders normally appoint the most competent legislators to chair them and their subcommittees. The membership tends to be more stable and experienced than that of other committees. The chairmen tend to be on the ladder to top leadership. Workhorses of the legislature, appropriations committees command respect from legislators and executive officials alike.

Moreover, they are assisted by the premier staffs of the legislature—for example, the Office of Legislative Analyst in California, the Department of Fiscal Services in Maryland, the Legislative Fiscal Bureau in Wisconsin, and the staffs of the senate and house appropriations committees in Florida. In addition, in many states, partisan staffs also back up majority and minority members on the committees and subcommittees. Staff analyses, suggestions, and recommendations play an important part in deliberations of the members.

Weeks of hearings and testimony by agency and public witnesses also furnish legislators with information that goes into their decisions. In the case of most members, experience comes in handy. If they have been through the process before, they already have an idea of how effectively agencies are in administering programs and where the difficulties lie. Often, members have traveled around the state, visiting sites and informing themselves when the legislature is not in actual session. The house appropriations committee in Maryland, for example, made seventeen site visits during the 1995 interim, five by the full committee and the rest by four subcommittees.

Just as with the policy committees in the legislature, those who chair the full committee and the subcommittees of appropriations bear much of the responsibility and play the largest role. Subcommittee and full committee chairs have to work out differences, just as do house and senate committee and subcommittee chairs. The majority leadership in the chamber is almost always closely involved in negotiations and decisions. During the process, Maryland's senate committee and subcommittee chairmen meet every week for lunch. House chairmen do likewise; in addition, they meet once a week with the speaker and others in a "leadership" group of about fourteen.[47]

Although leaders have the most say overall in the legislature's review, a number of members serve on the appropriations committee and come to grips with part of the budget. With the exception of a few states—like Wisconsin, where the Joint Finance Committee has only sixteen members— appropriations committees are the largest in the chamber and participation is reasonably broad. Illustrative is house appropriations in Maryland. In the old days only a few members were in on decisions. Then, under the chairmanship of Buzz Ryan, more and more members were included. The process opened up, debate increased, and more members felt included. Even nonmembers could get through. If they came forward with an amendment that looked good, the committee would absorb it. As a result, the budget bill was never amended on the floor and the committee never lost a bill.[48]

Elsewhere, too, membership of the fiscal committees tends to be large. One-third of the senators and representatives in Ohio sit on the committees that work over the budget. In North Carolina 75 percent of the senators and 60 percent of the representatives are on the budget committees, while the rest of the legislators are on the revenue committees. In a few states, essentially every legislator serves on the appropriations committees and can have some say about what goes into the budget. Of 150 legislators in Iowa, 125 are on one of nine joint subcommittees of appropriations (while the other 25 are on ways and means). Legislative leadership decides how many dollars are allocated to each subcommittee's jurisdiction. In Utah everyone but the speaker serves on one of ten joint appropriations subcommittees. In addition, a joint executive committee of eighteen members allocates dollar amounts for the subcommittees to assign to departments, agencies, and programs. The executive committee has the final word on subcommittee recommendations, not all of which are accepted in their entirety.[49]

In many states the budget bill, after being reported out of appropriations, also has to run the gauntlet of the party caucuses. It used to be that majority-party leaders had little difficulty steering the bill through their caucus, but nowadays caucus approval can require substantial work. Members do not automatically fall in line, and dissident elements challenge leadership abilities to negotiate a settlement. In Wisconsin, majority-party members for some years have managed to alter the budget bill as reported by the Joint Finance Committee. Members insist on their own provisions in return for their support.[50] This process in which the caucus engages, referred to as "auctioning off," involves giving enough members projects for their districts to achieve the fifty-one votes needed to pass the bill on the floor. The process is similar in Colorado, where the so-called long bill, developed by the Joint Budget Committee and reviewed by the appropriations committees, gets worked over by the majority-party caucus.[51]

After all of the preceding negotiations, the floor procedure in each chamber is usually perfunctory. Although the minority may offer amendments, few changes (that have not been agreed to beforehand) are allowed on the floor. In California, where a two-thirds vote of each house is required to pass the budget, even a few holdouts can threaten the process. These dissidents have to be pacified before the budget is voted on the floor.

The most critical stage is the end game, after the house and senate have each passed a bill and have to resolve not only their differences but also those they may have with the governor. If the executive and the legislature are in the same partisan hands, things are more likely to be worked out as the process proceeds and the final stage is less of a hurdle. Otherwise, the conference committee of senate and house members and the negotiations between the legislative leadership and the governor are apt to be intense.

Either way, participation in the final phase of resolution necessarily narrows. A conference committee consists of relatively few members from each house. They work in collaboration with the majority leadership and have considerable scope for shaping the fiscal budget settlement, no matter what went on before. In Mississippi the six-person conference committee in effect writes the appropriations bills during the last three days of the session.[52] In Oklahoma the leadership is said to exercise substantial power controlling its conferees, who can almost rewrite the budget from scratch.[53] In Florida the two houses have traditionally been adversarial in negotiating the budget, with each adopting bills that put it in the best bargaining position in conference. The house speaker and the senate president led the negotiations in what has been characterized as "an undue centralization of power in the system."[54]

In other states even the concluding stage has opened up. Maryland used to limit its conference to three members. Now more members have a say, more people are in the room, and a longer time is spent even on relatively noncontroversial issues. Most issues can be resolved by splitting differences or trading off cuts: "We'll take your cut on this, you take ours on that."[55] Conferees fight for the senate or house version behind closed doors, as in Ohio, but still quite a few people are present in the room. These are referred to as "unclosed, closed" meetings, where everything leaks out and all interested parties know what is transpiring. But because the conference is not held in public, there exists no official record reporting who supports what. Were positions on the record, the process would be altered, and the participants' ability to compromise would probably diminish.[56]

Meanwhile, of course, the governor's preferences have to be taken into account because in all but seven states he or she can item-veto budgetary provisions the legislature wants. California's negotiations in recent years usually involved what was called "the Big Five"—the speaker and minority leader of the assembly, the president pro tem and minority leader of the senate, and the governor. These participants would sit at the conference table in the governor's outer office, along with a few staff aides, and try to work out the final budget. In the 1994–1995 budget, the job was accomplished in the legislature and it was not necessary for the Big Five to meet.[57] The process in New York is roughly similar, with the governor (at times a Democrat and at times a Republican) trying to resolve differences with the Democratic speaker of the assembly and the Republican majority leader of the senate. Every year in Albany the end of the session is a time of last-minute bill trading where almost every important issue is tied to something else and everything is tied to the budget. Upstate Republicans try to get more money for their schools; Democrats try to get more environmental projects; and the governor withholds his support from a final budget deal until he obtains an agreement on workers' compensation and domestic-violence measures. "The second the budget is done, the session is over," declares one of Gov. George Pataki's advisers.[58]

However much the process narrows in the final stage to a few key participants, the rank-and-file cannot be ignored. Indeed, legislative leaders speak not so much for themselves, but for their caucuses. The conference committee report, and any agreements entered into, has to win a floor vote in each chamber in order for the budget to become law. So, as long as they have their votes, legislators have bargaining power and some say over what goes in and what stays out of the state budget.

The Legislature's Impact

In their study of budgeting in the states, Edward J. Clynch and Thomas P. Lauth categorize states in terms of executive-legislative power. At one end of the continuum are the executive-dominant states, such as California, Illinois, and Ohio. At the other are the legislative-dominant states, including Florida, Mississippi, Texas, and Utah. In the middle are states where the legislature has the ability to challenge the executive—Connecticut, Georgia, Idaho, Kentucky, and Minnesota.[59]

The balance within a state shifts depending on circumstances. When the executive and legislature are controlled by the same party, the governor tends to gain power. Tight revenues also favor the governor at the expense of the legislature. Under such conditions legislators frequently let governors take the lead raising revenues or cutting spending, neither of which is popular with their constituencies.[60] Divided government enhances the legislative role, as does favorable economic conditions with revenues in abundance.

Over time legislative involvement has increased practically everywhere. As one indication, consider control within a state over federal funds. Only since the early 1980s have legislatures been involved in the review and allocation of federal funds, which earlier had been deemed a gubernatorial prerogative. They became involved in order to gain control over state spending, advance their own priorities for use of the federal funds, exercise discretion over the purposes to which state matching funds would be committed, and limit future demands for state funds to pick up the costs of federally supported programs when federal funding ended.[61]

Not much of an annual or biennial budget is subject to change. Some of state spending takes the form of transfer payments to local governments and school districts, which are funded on a formula basis and not within the purview of the budgetary process. Other expenditures may also be mandated. Depending on the state, perhaps only 5 to 10 percent of total expenditures are susceptible, as a practical matter, to either gubernatorial or legislative control. Changes in levels of expenditure for specific agencies and programs tend to be incremental, with the past level of activity serving as a base from which the review proceeds in both the executive and legislative branches.

Therefore, we cannot expect the legislature to have a large impact on the total amount budgeted. In Connecticut, it is traditional that the legislature makes few changes in the budget. In one fiscal year, the amount was $23.64 million. That was only 0.38 percent of total spending. But the amount was 36 percent of all new and expanded programs in excess of $1 million that were ultimately approved.[62] Using the former percentage, the legislative role appears negligible. Using the latter percentage, the legislative role appears significant. In Ohio the legislature can affect about 5 percent of the budget. But that includes quite a few important initiatives, such as hospital-care insurance and day-care, that come through the budget.[63]

Ohio is one of a number of states that have increasingly made policy through the budget. Human services, education, an experimental voucher program all find their way into the budget. Sometimes this procedure suits the governor, sometimes the legislature, and sometimes both. It facilitates passage of legislation under the budget umbrella. Wisconsin has pioneered in this area, with its budget bill running to 1,557 pages in 1993 (having been 281 pages in 1973), filled as it was with nonbudget policy items.[64]

Even in Maryland, where the legislature cannot increase proposed expenditures or insert items of its own, its budgetary role is not to be minimized. It has a major say in determining the capital budget, through statute it determines aid to localities, by legislating it helps shape the budget for the following year, and it manages to inject considerable fiscal prudence into the process. The legislature establishes limits through its "spending affordability" process, and is not hesitant to reduce items that cannot be justified by the executive. Maryland's governors have the upper hand, in that their priorities constitute the principal budgetary agenda, but the general assembly rarely accepts as a given what the governor presents.

The influence of legislators in obtaining appropriations for special projects that are located in their districts and that benefit their constituencies is acknowledged—and criticized by virtually everyone outside the legislature. We discussed pork in chapter 1 in connection with representation by individual members. Here, our analytical perspective is that of the legislature and its impact on the budget.

Maryland's capital budget normally contains $15 to $20 million for projects of special concern to members and delegations. Florida's budget used to allot $150 to $250 million for "turkeys." New York allows for several hundred "member items" that in 1995 amounted to about $150 million, averaging $710,000 for each of the legislature's 211 members to use for local purposes.[65] Appropriations measures, in particular, serve as vehicles for items or amendments that fund pet projects for as many members as possible. A member of the minority party in New Jersey referred to the 1995–1996 budget as more than the traditional "Christmas tree" budget but rather, as "a whole winter wonderland of pork." That prompted the governor's chief of staff to respond most diplomatically: "There are some items in his budget which the legislature considers priorities in the local level. We can't forget that the legislature is closer to the local spending needs than, perhaps, we are."[66]

The press delights in exposing appropriations like that for the White Otter Fish and Game Club in the southern Adirondacks of New York. The club received $150,000 for a new clubhouse, thanks to the efforts of the local state senator, who was a club member. But many other items clearly have merit, even though they are not screened through the executive's bureaucratic process before insertion in the budget. In New York, as elsewhere, most of the pork goes to deserving organizations like art museums, volunteer fire companies, cub scout troops, and senior citizen centers, and to deserving projects like highways and convention centers. A sampling of member items in the 1996–1997 New York budget is illustrative. There is $95,000 for the Southeast Bronx Neighborhood Centers, $30,000 for the Seneca Chamber of Commerce, $25,000 for the Hispanos Unidos de Buffalo, $15,000 for the Town of Cicero Historical Society, and $10,000 for the Lion's Club of Katonah.[67] Critics of this practice question legislative judgment, condemn the politics involved in choosing local recipients, charge that much of the money is not well used, and deplore the fact that there is little oversight or public accountability.

The assault on pork has made headway, at least in some states. In Florida, every member used to have a share of the budget in the form of a "turkey." Due to Florida Tax Watch, continuing press criticism, and apparent public opinion, any line item with geographical identification is now out of bounds, unless the executive agency requests it. Whereas previously Florida legislators jockeyed for whose arts and cultural projects would be included in the budget, a newly enacted law authorizes the executive to rank projects. Legislators, of course, can lobby an agency to have their items selected for funding, but getting a turkey is tougher now than formerly; and, thus, fewer turkeys survive.[68]

One result of the diminution of pork in Florida is that it is much harder for legislative leadership to exercise leverage over members with regard to the budget and policy issues.[69] That is because, as much as anything else, pork affords leaders resources with which to build consensus among an increasingly independent membership. Local projects that benefit a legislator's district are an important currency in the log-rolling of the legislative process. If leaders control such currency, their power to get the additional votes necessary to pass the budget or enact a controversial bill is enhanced. Pork makes it easier for pluralities to become majorities. Not surprisingly, the new, meager portions of pork signal a decline in the power of legislative leadership.

The legislature's budgetary activity keeps the executive on its toes. Conflict is endemic in the process. When control of government is divided, settlements are more difficult to come by. Governors and legislatures have even failed to produce a budget by the constitutional deadline; namely, the beginning of the fiscal year being budgeted. California budgets were late in 1983, 1990, 1991, 1992, 1994, and 1995, in one of these years for sixty-three days and in another for thirty-three.[70] New York has had an even rockier road. For thirteen straight years, from 1985 to 1997, the governor and legislature failed to meet the state's March 31 deadline. In 1994 and 1995 they were 68 days late, and in 1996 they were 104 days late, apparently a national record, which they surpassed the very next year.[71]

In these struggles legislatures generally give as good as they take. They prevail over governors on some items, while losing on others. After the smoke settled in Albany in 1996, for example, the New York legislature had rejected many of Gov. George Pataki's proposed policy changes and restored about $1.4 billion to his original spending plan. The governor concluded: "I understand that whether you're a legislator, a speaker, a majority leader or the governor, you never get things 100 percent your way."[72]

On occasion, the legislature emerges from the budgetary process with a clear-cut victory rather than some wins and some losses. Rhode Island in 1996 is an illustration. The legislature opposed Gov. Lincoln Almond's retirement plan and his cuts in education. In the face of his refusal to negotiate, the legislature passed its own budget, sustaining most social services, implementing a plan to reduce the number of state employees, and adding slightly to spending for education. The legislature's proposal also contained provisions rescinding existing statutory authority of the governor to move budget allocations within agencies and to impound monies. Since Rhode Island does not provide the governor with a line-item veto, Almond vetoed the entire budget that the legislature had passed; the very next day the legislature overrode the veto.[73]

Legislative Follow-Through

The legislature's budgetary impact extends beyond the stages of formulation, deliberation, and negotiation to implementation itself. Legislatures have strengthened their control over what happens once the budget is enacted and signed into law. Nowadays, they never let go of the budget entirely.

Legislative control begins with the legislature specifying items that go in the budget bill, intending to guide implementation in that fashion. In Maryland, the Joint Chairmen's Report includes narrative language directing the agency on legislative intent with regard to the budget. Although the report does not have the force of law, agency heads know that they have to return for their funding to the appropriations and finance committees the following year. California gives direction in another way; it adopts a supplemental report conveying legislative intent with regard to the expenditure of funds. New Mexico's legislature has a "road memorial," which directs the highway department on the expenditure of funds appropriated.[74]

What has been termed "creeping legislative management" sometimes crosses the dividing line of executive-legislative power. New Jersey's Republican legislature not only cut Democratic governor Jim Florio's 1992–1993 budget, but it also tried to dictate which state workers would be laid off to make ends meet. The legislature mandated that managers rather than union members be axed, requiring about 1,300 layoffs among nonunion managers earning $50,000 or more a year. Florio vetoed the provision, but the legislature overrode the veto. The governor ignored the legislative mandate and challenged it in court. The New Jersey Supreme Court overruled the provision on the grounds that such legislative micromanagement intruded on the governor's constitutional authority.[75]

Thus, through specification in the act itself, accompanying directives, and other requirements, legislatures manage to maintain some control over administration of the budget. They exercise their muscle either through the committees that appropriate the funds in the first place or through special committees or commissions that operate when the legislature is not in session. Wisconsin's powerful Joint Finance Committee involves itself by drafting appropriations so as to require agencies to report before the committee releases money for a program; enacting provisions requiring committee approval of various aspects of financial management; and requiring by law executive branch studies, with reports submitted to the committee.[76] Ohio's mechanism is the Controlling Board, composed by seven members, of whom six are legislators. This board has authority to release appropriated funds that, by law, require board approval before expenditure; authorize expenditures from revenues not anticipated in the current appropriations act; and transfer funds and appropriations.

After enactment of the budget, governors have broad powers to reduce spending, and in forty-two states they can do so without legislative authorization.[77] In some states, legislative approval is required even for cuts, and for most anything else the legislature has to sign off. If the executive wants to transfer funds from one budgetary area to another, the legislature must agree. In a survey conducted by the National Conference of State Legislatures, thirty-two of the forty-one states reporting indicated that the executive could not transfer appropriations between departments without legislative approval. Of the forty-one reporting, twenty-eight needed the legislature to consent to transfers between programs and twenty-four needed consent for transfers between object classes within the same department.[78]

Legislative approval does not come easily. Legislative committees take their responsibilities seriously. As an example, consider Maryland's Policy Committee responding in 1995 to the request of the Department of Economic and Employment Development (DEED) to transfer $5.4 million from a "sunny-day fund" to four companies doing training and for a grant and a loan to assist a company in relocating. The questioning was vigorous, especially as to why the department was going beyond budgeted funds. The new secretary admitted culpability and pledged: "We are not coming back to you a year from now overspending this budget," and "We have to tighten up policy with respect to these grants."

Staff in the legislature's Department of Fiscal Services recommended going along with the transfer, but its analysis suggested that the department should "be encouraged" to develop better budget estimates for the industrial training program, rather than continue to use the sunny-day fund to supplement the budget. Fiscal Services added that the department ought to develop criteria to determine when matching funds will be required and, given the limited funds available for the training program, consider providing assistance only to companies with limited financial resources. All this was grist for the legislators' mill, and members of the Policy Committee piled on with criticism for the agency. The committee's demonstration was intended partly for the statehouse press, but it was also designed to get an unambiguous message across to the new secretary as to what the legislature expected from his department.[79]

Beyond day-to-day control, legislatures currently are also apt to engage in postexpenditure review of executive budget performance. This is part of legislative oversight, a function that legislatures have developed since the 1970s. Currently forty-three states are involved in the evaluation of programs, and in twenty-five of them evaluation is linked to the budget.[80] Reviews and evaluations are conducted by the fiscal committees, by special agencies (such as Virginia's Joint Legislative Audit and Review Commission and Connecticut's Program Review and Investigations Committee), and by performance audit operations in the offices of legislative auditors (as is done in Minnesota, Wisconsin, and Florida).

DEMOCRATIC TENDENCIES

Without an assertive legislature, the power of the governor would tip the balance scales dramatically. The democratic inclination is to be wary of centralized power, even with the safeguard of periodic elections. With a legislature, the executive is at least balanced, if not always checked. Democratically, also, the legislature represents different constituencies and represents them in a different fashion. Local interests and groups have more of a voice in the legislature than they do in the executive. The minority party is not shut out of the legislative branch, although it may be represented only covertly by the bureaucracy in an executive controlled by the other party. The legislature also brings to the governmental process different values and perspectives—a more political and less bureaucratic approach.

There can be no question that the legislature acts as an instrument of democracy in the larger political system of the state. Yet as legislatures become more democratic themselves—more internally fragmented—their power to balance the executive will likely diminish. It is difficult enough for a multimember body to coalesce. But the more independent individual members become and the weaker the leadership, the easier it will be for governors to dominate. The resources that executives have at their disposal can prove terribly alluring to legislators who are perpetually running for office. Legislators without leadership are easy targets for chief executives to pick off. The way things are going, the empowerment of legislatures of the past thirty years has run its course. Ironically, the further democratization of the state legislature probably will lead to the further empowerment of the executive.

NOTES

1. Joseph M. Besette, *The Mild Voice of Reason: Deliberative Democracy and American National Government* (Chicago: University of Chicago Press, 1994), 16.

2. This section is based in part on Alan Rosenthal, *Governors and Legislatures: Contending Powers* (Washington, D.C.: CQ Press, 1990).

3. Burdett A. Loomis, *Time, Politics and Policies: A Legislative Year* (Lawrence: University of Kansas Press 1994).

4. E. Lee Bernick and Charles W. Wiggins, "Executive-Legislative Relations: The Governor's Role as Chief Legislator," in *Gubernatorial Leadership and State Policy,* ed. Eric B. Hezik and Brent W. Brown (Westport, Conn.: Greenwood, 1991), 75.

5. Laura Van Assendelft, "Gubernatorial Agenda Setting and Divided Government in the South," *Journal of Political Science* 23 (1995): 29–63.

6. *New York Times,* December 27, 1994.

7. Glenn Abney and Thomas P. Lauth, "Governors and the Line-Item Veto" (paper prepared for delivery at the annual meeting of the American Political Science Association, Atlanta, Georgia, November 3–5, 1994).

8. Edward J. Clynch, "Mississippi: Does the Governor Really Count?" in *Governors, Legislatures, and Budgets,* ed. Edward J. Clynch and Thomas P. Lauth (Westport, Conn.: Greenwood, 1991), 133.

9. Jack Van Der Slik and Kent D. Redfield, *Lawmaking in Illinois* (Springfield, Ill.: Sangamon State University Press, 1986), 165–166.

10. *State Net Capitols Report,* March 7, 1997.

11. William K. Muir Jr., *Legislature: California's School for Politics* (Chicago: University of Chicago Press, 1982), 169–171.

12. Thomas H. Kean, *The Politics of Inclusion* (New York: Free Press, 1988), 88.

13. Jay Perkins, "Toeing the Line in Louisiana," *State Legislatures,* July–August 1996, 26; interview with the author, June 20, 1995.

14. George W. Scott, "Legislator." Photocopy. See also Peverill Squire, "Changing State Legislative Leadership Careers," in *Changing Patterns in State Legislative Careers,* ed. Gary F. Moncrief and Joel A. Thompson (Ann Arbor: University of Michigan Press, 1992), 179–180.

15. David R. Colburn and Richard K. Scher, *Florida's Gubernatorial Politics in the Twentieth Century* (Tallahassee: University Presses of Florida, 1980), 158.

16. Interview with the author, March 30, 1995.

17. Morris P. Fiorina, "Divided Government in the American States: A By-product of Legislative Professionalism?" *American Political Science Review* 88 (June 1994): 305.

18. Don W. Driggs and Leonard E. Goodall, *Nevada Politics and Government* (Lincoln: University of Nebraska Press, 1996), 75.

19. Van Assendelft, "Gubernatorial Agenda Setting."

20. Edward J. Clynch and Thomas P. Lauth, "Conclusion: Budgeting in the American States—Conflict and Diversity," in *Governors, Legislatures, and Budgets,* ed. Edward J. Clynch and Thomas P. Lauth (Westport, Conn: Greenwood, 1991), 150.

21. See David R. Mayhew, *Divided We Govern: Party Control, Lawmaking, and Investigations, 1946–1990* (New Haven, Conn.: Yale University Press, 1991); also Peverill Squire, "Divided Government and Public Opinion in the States," *State and Local Government Review* 25 (fall 1993): 150–154.

22. *New York Times,* May 20, 1994.

23. George Weeks and Don Weeks, "Taking Turns," *State Legislatures,* July 1993, 20; Carol S. Weissert, "Michigan: No More Business as Usual With John Engler," in *Governors and Hard Times,* ed. Thad L. Beyle (Washington, D.C.: CQ Press, 1992), 161.

24. Peter Eichstaedt, "No, No, Two Hundred Times No," *State Legislatures,* July–August 1995, 49.

25. Interview with the author , May 16, 1995.

26. *Richmond Times-Dispatch,* March 6, 1995.

27. *Daily Press,* March 6, 1995; *Washington Post,* January 18 and February 27, 1995.

28. Rochelle L. Stanfield, "Just Do It," *National Journal,* March 30, 1996, 698.

29. Dall W. Forsythe, *Memos to the Governor: An Introduction to State Budgeting* (Washington, D.C.: Georgetown University Press, 1997): 75.

30. *New York Times,* March 9, 1988.

31. James E. Jernberg, "Minnesota: Searching for Stability," in *Governors, Legislatures, and Budgets,* ed. Edward J. Clynch and Thomas P. Lauth (Westport, Conn: Greenwood, 1991), 73, 75.

32. Malcolm E. Jewell and Penny M. Miller, *The Kentucky Legislature* (Lexington: University Press of Kentucky, 1988), 141–142.

33. Clynch, "Mississippi," 127; Gloria A. Grizzle, "Florida: Miles to Go and Promises to Keep," in *Governors, Legislatures, and Budgets,* ed. Edward J. Clynch and Thomas P. Lauth (Westport, Conn: Greenwood, 1991), 95.

34. Irene S. Rubin et al., "Illinois: Executive Reform and Fiscal Conditions," in *Governors, Legislatures, and Budgets,* ed. Edward J. Clynch and Thomas P. Lauth (Westport, Conn: Greenwood 1991), 22.

35. Interview with the author, June 5, 1995.

36. Glen Hahn Cope, "Texas: Legislative Budgeting in a Post–Oil Boom Economy," in *Governors, Legislatures, and Budgets,* ed. Edward J. Clynch and Thomas P. Lauth (Westport, Conn.: Greenwood, 1991), 117.

37. Clynch, "Mississippi," 126, 131.

38. John A. Straayer, *The Colorado General Assembly* (Niwot: University Press of Colorado, 1990), 107, 219–230.

39. Interview with the author, May 17, 1995.

40. F. Ted Hebert, "Utah: Legislative Budgeting in an Executive State," in *Governors, Legislatures, and Budgets,* ed. Edward J. Clynch and Thomas P. Lauth (Westport, Conn.: Greenwood, 1991), 110–111.

41. Interview with the author, March 30, 1995.

42. James J. Gosling, "Budget Procedures and Executive Review in State Legislatures," in *Encyclopedia of the American Legislative System,* ed. Joel H. Silbey (New York: Scribner's, 1994), 766.

43. Interview with the author, May 17, 1995.

44. Rubin, "Illinois," 22.

45. Jernberg, "Minnesota," 76.

46. Gosling, "Budget Procedures and Executive Review," 769.

47. Interview with the author, June 5, 1995.

48. Ibid., March 6, 1996.

49. Hebert, "Utah," 112–113; also Ronald K. Snell, "Bringing More Legislators into the Budget Process," National Conference of State Legislatures, March 1994. Photocopy.

50. Rich Jones et al., "Review of Legislative Operations in the Wisconsin Legislature," National Conference of State Legislature, May 1994. Photocopy.

51. Straayer, *Colorado General Assembly,* 214.

52. Clynch, "Mississippi," 132.

53. Ronald M. Peters and Elizabeth Himmerich, "Policy Shift and Leadership

Coalition: The Revolt Against Speaker Barker in Oklahoma" (paper prepared for delivery at the annual meeting of the American Political Science Association, San Francisco, August 30–September 2, 1990).

54. Grizzle, "Florida," 96–97.

55. Interview with the author, June 5, 1995.

56. Ibid., February 24, 1995.

57. Ibid., March 16, 1995.

58. *New York Times,* July 3, 1996.

59. Clynch and Lauth, "Conclusion," 152–155.

60. Ibid., 151–152.

61. Gosling, "Budget Procedures and Executive Review," 774–775.

62. Carol W. Lewis, "Connecticut: Prosperity, Frugality, and Stability," in *Governors, Legislatures, and Budgets,* ed. Edward J. Clynch and Thomas P. Lauth (Westport, Conn.: Greenwood, 1991), 48.

63. Interview with the author, February 24, 1995.

64. In 1993 some of these items started to be removed from the budget and treated as regular legislation. See Jones et al., "Review of Legislative Operations in the Wisconsin Legislatures."

65. *New York Times,* July 14, 1996.

66. Ibid., June 20, 1995.

67. Ibid., July 14, 1996.

68. Interview with the author, March 25, 1995.

69. Ibid. See also Forsythe, *Memos to the Governor,* 70.

70. Steve Scott, "The 1995–96 Budget," *California Journal,* September 1995, 8.

71. *New York Times,* July 14, 1996.

72. Ibid.

73. Maureen Moakley, "The Rhode Island Legislature: The Center Still Holds" (paper prepared for delivery at the annual meeting of the American Political Science Association, San Francisco, August 29–September 1, 1996).

74. Interview with the author, May 17, 1995.

75. *New York Times,* December 30, 1992.

76. Remarks of Marlin Schneider, cochair, Joint Finance Committee, Wisconsin, July 26, 1988.

77. Richard Briffault, *Balancing Acts: The Reality Behind State Balanced Budget Requirements* (New York: Twentieth-Century Fund Press, 1996), 32.

78. Corina L. Eckl, *Legislative Authority Over the Enacted Budget* (Denver: National Conference of State Legislatures, July 1992), 25–35.

79. Policy Committee meeting, Annapolis, June 6, 1996.

80. Eckl, *Legislative Authority,* 16.

CHAPTER 9

The Democratic Challenge

After examining state legislatures and their milieu, one conclusion stands out: These are institutions with democratic features being buffeted by democratic forces. This is not to say that legislatures are perfectly democratic. In fact, they have antidemocratic blemishes that repel democracy's advocates—backroom negotiations despite proclamations of openness, campaign contributions that facilitate access, and inequalities in the internal distribution of influence, to name a few. Yet as far as process, participation, and power are concerned, legislatures are notably democratic.

In this concluding chapter, we shall bring together the bits and pieces of description and analysis that appear in the preceding pages, making the argument about legislative democracy. Then we shall point out the perils that contemporary legislative democracy poses for representative government, each of which has been touched on or inferred in chapter-by-chapter discussions. The final section will specify the options that face legislative assemblies and their constituencies, and what—if anything—can be done about what appears to be the decline of representative democracy.

THE PROGRESS OF DEMOCRACY

Americans feel the governmental process simply does not work to represent them or to respond to their needs. According to the populist spirit raging throughout the states, only the special interests have access, and only they are indulged by an otherwise unrepresentative and unresponsive system. "Soured on pluralism," one expert on public opinion writes, "voters are voicing anger and resentment at how representative democracy is working."[1] Although populism draws a sharp line between the people on the one hand and the professional politicians on the other, that line—as we have tried to show throughout this book—is becoming blurred. The realities of the legislature and legislative process are not what they are popularly conceived to be.

Representation in legislative assemblies is more democratic than formerly. Since the judiciary intervened in reapportionment, political and legal representation has been equalized. Each person has a vote equivalent to that of any other person. Some Republicans in overwhelmingly Democratic districts and some Democrats in overwhelmingly Republican districts feel disenfranchised from a practical point of view, but their votes count equally in theoretical terms. The trend toward single-member districts has also worked to equalize the influence of voters; there are fewer instances in which some voters in a state can cast ballots for two representatives while others can cast ballots for only one.

Descriptively as well, legislatures are more representative than earlier. Lawmakers still do not mirror the publics they represent, but they come closer. Women and minorities are no longer absent from the ranks of state senates and state houses (and attorneys are less present than formerly). This means that issues which have previously had little steam now find a place on the agenda.

The system of representation is rooted in periodic elections, with most of members of state houses running every two years and most members of state senates running every four years. Assuming that incumbents desire to be re-elected, there is no getting away from accountability to the voters. Even though the majority of incumbents have seats that can be considered statistically safe, psychologically few of them feel or behave as if their reelection is a sure thing. They have seen overconfident colleagues upset by challengers, and they consider themselves unsafe whatever their previous margins. Always in peril because of the impending election, they campaign continuously, doing whatever seems necessary to hold together the coalition that elected them and giving as few voters and groups as possible cause for supporting their opponent.

If there were not sufficient pressure on individual lawmakers, the legislative parties are also feeling the strain. Only a minority of electoral districts throughout the nation can be categorized as competitive; yet currently two out of three legislative bodies in the fifty states can be won by either the Democrats or the Republicans. The majority party in the chamber is intent on maintaining its majority; the minority party is intent on winning a majority. The incentives that drive the two parties are collective and individual—gaining power, achieving leadership positions, and enacting legislation that most legislative party members favor and bills that benefit their districts. The rewards of victory are not inconsiderable, so it is little wonder that the legislative parties have become—among other things—campaign organizations. Indeed, their leadership and party PACs help them function as such and tend to increase competition in those districts where each party has a reasonable chance of winning. The legislative parties, like their legislator members, concern themselves with maintaining their electoral bases, picking up voters wherever they can and hanging on to their more peripatetic supporters.

In large part because of competition at the polls, legislators and legislatures constantly survey the political landscape so they can be in tune with voters' desires. Now that most members represent single-member districts, there is no longer the possibility of hiding behind a unified delegation. Lawmakers are alone and exposed. They try to reduce the risks they face on issues of public policy by attending to constituency service—doing casework, bringing home the bacon, and making their presence felt at home. Today they are, both by choice and necessity, more parochial, more localistic, and more responsive in their perspectives.

One political scientist summed up the problem as far as the American people are concerned in the following way: "A crucial element in the restoration of public trust is the recognition by our leaders that they must somehow attend more closely—or at the very least appear to attend more closely . . .—to the needs and wishes of ordinary citizens."[2]

As applied to individuals holding state legislative office, the idea that they do not attend to the needs and wishes of ordinary citizens is almost preposterous. If anything, they are overly attentive and too responsive. But, much as they try, individual lawmakers cannot please everyone; there will always be dissatisfied groups and disgruntled constituents.

It is even more difficult for legislatures than for legislators to please everyone, even though they too are quite responsive. They respond with legislation for practically every interest group that makes an appeal. They respond when the problems of ordinary citizens are brought to their attention. Sometimes, it is true, they avoid issues. This is not because they are recalcitrant, but because the divisions in the legislature cannot be overcome and all-out combat would produce more losers than winners. In such cases, legislatures are not creating differences, but are reflecting sharp differences in their states and in society. Occasionally, legislatures will sidetrack something that most citizens seem to want—lower taxes, term limits, or whatever. In these cases, lawmakers agree, at least tacitly, that the most responsible action is not to accede to citizens' desires because such action is not in citizens' interests.

The acid test of responsiveness relates to the policies that legislatures produce. It is virtually impossible to obtain agreement on just what should emerge from the process, since different values and approaches naturally lead to different outcomes. But a recent study linking public opinion and public policy in the states found that "at the ballot box, state electorates hold strong control over the ideological direction of policies in their states. In anticipation of this electoral monitoring, state legislatures and other policymakers take public opinion into account when enacting a state policy."[3] Such a finding flies in the face of conventional wisdom. Far more than "electoral monitoring" takes place. "Public opinion," or rather, the opinions of all sorts of publics, do not wait passively to be discovered. They are made known.

Public participation in state policy-making has been increasing, while the separation between those who govern and those who are governed has been diminishing. Despite low voting turnout, various publics have ample opportunity to get their messages across. Legislators today have more information about what people believe and want than was ever available before. Public-opinion polls, e-mail, 800 numbers, call-in radio and television have exponentially increased the contact representatives have with their constituents. All this makes for greater responsiveness and less independence of judgment on many issues. Independence of judgment is what distinguishes representative democracy from popular rule. As constituents' preferences increasingly constrain legislators, representative democracy gives way.[4]

The distance between legislators and their publics has narrowed, so that little space currently separates them. Directly or indirectly, people are in the legislature's face. Polling is ubiquitous. Statewide polls are not without impact; district polls, which are still relatively rare, can be most intimidating. Electronic democracy and teledemocracy hold out prospects of legislators receiving more instructions from their electorates in the future than they do now. The day is not far off when interactive television or the Internet will be used for holding referendums on issues, state by state, with the results tallied and publicized district by district. Legislators will be hard pressed to act contrary to the majority opinions in their district, lest they be attacked by an opponent in the forthcoming campaign for rejecting the will of their constituents—particularly when they knew what it was.

If legislatures do not give citizens what they want, then, in half the states, people have recourse to the ballot by way of the initiative. Conversely, citizens can resort to the referendum, if the legislature has given them what they do *not* want. The initiative has been heavily used only in several states, but its impact reaches further. It has been employed in imposing restrictions on the legislatures—in particular, term limits. Moreover, the threat of an initiative has forced legislatures in a number of places to enact laws that they otherwise would not have condoned.

A principal player in legislative democracy nowadays is the press. The contemporary legislature is open to scrutiny by the press, which subsequently communicates its views to the public. The print and electronic media shape public perceptions of political institutions and processes, contributing substantially to the cynicism and distrust that the public expresses today. The media, moreover, affect both legislative behavior and the management of the legislature as an institution in a rather direct fashion. The decisions that legislators make on staffing, compensation, travel, and ethics are routinely influenced by what they think will be the media's response.

Unelected and unaccountable, the media are nevertheless exercising a great deal of influence. Journalists and editors claim to be acting as watchdogs for and as representatives of the public, and that they are therefore serving to ensure that elected public officials are accountable. The media both respond to and shape public tastes, but the very nature of their enterprise puts a peculiarly negative spin on how the governors come across to the governed.

The main avenues of participation in policy making per se are through the many groups that are promoting their interests in the legislature. Directly or indirectly these groups represent practically every imaginable interest and the interests of practically every conceivable person. This interest-group system has been characterized as "hyperpluralism," a system in which a proliferation of groups compete with one another.[5] Although they are not equal in strength, the resources they draw on are varied and dispersed. Just about any organized group has access to the legislative process and is able to get one sort of hearing or another for its ideas and needs. Those with the most members, the most resources, and good, persuasive arguments tend to win more often than not.

Interest groups are highly participative. Many involve themselves in elections, hoping to wind up with lawmakers friendlier to their cause. Even more lobby at the capital, hoping to persuade lawmakers to enact policies that are helpful to them and to defeat those that are harmful. Lobbying used to be an inside game, restricted to a relative few and depending heavily on the relationships among lobbyists and legislators. The line between social and professional often became blurred. Recently lobbying has been evolving into more of an outside game, employing grassroots techniques and drawing on organizational memberships. Lobbying has broadened beyond its immediate membership. Now, on issues where the stakes are high, groups are likely to launch public relations and media campaigns, with issue advertisements aimed at the general public. These campaigns are designed to win over people, or at least to give the impression that the legislators' publics are on the group's side. Actively or passively, more people are involved in the lobbying enterprise than ever before.

Power within legislatures, which was never highly concentrated, is now even more dispersed. Just as the legislature's external environment is fragmented, so is its internal environment. Connected as they are to their constituencies, members maintain independence of party and of leadership in the legislature. They have their personal careers and individual agendas to promote. Each has his or her own bottom line, which legislative leaders are obliged to respect. Formerly, legislators developed ties with one another by virtue of shared social life in the capitol community. Little community exists anymore, with legislators scattered and the few norms that previously existed now eroding.

On the basis of surveying veteran legislators about a number of internal matters, three political scientists portray not only a new breed of legislator but also a changed institution—one in which they see power having devolved in a centrifugal fashion.[6] That is certainly an apt description of most legislative bodies, where power is distributed among committees, subcommittees, and individual members. Nowadays every legislator can expect a meaningful committee assignment, and many returning members can expect a leadership position of some type. Just about everywhere appropriations committees have been enlarged and more legislators now have some say on the budget.

Just as committee chairmen are granted greater autonomy by the top leadership, so committee members are granted a larger role by committee chairmen. Each person in a leadership position is responsive to those below, those people upon whom his or her position and success depend. More bills are reported, more amendments accepted, and more accommodations made. Rank-and-file legislators have influence, if they choose to exploit it, as they only occasionally had before. And in those states with term limits, further equalization will occur as differences among members that are attributable to tenure and knowledge diminish further.

As evident as anything else internally is the diminution of leadership power. The presiding officers can no longer depend on a docile or a loyal following. There are too many examples of house speakers or senate presidents (or presidents pro tem) being repudiated by their own caucuses or by bipartisan coalitions. Their following cannot be assumed; it must be constantly recreated. To ensure their positions and their power, leaders have to do more and more service for their members, catering to their individual needs even at substantial cost. There is little threat nowadays, if there ever was, of autocratic legislative leadership; the greater threat is of more demanding members and more submissive leadership.

THE DANGERS OF DEMOCRACY

The legislature and the legislative process are democratic to begin with, and have become more so in recent years. Some of the democratic changes that have come about are salutary, but some of them—especially if carried too far—endanger the legislature's ability to function in a representative and authoritative capacity. The dangers of democracy are already upon legislatures; they are real, and not merely hypothetical.

1. The danger of inequality. Not everyone shares equally when it comes to political clout. Large stakeholders usually have more to say about public policy than do small stakeholders. Participatory democracy, as expressed through the initiative, is not the panacea its advocates claim it to be. Organized interests, and not common folks, are most frequently the initiators. As a leading student of I&R writes, "The people who rule in the initiative and referendum process are first and foremost the people who set the agenda for voters to decide at the next election."[7] They are not the spectators in our political system.

The knowledge and self-confidence requisite for participation in issue campaigns is unequally distributed. Anthony King points to the problems inherent in participatory democracy: first, the problem of time, with most people unwilling to devote the time required; second, the problem of bias, with much greater participation by those with leisure time and by the educated, the articulate, and the aggressive.[8]

2. The danger of manipulation. The "inside game," in which legislators and lobbyists exchange information and deal with one another, may well represent the public's interest better than the "outside game," in which an appeal is made to the public for votes and/or support. Given the powerful electoral connection between voters and legislators, it is unlikely that representatives will stray far from the interests of their constituents. Given the requirements of the process, it is unlikely that lobbyists will mislead legislators. Within the legislative framework, information is reliable and efficiently transmitted by lobbyists to legislators. All of this can go on with relatively few people involved.

Grassroots lobbying broadens participation. Many citizens are involved in campaigns waged by the groups to which they belong, and many more are influenced, and even mobilized, by such campaigns. Others take in the messages directed at them. Mobilization is not really necessary. What matters is that legislators get the impression both that citizens favor a measure proposed by a campaigning group and that citizens will retaliate against contrary legislators. PR and media campaigns are designed to intimidate, not to communicate.

3. The danger of a coherent "public interest." Legislators have their own rationales, and their own peculiar calculations for figuring out what benefits their constituencies and the state as a whole. The procedures they use are neither scientific nor holistic. Legislators tend to see things in terms of increments and fragments. Moreover, they recognize the group basis of politics and the inevitable conflict among various interests and points of view. Their model of political democratic reality is being challenged today by those who claim to represent the public at large.

These claimants advance the proposition that there exists a general will that petty and parochial legislators cannot help but recognize yet do not acknowledge. The so-called public interest groups, like Common Cause, assume the mantle of public representation on issues such as ethics and campaign finance. The media, including both the reportorial and editorial press, also speak loudly on behalf of what they declare to be the public on many governmental and policy issues. Although they are neither elected nor otherwise accountable, members of the media maintain that they—and not the politicians—can be trusted to articulate the public interest.

Apparently no less authoritative are public opinion polls, which, it is argued, convey the most persuasive information about what people want and need. Polls do provide opportunities for citizens to increase their influence on the political process.[9] But the reliability of issue polls is always open to question. Respondents frequently have little sense of the issue about which they are being polled. But the very process suggests they *should* have opinions, and consequently they respond one way or the other. When a respondent's opinions are weakly grounded, the placement and wording of questions have much to do with the distribution of positive and negative responses. Polls do provide lawmakers with useful information, particularly that of a cautionary nature. But polls cannot stand alone; they have to be taken with considerable doses of judgment and integrated with other information on what or even whether people feel about a subject.

4. The danger of unworkable policy. Legislators do not deserve a grade of A or B for producing rational public policies, all of which fit together in a coherent whole. The legislative process is rarely up to such an achievement. Still, those who take their leadership responsibilities to heart have an idea of which measure must be traded off for something else, which one is inconsistent with another, how today's agenda is informed by yesterday's experience, and what the possible consequences are for the future. Legislators may not make enough connections, but at least they make some.

The more the legislature is constrained by public participation, the less any one policy will be decided in connection with the larger policy picture. Mobilized combatants leave scant leeway for legislators. The focus is on the single issue, and not on the broader spectrum. The initiative is an extreme case of this point. Once sufficient signatures have been collected, the petition has withstood legal review, and the question has been put on the ballot, the legislature is no longer involved.[10] Disputants battle it out, with virtually no consideration of how the issue in question relates more broadly to governance and policy.

If one looks at the California's constitutional reform process through the initiative, the policy dangers are evident. Peter Schrag reviews what he calls the "orgy" of reform, which really began in 1978 with Proposition 13, limiting property taxes. This was followed in 1979 by a prohibition on unfunded mandates and also on spending limits for state and local governments. Then, in 1988 a requirement was adopted that the state spend a large percentage of its general-fund budget on schools. In 1990 term limits and limits on legislative spending further compounded the damage. "All that reforming," writes Schrag, "has produced a Rube Goldberg machine of truly baroque proportions," which pulverizes governmental authority and makes it almost impossible for state and local officials to set priorities and deal with the issues they were elected to address.[11] It is not surprising that California citizens are dissatisfied with how their governments work. They do not work well at all. Nor is it surprising that California citizens do not acknowledge that they themselves bear major responsibility for the quality of governmental performance.

5. The danger of enfeebled leadership. "A representative democracy," writes political scientist John Geer, "must walk a tightrope between excessive leadership and the absence of leadership."[12] There is not much danger of excessive leadership today. Individual legislators, to an alarming degree, have abandoned their leadership role in favor of being responsive. Their problem is not that they attend too little, but that they attend too much—to anything that purports to be the voice of people.

Nor is it that legislators know too little about what their electorates feel, but that they know too much.[13] Although much of what they know may not be terribly reliable, they feel that they ignore it at their peril. Frank Luntz, a GOP pollster, made the case for the primacy of public opinion when he admonished Republicans:"We must not look at our party as speaking for the American people. . . . We must begin to see ourselves as a conduit through which the people speak for themselves."[14] There is no place for political leadership in Luntz's conception of governance.

Instead of leadership, legislators under intense pressure from democracy are more inclined to engage in symbolic politics and make the rhetorical case. They are also reluctant to make tough decisions, to ask for sacrifices, to impose losses—thereby courting unpopularity and risking defeat at the polls.[15]

Tom Loftus, who had been there as a Wisconsin legislative leader, challenged legislators gathered at a national meeting to be willing to lose for something they believe in. "Someone needs to take a dive," Loftus said, "because they showed courageous leadership on an issue that counts." There is no reason to expect that many legislators will follow Loftus's advice. Lawmakers who like being where they are and worked hard to get there are not likely to sacrifice themselves in order to exercise their own judgment rather than follow the electorate's. Anthony King has similar concerns but proposes a different solution. For him, elective officeholders must somehow be permitted to spend more time and energy on *actually governing* and to have more leeway, more discretion, in the making of policy.[16] How this will happen under present conditions is the big question.

Legislative leadership still leads, but probably not enough. The increasing independence and individualism of members have left elected leaders with uncertain support. Their tenure today is limited—by constitution, law, custom, or by the ambitions of their colleagues. While their resources remain substantial, they are inhibited from using them to enforce discipline in the legislative party. Much of their energy has to be spent serving their followers and maintaining their support. Much also has to be devoted to getting their partisan colleagues reelected. The legislative election campaign, along with serious fund-raising, is now a critical part of the leadership job. If members have only limited leeway on policy, leaders are on their way to having even less.

6. The danger of less deliberation. American legislatures have long been criticized for their inadequate debate and insufficient deliberation. They deserve the criticism. The pressures of democracy, however, push the legislature in entirely the opposite direction. The initiative is antithetical to a deliberative process. In the legislature, diverse views are brought to bear on a problem; measures are reviewed and modified at stage after stage. Hearings and floor debate in one house and then in the other and in conference all encourage deliberation and bargaining.[17] Under the initiative, a measure is formulated by one side or the other, the campaign is waged, with both sides arguing their case, and the electorate votes the measure up or down. There is little exchange, little or no negotiation, and scant modification.

Even without the initiative, an excess of public participation hamstrings deliberation. Political forces become overwhelming and legislators succumb. Why talk? Michael Wines of the *New York Times,* referring to Washington, D.C., writes that "a somewhat slow and contemplative system" has been turned into "something more like a 500-channel democracy, with the clicker grasped tightly in the hands of the electorate."[18] Things may be less sophisticated at the state level, but here too lawmakers are becoming, if not slaves to public opinion, then prisoners of public sentiment. In North Dakota, a state known for its democratic politics, it is reported that the pressure of increased citizen access to the legislature has tended to reduce the time and inclination of legislators to engage in deliberation on the issues.[19] If lawmakers attend more to messages coming at them from outside the legislature, they will be less disposed to attend to messages from one another inside the legislature.

7. The danger to consensus building. A number of democratic features make it difficult for the legislature to build consensus today. The openness of the contemporary legislature militates against straight talk on the one hand and deal-making on the other. Much of the legislative process is required to take place in public view. Committee meetings, for instance, have to be open. The comments of committee members become part of the public record, so legislators can easily be held accountable for their statements, as well as for their votes.

Political compromise is a lot harder than it was when legislators could simply work things out among themselves. Once a position becomes public, a legislator becomes frozen in it. On some issues there is no longer enough wiggle room to reach accommodation. Efforts to settle disagreements by splitting differences and negotiating compromises normally have to take place behind the scenes. The concerned public views these necessarily unseen activities as proof that their leaders are selling out.[20] It is perilous for legislators to be themselves—if they still have selves to be—when they are fully exposed to the media and, thus, to the public. "In a world where interest groups and the media will pounce and tear apart any controversial statement," writes Bruce Adams, "there will be precious few elected or top appointed officials willing to brainstorm in public."[21]

The broader and more intense the involvement of publics, the more an issue tends to become polarized. Neither side can afford to give without abandoning principle, without suffering loss of face. Legislators who are allied with a group and dependent on its members for support also stiffen up. After all, to win reelection, they need votes from members and the best way to ensure votes is to attack the group's enemies. This may pay electoral dividends, but it does not bring together the parties in conflict.

The antithesis of consensus building is when one side wins and the other loses, with little or no effort to settle on a position somewhere in the middle. This is a distinguishing characteristic of direct legislation—the initiative—which leads to an all-or-nothing decision on the question, a decision reached without compromise or accommodation along the way.[22] When legislatures broker a settlement, opposing interests can wind up endorsing the outcome. That way they can put the battle behind them and get together on something they can support. When legislatures are cut out of the action, the possibility of joint endorsement is negligible. The losers will challenge the outcome directly in court or try to undermine it indirectly in the process of implementation.

8. The danger of a weak political institution. One effect of democratization is the deinstitutionalization of the legislature. No longer are legislatures bounded from their environments, and no longer do they have control over their own internal affairs. The press has intruded into matters that had previously been left to legislatures to manage for themselves. Now the press, and presumably the public, want things done their way. Legislators are reluctant to travel out of state, hesitant to socialize with lobbyists, and fearful that their ethics will be impugned.

Today's lawmakers are demoralized. They have to be on the defensive and cannot afford to strengthen their institution, especially if public monies are required for institutional improvement. Although hard data are elusive, it would appear that those legislators who have general concerns and institutional inclinations will be less apt to stay for very long. The climate is too hostile. It is less likely that people like themselves will be recruited in the future. The sacrifices legislators make are greater than they used to be, and risk to one's reputation has become part of the equation.

With term limits in some places and briefer tenure in most, legislators will have little experience, little disposable time, and probably little patience. There will not be much to bond them with the legislature. Institutional loyalty, which has been in short supply, may be even rarer in the future. As the institutional fabric frays even further, there may be no *there* there in the not-too-distant future.

9. The danger of unchecked power. As chapter 8 suggests, the development of legislatures, especially their increase in capacity, has served to balance and check the power of the executive. Legislatures now share in making policy, in determining budgets, and to a lesser extent in administering government. Although governors have marked advantages, legislatures have had sufficient resources and incentives to counter the weight of the executive. They have therefore acted to prevent an undue centralization of power.

If they lose strength, legislatures will be unable to continue as a democratizing force in the governmental system. The panoply of interests that the legislature represents differs from that of the governor. The legislative approach is more political, more personal. Its members have different perspectives. As the legislature loses power, these values will lose out, while executive values will gain. Perhaps that would be beneficial. Perhaps that is what people want. But it is doubtful that, were the public better informed of possible consequences, it would choose weaker legislatures if these meant more powerful governors.

What I refer to here as "the dangers of democracy" are not the only problems contemporary legislatures face. Nor do the problems listed above result entirely from democratic tendencies. Usually a combination of factors accounts for institutional pathology, not any single, identifiable factor. But, in light of the pressures of democracy, these dangers are most pertinent. They suggest the question, what can be done about it?

ADAPTING TO DEMOCRACY

The conventional prescription for legislative illness is to change the legislature. Reform, democratization, and public participation are supposed to cure what is ailing the legislature. Another prescription, however, is to change the public. Those advocating this course are few and far between. The position advanced here is that both types of change are necessary, but the latter is even more critical than the former.

Changing the Legislature

Although the Whigs believed that considerable distance should separate rulers and ruled, the amount of insulation they had in mind is out of the question today. Participatory democracy is here to stay; there is no prospect of going back. It rests on the principles of popular consent and majority rule, and the populist belief that decisions made by ordinary people have greater validity than those made by their elected representatives.[23] The question, however, is how much further it should proceed, and how can the legislature best adapt to the democracy already upon it.

Recommendations for legislative reform abound. Constitutional revision, unicameralism, term limits, ethics laws, and, campaign-finance reform are among them. It is not possible to examine each and every proposal here. The ones of special relevance to this analysis are those that call for more democracy, mainly by providing citizens with further means of participating in the governing process. The popular view, as expressed by the National Commission for the Renewal of American Democracy, holds that participation must involve more than voting for candidates, with citizens having "an active, meaningful role" in the governing process.[24] The assumption is that citizens do not presently have such a role.

There can be little doubt that the public—as elicited in polls and focus groups—feels aggrieved, shut out of the process. The Kettering Foundation, among others, reports that people are eager to participate, but feel that the system keeps them out. This is the dominant finding; yet a focus-group study, conducted by two political scientists examining public attitudes toward Congress, found that people admitted they were unwilling to engage in politics not because they were barred from participation but because they were uninterested and had other priorities.[25] People feel shut out if they say they do, but it is not necessarily because they *are*.

Reformers maintain that political institutions do not take the views of citizens into account when deciding on policies that affect them. But that is just what legislators do, almost religiously. Reformers would go further, making lawmakers even more responsive to the public by figuring out additional ways of bending lawmakers to the people's will (whatever that may be). King recoils at proposals that go in that direction. For him, the political system is too responsive. "America suffers," he writes, "not from an insufficiency of democracy but from a surfeit of it." It is his view that less democracy might well mean better democracy and better government.[26]

Our judgment is that while it is possible to improve legislatures, it is not likely that we will be able to improve *on* legislatures. Neither increased participatory democracy nor further steps toward direct democracy is the way. Instead, legislators have to take responsibility for their own institution. That entails any number of things: nurturing civility; keeping partisanship from damaging the legislature or the legislative process; maintaining the strength of the institution; and providing for enough centralized power to facilitate consensus building. Each legislature has to deal with these issues in its own way. But each ought to accord them substantially more attention than is done now.

Most important, in the context of this discussion, legislatures must take upon themselves the function of civic education. The principal functions of legislatures, most political scientists would agree, are making policy, deciding on budgets, exercising oversight, and serving constituents. Other, more limited, functions—such as reviewing executive nominations—also require legislative attention. Civic education should also be considered a legislative responsibility. Yet it has been given relatively short shrift. If legislatures are to help rebuild public trust and thus maintain the well-being of representative democracy, they will have to devote a lot more than passing attention to the education of citizens.

Changing the Public

In his foreword to Lawrence Grossman's book, *The Electronic Republic,* Richard Leone of the Twentieth-Century Fund ventures an ominous prediction for representative government: "The real question, then, may not be whether an increase in electronic democracy is desirable, but how to make the best of what is sure to be part of our future."[27] Electronic democracy in some forms is already upon legislators, who are becoming more exposed to individual and group communication by telephone, fax, and most recently e-mail. As of 1997, at least two-thirds of the legislators in thirty-nine of the ninety-nine legislative chambers could be reached by e-mail.[28] More advanced forms of electronic democracy are waiting in the wings. Even proponents of increased public participation acknowledge its dangers, particularly if we cannot develop a concerned and educated public. A number of suggestions have recently been made, and projects launched, in order to improve public competence. With more opportunities for people to increase their influence on the political process, much rests on their ability to make good judgments.[29]

Political scientist Robert Dahl recognizes that although technology will allow citizens to vote directly on issues, voting without adequate understanding would not ensure that the policies adopted would protect or advance their interests. He recommends what he refers to as a "minipopulous"; that is, one thousand randomly selected citizens who would deliberate for a year and then announce their choices. Several such groups would operate as a complement to the legislature, expressing the informed, deliberative judgment of the demos.[30] Popular deliberation is also being promoted by the National Issues Forum of the Kettering Foundation and Public Agenda. The Jefferson Center for New Democratic Processes in Minnesota has experimented with "policy juries," which deliberate and then elect representatives to a statewide body that makes final recommendations. A similar mechanism, the "deliberative poll," developed by James Fishkin, allows for a knowledgeable and deliberative community representing what the electorate would be if it could take the time and explore the issue.[31]

These mechanisms are useful if their purpose is to educate people on the issues. Those individuals who engage in the enterprise will come to realize how much of a difference information and deliberation can make. They will also become more tolerant of different views. These mechanisms also can assist elected public officials, who want to know what informed citizens are thinking on particular issues. But deliberative polls are no substitute for public opinion polls, because they reflect a citizenry that is unrepresentative of the general public in its knowledge and deliberative experience. That is not the normal state of affairs, nor will it ever be. Most important, deliberative polls are no substitute for the legislature. Deliberative polls and their ilk take place in experimental, not natural, environments. Those who are part of such experiments have no constituencies to represent, no interests pulling in different directions, no opponents to beat back, no other issues that have to be addressed, no trade-offs that have to be made, no revenues that have to be raised, no negotiations that have to transpire, and no responsibilities to fulfill. The deliberation that takes place in a legislature and the linkages that lawmakers have are of a radically different order, influenced as they are by so many factors.

Proposals to strengthen the power of the governed by weakening the authority of the governors are in high fashion today.[32] Educating citizens about the issues their states and representatives face is worthwhile. But there is a far greater need for citizens to be educated as to how their political system works and what representative democracy entails. This is not to defend the institutional status quo, but to be concerned about demands for wholesale governmental reform that result, in large part, from a lack of understanding of how government operates. Nor is this to challenge public skepticism, a reasonable amount of which is healthy in a democratic polity. But too much skepticism, cynicism, and distrust add up as a threat to the health of the polity.

The problem is that the public is completely disconnected from an understanding or appreciation of the political process. So, we talk about changing the process to please the public on the assumption that the public cannot be changed. It may appear elitist, politically incorrect, and practically foolish to even think about educating the public in politics. Only ivory-tower scholars would be so presumptuous as to pursue such a path. In a fascinating study of public attitudes toward Congress, John Hibbing and Elizabeth Theiss-Morse conclude that people profess a devotion to democracy in the abstract but have little appreciation for how it operates. They have scant tolerance for uncertainty, conflicting options, long debate, competing interests, confusion, bargaining, haggling, compromise, slowness, and imperfect solutions. "The big failing of Americans," these political scientists write, "is that they lack an appreciation for the ugliness of democracy."[33]

Representative democracy is indeed a messy form of government, one that is almost unfathomable to anyone but a participant or close observer. And it is by no means easily understandable even to them. Ordinary people cannot appreciate such a chaotic process or bizarre form of life. Furthermore, to individual constituents, the legislature is a bunch of faraway politicians and is therefore easy to condemn, while their own representative comes closer to flesh and blood and human life, and is easier to tolerate. Moreover, the legislature is constituted to give rise to disagreement and fated to be disagreeable, annoying at least some people both when it acts and when it fails to act.[34] Congress, in fact, "embodies practically everything Americans dislike about politics." It is large, ponderous, open, and based on compromise.[35]

Another study of the public approval ratings of Congress showed that when Congress is doing its job—passing legislation, overriding vetoes, and engaging in conflict—the public is more disapproving. "Ironically," write the investigators, "when Congress performs its function of lawmaking and deliberation, it is debased in the eyes of those it is intended to represent." The process is so unappealing that public respect for the institution declines.[36]

State legislatures resemble Congress in the emotions they arouse in the public. What people know about their state legislatures is even less than what they know about Congress. Information about legislatures, like that about Congress, is filtered through the lens of the media. Given the nature of "news" and the incentives of the media, it is hardly surprising that legislative bodies are held in low esteem.

The challenge, of course, is to provide the public with fair-minded information about legislatures. But, even more important, citizens have to have a better idea of what representative democracy is supposed to be about, how it works, and what we can reasonably expect from its functioning. If we can understand the system we have in place and assess how it is working, we will be in a better position to decide whether and how to change it. Currently, our assaults on representative democracy are doing damage to the system we have, while offering nothing in its place.

Education in representative democracy is an imposing task. Thus far, those of us in elementary, secondary, and higher education have not been doing a very good job as far as civic education is concerned. Our emphasis has been on rights, while little attention has been devoted to responsibilities. Citizen participation and the articulation of demands have been encouraged, while an understanding of the consensus-building aspects of the political system has been neglected. In their study, for instance, Hibbing and Theiss-Morse found that there is no correlation between years of schooling on the one hand and willingness to appreciate the importance of debate and compromise on the other.[37] Education has not fostered dispositions that are compatible with representative democracy.

Civic education cannot be left to the tender mercies of the media. Nor can sole reliance be placed on the schools. The schools require a jump start, and perhaps then they will do better at these tasks. A lot can be done by higher education—by institutes, centers, and bureaus whose missions encompass public service and citizen training. Many of these institutions are already involved in one way or another—with legislatures and with citizens—but not to any large extent in trying to portray and explain representative democracy.

If the public is to gain some sense and appreciation of the system that serves them, state legislatures will have to take the lead role. As mentioned earlier, in addition to their other functions, they have to take responsibility for the education of the public. To some extent they are already engaged in educational activities. Many legislative bodies, through public information offices and the equivalent are reaching out to the citizenry, speaking positively about the things they are doing and why they are doing them. Many of them have encouraged C-SPAN type coverage of legislative proceedings. A 1992 survey by the National Conference of State Legislatures found that gavel-to-gavel coverage of legislatures was under way in California, Maine, Minnesota, Nebraska, and Rhode Island, while programs focusing exclusively on the legislatures were televised in twenty-eight states, and legislative issues were included in broader public affair programs in thirty-nine.[38] TVW in Washington does an especially noteworthy job.

Some of these television programs do reach the public. Surveys suggest that one out of four Kentuckians claimed to have watched coverage of the legislature at least some of the time and more than half the Nebraskans reported watching the nightly legislature wrap-up at least occasionally (while one-third watched it often or sometimes). Lately, however, commercial and public television coverage of the legislature has been on the decline, mainly because of budget cuts, while cable programming is on the rise.[39]

All these efforts to communicate the legislature to the public are to be commended. If we assume that familiarity breeds understanding and perhaps empathy, instead of contempt, then greater visibility of the process can help. But much more is required if citizens are to become familiar with the institutions of representative democracy. Educational materials—disseminated over public and cable television and to the schools, town meetings, and organized groups—must portray legislators and legislatures at work in order to communicate the essentials of contemporary representative democracy. These essentials are:

1. The public is divided; public opinion is divided.
2. Public officials, reflecting the publics and their opinions, are also divided.
3. Ordinary people are represented by groups and also by legislators who do their best to be responsive to their constituents.
4. Debate is good, allowing as it does opposing sides to be heard.
5. Compromise is essential, if consensus is to be built and progress is to be made.
6. Competition and conflict are normal and healthy.
7. People cannot get everything they want.
8. Working through to a settlement takes time.
9. Although settlements are reached, closure is rare; the process continues.
10. Through it all, tolerance helps.

This is what needs to be taken into account if we want a responsible, as well as participant, citizenry engaged in the legislative processes.

CONCLUDING NOTE

The conclusion to this account of participatory democracy in and around state legislatures is in the same spirit as the conclusion to the earlier account of *Legislative Life*. Both works offer sympathetic descriptions of a remarkable, but poorly understood, institution. What seems necessary, given the overall record of representative democracy, is greater understanding by the public of their political institutions—particularly ones that have proven as democratic and responsive as have state legislatures. The ways in which legislatures reflect and respond to their environments have proved to be their peculiar strength. It may also be their peculiar weakness today, in that it saps their ability to take a broader and longer-range perspective in trying to further the interests of the people state legislatures represent.

People have the right to criticize their political institutions. They have the right to press for their refashioning. But along with these rights, people have the responsibility to be knowledgeable about their political system and how it works, and to be aware of the possible consequences of change.

Legislatures have lived up to their end of a bargain with the public. It is time for the public to live up to its end. Otherwise, representative democracy, which has served us well for quite a while, will fade further away.

NOTES

1. Jack Citrin, "Who's the Boss? Direct Democracy and Popular Control of Government," in *Broken Contract? Changing Relationships Between Americans and Their Government,* ed. Stephen C. Craig (Boulder: Westview, 1996), 268.

2. Stephen C. Craig, *The Malevolent Leaders: Popular Discontent in America* (Boulder: Westview, 1993), 158–159.

3. Robert S. Erickson, Gerald C. Wright, and John P. McIver, *Statehouse Democracy: Public Opinion and Policy in the American States* (New York: Cambridge University Press, 1993), 247.

4. Steven Stark, "Too-Representative Government," *Atlantic Monthly,* May 1995, 93–94; Bernard Manin, *The Principles of Representative Government* (New York: Cambridge University Press, 1997), 163, 237.

5. Jonathan Rauch, *Demosclerosis: The Silent Killer of American Government* (New York: Times Books, 1994).

6. Gary F. Moncrief, Joel A. Thompson, and Karl T. Kurtz, "The Old Statehouse Ain't What It Used To Be: Veteran State Legislators' Perceptions of Institutional Change" (paper prepared for delivery at the annual meeting of the American Political Science Association, Washington, D.C., September 2–5, 1993). Peverill Squire argues that decentralization is to be expected in a maturing legislature. See his "Theory of Institutionalization and the California Assembly," *Legislative Studies Quarterly* 54 (November 1992): 1026–1054.

7. David B. Magleby, *Direct Legislation: Voting on Ballot Propositions in the United States* (Baltimore: Johns Hopkins University Press, 1984), 182.

8. Anthony King, *Running Scared* (New York: Free Press, 1997), 166–167.

9. John G. Geer, *From Tea Leaves to Opinion Polls* (New York: Columbia University Press, 1996), 195.

10. This does not mean that legislators themselves may not be involved in the initiative campaign. A number of them are very much involved. Nor does it mean that the legislature has no role afterwards. Under the indirect initiative, it still has authority to legislate, and under the direct initiative, it will reenter the process when implementing legislation is required.

11. Peter Schrag, "When Government Goes on Auto-Pilot," *New York Times Magazine,* February 16, 1995.

12. Geer, *From Tea Leaves to Opinion Polls,* 19.

13. Stark, "Too Representative Government," 94.

14. Elizabeth Kolbert, "Frank Luntz," *New York Times Magazine,* March 26, 1995.

15. King, *Running Scared,* 84–89.

16. Ibid., 166, 187.

17. Magleby, *Direct Legislation,* 184–187.

18. *New York Times,* October 16, 1994.

19. North Dakota Consensus Council, "The Strengths and Weaknesses of the North Dakota Legislative Assembly," draft, August 26, 1994.

20. Lawrence K. Grossman, *The Electronic Republic* (New York: Viking, 1995), 106.

21. Bruce Adams, "Building a New Environment," *Kettering Review* (fall 1995): 17. This is written by an elected public official who used to be the national issues director of Common Cause.

22. Magleby, *Direct Legislation,* 184–185.

23. See Citrin, "Who's the Boss?"

24. National Commission for the Renewal of Democracy, "The Portland Agenda: Principles and Practices for Reconnecting Citizens and the Political Process," December 1993, 10.

25. John R. Hibbing and Elizabeth Theiss-Morse, *Congress as Public Enemy: Public Attitudes Toward American Political Institutions* (New York: Cambridge University Press, 1995), 104.

26. King, *Running Scared,* 90, 162.

27. Grossman, *Electronic Republic,* xiii.

28. *State Net Capitols Report,* June 6, 1997, 9–10.

29. Geer, *From Tea Leaves to Opinion Polls,* 195–196.

30. Robert A. Dahl, *Democracy and Its Critics* (New Haven, Conn.: Yale University Press, 1989), 339–340.

31. James S. Fishkin, *Democracy and Deliberation* (New Haven, Conn.: Yale University Press, 1991).

32. King, *Running Scared,* 162–165.

33. Hibbing and Theiss-Morse, *Congress as Public Enemy,* 147–157.

34. Hans A. Linde, "On Reconstituting 'Republican Government'," *Oklahoma City University Law Review* 19 (summer 1994): 207.

35. Hibbing and Theiss-Morse, *Congress as Public Enemy,* 60.

36. Robert H. Durr, John B. Gilmour, and Christina Wolbrecht, "Explaining Congressional Approval," *American Journal of Political Science* 41 (January 1997): 183–200.

37. Hibbing and Theiss-Morse, *Congress as Public Enemy,* 157.

38. Mary Renstrom, "Legislative Television Programming in the States," *State Legislative Report* 17 (July 1992): 1.

39. Karen Fisher, "Legislatures in the Living Room," *State Legislatures,* August 1991, 17; Renstrom, "Legislative Television Programming in the States," 2.

Select Bibliography

American Society of Legislative Clerks and Secretaries. *Inside the Legislative Process.* National Conference of State Legislatures. Denver: the Conference, 1991.

Benjamin, Gerald, and Michael J. Malbin, ed. *Limiting Legislative Terms.* Washington, D.C.: CQ Press, 1992.

Berg, John C. "Massachusetts: Citizen Power and Corporate Power." In *Interest Group Politics in the Northeastern States.* Edited by Ronald J. Hrebenar and Clive S. Thomas, 167–198. University Park: Pennsylvania State University Press, 1993.

Bernick, E. Lee, and Charles W. Wiggins. "Legislative Norms in Eleven States." *Legislative Studies Quarterly* 8 (May 1983): 191–200.

————. "Executive-Legislative Relations: The Governor's Role as Chief Legislator." In *Gubernatorial Leadership and State Policy.* Edited by Eric B. Herzik and Brent W. Brown, 73–91. Westport, Conn.: Greenwood, 1991.

Bessette, Joseph M. *The Mild Voice of Reason: Deliberative Democracy and American National Government.* Chicago: University of Chicago Press, 1994.

Beyle, Thad L., ed. *Governors and Hard Times.* Washington, D.C.: CQ Press, 1992.

Bibby, John F., and Thomas M. Holbrook. "Parties and Elections." In *Politics in the American States: A Comparative Analysis,* sixth ed. Edited by Virginia Gray and Herbert Jacob, 78–121. Washington, D.C.: CQ Press, 1996.

Blair, Diane D. *Arkansas Politics and Government.* Lincoln: University of Nebraska Press, 1988.

Bolotin, Frederic N. "Ohio: A Plethora of Pluralism." In *Interest Group Politics in the Midwestern States,* 243–262. Edited by Ronald J. Hrebenar and Clive S. Thomas. Ames: Iowa State University Press, 1993.

Brace, Paul, and John A. Straayer. "Colorado: PACs, Political Candidates, and Conservation." In *Interest Group Politics in the American West.* Edited by Ronald J. Hrebenar and Clive S. Thomas, 49–57. Salt Lake City: University of Utah Press, 1987.

Browne, William P., and Kenneth Ver Burg. *Michigan Politics and Government.* Lincoln: University of Nebraska Press, 1995.

Bryant, William R., Jr. *Quantum Politics: Greening State Legislatures for the New Millennium.* Kalamazoo: New Issues Press, Western Michigan University, 1993.

Calvert, Jerry W. "Reform, Representation, and Accountability—Another Look at the Montana Legislative Assembly." In *Legislative Reform and Representative Government in Montana.* Edited by Jerry W. Calvert. Bozeman: Burton K. Wheeler Center, Montana State University, September 1993.

Campbell, Ballard C. *Representative Democracy: Public Policy and Midwestern Legislatures in the Late Nineteenth Century.* Cambridge: Harvard University Press, 1980.

Cigler, Allan J., and Dwight C. Kiel. *The Changing Nature of Interest Group Politics in Kansas.* Topeka: Capitol Complex Center, University of Kansas, June 1988.

Cingranelli, David L. "New York: Powerful Groups and Powerful Parties." In *Interest Group Politics in the Northeastern States.* Edited by Ronald J. Hrebenar and Clive S. Thomas, 251–277. University Park: Pennsylvania State University Press, 1993.

Citizens Conference of State Legislatures. *The Sometime Governments.* New York: Bantam, 1971.

Citrin, Jack. "Who's the Boss? Direct Democracy and Popular Control of Government." In *Broken Contract? Changing Relationships Between Americans and Their Government.* Edited by Stephen C. Craig. Boulder: Westview, 1996.

Clucas, Richard A. "Legislative Leadership and Campaign Support in California." *Legislative Studies Quarterly* 17 (May 1992): 265–283.

———. "The Effect of Campaign Contributions on the Power of the California Assembly Speaker." *Legislative Studies Quarterly* 19 (August 1994): 417–428.

———. *The Speaker's Electoral Connection: Willie Brown and the California Assembly.* Berkeley: Institute of Governmental Studies Press, University of California, 1995.

Clynch, Edward J. "Mississippi: Does the Governor Really Count?" In *Governors, Legislatures, and Budgets.* Edited by Edward J. Clynch and Thomas P. Lauth, 125–136. Westport, Conn.: Greenwood, 1991.

Clynch, Edward J., and Thomas P. Lauth. "Conclusion: Budgeting in the American States—Conflict and Diversity." In *Governors, Legislatures, and Budgets.* Edited by Edward J. Clynch and Thomas P. Lauth, 149–155. Westport, Conn.: Greenwood, 1991.

Cohen, Jeffrey E. "Perceptions of Electoral Insecurity Among Members Holding Safe Seats in a U.S. State Legislature." *Legislative Studies Quarterly* 9 (May 1984): 365–369.

Collins Center for Public Policy. *Making Florida Democracy Work.* Tallahassee: Collins Center, Florida State University, 1996.

Cook, Corey. *Campaign Finance Reform.* Sacramento: California Research Bureau, California State Library, 1994.

Cope, Glen Hahn. "Texas: Legislative Budgeting in a Post–Oil Boom Economy." In *Governors, Legislatures, and Budgets.* Edited by Edward J. Clynch and Thomas P. Lauth, 115–124. Westport, Conn.: Greenwood, 1991.

Cornwell, Elmer E., Jr. "Rhode Island: Bruce Sundlin and the State's Crisis." In *Governors and Hard Times.* Edited by Thad L. Beyle, 163–177. Washington, D.C.: CQ Press, 1992.

Cox, Gary W., and Scott Morgenstern. "The Increasing Advantage of Incumbency in the U.S. States." *Legislative Studies Quarterly* 18 (November 1993): 495–514.

Craig, Stephen C. *The Malevolent Leaders: Popular Discontent in America.* Boulder: Westview, 1993.

Cronin, Thomas E. *Direct Democracy: The Politics of Initiative, Referendum, and Recall.* Cambridge: Harvard University Press, 1989.

Cronin, Thomas E., and Robert D. Loevy. *Colorado Politics and Government.* Lincoln: University of Nebraska Press, 1993.

Crotty, Patricia McGee. "Pennsylvania Individualism Writ Large." In *Interest Group Politics in the Northeastern States.* Edited by Ronald J. Hrebenar and Clive S. Thomas, 279–300. University Park: Pennsylvania State University Press, 1993.

Dahl, Robert A. *Democracy and Its Critics.* New Haven, Conn.: Yale University Press, 1989.

Dow, Jay K., and James W. Endersly. "Campaign Contributions and Legislative Voting in the California Assembly." *American Politics Quarterly* 22 (July 1994): 334–353.

Driggs, Don W., and Leonard E. Goodall. *Nevada Politics and Government: Conservatism in an Open Society.* Lincoln: University of Nebraska Press, 1996.

Ehrenhalt, Alan. *The United States of Ambition.* New York: Times Books, 1991.

Erikson, Robert S., Gerald C. Wright, and John P. McIver. *Statehouse Democracy: Public Opinion and Policy in the American States.* New York: Cambridge University Press, 1993.

Eulau, Heinz. "Legislative Norms." In *Encyclopedia of the American Legislative System.* Edited by Joel H. Silbey, 585–601. New York: Scribner's, 1994.

Everson, David H., and Samuel K. Gove. "Illinois: Political Microcosm of the Nation." In *Interest Group Politics in the Midwestern States.* Edited by Ronald J. Hrebenar and Clive S. Thomas, 20–49. Ames: Iowa State University Press, 1993.

Feig, Douglas G. "The State Legislature: Representatives of the People or the Powerful?" In *Mississippi Government and Politics.* Edited by Dale Krane and Stephen D. Shaffer, 111–131. Lincoln: University of Nebraska Press, 1992.

Fiorina, Morris P. *Divided Government.* New York: MacMillan, 1992.

———. "Divided Government in the American States: A By-product of Legislative Professionalism?" *American Political Science Review* 88 (June 1994): 304–316.

Fishkin, James S. *Democracy and Deliberation.* New Haven: Yale University Press, 1991.

Fleer, Jack D. *North Carolina Government and Politics*. Lincoln: University of Nebraska Press, 1994.

Fowler, Linda L. "Constituencies." In *Encyclopedia of the American Legislative System*, 399–418. Edited by Joel H. Silbey. New York: Scribner's, 1994.

Francis, Wayne L. *The Legislative Committee Game: A Comparative Analysis of Fifty States*. Columbus: Ohio State University Press, 1989.

————. "Floor Procedures and Conference Committees in State Legislatures." In *Encyclopedia of the American Legislative System*, 721–729. Edited by Joel H. Silbey. New York: Scribner's, 1994.

Francis, Wayne L., and John R. Baker. "Why Do U.S. State Legislators Vacate Their Seats?" *Legislative Studies Quarterly* 11 (February 1986): 119–126.

Freeman, Patricia, and William Lyons. "Female Legislators: Is There a New Type of Woman in Office?" In *Changing Patterns in State Legislative Careers*. Edited by Gary F. Moncrief and Joel A. Thompson, 59–70. Ann Arbor: University of Michigan Press, 1992.

Freeman, Patricia K. "A Comparative Analysis of Speaker Career Patterns in U.S. State Legislatures." *Legislative Studies Quarterly* 20 (August 1995): 365–376.

Funderburk, Charles, and Robert W. Adams. "Interest Groups in Ohio Politics." In *Ohio Politics*. Edited by Alexander P. Lamis, 303–330. Kent, Ohio: Kent State University Press, 1994.

Gable, Richard W. "California: Pete Wilson, A Centrist in Trouble." In *Governors and Hard Times*. Edited by Thad L. Beyle, 43–59. Washington, D.C.: CQ Press, 1992.

Gais, Thomas L., and Michael J. Malbin. "Administering Campaign Finance Reform: What Happens After the Law Is Signed?" in *Rockefeller Institute Bulletin 1996*, 57–69. Albany: Nelson A. Rockefeller Institute of Government, 1996.

Geer, John G. *From Tea Leaves to Opinion Polls*. New York: Columbia University Press, 1996.

Gerber, Elizabeth R. "Legislatures, Initiatives, and Representation: The Effects of State Legislative Institutions on Policy." *Political Research Quarterly* 49 (1996): 263–286.

Gierzynski, Anthony. *Legislative Party Campaign Committees in the American States*. Lexington: University Press of Kentucky, 1992.

————. "Elections to the State Legislatures." In *Encyclopedia of the American Legislative System*. Edited by Joel H. Silbey, 435–449. New York: Scribner's, 1994.

Gierzynski, Anthony, and David Breaux. "Money and Votes in State Legislative Elections." *Legislative Studies Quarterly* 16 (May 1991): 203–217.

Gierzynski, Anthony, and Malcolm Jewell. "Legislative Caucus and Leadership Campaign Committees." In *Changing Patterns in State Legislative Careers*. Edited by Gary F. Moncrief and Joel A. Thompson, 107–126. Ann Arbor: University of Michigan Press, 1992.

Gosling, James J. "Budget Procedures and Executive Review in State Legislatures." In *Encyclopedia of the American Legislative System,* 765–781. Edited by Joel H. Silbey. New York: Scribner's, 1994.

Gove, Samuel K., and James D. Nowlan. *Illinois Politics and Government: The Expanding Metropolitan Frontier.* Lincoln: University of Nebraska Press, 1996.

Graham, Cole Blease, Jr., and William V. Moore. *South Carolina Politics and Government.* Lincoln: University of Nebraska Press, 1994.

Gray, Virginia, and David Lowery. "Reflections on the Study of Interest Groups in the States." In *Representing Interests and Interest Group Representation.* Edited by William Crotty, Mildred A. Schwartz, and John C. Green. Lanham, Md.: University Press of America, 1994.

Grizzle, Gloria A. "Florida: Miles to Go and Promises to Keep." In *Governors, Legislatures, and Budgets.* Edited by Edward J. Clynch and Thomas P. Lauth, 93–102. Westport, Conn.: Greenwood, 1991.

Grossman, Lawrence K. *The Electronic Republic.* New York: Viking, 1995.

Hackbart, Merl M. "Kentucky: Transitions, Adjustments, and Innovations." In *Governors, Legislatures, and Budgets.* Edited by Edward J. Clynch and Thomas P. Lauth, 83–91. Westport, Conn.: Greenwood, 1991.

Hale, Dennis. "Massachusetts: William F. Weld and the End of Business as Usual." In *Governors and Hard Times.* Edited by Thad L. Beyle, 127–150. Washington, D.C.: CQ Press, 1992.

Hamm, Keith E., and Robert Harmel. "Legislative Party Development and the Speaker System: The Case of the Texas House." *Journal of Politics* 55 (November 1993): 1140–1151.

Hamm, Keith E., and Ronald D. Hedlund. "Committees in State Legislatures." In *Encyclopedia of the American Legislative System.* Edited by Joel H. Silbey, 669–699. New York: Scribner's, 1994.

Hamm, Keith E., Ronald D. Hedlund, and R. Bruce Anderson. "Political Parties in State Legislatures." In *Encyclopedia of the American Legislative System.* Edited by Joel H. Silbey, 947–981. New York: Scribner's, 1994.

Hamm, Keith E., and Charles Wiggins. "Texas: The Transformation From Personal to Informational Lobbying." In *Interest Group Politics in the Southern States.* Edited by Ronald J. Hrebenar and Clive S. Thomas, 152–180. Tuscaloosa: University of Alabama Press, 1992.

Hanson, Royce. *Tribune of the People.* Minneapolis: University of Minnesota Press, 1989.

Heard, Alexander, ed. *State Legislatures in American Politics.* Englewood Cliffs, N.J.: Prentice-Hall, 1966.

Hebert, F. Ted. "Utah: Legislative Budgeting in an Executive Budget State." In *Gover-*

nors, Legislatures, and Budgets. Edited by Edward J. Clynch and Thomas P. Lauth, 103–113. Westport, Conn.: Greenwood, 1991.

Hedlund, Ronald. "Accommodating Member Requests in Committee Assignments: Individual-Level Explanations." In *Changing Patterns in State Legislative Careers.* Edited by Gary F. Moncrief and Joel A. Thompson, 149–174. Ann Arbor: University of Michigan Press, 1992.

———. "Wisconsin: Pressure Politics and a Lingering Progressive Tradition." In *Interest Group Politics in the Midwestern States.* Edited by Ronald J. Hrebenar and Clive S. Thomas, 305–344. Ames: Iowa State University Press, 1993.

Hibbing, John R. "Modern Legislative Careers." In *Encyclopedia of the American Legislative System.* Edited by Joel H. Silbey, 497–512. New York: Scribner's, 1994.

Hibbing, John R., and Elizabeth Theiss-Morse. *Congress as Public Enemy: Public Attitudes Toward American Political Institutions.* New York: Cambridge University Press, 1995.

Hirsch, Eric. *State Legislators' Occupations, 1993 and 1995.* Denver: National Conference of State Legislatures, March 1996.

Hrebenar, Ronald J., and Clive S. Thomas, eds. *Interest Group Politics in the American West.* Salt Lake City: University of Utah Press, 1987.

———. *Interest Group Politics in the Southern States.* Tuscaloosa: University of Alabama Press, 1992.

———. *Interest Group Politics in the Midwestern States.* Ames: Iowa State University Press, 1993.

———. *Interest Group Politics in the Northeastern States.* University Park: Pennsylvania State University Press, 1993.

Hyde, Mark S. "Rhode Island: The Politics of Intimacy." In *Interest Group Politics in the Northeastern States.* Edited by Ronald J. Hrebenar and Clive S. Thomas, 301–321. University Park: Pennsylvania State University Press, 1993.

Jernberg, James E. "Minnesota: Searching for Stability." In *Governors, Legislatures, and Budgets.* Edited by Edward J. Clynch and Thomas P. Lauth, 71–81. Westport, Conn.: Greenwood, 1991.

Jewell, Malcolm E. *Representation in State Legislatures.* Lexington: University Press of Kentucky, 1982.

———. "State Legislative Elections: What We Know and Don't Know." *American Politics Quarterly* 22 (October 1994): 483–509.

Jewell, Malcolm E., and David Breaux. "The Effect of Incumbency on State Legislative Elections." *Legislative Studies Quarterly* 13 (November 1988): 495–514.

Jewell, Malcolm E., and Penny M. Miller. *The Kentucky Legislature.* Lexington: University Press of Kentucky, 1988.

Jewell, Malcolm E., and Marcia Lynn Whicker. *Legislative Leadership in the American States.* Ann Arbor: University of Michigan Press, 1994.

Johnson, Janet B., and Joseph A. Pika. "Delaware: Friends and Neighbors Politics." In *Interest Group Politics in the Northeastern States*. Edited by Ronald J. Hrebenar and Clive S. Thomas, 61–93. University Park: Pennsylvania State University Press, 1993.

Jones, Ruth S., and Katheryn A. Lehman. "Arizona: The CEO Approach of J. Fife Symington III." In *Governors and Hard Times*. Edited by Thad L. Beyle, 29–42. Washington, D.C.: CQ Press, 1992.

Kettering Foundation. *Citizens and Politics: A View From Main Street America*. Dayton, Ohio: Kettering, 1991.

King, Anthony. *Running Scared*. New York: Free Press, 1997.

Kurtz, Karl T., ed. "The Changing State Legislatures (Lobbyists Beware)." In *Leveraging State Government Relations*. Edited by Wesley Pedersen, 23–32. Washington, D.C.: Public Affairs Council, 1990.

———. "The Old Statehouse, She Ain't What She Used to Be." National Conference of State Legislatures, July 26, 1993. Photocopy.

Lamis, Alexander P., ed. *Ohio Politics*. Kent, Ohio: Kent State University Press, 1994.

Lauth, Thomas P. "Georgia: Shared Power and Fiscal Conservatives." In *Governors, Legislatures, and Budgets*. Edited by Edward J. Clynch and Thomas P. Lauth, 53–62. Westport, Conn.: Greenwood, 1991.

Lewis, Carol W. "Connecticut: Prosperity, Frugality, and Stability." In *Governors, Legislatures, and Budgets*. Edited by Edward J. Clynch and Thomas P. Lauth, 41–52. Westport, Conn.: Greenwood, 1991.

Lippincott, Ronald C., and Larry W. Thomas. "Maryland: The Struggle for Power in the Midst of Change, Complexity, and Institutional Constraints." In *Interest Group Politics in the Northeastern States*. Edited by Ronald J. Hrebenar and Clive S. Thomas, 131–165. University Park: Pennsylvania State University Press, 1993.

Little, Thomas H. "Electoral Competition and Legislative Minority Parties: Schlesinger's Parties in a Legislative Setting." *American Review of Politics* 16 (fall–winter 1995): 299–316.

———. "Understanding Legislative Leadership Beyond the Chamber: The Members' Perspective." *Legislative Studies Quarterly* 20 (May 1995): 269–289.

Loftus, Tom. *The Art of Legislative Politics*. Washington, D.C.: CQ Press, 1994.

Loomis, Burdett A. "The Motivations of Legislators." *Encyclopedia of the American Legislative System*. Edited by Joel H. Silbey, 343–352. New York: Scribner's, 1994.

———. *Time, Politics and Policies: A Legislative Year*. Lawrence: University Press of Kansas, 1994.

McBeath, Gerald A., and Thomas A. Morehouse. *Alaska Politics and Government*. Lincoln: University of Nebraska Press, 1994.

McCaffery, Jerry L. "California: Changing Demographics and Executive Dominance." In *Governors, Legislatures, and Budgets*. Edited by Edward J. Clynch and Thomas P. Lauth, 7–16. Westport, Conn.: Greenwood, 1991.

MacManus, Susan A. "Ohio: Impact of Economic and Political Conditions." In *Governors, Legislatures, and Budgets.* Edited by Edward J. Clynch and Thomas P. Lauth, 31–39. Westport, Conn.: Greenwood, 1991.

Magleby, David B. *Direct Legislation: Voting on Ballot Propositions in the United States.* Baltimore: Johns Hopkins University Press, 1984.

———. "Direct Legislation in the American States." In *Referendums Around the World: The Growing Use of Direct Democracy.* Edited by David Butler and Austin Raney. Washington, D.C.: AEI Press, 1994.

Manin, Bernard. *The Principles of Representative Government.* New York: Cambridge University Press, 1997.

Miller, Mark C. *The High Priests of American Politics: The Role of Lawyers in American Political Institutions.* Knoxville: University of Tennessee Press, 1995.

Moncrief, Gary F., and Joel A. Thompson, eds. *Changing Patterns in State Legislative Careers.* Ann Arbor: University of Michigan Press, 1992.

Moncrief, Gary F., Joel A. Thompson, Michael Haddon, and Robert Hoyer. "For Whom the Bell Tolls: Term Limits and State Legislatures." *Legislative Studies Quarterly* 17 (February 1992): 37–47.

Moncrief, Gary F., Joel A. Thompson, and Karl T. Kurtz. "The Old Statehouse, It Ain't What It Used to Be." *Legislative Studies Quarterly* 21 (February 1996): 57–72.

Mooney, Christopher Z. "Measuring U.S. State Legislative Professionalism: An Evaluation of Five Indices." *State and Local Government Review* 26 (spring 1994): 70–78.

Morehouse, Sarah McCally. "Executive Leadership and Party Organization in State Legislatures." In *Encyclopedia of the American Legislative System.* Edited by Joel H. Silbey, 621–640. New York: Scribner's, 1994.

Morgan, David R., Robert E. England, and George G. Humphreys. *Oklahoma Politics and Policies: Governing the Sooner State.* Lincoln: University of Nebraska Press, 1991.

Muir, William K., Jr. *Legislature: California's School for Politics.* Chicago: University of Chicago Press, 1982.

Murphy, Russell D. "Connecticut: Lowell P. Weicker Jr., A Maverick in the 'Land of Steady Habits'." In *Governors and Hard Times.* Edited by Thad L. Beyle, 61–75. Washington, D.C.: CQ Press, 1992.

Palmer, Kenneth T., G. Thomas Taylor, and Marcus A. Librizzi. *Maine Politics and Government.* Lincoln: University of Nebraska Press, 1992.

Patterson, Samuel C. "Legislative Politics in Ohio." In *Ohio Politics.* Edited by Alexander P. Lamis, 233–257. Kent, Ohio: Kent State University Press, 1994.

———. "Representation." In *Encyclopedia of the American Legislative System.* Edited by Joel H. Silbey, 3–21. New York: Scribner's, 1994.

———. "Legislative Politics in the States." In *Politics in the American States,* sixth ed. Edited by Virginia Gray and Herbert Jacob, 159–206. Washington, D.C.: CQ Press, 1996.

Patterson, Samuel C., Randall B. Ripley, and Stephen V. Quinlan. "Citizens' Orientations Toward Legislatures: Congress and the State Legislature." *Western Political Quarterly* 45 (1991): 315–338.

Pedeliski, Theodore B. "North Dakota: Constituency Coupling in a Moralistic Political Culture." In *Interest Group Politics in the Midwestern States.* Edited by Ronald J. Hrebenar and Clive S. Thomas, 216–224. Ames: Iowa State University Press, 1993.

Pitkin, Hanna F. *The Concept of Representation.* Berkeley and Los Angeles: University of California Press, 1967.

Polsby, Nelson W. "The Institutionalization of the U.S. House of Representatives." *American Political Science Review* 62 (March 1968): 144–168.

Price, Kent C. "Instability in Representational Role Orientation in a State Legislature: A Research Note." *Western Political Quarterly* 38 (March 1985): 162–171.

Rauch, Jonathan. *Demosclerosis: The Silent Killer of American Government.* New York: Times Books, 1994.

Rausch, John David, Jr. "Anti-Representative Direct Democracy: The Politics of Legislative Constraint." *Comparative State Politics* 15 (April 1994): 1–16.

Reingold, Beth. "Conflict and Cooperation: Legislative Strategies and Concepts of Power among Female and Male State Legislators." *Journal of Politics* 58 (May 1996): 464–485.

Richardson, H. L. *What Makes You Think We Read the Bills?* Ottawa, Ill.: Green Hill, 1978.

Richardson, James. *Willie Brown: A Biography.* Berkeley and Los Angeles: University of California Press, 1996.

Rosenthal, Alan. *Legislative Life: People, Process, and Performance in the States.* New York: Harper and Row, 1981.

———. *Governors and Legislatures: Contending Powers.* Washington, D.C.: CQ Press, 1990.

———. *The Third House: Lobbyists and Lobbying in the States.* Washington, D.C.: CQ Press, 1993.

———. "Legislative Reform." In *Encyclopedia of the American Legislative System.* Edited by Joel H. Silbey. New York: Scribner's, 1994.

———. *Drawing the Line: Legislative Ethics in the States.* Lincoln: University of Nebraska Press, 1996.

———. "The Legislature: Unraveling of Institutional Fabric." In *The State of the States,* third ed. Carl E. Van Horn, 108–142. Washington, D.C.: CQ Press, 1996.

———. "State Legislative Development: Observations From Three Perspectives." *Legislative Studies Quarterly* 21 (May 1996): 169–197.

Rueter, Theodore. *The Minnesota House of Representatives and the Professionalization of Politics.* Lanham, Md.: University Press of America, 1994.

Sanford, Terry. *Storm Over the States.* New York: McGraw-Hill, 1967.

Schlesinger, Joseph A. *Ambition and Politics: Political Careers in the United States.* Chicago: Rand McNally, 1966.

Searle, Rod. *Minnesota Standoff.* Waseca, Minn.: Alton, 1990.

Shan, Chao-Chi, and Jeffrey M. Stonecash. "Legislative Research and Electoral Margins: New York State Senate, 1950–1990." *Legislative Studies Quarterly* 19 (February 1994): 79–93.

Shea, Daniel M. *Transforming Democracy.* Albany: State University of New York Press, 1995.

Smallwood, Frank. *Free and Independent.* Brattleboro, Vt.: Stephen Greene, 1978.

Squire, Peverill. "Career Opportunities and Membership Stability in Legislatures." *Legislative Studies Quarterly* 13 (February 1988): 65–82.

———. "Changing State Legislative Leadership Careers." In *Changing Patterns in State Legislative Careers,* 175–193. Edited by Gary F. Moncrief and Joel A. Thompson. Ann Arbor: University of Michigan Press, 1992.

———. "Legislative Professionalization and Membership Diversity in State Legislatures." *Legislative Studies Quarterly* 17 (February 1992): 69–79.

———. "The Theory of Legislative Institutionalization and the California Assembly." *Journal of Politics* 54 (November 1992): 1026–1054.

———. "Professionalization and Public Opinion of State Legislatures." *Journal of Politics* 55 (May 1993): 479–491.

Stonecash, Jeffrey M. "Campaign Finance in New York Senate Elections." *Legislative Studies Quarterly* 15 (May 1990): 247–261.

Stonecash, Jeffrey M., and Anna M. Agathangelou. "Trends in the Partisan Composition of State Legislatures: A Response to Fiorina," *American Political Science Review* 91 (March 1997): 148–155.

Straayer, John A. *The Colorado General Assembly.* Niwot: University Press of Colorado, 1990.

Suddes, Thomas. "Panorama of Ohio Politics in the Voinovich Era, 1991–." In *Ohio Politics.* Edited by Alexander P. Lamis, 157–180. Kent, Ohio: Kent State University Press, 1994.

Syer, John. "California: Political Giants in a Megastate." In *Interest Group Politics in the American West.* Edited by Ronald J. Hrebenar and Clive S. Thomas, 33–48. Salt Lake City: University of Utah Press, 1987.

Thielemann, Gregory S. "State Legislative Support Staffs and Administration." In *Encyclopedia of the American Legislative System.* Edited by Joel H. Silbey, 801–813. New York: Scribner's, 1994.

Thomas, Clive S. "Conclusion: The Changing Pattern of Interest Group Politics in the Western States." In *Interest Group Politics in the American West.* Edited by Ronald J. Hrebenar and Clive S. Thomas, 143–152. Salt Lake City: University of Utah Press, 1987.

Thomas, Clive S., and Ronald J. Hrebenar. "Interest Group Power in State Politics: A Complex Phenomenon." *Comparative State Politics* 15 (June 1994): 7–18.

———. "Interest Groups in the States." In *Politics in the American States,* sixth ed. Edited by Virginia Gray and Herbert Jacob, 122–158. Washington, D.C.: CQ Press, 1996.

Thomas, Sue. *How Women Legislate.* New York: Oxford University Press, 1994.

Thompson, Joel A., and Gary F. Moncrief. "The Evolution of the State Legislature: Institutional Change and Legislative Careers." In *Changing Patterns in State Legislative Careers.* Edited by Gary F. Moncrief and Joel A. Thompson, 195–206. Ann Arbor: University of Michigan Press, 1992.

Van Assendelft, Laura. "Gubernatorial Agenda Setting and Divided Government in the South." *Journal of Political Science* 23 (1995): 29–63.

Van Der Slik, Jack, and Kent D. Redfield. *Lawmaking in Illinois.* Springfield, Ill.: Sangamon State University, 1986.

Wahlke, John C., Heinz Eulau, William Buchanan, and LeRoy C. Ferguson. *The Legislative System: Explorations in Role Behavior.* New York: Wiley, 1962.

Weber, Ronald E., Harvey J. Tucker, and Paul Brace. "Vanishing Marginals in State Legislative Elections." *Legislative Studies Quarterly* 16 (February 1991): 29–47.

———. "New Course in Sacramento." *State Legislatures* (July–August 1996): 28–33.

Weissert, Carol S. "Michigan: No More Business as Usual With John Engler." In *Governors and Hard Times.* Edited by Thad L. Beyle, 151–162. Washington, D.C.: CQ Press, 1992

West, Sharon Crook. "The News Media and Ohio Politics." In *Ohio Politics.* Edited by Alexander P. Lamis, 181–195. Kent, Ohio: Kent State University Press, 1994.

Whicker, Marcia Lynn. "South Carolina: The Demise of Legislative Dominance?" In *Governors, Legislatures, and Budgets.* Edited by Edward J. Clynch and Thomas P. Lauth, 137–148. Westport, Conn.: Greenwood, 1991.

Wohlstetter, Priscilla. "The Politics of Legislative Oversight: Monitoring Educational Reform in Six States." *Policy Studies Review* 9 (autumn 1989): 50–65.

Wright, Ralph. *All Politics Is Personal.* Manchester Center, Vt.: Marshall Jones Co., 1996.

Zisk, Betty H. *Money, Media, and the Grass Roots: State Ballot Issues and the Electoral Process.* Newbury Park, Calif.: Sage, 1986.

Index